A Life
of Unlearning

A Journey to Find the Truth

Anthony Venn-Brown

Dedication

To my wonderful daughters Rebekah and Hannah, who showed me unconditional love through times of confusion, public humiliation and pain. In similar circumstances, other children have disowned their fathers, but mine stuck by me. To my family, who have also shown me acceptance and supported me to tell my story. To my wonderful network of friends, who are the most amazing group of quality people anyone could choose to have in their lives. I'm grateful for you all.

I'd like to make a special dedication to those we have sadly lost already through suicide. GLBTI (gay, lesbian, bisexual, transgender, intersex) youth are four to six times more likely to suicide than other young people. I could so easily have been one of those statistics.

Thank you to the amazing array of community groups that support us. Thank you to all the churches that have broken through ignorance and prejudice and opened their doors and hearts. Truly you understand Divine love and grace. Thank you to the politicians who fight to ensure we are no longer treated with inequality and that our relationships are given the respect and recognition they deserve.

Rosa Parks, my inspiration. Thanks.

Acknowledgments

Writing *A Life of Unlearning* has been an amazing journey in itself, which began with the first chapter being written in 1997. The series of synchronistic events quickly reinforced my belief that there was a greater purpose in telling my story, far beyond detailing a series of events. It began with the encouragement of my friends, and then with Colin Schumacher arriving in my life and offering to be my first draft editor. The meetings, deadlines, exercises and readings meant I went from telling a story to writing a book—a quantum leap. In moments of confusion, Colin has also been a valuable sounding board for this revised second edition, offering editing suggestions and helping me find clarity over a warm drink or glass of wine. Being within five minutes walk of each other was most convenient.

Thanks to my dear friend Tim McGarry who gave up his time in the midst of his very busy schedule to help with a final proofread of the first edition. Sue Kentlyn also deserves as special mention as she invested hours to look at the additions to the revised second edition. Her suggestions were most useful and ensured that what went to the publisher's editor was a much higher standard. Finally thank you to the others, too numerous to mention, who have added in some way to the writing, publication or promotion of this book: you know who you are. Thanks for playing your part.

Foreword

This is a book in which the author tells of how he 'unlearnt the truths I'd been taught about myself and discovered how to live as the real me'. It is the story of his quest to find not only self-acceptance but one of the most powerful forces in nature—human love.

For most people, their search for love follows a predictable pattern. There are ups and downs. But heterosexuals do not generally feel a need to proclaim their sexual identity as such. It is just taken for granted. Society and its institutions are built around it.

Anthony Venn-Brown grew up in a loving family, within the Anglican tradition of Christianity. At puberty he discovered his attraction to his own sex. His book is the story of his fight against these feelings; and his attempts to combat them by joining (and later ministering in) fundamentalist and Pentecostal churches, by marrying and fathering children, and denying the reality of his inner-being. In the end, he accepts who he is; rejects the centuries-old endeavours to make him feel ashamed of himself; seeks love to complete his life; and finds new paths for his spiritual journey. His is a rocky road; but it is the only one made for him.

Not long ago, nor far away, Anthony Venn-Brown would have been stoned to death or burned at the stake, imprisoned or universally shunned. However, his life coincided with changes in knowledge about sexuality. Twentieth-century science, through the work of Havelock Ellis, Sigmund Freud, Alfred Kinsey, Evelyn Hooker and countless others disclosed the existence of a proportion of people who, like the author, are homosexual or bisexual. Many debates continue: the precise segment of a population that identifies with that minority; whether the cause is always, or only sometimes, genetic; and which of society's rules need to adapt to the new reality. In most Western countries, under the influence of education and the new media and human rights law, great changes have occurred that have made the journey of self-acceptance easier for people like the author of this book. Yet for most individuals it is still a painful journey, as this book reveals. It can be painful for the person at the centre of the journey; but also for their family and for society itself.

Despite his difficult experiences, the author emerges from this book as a lucky man. He was blessed with the love of his family and of his wife, now remarried: herself a victim of his earlier struggles. His daughters' love and that of companions who have helped him to discover himself, all taught him lessons. He shares them with us. The churches with which he was successively associated do not always seem to have fulfilled the loving message they were established to preach. The dramatic stories of attempted exorcisms and public humiliations are, in some ways, modern counterparts to the burnings with faggots in earlier times and the executions by stoning that still take place in some parts of the world.

The author is careful not to condemn people of religion. For the most part they themselves emerge from this book as victims of old traditions and past misunderstandings. Just the same, they are sometimes the cause of pain, violence and many tears. They live on the fault line that divides our world between knowledge and ignorance, rigidity and kindness. To force people to deny their identity, as God or nature made them, is wrong and doomed to fail. Truly, the hearts of those who persist with such error, against the discoveries of science, may be in need of reparative therapy of their own.

Some 'truths' require unlearning, either because of past misunderstanding or misinterpretation, and we must accept this unlearning as part of the search for enlightenment that we are designed to seek incessantly. Human stories, like the one in these pages, play a part in advancing understanding and acceptance. The search for love is deeply imprinted in our being. It is part of our human nature; the wellspring of all religions and of spiritualism; and it is the foundation of universal human rights.

The Hon. Michael Kirby,
Sydney, 18 March 2004

Contents

Prologue

In 2004, standing before the 350 people who had gathered to celebrate the launch of my book *A Life of Unlearning*, I had a strong sense that my story would impact on lives. I was unaware however, just how many lives would be changed and also the vast range of backgrounds readers would come from. The emails began arriving the first week *A Life of Unlearning* hit the shelves, and continue to this day. My publisher has never seen anything like it. Some emails share their own personal tragedy or struggle while others tell me of the healing they experienced as they reached the final chapters. I'd suspected my story was much more than just the conflict of same-sex-orientation and Christianity; it was essentially about the struggle every human being faces in order to live authentically. Being true to yourself.

As Gary Fishlock, the editor of *SX magazine*, said in his review, 'Ultimately, as the theme that emerges is about being true to yourself, *A Life of Unlearning* should be compulsory reading for every man, woman and child, whether they're gay or straight, young or old, religious or non-religious.'

Each of us experience conditioning and pressures from family, friends, church, society, corporations, marketers, to be and act in a certain way in order to be accepted. To be true to yourself in this environment, to have personal integrity and live authentically, will come at a price.

The emails come from parents whose children are gay or lesbian, devastated wives whose husbands have come out, parents of young children who are determined to allow their kids to be who they are meant to be, parents who had rejected their children but now are reconciled, people who had lived with a sense of shame and failure but now have courage and hope. The word 'inspired' appears repeatedly.

Even more surprising are the emails from straight people and others with no religious background, saying how much they related to my journey.

And so in 2004 I entered the most fulfilling time of my life knowing that my complete and, as one radio announcer called it 'brutal', honesty had created a space for people to face their own demons and experience transformation. *A Life of Unlearning* is a total exposure because I'm convinced this story has no value unless the entire truth is told. I'm not proud of everything I've done but these chapters contain the pieces that make up the whole picture of my life. This is the truth.

When I left my Christian world in 1992, the new world I entered knew nothing of my previous existence as a preacher. Eventually, when I felt comfortable enough to talk about the past, the frequent response was, 'Oh my God, why don't you write a book?' My immediate reaction was that it would be too painful to dig into the past and look again at incidents I'd intentionally buried and intended to forget. Others suggested the act of writing would be therapeutic and cathartic, but I needed a greater reason to write. In the May of 1999 that reason came.

Up until this point my life was like an incomplete jigsaw puzzle, and while some pieces were rich in colour, representing many wonderful experiences, others were incredibly dark and distorted. I'd often tried to make sense of what had happened and put the pieces together, but they just didn't fit. Amazingly, while attending a spiritual leadership program in Mexico, clarity came out of chaos and each piece came together. With the picture unfolding before me, a sense of mission awakened. 'I must tell my story' was all I could think about. The first edition of *A Life of Unlearning* in 2004 was the end result, telling the story of how everything I believed about myself was challenged in order to finally arrive at that place of resolution, integrity and authenticity.

I write at the risk of being misunderstood, as some people will make judgements based on their own preconceived ideas and prejudices. Christian activist groups have launched email campaigns against me. That's fine. I know who I am and what I've done. Most of my life was spent pleasing others by saying and doing the things they wanted, but I was living a lie. Facing the truth meant I would hurt the people I loved the most and become an object of embarrassment, ridicule and shame. The amazing peace and freedom I have today cost me too much to consider retreating to the safety of partial disclosure.

According to my old belief system, being a Christian and homosexual was not possible. The two were incompatible; in total opposition, in fact. The constant conflict of being one person inside but presenting another on the outside for twenty-two years eventually took its toll. The real person was being suppressed, denied and hated. I spent most of my life trying to destroy the real me, doing all I could to ensure he never found expression. A suicide of the soul.

When I was forced to be honest with myself, it became impossible to resolve the beliefs that had been foundational to my life and my current reality. Many of us have had to work through years of conditioning and the consequences of accepting 'truth' without ever challenging it. But on my journey, I was led step by step to the resolution of ALL these issues. Some churches and denominations have yet to take that journey. It's very confronting and challenging for them to think they got it wrong about homosexuality. To analyse that could mean being wrong about other issues of substance as well. They fear that if one thing is proved false, then everything is up for challenge and it may all come tumbling down. Looking back though, the church has surprisingly survived the wrongs of the past: fighting the abolition of slavery, banning interracial marriages, refusing women the vote or a place in the church, and even denying that the world revolved around the sun, to name a few. I can list at least twenty issues (including divorce) that, during my twenty-two years in the church, were considered evil and against scriptural standards but are now commonplace and accepted.

The church has been wrong, very wrong. Believing you were right, you hurt people and caused unnecessary suffering. Your rightness is a poor substitute for righteousness. Maintaining a stand of rigidity and denial will not serve anyone—we need to engage in an open, informed, intelligent, respectful dialogue. This is my goal.

A Life of Unlearning will be a story of hope for those who wonder why life can be so unfair and a story of inspiration for those seeking a higher purpose in their lives. It will give insight and understanding to people from religious backgrounds, while others will find it incredibly challenging and confronting. It's estimated that nearly eighty per cent of the population know someone who is gay or lesbian. Perhaps the remaining twenty per cent do as well but are just not aware of it. So for those related to or associated with same-sex oriented people, these pages can help you draw closer to the ones you know and love. For the gay person, being true to yourself usually comes at a price, so I hope my story will bring healing if you're carrying the scars from your battle to gain acceptance. Most of all, I trust that by sharing my life so openly, it will take us another step closer to the day when all GLBTI (gay, lesbian, bisexual, transgender and intersex) people will experience the rights and privileges every human being is entitled to. A day when prejudice, inequality and discrimination will be no more. This is the reason I tell my story.

CHAPTER 1

The confession

It was a tragic way to end a successful and rewarding career. At the age of forty, my entire world was caving in. I'd lived most of my life with only one ambition—to serve God and preach His word—living sacrificially in order to achieve it. During the last eight years especially, I'd seen the fulfilment of this lifelong dream. Now my twenty-two years of struggle, sacrifice and achievements were coming to a horrifying conclusion. Watching everything I'd accomplished crumble away by the hour left me weak and in a state of shock. I wept frequently and wondered how I could have lost all I valued in such a short space of time. That one event, ten days earlier, had caused my life to collapse like an endless line of dominoes. Deep down inside I'd feared this might happen, but like so many things in my life I had put it out of my mind, unwilling to face reality. Now reality was screaming in my face, refusing to be ignored.

I'd invested my life in becoming one of Australia's leading evangelists for the Assemblies of God Church. I was in great demand—my calendar was always booked out twelve months in advance and every weekend was spent flying all over the country, preaching at youth rallies and Australia's mega-churches. Standing before thousands of young Christian people hanging on every word I spoke was exciting and rewarding. Leading bible colleges booked me regularly for a week of lectures for their entire student body. On other occasions I'd been the guest speaker at national leaders' conferences and even been invited as the Australian representative for international religious events. My message was preaching the relevancy of Jesus Christ to a world in need, and sharing the power of God to change lives. People valued my insight because I'd successfully accomplished what so many had previously failed to do—I was a full-time evangelist. This was a common occurrence in the United States but Australia was a different story. Many prominent preachers in Pentecostal circles had tried to function as full-time evangelists, but quickly retreated to the security of a regular salary, pastoring a church. The financial pressures and demands of an itinerant ministry proved too much for many a 'starry-eyed' preacher. When I'd established my organisation, Every Believer Evangelism, eight years earlier in 1983, I had one mission—to break through the preconceived ideas and concepts of evangelism and establish the role of the itinerant evangelist as a vital and permanent ministry in the church in Australia. I really believed breaking through these barriers would make it easier for others to follow. The influence and credibility I enjoyed was no overnight success. My family and I had paid a high price to overcome the obstacles, but for some reason I'd succeeded where others had failed.

Thousands of people attended my seminars and weekend camps, and the sale of my tapes and videos had added to the impact. What thrilled me most of all was that so many had become Christians after hearing me preach, now convinced God was real and Jesus Christ could change their lives. I gained great satisfaction from the opportunities to travel overseas and lead church study tours to the United States, knowing I was bringing significant change to individuals and the denomination. But it had all come to an end.

That April Sunday morning in 1991 was beautiful. The sun was shining, the sky a cloudless, rich blue and the slight chill of the early autumn morning had abated. My family loved living on the Central Coast of New South Wales, as it was always a few degrees warmer than

Sydney, people were more laid back, and life not as rushed. My wife, Helen, and I had moved there in 1988 with our daughters Rebekah and Hannah after being based in Sydney for four years. Living in Sydney had not worked out. I was away preaching for six months of the year, and the large, busy city church at Waterloo (Pastored by Frank Houston and later to become Hillsong), while supporting us in many ways, seemed unaware of the loneliness and isolation Helen felt, trying to raise the girls on her own. Moving to the Central Coast meant our family had a church they could call home and more importantly connect with, while providing me with a retreat from my hectic schedule.

All over the coast, families were getting ready for the regular morning service of celebration, oblivious to what they were about to encounter. During the week, Helen and I had joined the local church leaders in Sydney for the Assemblies of God National Conference at the Darling Harbour Convention Centre so I'm sure everyone was expecting to hear glowing reports about the wonderful things happening in the denomination.

The Assemblies of God denomination is part of the Pentecostal stream of Christendom (the others being Catholicism and Protestantism). About twenty-five per cent of the world's Christians today are Pentecostal or Charismatic. In each of these streams there are a variety of groups and denominations, but the Assemblies of God is by far the largest denomination in the Pentecostal stream. The Pentecostal movement began at the beginning of the twentieth century in the United States, with a revival of the supernatural manifestations mentioned in the New Testament, such as healing, miracles, prophecy and speaking in tongues. There are 11,000 different Pentecostal or Charismatic denominations worldwide, including the Apostolic churches—Elim, Foursquare Gospel and The Church of God in Christ, The United Pentecostal Church—just to name a few. There are also thousands of independent churches with no affiliation to a particular group. Surprisingly, the Assemblies of God in Australia began independently of the American movement. In Australia over the last forty years, the Assemblies of God has experienced a renewal, rising out of institutional religiosity to become the fastest-growing denomination in the country. The name, Assemblies of God, was relatively unknown in Australia; most Pentecostal churches chose more contemporary names like Christian Life Centre or Christian Centre, with Hillsong being the most famous of all. The growth of Hillsong and the introduction of the Family First party to Australian politics, led by the former Assemblies of God superintendent the Hon. Andrew Evans, suddenly put the Assemblies of God in the media and public awareness in 2004.

The conference and days of turmoil were now behind us, it was Sunday and time for church. I dragged myself out of bed and showered. No breakfast that morning—I'd been unable to eat for days. I sat on the lounge with my *Bible* on my lap, trying to get some words of encouragement from the scriptures to help me through the next few hours. I wistfully flicked through the light rice paper pages of my well-worn *Bible* but they appeared transparent, as my eyes focused beyond the page, unable to settle on any particular words or phrases, whilst I fought back tears. An air of grief permeated our house, not unlike the heavy, uneasy silence that settles on a house full of relatives waiting to go to a funeral. We moved slowly and solemnly around the house, only speaking when it was absolutely necessary. Being away preaching constantly meant we treasured the rare opportunities of attending church as a family, but not this Sunday morning. Normally we'd also be early for church; this morning we'd left it until the last minute to leave … but now it was time to go. It must be done. The leaders of the Assemblies of God told me it must be done, as this would demonstrate I was truly repentant and be a part of my healing and restoration. It was useless arguing with them as I had no emotional energy in me to oppose their decision.

The girls looked beautiful as usual, dressed in their Sunday best.

Rebekah, from her moment of birth, was the type of child who attracted people with her bright personality and was often called 'little Tony', after me. Now, at the age of fifteen, she had her first perm and her sunbleached hair frizzed uncontrollably at the sides. Hannah had inherited more of her mother's personality and, even at thirteen, had already established herself as the more conservative one, which was reflected in her hairstyle, a straight bob. She always had an inner quality that shone in her face, and the strong cheekbone structure she'd inherited from her mother's Ukrainian family meant she constantly fought off people trying to pinch her gorgeous cheeks. Spending most of our lives in the ministry meant there was little money for luxuries such as the latest fashionable labels, but Helen had an amazing knack of making the girls look a million dollars. We prided ourselves on being a very trendy, contemporary Christian family.

Helen was putting on a brave face and doing everything she could to pretend this was a normal Sunday morning. Over the last few days, I'd witnessed a strength in her I'd never seen before but it was difficult to determine what she was really feeling. Her emotions were put aside in order to sustain family cohesion. She really worried me though, knowing the stress of our crisis was driving both of us to breaking point. Only a few days earlier she'd collapsed on my office floor after making the frightening discovery, and I had to revive her. The doctor had put her on medication. There's only so much a person can take. It was also difficult to determine what my girls were really thinking. I was hoping they were too young to fully realise the implications of the day ahead, but I'm sure they were feeling confused and betrayed. Confused because of the secrecy of what was really going on, and betrayed because I'd let them down so badly; surely this could not be happening in our family. They had placed me on a pedestal, a Daddy who could do no wrong as a man of God and devoted father. Our close friends saw us as the ideal Christian family—our relationships appeared strong and we had successfully balanced family life and the demands of the ministry. The name Venn-Brown once well respected, after today, would be associated with shame and failure.

The girls had seen some highly unusual behaviour from their Daddy over the last few weeks. Sometimes I'd be happy and bubbly, then without warning plunge into silence and depression—so unlike me and the usual cheerfulness they'd known. Two weeks before, in a restaurant, I'd broken down and cried over dinner, acknowledging the sacrifices they'd made for the Kingdom of God, announcing I'd no longer put them through this struggle. Bizarre behaviour, considering they had only ever known me as a man with a consuming sense of mission.

Sometimes, when I'd call from overseas or somewhere in Australia, they'd ask me when I was coming home and we'd cry because we missed each other so much. I'd always reassured them the sacrifices we were making were important for the Kingdom of God. Don't worry, giggles (I often called the girls 'my giggles'), your Daddy is going to become a normal Daddy and be home all the time from now on. Three days ago we'd had a family conference to discuss what had happened and I'd explained, the best I could, what the consequences would be. How does a father tell his children he's failed and because of his actions their lives would change forever? They hadn't asked any questions, just took it all in their stride, but now they were being placed under enormous pressure because of me.

We walked out into the warm sunlight and onto the pine deck. We'd been so fortunate in finding homes to rent and once again we'd been provided with a gem, nestled among a well-established tropical garden with banana trees flagging one side of the huge deck that covered the two-car garage. During summer nights we made the most of every opportunity to eat out on the deck and in the early mornings flocks of rainbow lorikeets, with their vibrant colours, visited to feed on the seeds we provided for them. The well-established trees created privacy, making our home feel like a retreat, an oasis. And only a five-minute walk to the golden sands of Terrigal Beach.

Walking underneath the deck to the carport we got into our stylish white Fairlane. The registration plate, EBE 777, had been especially chosen as an acronym of the name of my organisation Every Believer Evangelism and God's number 777 (as opposed to the devil's number 666). We'd been unable to afford a classy vehicle previously because of our lack of finance, but as the ministry became more successful, the board of trustees approved the purchase. The plush velour seating, climate and cruise controls along with the great sound system made journeying less tiring. For us this vehicle was a luxury but the purchase was justified by buying a car that was second-hand instead of brand new.

I gave Helen the keys and asked her to drive. Normally, I'd be more in control, seeing the role of driver as a reflection of my position as the biblical leader in the family unit, but this morning I was feeling physically weak. Arriving at church and walking through the crowd I tried to deflect eye contact as the briefest glance made me feel like people could see right into my soul. I didn't want it to be obvious that something was wrong but just get inside and sit down. Helen knew the fewer people I had contact with, the better, and with a firm grip on my arm manoeuvred me through the crowd. The foyer was the usual scene for a Sunday morning at 9.55am. People hugging each other, saying 'God bless you', 'Nice to see you, Tony', 'How's the ministry going?' and 'Are you preaching this morning?' My poor efforts to smile made it obvious to most people that something was drastically wrong.

I'd already spoken with the leaders of the church so maybe the word had circulated and people were just pretending to be normal. My closest friends came to say hi one by one and seeing the sadness in their eyes and feeling their touch was almost too much. Engulfing feelings of failure as a preacher, husband, father and even as a Christian were rising within me like a flood. No. I can't break down now, I must be strong and stay in control.

People could tell something wasn't right, just by my walk and demeanour—it was the posture of a broken man—so our attempts to be inconspicuous failed as eyes followed us making our way towards the front of the auditorium.

Central Coast Christian Life Centre was one of the new Assemblies of God churches that had sprung up around Australia and this particular congregation had grown to around eight hundred people. Many of these churches leased warehouses or factories and converted them into auditoriums for the large congregations. Externally it still looked like a factory but an attempt had been made to tastefully appoint it inside. The cement floor had been covered with a deep charcoal carpet, though the building lacked comfort in extremes of temperature. The congregation froze in winter and sweltered in summer, but that was okay, we were Christians and supposed to make sacrifices. Three six metre banners hung at the front in a variety of colours with the words 'LOVE, JOY, PEACE' embroidered on them, but the contrast of the strong lines of corrugated iron roofing and large cement blocks in the walls overwhelmed the attempts to transform the large space.

For most people it would be difficult to think of this as a church as there were no crosses, crucifixes, stained glass windows or religious paraphernalia. Central Coast Christian Life Centre had developed a strong family emphasis with the largest portion of the congregation under thirty. The congregation's casual dress reflected the surfie/holiday culture of the coast. The Hawaiian prints, colourful T-shirts and shorts clashed with a few old faithfuls who felt that church was a place where one should wear their Sunday best. These people were leftovers from an era when men went to church in suits, women wore modest, stylish dresses and hats, and the children dressed in clothes reserved for that once-a-week event.

Pentecostal churches had long ago moved beyond the traditions of organs and hymns and the service usually commenced with half an hour of lively singing, clapping and vibrant worship, similar to the black churches of America. A ten-piece band, consisting of guitars, bass, drums, percussion and keyboards, led the worship, pumping out a contemporary sound not unlike a rock concert. The church attracted talented musicians and singers who contributed to the professional standard of the worship and members of the congregation had composed many of the songs we sang.

I tried to join in the familiar songs but every attempt made me cry. Helen stood on one side and Paul (one of my best friends and a board member of my evangelistic organisation who'd come from Sydney especially to support me) on the other. The girls sat with their friends elsewhere in the congregation. There were moments when I thought I wouldn't make it through the service. I'd never known one could feel so numb and yet be in such pain at the same time.

Kevin, the pastor, moved up to the clear perspex pulpit to preach. Kevin was a trendy forty-year-old, part of the new breed of Assemblies of God pastors who'd rejected the conservative look of a minister, always leading the service and preaching in casual outfits. He was constantly reinventing himself with new looks, hairstyles, clothes and cars but this morning he'd chosen to wear a suit, adding to the gravity of what was going to happen. Kevin was obviously struggling as he preached the sermon; his casual, conversational style lacked its normal flow. As the service was ending, a feeling of nausea overwhelmed me, realising my time had come. What was about to happen was justified, I believed. I'd done the wrong thing. Kevin closed the service with a special announcement, 'Those of you who feel Christian Life Centre is your home church, we'd like you to stay for a few moments please, we have some church business to attend to. People that are visiting today, thank you for coming, we hope you enjoyed the service, you're free to leave.'

What was about to happen would be traumatic for all concerned and certainly something not to be witnessed by visitors or non-Christians.

Helen and Paul's grips on my arms strengthened. I began to sob, an uncontrollable sobbing, beginning deep within and shaking my entire body. No, Tony, you can't let go now. Be strong.

Kevin's statement, 'Sometimes difficult things need to be done in churches and I have to let you know today that one of our leaders has fallen,' brought an instant gasp from various parts of the congregation. He then motioned for me to come forward. Suddenly I felt like an old man as I slowly rose to my feet and shuffled towards the front. Reaching the podium, I turned around to face the congregation.

I will never forget those faces.

Whenever in town, I'd preached messages of encouragement and hope from this pulpit but the usual responsive faces were now replaced with wide eyes and mouths open in shock. Some who'd already heard the news began crying, others placed their heads in their hands and began to sob.

Husbands and wives clutched each other tightly. Helen had lost her composure and was being comforted by friends. Rebekah and Hannah were sitting near the front, crying as well. The weight of my humiliation instantly increased as I became even more aware of the suffering I was causing my wife and girls. It wasn't fair. I deserved to be punished, not them.

I leant on the pulpit to support myself and counteract the weakness in my legs. I'd rehearsed the brief statement over and over again in my mind even though I knew it would take less than sixty seconds. I'd been directed to make my confession general and concise, and not to give excuses. Thank God I didn't have to mention the most horrifying detail of all—the one that would have made me the worst of all sinners. My voice trembled as I commenced. 'Last week I preached my last sermon. I'm resigning from the ministry today. I'm sorry that I have to confess to you I've committed the sin of adultery and I ask you to forgive me. I'm so sorry for the shame I have caused my wife and family, the church and God. Please forgive me.'

I wished I could have said more, even some words of justification. Or make mention of a midlife crisis or being on the edge of a nervous breakdown, or burnt out. I wanted to scream, 'Oh God, if only you knew the battles I've been through, that I've fought every single day for the last twenty-two years as a Christian.'

Now exposed and humiliated, I sobbed uncontrollably. Of course, that wasn't the entire story. I'd transgressed beyond other disgraced ministers. Kevin and other leaders from the church rushed to my aid, trying to console me, the support of their arms stopping me from collapsing on the stage. People began to weep loudly, while others sat in stunned silence. Friends helped Helen to the stage, and she stood beside me. Kevin took the microphone and began to pray. 'We thank you God for Tony's life and ministry and we ask you to heal and restore him. We pray also for Helen, Rebekah and Hannah and ask you to give them strength at this time and to let them know your love. We ask your love, power and forgiveness to surround Tony.' Prophetic words of encouragement came from various leaders saying God would take this experience to strengthen, restore and give me a ministry beyond anything I'd known before. I knew that was impossible so the words brought little comfort. I'd failed God and my time was up.

The entire congregation was now in tears—people were devastated, some shaking their heads in disbelief. This could never have happened. Tony was such a good preacher, loving husband and father. My brief confession had actually created more questions in the minds of many people. Who was it with? Was it someone in the congregation? When did it happen? How long had it been going on? Was it a once-only fall or an affair over a period of time? I knew the gossipers would fill in all the gaps.

The congregation slowly dispersed; some moved to the foyer, others walked down the front to offer words of support, and a few just held me and wept. I didn't want anyone to talk to me or touch me, let alone tell me they loved me. I was so unworthy. If ever there was a time I wished the ground would open up and swallow me, it was then.

It was done. I'd made my public confession and hoped things might become a little easier. There should have at least been a feeling of relief, like a load lifted off me. But there wasn't—just numbness. It was like a funeral and I was the corpse. In order to please God, my family and friends, I had become a person who met their expectations. So much of what I'd loved had died and the man that people had perceived me to be now ceased to exist. Had my entire life been a lie? It felt like I'd just given away the last thing I owned, my self-respect. What would be left? Was there anything worth living for?

I wondered, in view of what I'd done, if I could ever be forgiven— surely I'd live with the shame and humiliation the rest of my life? I wanted so desperately to save my family and myself from the pain and darkness ahead, but no, sin has its consequences and I must pay. That chance meeting with Jason, only weeks earlier, had set my life on a course I could no longer control.

CHAPTER 2
It all began when …

In 1954, Neutral Bay was not the trendy suburb it has since become but more a staid, middle-class one. There wasn't a lot of room for a family of five in our two-bedroom flat. My sisters Sue and Cathie were nine and four, making me the three-year-old baby of the family. Dad worked in the city for Bradley Bros., a spare parts distributor with a couple of country branches. He began working as a messenger boy when he left high school and retired as a director of the company—an unusual concept in today's society. The only time Dad didn't work for Bradley Bros. was for six years during World War II. After returning from fighting in the Middle East, he met and married Mum, but on the third day of their honeymoon his division was sent to fight the Japanese in Papua New Guinea. Mum didn't see him for another year, always wondering if three days might be the only time she'd have with the man she'd vowed to spend the rest of her life with.

Life was simple for us. We didn't have enough money to buy a refrigerator so the iceman came every few days to give us a new block for our ice chest and he always chipped off a piece of ice for me to suck on. That was my iceblock. While my sisters attended Neutral Bay Primary School, I spent my time amusing myself by visiting our neighbour, Mrs Kirkwood, affectionately known to us as 'Kirky', a stout elderly lady with wispy grey hair who, I regularly reminded, smelt nice. I also played with my friend David, down the road. David's mother draped sheets over the furniture for us to play cubby houses, and then when Sue and Cathie came home, I played Mummies and Daddies with them. We'd get all their dolls out (they were our children) and the toy prams, and have dinner parties with the tiny china tea sets our grandparents had given the girls. More than once, when Dad caught me, he scolded me for playing with dolls and the look of disgust and anger made me aware I'd done something very wrong. It would have been difficult, as a preschooler, to understand my father's socialisation and his need to police gender roles; I was just having fun. In fact, no one questioned gender roles in the 1950s. Everyone just knew their place.

Three memories stand out from my brief time at the local Anglican Church's preschool: peanut butter and honey sandwiches, playing 'Simon Says', and painting on the walls of the church. It wasn't real paint though; we created images on the exterior brick walls with a brush, holding a small, used Heinz spaghetti tin filled with water. The water left a dark mark on the rich, brown brickwork. What wonderful masterpieces I created! Sadly they evaporated in five minutes, which made it difficult to take my artwork home. Before going to preschool, I'd wait outside the flat for the baker to deliver fresh bread and watch his horse saunter down the road, amazed that he automatically knew when to stop at the houses that bought bread. Large animals scared me so I didn't pat the horse like the other neighbourhood kids did.

Dad's car was an old Page and even for that time it had a vintage air about it with its wooden spokes and canvas roof—as there were no windows we'd have to shield ourselves with umbrellas when it rained. The car was a gift from his father; there was little money to spare after feeding a family of five on one wage. Our luxuries included occasional milkshakes, owning a full set of Derwent colouring-in pencils in a shiny steel box, and going on family picnics. I don't remember, though, ever having a sense of lack or need for something more. We were happy, we were loved, and we were fed.

Dad's parents lived at Longueville, about ten kilometres away, and owned a very large five-bedroom home, always had a new car and seemed to want for nothing. They were perfect grandparents, spoiling me at every opportunity. But who wouldn't? I was so cute. Every Sunday we visited them for a roast dinner, a ritual that lasted for as long as I can remember, at least until Grandma became too frail to cook. Grandma's cooking was legendary; her Yorkshire pudding always crunchy, the homemade gravy made from flour and the juices left in the roasting pan—the best I've ever tasted. The thought of it still makes me salivate. After lunch Dad and Grandpa usually retired to comfortable lounge chairs to nod off and snore a duet while the ladies did the dishes. As soon as dinner finished, Cathie and I went for walks to the terminus at Lane Cove and watch the trams arriving from the city, or visited Grandpa's sister, Great Aunty Isabelle (Aunty Bell, as we called her) just a kilometre away. Other times we'd walk down to the park at Tambourine Bay, hoping it was low tide so we could explore the rock pools and chase the myriad soldier crabs scampering across the sand back into their holes.

My grandparents' lounge/dining room extended twenty metres down one side of the house and against the wall, and in the middle was a piano. Grandma played the organ at the local Anglican Church and occasionally gave piano lessons. Some Sundays, if she'd managed to finish clearing up before the gentlemen nodded off, we'd gather around the piano and sing 'Bless this house, Oh Lord we pray', 'Onward Christian soldiers' and other hymns. Almost like an Australian version of *The Waltons*.

Christmas at my grandparents' was always a special time. It was an open house every Christmas Eve at 'Rimaru', Arabella Street, Longueville. Aunts, uncles, cousins, friends and people from the church descended on my grandparents' home where we'd sing Christmas carols and eat lots of nuts, sweets and Christmas cake. The three steps at the end of the lounge room leading to the dining room were perfect as an impromptu stage, so my sisters and I sang and performed for the crowd of fifty or so. Some guests sang in groups or solo, while others recited verses or told jokes. Everyone was expected to contribute to the evening's entertainment. The performance standards weren't high but the kids' ad lib plays always received the loudest applause, which meant we'd get overexcited and have to be reminded that 'children should be seen and not heard'.

One Christmas became a classic in family storytelling. Everything was prepared, the food laid out, and we all waited eagerly for the guests to arrive. People usually started arriving between 7pm and 7.30pm, but by 8pm the adults became concerned. By 8.30pm, sitting on the veranda waiting with the handful of guests that had arrived, my grandparents discussed what could be wrong.

Grandpa said to Grandma, 'You did send out the invitations, didn't you?'

'No, I thought you'd sent them out!' she quickly snapped back. Frantic telephone calls were made and a few more people arrived, but it wasn't the same.

Our grandparents' block of land was quite large with sweeping views of the Lane Cove River, Greenwich, Hunters Hill and across to the city. After his Sunday nap, Dad often helped out by mowing the lawns. The lawns took at least two hours to mow and when Dad had finished mowing the large banks at the front of the house we'd slide down the grass on pieces of cardboard. The kids were given the task of raking up the cuttings and placing them down at the bottom of the garden. Cathie and I gathered these together and, under the large hydrangea bushes, created 'fairy castles', decorated with sticks and leaves with little paths for the fairies to walk along. Grandma encouraged my vivid imagination and, while I wasn't looking, made tiny footprints along the paths and then told me the fairies had visited.

After preschool, I commenced kindergarten at the local primary school, which meant I had to ride with my sisters on the double-decker bus with all the big kids—a scary thought when you're only a little tot. I was never excited about going to school like this as it usually meant I'd fall over when the bus drove off, lurching as the driver ground the gears. Driving around corners was frightening and no matter how much Mum tried to reassure me, I was convinced those huge double-decker buses could tip over. I always survived the journey but never looked forward to it.

Even at this young age I had a career path worked out and whenever asked by adults what I wanted to be when I grew up, I only ever gave two answers: a fireman or a ballerina man. Quite a contrast. I remained focused and never wavered from these two professional goals during my early schooling.

Two memories remain of my year in kindergarten. One of those was my first Education Day when the school had an open day for family, and our class had prepared a special musical performance. With our percussion instruments, we accompanied the piece of rousing marching band music, something like the *1812 Overture*, being played on the wind-up gramophone. My mother and grandmother were a part of the auspicious audience and Dad, taking the afternoon off work, reinforced the importance of this event. My part was critical, as I was to bang the big cymbals at the climax of the piece. Parents looked on with pride and delight as the music reached a crescendo.

Now! Uh oh. No bang of the cymbals. The excitement had proved too much for my bladder and I'd gone to the toilet. The piece was terribly incomplete without my contribution and for many years after the event, every time I brought someone home to meet the family, this story was repeated. Why do families insist on making sure you don't forget the most embarrassing moments of your life?

The other unfortunate memory of kindergarten at Neutral Bay Primary School is the day I projectile vomited on the girl in front of me. It wasn't my fault—it just came out. I'd informed the teacher I wasn't feeling well and was quickly marched into the corridor, she was going to call my mother to come and pick me up when … Oh no, not again. The boys laughed and the girls squealed as I slipped on the vomit and fell on the floor. This was too much and in a fit of anger I took off home to Mum. It's amazing how, as a young boy of nearly five, I managed to find my way through the busy shopping centre and across main roads—I walked a total of three kilometres home. (This amazing skill of finding my way home when I was unwell was an ability that proved valuable to me later in life, when returning home after an excessive night of partying.)

In 1956, before I completed kindergarten, we moved to the picturesque suburb of Hunters Hill, a peninsula on Sydney Harbour, only ten kilometres from the city, with the Lane Cove River on one side and the Parramatta River on the other. The Aboriginal name for Hunters Hill was Moocooboolah, meaning 'land between two waters'. Originally, Hunters Hill had been settled by French stonecutters who arrived at the colony to assist with the construction of sandstone buildings. Many of the original sandstone cottages and mansions remain today along with the quaint, narrow streets and lanes, creating a French provincial and village atmosphere.

Everything we needed was within a few blocks of our house. Mussetts' newsagency carried every conceivable item from newspapers to hardware. The lighting was poor and the shop further darkened by items hanging from the ceiling. Whatever you needed—toys, fuse wire, globes, art materials, reels of cotton, ice creams and sweets—Mr Mussett was sure to find it hidden away somewhere in his shop. The rolled morning newspapers were delivered in his old Plymouth car, thrown out by his sons through the doors that had been removed for the purpose. Mr Bliss senior and his sons owned the corner grocery store and looked very smart in their shirts, ties, and white aprons. If I'd ask politely they often gave me a small brown paper bag containing the broken biscuits they couldn't sell from the colourful Arnott's biscuit tins.

Hunters Hill Bakery was directly opposite and every weekday

morning we woke to the sound of smashing bread tins as the hot loaves were removed from their containers, and the aroma of freshly baked bread wafting across the street. Before breakfast, Mum sent us over to buy a loaf so she could make sandwiches for our lunch. Sometimes the temptation of pulling small, warm wads of fresh white bread out of the centre of the loaf proved too much and Mum scolded us when we returned. The bakery was in the process of converting from delivering the bread by horse to using motor vehicles, so we made sure to visit the horses in the stables behind the bakery. Miss Cynthia Crop, an austere lady in her late thirties, flat-chested with prematurely greying hair tightly pulled back into a French bun, worked in the attached shop. I think it was the only job she'd ever had. She lived down the block with her sick mother. I noticed she always smiled at the adults but if I went to the shop by myself she scowled, making me feel like she resented her lot in life—an unattractive, ageing, childless spinster trapped into looking after her invalid mother.

Another spinster, of a totally different disposition, Miss Stoltzenburg, owned a private library two doors down, housed in the front garage her father had converted by building floor-to-ceiling shelves. She'd personally purchased the hundreds of books that made up her library and earned her living lending them out for a weekly fee. Mr Stoltzenburg, her father, was an eccentric man who collected junk and repaired broken things. This worked well for us, as we were blessed with a constant supply of second-hand scooters, pedal cars and tricycles. Mr Stoltzenburg's twisted body caused him to walk with a pronounced limp, but his greatest claim to fame was chasing fire engines. The beauty of living on the main road of the peninsula was that we heard every fire engine that came to Hunters Hill before it arrived. Immediately we heard the siren in the distance, all the children ran out onto the street, Mr Stoltzenburg hobbled out of his house calling all the neighbourhood kids to hop into his beaten-up Holden station wagon, and then we'd follow the fire engine down the winding main road till we found the fire.

The old man always made sure we kept a safe distance but were still close enough to enjoy the excitement of watching firemen pull hoses out of the engine and attack the blaze. His heart of gold and generous spirit ensured him pride of place as the neighbourhood grandfather.

The post office was a block away and the local primary school just up the hill. A ten-minute walk down the steep hill of Alexandra Street took me to a wharf where I spent endless hours and days fishing for leatherjackets, yellowtail and bream. Woolwich Swimming Baths was affectionately known to the locals as Mooney's Mud Hole, because it was leased from the local council and maintained by Mr Mooney, and at low tide was nothing more than mudflats. Situated on the edge of the Lane Cove River, it was either a fifteen-minute walk or a quick bus ride from home. During summer holidays, Mum gave me sixpence for my day's excursion to the pool, which meant I had a penny ride each way on the bus, a penny to get into the pool and a little extra to buy Choo Choo bars, rainbow balls and sherbet bags. The many days I enjoyed at the local pool ensured I had a rich tan and a slim swimmer's build.

My two older sisters were good playmates but they didn't play boy games. Cathie was only a year older than me so we managed to get up to lots of mischief together. We'd always muck around but Dad's words of, 'Stop that or someone will get hurt!' often curtailed our enjoyment. When I was seven, it was announced that Mum was going to have another baby and immediately I thought, at last I'm going to have a little brother to play with. Two boys and two girls—I thought that was fair. Months later, when the wonderful news was announced that I had another sister, Phillippa, apparently I screamed, 'When she comes home I'm going to put her in the garbage bin, I don't want a sister, I want a brother!' then ran away and cried. Another thing I've been repeatedly reminded of by the family.

I found it difficult to make friends during my early primary school days. Soon after making a friend, it wasn't long before we'd fight and the friendship ended. This happened so many times I lost count and it made me wonder why I couldn't maintain friendships. Two friends stand out though: Ian Drysdale and Kenny Campbell. Ian was a bit of a sissy and didn't like to get dirty. Our families had a connection through social activities on the Hill so I found myself playing with Ian a lot, but it was a very volatile friendship. Kenny was different—a real boy's boy, coming from a big family with older brothers—he was like the little brother I wanted so much. He had a strange combination of dark hair and freckles across his nose and was forever flicking his over-grown fringe out of his eyes. Kenny was not only cute, I admired the fact that he was mischievous and would attempt things that scared the life out of me. One day in class, he tapped me on the shoulder, looked down under the desk, then pulled the side of his shorts up and showed me his willy. I don't really know why he did it. I hadn't asked to see it. It was a fine willy—no wonder he was proud of it. Kenny taught me many things but one of his greatest contributions to my life was that he taught me how to smoke. Kenny stole Peter Stuyvesants from his mother and we'd smoke them behind the toilets of the Congregational Church across the road from school. My initial attempts predictably made me feel nauseous and gave me terrible head spins, but I persevered and before long I'd mastered the skills of drawing back and blowing smoke rings. I liked Kenny. I really liked Kenny.

My father was typical of most men of that era. As a husband and father, his main role was provider, and he left for the city soon after 7am before we got up for school, worked all day and went to the pub for a couple of beers with his mates on the way home. He was not an excessive drinker; in fact, Dad was never excessive in anything. We'd usually eaten by the time he returned home about 7pm; otherwise he arrived just in time for dinner, then we'd say goodnight and go to bed. Dad's other role was as the maintainer of patriarchal power—whenever I misbehaved Mum reminded me, 'Wait 'til your father gets home, young man.' We knew who was boss.

I'm sure he felt proud of the job he did as a provider and authority figure—the role every decent man took on at that time. Memories of my father aren't warm, but not harsh either. It just always seemed like we were worlds apart. I saw no other examples of father-son relationships different to ours. That's just the way it was.

During my primary school days he was obviously concerned about this cute little boy, Tony, who needed toughening up. As soon as I turned eight, I was made to join the Cub Scouts but if it had been up to me, I wouldn't have been there. Another attempt to make a 'real boy' out of me was to enrol me in the local church soccer team. I didn't mind soccer because it wasn't like rugby—it was the lesser of two evils—not as rough and I was less likely to get hurt. The fact I was playing in a team with other boys I went to primary and Sunday school with made me feel more comfortable. Tony wasn't a star player though. In fact, I was a bit of a dud. Playing left or right back meant my role was to defend the goals but when the opposing forwards came thundering down towards our goal, I usually failed to stop them.

I never missed a practice though. Commitment was always one of my strong points, and every Wednesday afternoon I'd catch the red and yellow bus to Boronia Park, run around the oval eight times, practice passing, kicking and heading, then return home as it was turning dark.

After playing with the team for some time I began dreading soccer on Saturday mornings. I'd get up early and put on my All Saints soccer uniform, which consisted of a white shirt (that Mum always starched), with one diagonal blue stripe across the chest, black shorts and blue and white socks. I knew I looked good in my crisp uniform and after packing my soccer boots and shin pads, I joined Mum for breakfast. Mum and I had a ritual we went through every morning.

'What would you like for breakfast, Tony?' she'd ask.

'Rice Bubbles,' I'd reply.

'That's not enough,' she'd respond, but after sixty seconds of arguing,

Mum's determination to give me a more substantial breakfast weakened and I had my Rice Bubbles. We did this every morning for years.

Parents were usually well represented at the game and I hoped every Saturday morning this might be the time my parents would watch me play soccer, but that time never came. I didn't think it was fair—to make me do something I didn't want to do and then not support me. Dad worked all week and women were considered inferior drivers, so Mum had never thought of getting a driver's licence. At the time, there was no late night shopping or Sunday trading and everything closed at noon on Saturday. This meant Saturday mornings were spent shopping for the family groceries. Although I wanted Mum and Dad to come and watch me play soccer, our weekly provisions were a higher priority.

Team selection on Saturday mornings was difficult for me because all the best players were allocated their positions first. I couldn't kick goals like the coach's son Greg, Bobby was brilliant at dribbling the ball, nor could I save goals like Allan; he was a hero. One by one, the players were chosen, usually leaving me with the position of reserve. The weekly ritual of rejection only reminded me I wasn't quite good enough and often made me cry, then I'd run home. I was told on many occasions that no one liked a cry-baby, so as the season progressed I became stronger, and helped hand out oranges at half time and ran up and down the field yelling 'Come on Saints!' I always got a medal for being a team member at the end-of-season prize-giving but the family thought I should get a special banner for being 'Best Reserve of the Year'.

The local Anglican Church, All Saints, a very impressive sandstone building with beautiful gothic architecture and colourful stained-glass windows (almost like a mini-cathedral), was around the corner from our house. Family life for the Venn-Browns revolved around the local church, as we had a strong Anglican heritage. My great-grandfather had been an archdeacon, my grandfather on my mother's side was an Anglican priest in Brisbane and my grandfather on my father's side was a lay reader in the local church. Dad trained the servers, as well as being Sunday school superintendent and rector's warden. Sunday was a busy day, which commenced with Holy Communion at 8am, and then on to Sunday school.

Singing in the church choir was something I really enjoyed, especially when we were paid for singing at weddings—having extra pocket money was always helpful. Some people told me I had the voice of an angel and occasionally I sang solos during the special events of Christmas and Easter. We may have looked like angels in our robes and starched ruffles around our necks, but we were devils in disguise; absolute brats. Mr Beadman J Fox, the choirmaster, a plump, English bachelor in his late forties who'd been trained in the finer points of the choral arts, was constantly driven to distraction by our mischievous behaviour. There were twelve boys when we had a full contingent, but this rarely happened. Practices on Wednesday nights began at 7pm for the boys, and the adults joined us at 8pm for another hour. With no other adults around to keep a check on our behaviour, we placed whoopee cushions under Mr Fox's chair, hid under the pews, stuck signs on his back and took turns to disappear for a quick cigarette when his back was turned. When our behaviour became unbearable, he'd threaten to resign, the rector would come over and give us a stern lecture, then we'd sing like angels and all would be forgiven.

In 1963 I went to Hunters Hill High School, and was surprised to find myself placed in the 1A class. I couldn't understand it. I knew I wasn't stupid - maybe lazy, undisciplined and brattish but not stupid - but still I wondered why I was placed among the intelligentsia of Hunters Hill's children. During my early high school days Dad's mission to ensure I became a man continued and I was told I MUST join the military cadets. My protests were unsuccessful. For most young men learning to fire a 303 rifle (left over from World War II), the prospect of camps and manoeuvres were exciting adventures, but they filled me with fear. As we approached these events, stories circulated about the things that could go wrong, like the rifles that exploded or about the broken and bruised shoulders caused by the severe kickback from the antiquated weapons.

The night before going to the practice range I'd been unable to sleep and tried to get out of the activity by any means, including pretending to be sick, but everything failed. When it was my turn to mount the firing range, I was trembling and praying hard that nothing would happen. The sergeant yelled 'Fire!' and I pulled the trigger without even thinking about aiming because I wanted to get it over and done with as soon as possible. The almighty explosion sent my ears ringing as the rifle kicked with immense force into my shoulder. At that moment, I was convinced I'd never make a soldier. I survived the experience without any injuries except to my ego. Returning from the day on the rifle range with my paper target in hand, my grandmother complimented me about there not being a mark on it. I think she missed the point.

Our annual camp at Singleton brought other trials that crippled me with fear. Such as the night manoeuvres during which I'd hide in a bunker in the pitch black praying I wouldn't be discovered or attacked by the older cadets who bashed me up. Like dogs, they always seem to sense my fear. There was also the humiliation of the medical examination known as the 'Greatcoat Parade' to contend with. We were ordered to strip and appear in nothing but our huge woollen greatcoats and boots outside the barracks. Inside the barracks, we had to remove everything and stand with our arms out in a crucified position, coat in one hand and boots in the other, while the medical officer checked for skin diseases, and made sure we had two testicles and no hernias. Being a late developer, I found this especially embarrassing and the situation was made even more intimidating by the stories I'd heard about what happened to the guys who got an erection during the examination.

I quickly learnt I could avoid most of the activities I hated about the cadets by joining the band and playing the bugle. It's much better to play music than to practise killing people, I thought. The practise sessions, blasting away in my bedroom or backyard, brought complaints from all the family and neighbours, but I wasn't worried; it was my parents' choice that I was in the cadets, not mine.

Looking back, I realise how much of my early life was lived in fear, always being pressured to conform to an image of masculinity that wasn't me and being reminded that I wasn't quite making the grade. It would have been so much easier if I could have been just like everyone else. Conformity is what gets you acceptance, not difference.

CHAPTER 3

The drama begins

During the early years in high school, most of my friends were not interested in girls. Sometimes I looked at magazines, but was only mildly stimulated by the sights I saw. My curiosity in women's body parts was fuelled more by a desire to conform than an awakening of sexual appetite to lay Cheryl, Yvonne or Carol. Girlfriends I had were purely platonic relationships and I put my lack of interest down to the fact that I was maturing later than the rest of the guys. I told the dirty jokes and spoke of girls in sexual terms in order to appear normal but it never did seem right to me. Occasionally I was called names like sissy: a label I didn't want to attract but knew was justified because I related so well to girls (with three sisters, I'd been surrounded by them all my life).

One afternoon, after a school soccer match, we were getting changed after the game. One of the guys began clowning around by humping his mate while he bent over to undo his boots.

'Get off me, you homo!' the guy protested and I laughed along with everyone else, not really knowing what the joke was about. Curious about this word 'homo', I asked Mum what it meant when I got home.

'Mum,' I asked cautiously (asking my parents such a probing question was not the usual thing), 'What's a homo?' I remember the look of concern, almost fear, on my mother's face.

'Why are you asking?' she responded. Sensible reply, Mum.

'I heard some of the boys at soccer calling someone a homo.'

'Was it you?' she responded quickly.

'No, Mum,' I protested, sensing immediately this was a label to be strongly denied. Mum looked relieved as she carefully gave her response.

'A homo is a man that likes other men.' She didn't say the word 'homosexual' as that may have led to further questioning. This inadequate answer satisfied me at the time but I knew there was more that I needed to know. In fact, there was a lot I needed to know about, like 'the birds and the bees' for instance, but we didn't talk about those things in our family, being still under the influence of the Victorian mindset that sex, religion and politics should never be discussed. It was surprising that Mum could actually tell me anything about such a strange subject.

In Year 9 I found a real friend. I met Luke Horsely when he and his family moved into the suburb. For some unknown reason (maybe because I was a good church boy), Luke's mother thought I'd be a good influence on him, being two years older. She actively encouraged the friendship and finally invited me to have lunch with them after church one day. Luke and I often laughed afterwards about the concept of me being a good influence—if only she knew.

The Horselys lived in a waterfront house on the Parramatta River side of Hunters Hill and owned several boats. As soon as lunch was over, Luke and I went for a row in the dinghy to a bush reserve further up the shore from the house. The tide was rising so we secured the dinghy and I followed Luke as we made our way through the scrub. About ten metres in from the shore was a clearing and a cubbyhouse made with scrap pieces of wood and corrugated iron. It was a magnificent structure, a boy's dream come true, a secret hideaway and fortress, reminding me of *Robinson Crusoe* and *Tom Sawyer* stories. All afternoon we smoked cigarettes while I sat engrossed in Luke's impressive stories about his daring exploits. There was nothing sissy about Luke—we bonded immediately and from that day became inseparable.

Luke was like a little brother and my life took a completely new turn. I became braver and more adventurous. We spent every school holiday together swimming, fishing, boating, hiking and going on bicycle trips. Being with Luke was like living on the set of an adventure movie, always exciting. There were times when I contemplated the strangeness of our friendship (the fact that I was in Year 9 and Luke in Year 7) but didn't concern myself, as the age difference was never an issue. We were incorrigible. I did things with Luke I had never considered doing before, like making 'bunger' guns out of plumbing pipe and shooting glass marbles out of them across the river. This of course was highly dangerous, but you don't consider those things when you're young. If we took a dislike to somebody then we'd blow up their letterbox. This was done by taking a 'tuppeny bunger' (a firework the size of a sausage) and attaching a small piece of mosquito coil to the wick. This meant we could light the coil, walk past the house, secretly drop the bunger into the letterbox, find a spot to hide and wait five minutes for the coil to ignite the wick. The owners ran out screaming, ready to deal with the culprits, but Luke and I were well hidden, trying to hold back the laughter so as not to be detected. People we didn't particularly like had their letterboxes blown up several times.

One of the worst things we ever did was the 'milk run'. Luke suggested I meet up with him after everyone had gone to sleep, so once all the activity ceased in the house and I heard Dad turn the key in the back door, I dressed, quietly lifted the window and climbed out. Our house was a semidetached property with a lane running down one side, so I was able to quietly creep past my sisters' bedroom windows, jump over the neighbour's fence and slip out onto the main street without disturbing anyone. Luke was waiting for me on the corner as arranged.

At that time, milk was home delivered in the early hours of the morning, so Luke showed me how to steal the money people left out ready for the morning delivery. Sometimes it was very lucrative as people paid their bills on a weekly and even monthly basis; you just had to be lucky on the night. After we finished the 'milk run', we'd get a bus to Kings Cross, the red light area of Sydney, and walk the streets, for no particular reason except to look at the prostitutes and spruikers and for the sheer excitement of being in a forbidden place. We'd sit for an hour or so in a coffee shop watching the passing parade and sip on cappuccinos (a new trend), then return home to catch a few hours' sleep before school the next day. The 'milk run' was my only participation in crime, but Luke later became involved in car theft and acquired a criminal record. I've often felt guilty thinking about those poor people who must have had numerous arguments with the milkman, adamant they'd left their money out.

Sometimes on Friday or Saturday nights I'd go to Luke's to watch television, and while sitting on the lounge together, we'd hop under a blanket to keep warm. One night, sitting close to Luke, I became very conscious of our bodies touching and became aroused. It was a strange feeling, something I hadn't experienced before. Those first experiences when sexual energy awakens within you can be so memorable. It was a warm energy and certainly very powerful—a sensation that invigorated every cell of my body. What the *Playboy* magazines had failed to achieve was now rising eagerly. I felt hot, like I was blushing, as Luke's leg began to move slowly against mine. I was scared and unsure how to react. Did Luke want to touch me? Was he conscious of the movement too? Was he consciously moving his leg against mine? I carefully moved my leg a little to see how he would react. He moved again. I moved, then he moved, and after thirty minutes our legs were firmly pressed against each other's. I moved my arm so that it accidentally touched Luke's leg; he did the same. Every move produced a corresponding response, until there was no doubt that what was happening was not accidental. We wanted to touch each other but were too scared to take the next step as we learnt the language of sexual communication.

That inner force urged me on as I slowly moved my hand up his leg until it was in his crotch, expecting him at any moment to yell out, 'What do you think you're doing?' but there was no protest. Luke's eyes remained fixed on the television as I fumbled through the fly of his pyjamas. He sat still, allowing me the opportunity to explore, and then moved his hand inside my shorts. I had never had anyone touch me before. For the next thirty minutes no words were spoken and our eyes never met, while we experienced the pleasure of touching and being touched: enjoying the thrill of new sensations. Finally we moved apart and when it was time for me to go home, I got out from under the blanket and said goodnight, acting as if nothing unusual had happened. Luke acted accordingly.

I think that this was Luke's first sexual experience too but we never discussed it. Every time we got under the blanket on the lounge, it happened. We were unable to improve our technique or speed up the process. We did get a little bolder and sometimes smiled in anticipation of what was about to happen when we spread the blanket over our legs. This boldness increased to the point where I began asking Luke if he wanted me to come back to his place after everyone had gone to bed, and a few times I sneaked out at night, and hopped into his bed and we played with each other. It was very intense but still had a little-boy innocence about it as we were at the same point of sexual development. The strange thing was that we never reached orgasm; maybe if we were capable of coming we would have stopped the behaviour. There was no one else in my life like Luke; what we shared didn't seem wrong, we were so close.

We continued a limited sexual exploration for about twelve months until Luke finally said he didn't want to do it any more, realising we could be called poofters because of what we were doing. I know his older brother Greg was suspicious and yelled at us one night when he noticed movement under the blanket. A quick move and strong protest of denial seemed to deal with the accusation. As I moved into Year 11,

I became aware of the need to grow up a bit and not spend so much time with Luke. We never fought or had an official breakup, just drifted apart. I was totally unaware I had just had my first relationship and that what my schoolmates talked about happening with girls I had experienced, only with a boy. Last time I saw Luke he had been married and divorced. Straight, not gay. I think.

Friendships were not as difficult in my senior years, even with the 'real boys'. Two of my strongest friendships were with 'macho' men who would never have been suspected of any homosexual behaviour. They loved football, had sex with their girlfriends and were regarded admiringly by the majority of the school population: 'jocks' in a modern idiom. Usually I was protected from accusations of being queer because of Cyril. Everyone knew he was the school poof as he was tall, lanky and limp-wristed, with a high whiny voice. He loved wearing black and constantly flicked his long, blond fringe from his eyes as he minced across the schoolyard. Cyril's strong feminine characteristics meant all verbal abuse and harassment focused on him. Cyril's victimisation meant I could safely hide behind my friendships with the straight boys and avoid discovery. Occasionally I joined in the ridicule, reinforcing my position as one of 'the boys'. Tragically, the bullying and stigma of being homosexual caused Cyril such unhappiness that he committed suicide soon after leaving school. He was not the first student to have taken that dreadful step though. 'Big Bill' hung himself after school one day when the continuous taunts over his size, clumsiness and lack of girlfriend made him decide it would be better to be dead than to live. When the principal questioned us the next day, none of us knew how unbearable our words had made Bill's life. It was sobering to think we had ostracised him with our words and actions to the point where his loneliness became intolerable. All bullying stopped for two weeks.

The message was clear to me—through every derogatory term such as pansy, poofter, fairy, queer, homo and faggot—that being homosexual was a curse. I'd learnt already that homosexuals were gaoled as criminals, considered sexual perverts and given shock treatment by psychiatrists and that respectable people would not even mention such a disgusting term in public. Certainly no-one would ever choose to be queer; it was a sinister accident of nature. Homosexuals were destined to a life of rejection, and if by some wicked twist of fate a person was one, they must do everything possible to conceal it from everyone else. Maybe this idea of the need for secrecy was the motivator behind an unusual change in my behaviour—I'm not sure why it happened, it just did.

It was a warm summer's night, stillness had settled on the house. Feeling restless, I dressed and climbed out the window to go for a walk. Where was I going? Nowhere in particular, I just wanted to be out. As it was after midnight, the traffic on Alexandra Street had ceased and the only noises I could hear were the croaking of the frog that lived under the dripping tap in the front garden and the mild hum of distant traffic somewhere beyond the peninsula. Walking along the street, I'd turn around and watch the occasional car drive past, instinctively knowing this was why I was walking—to have one of those cars stop.

A small black Morris slowed down as it drove past, then within minutes returned, going in the opposite direction. My heart began to race with a combination of fear and sexual excitement as the car finally stopped a few metres in front of me. As I walked past the car, I heard the engine start and watched as it drove off and turned left at the post office, thirty metres in front of me. I continued along the main road past the corner then stopped, my heart pounding at a forceful pace. My curiosity became stronger than the fear so I walked back to the corner and saw the Morris parked in the darkness of the side road.

I walked in his direction (I was hoping it was a he) and as I passed the car he leant over and unlocked the passenger door. All logical thoughts of the possible frightening consequences had faded as I opened the door, and although this was my first experience, my actions were automatic and instinctive.

'Hello.' His voice emerged from the darkness—deep, masculine, seductive and appealing. He leant over closer and now with the help of the streetlight I could see he was a handsome man in his late twenties with thick black hair and his cheeks a little flushed by the excitement of the chase.

'What are you doing?' he asked.

'Just going for a walk,' I replied.

'Like to go for a drive?' he quickly responded. With my nod of agreement and immediate move into the passenger seat, he turned on the engine and drove off. As we drove the few kilometres towards the end of the peninsula, he introduced himself. 'My name's Allen.'

'I'm Brian,' I said. I wouldn't want the stranger knowing my real name.

His questioning and my responses were awkward as he took his left hand off the wheel and fondled me as we drove. He'd obviously done this before as when we arrived at a park he knew exactly where the car would be most concealed. I sat stiff and frozen. Allen smiled as he undid his fly and began masturbating. I knew that the large, erect penis I was gazing at for the first time was what I had been waiting to see and touch. This was so different from my experiences with Luke. He pulled down my fly and began touching, pulling, fondling. Within sixty seconds I'd exploded but it seemed like forever while I waited for him to come as he tried to coax me into touching and kissing. I watched in amazement as he shrieked while bizarre spasms jolted his body. He smiled as he sighed deeply, pulled out a handkerchief from his pocket, cleaned himself up, and turned on the engine.

I was glad it was over and then began to realise the danger I'd placed myself in. I prayed he wouldn't hurt me or leave me alone in the park. Allen asked where I lived so I gave him a false address and he drove me within a few blocks of my house.

'Did you enjoy that?' he asked as he pulled on the handbrake.

'Not really. I just wanted to see what it would be like. I don't think

I'll do it again,' I replied, guaranteeing what had happened would not be repeated. I certainly felt like that, so I got out of the car and when he was out of sight, hurried home, fearful he may reappear and discover where I really lived. The initial thrill and excitement of my first encounter with a man quickly vanished under a fog of guilt.

I was quite shaken the next day at school but there was no-one to talk to about the confusion and gnawing guilt that clouded my mind. Who could I really trust with that type of information? Convinced it wouldn't happen again, I knew I just had to get through this by myself.

In Year 12, my closest friend, Glenn, was ruggedly handsome with a strong beard line. His solid masculine chest, furred like a mohair rug, made me think he'd begun developing when he was nine. He was extremely popular; an athlete and football player who oozed sexuality. With his girlfriend, Kate, we attended many of the same classes and got along famously.

Kate loved Glenn and so did I, even though I was unaware of it at the time. I always looked forward to being with him, especially alone, and created as many opportunities as I could. We were as much a couple as he and Kate. Being with Glenn was a little awkward at times as I was extremely conscious of him physically. He often captivated me visually and I know I touched him more than I should have but his magnetism was difficult to resist. He didn't seem to mind that I wasn't a 'butch' thing; in fact, I think he almost liked the role of being my protector. People often referred to Glenn as a 'ladies' man' and even though I wasn't quite sure what that meant, I understood why he was popular with the ladies. Glenn turned me on but I tried not to think about it because I wasn't supposed to feel that way about men.

Glenn and I left the school campus and went to my place during our free periods at school or visited the local hotel for a beer at lunchtime. One day when Glenn and I returned from spending lunch hour at my place, some of the guys from our year yelled out from the stairs to the classroom, 'Hey, homos!' Glenn laughed, bent over and rubbed his bum, playing to their taunts, confident no-one would believe such allegations. I blushed and smiled uneasily, trying to look as if the thought of having sex with him had never crossed my mind. The guys in my year knew there was a limit as to how far they could push this with Glenn, as he'd punch their heads in. It was a wonderful feeling of security knowing I had a man who was more than capable of defending any accusations against me.

Glenn and I worked back one afternoon after school in one of the classrooms on a project for the final exams. Sitting side by side, I became aware of our legs touching and the accidental, prolonged touch aroused me. Glenn didn't move away but moved his leg harder against mine. I was more familiar now with these steps. The thing I had secretly desired was happening but it was inconceivable that Glenn wanted the same thing.

I'm sure many gay men are crippled by fear during their initial sexual experiences—I know I was. Fearful of being rejected, bashed, or worse still, identified as a queer and exposed to your peers. Glenn seemed to sense my concerns and reassuringly said, 'Why don't we get out of here and go to my place?' He'd never invited me to his home before but, knowing both his parents worked, we would be alone in the house. We quickly packed up and walked to his car.

The drive to Glenn's house was unusually quiet and we discussed nothing about what had happened or might happen. I began to tremble in the passenger's seat, still wondering if the thoughts I'd regularly dismissed might now possibly come true. When we arrived at Glenn's, he showed me through the house, and then led me to the kitchen where he made us cups of coffee; he still said nothing. Maybe I was imagining his intentions?

Glenn walked into the bedroom with his coffee and I followed close behind, trying to steady my shaking mug with both hands. I'd always admired Glenn as being much more mature and experienced than me and I needed him to take the initiative. But being the initiator placed him in a vulnerable position; if anyone found out, he could never deny that he was the innocent party. Glenn's next question gave me the courage to move forward.

'How long have you felt like this?' he said, pretending to be my shrink as I lay on the couch next to the window. It wasn't very original or creative but it was a start.

'For quite some time now,' I replied.

Glenn continued, 'Have you seen my new jeans?' and moved towards the wardrobe, both of us now naturally slipping into roles in a play moving quickly towards the climax of the final act. With his back turned, I took the opportunity to admire the movement of his solid, V-shaped body as he searched through the wardrobe. Glenn turned around and I watched as he undid the fly of his Levi jeans button by button, and moved his hands over the stiffness of the heavy-gauge denim. The contrast of the white bikini briefs emerging from the blue denim kept my focus. Bikini briefs were such a turn-on; I'd often admired the muscular bodies of the male models depicted on the labels in shops. Unfortunately they were not on my mother's shopping list. Glenn dropped his jeans to the floor, stepped out of them, looked up and smiled.

Standing almost naked in front of me, Glenn was a sensual, visual feast. I moved from the couch to his side and placed my hand on the bulge in his briefs. He immediately became aggressive and undressed me, pushed me on the bed, and rolled me onto my stomach. I'd heard about this in jokes and derogatory remarks but never believed men would do such a thing. Every time he pushed, I squirmed and wriggled. Fear and pain quickly extinguished the desire that only moments before had overwhelmed me.

'No, Glenn, stop it, I don't want to do this!' I protested, but he ignored me and kept on trying. Finally, I screamed and Glenn gave me a look of disgust as he dismounted then disappeared into the bathroom. I picked up my clothes to dress and calling to him in the bathroom said,

'I'm sorry but I can't do this. I've never done it before.' Glenn's anger was something I'd never experienced and I knew I'd failed him. I was willing to give him so much— love, friendship, support, a listening ear—but I knew if this is what I had to do to, I could never succeed.

'You're going to get your head bashed in doing things like that,' he said, suggesting I had led him on. 'You'd be in big trouble, if you did that to ...' he said, breaking a code of silence as he mentioned the names of several guys at school I would never have suspected of having sex with other guys. There was obviously more going on amongst 'the boys' at school then I had ever imagined. His warning was confusing. My intention was not to make myself available to every guy at school who wanted to fuck a boy or experiment. The point was that I wanted to be close to him. I dressed and waited for Glenn's offer to drive me home. The journey home to my place was torturously quiet.

It was very uncomfortable the next day at school and Glenn and I avoided each other. Maybe Glenn had said something to some of our friends and accused me of trying to have sex with him. After all, it was my fault; I should never have allowed it to happen. No, Glenn wouldn't say anything to jeopardise his reputation. Gradually, over the next couple of weeks, we began talking to each other, but never about what happened. Within three months, everything had returned to normal with the usual trips to the local hotel, parties and lunchtimes together.

Glenn and Kate's relationship was always volatile and often, when they had difficulties, Glenn became violent or plummeted into the depths of depression. I took on the role of mediator but, in the midst of one of their heated exchanges, Kate broke it off. Glenn was devastated, so I invited him to come to my place on Saturday night to watch television. A Saturday night alone in the house without my parents was unusual and Glenn arrived with a bottle of Bacardi and I provided the Coke. We talked about the breakup while we watched television and Glenn became increasingly morose. I felt sorry for him knowing he loved Kate so much but while we talked, Glenn made strange comments that aroused my curiosity.

Was it just my imagination or was Glenn trying to come on to me again? His comments about feeling horny could be taken two ways and even though I didn't want another experience like the last one, I still was incredibly attracted to the man. After several drinks, Glenn said, 'I'm going to lie down for a while,' then disappeared into my bedroom. What was he really saying? What did he want? Was this his way of inviting me to come and join him in the bedroom? I sat wondering for ten minutes if I should take the risk again and respond to Glenn's possible baiting, until eventually the strong, hormonal push of puberty gained control. I was too curious and aroused to stay in front of the television another minute.

The bedroom was dark but I could make out Glenn's figure lying face up on my bed so I sat down next to him.

'Are you okay?' I asked. Glenn lay motionless and inviting. The light from the hallway enabled me to see he had already half undone his fly. I tried to rouse him again but all I got was a moan that reminded me of the mornings I pretended to be asleep when Mum tried to wake me for school. I placed my hand cautiously on his leg rubbing the tough denim and looked for a reaction. He groaned and moved in a seductive manner that said 'go ahead' so I moved up to his crotch. Glenn groaned again as I rubbed the strong line of hair that ran from his navel to his groin and within seconds I felt the wetness of his cum in my hand.

I quickly retreated to the lounge room, not knowing what to say or do, fearing the outcome of having once again crossed the boundaries and trying to figure out how I would explain what I'd done. Nearly thirty minutes passed and when Glenn had not emerged, I returned to the bedroom and saw the window open and Glenn gone. Panicking, I searched frantically for him in every room and down the lane beside the house, eventually finding him in his car outside. It was difficult to make sense from what he was saying as he was slurring his words, but something was terribly wrong.

'Tell me Glenn, what's the matter?' He mumbled something about pills and mentioned medication I was unfamiliar with. When I reached over to touch his arm it felt wet. Looking at my palm, I saw the darkness that could only be blood. There were scratches all over his wrists.

Oh my God! What have I done? When I tried to find out what had happened, Glenn's responses were disjointed, so I ran into the house and grabbed a towel to clean up the blood. But when I returned the car was gone. I rang his mother to tell her what had happened and when my parents returned, I tried to explain away the calls I was making and my stress. After a long and sleepless night, Glenn eventually arrived home safely but the night's events took their toll on me.

I was having a difficult time dealing with the previous weekend and felt guilty that I'd contributed to Glenn's trauma. It was becoming increasingly obvious that any attraction to the same sex would only ever produce drama in my life. Depression took over as this conflict plagued my mind. I couldn't study, lost my appetite and began spending more time alone as thoughts of suicide increased. At this point the most beneficial thing would have been to talk to another person who understood what I felt, but the only other homosexual in my world was Cyril and there was no way I could align myself with him. I needed to talk but who could I trust with my darkest secrets?

After days of engulfing depression, one night, alone in my room, I concluded Glenn's lead was the way to go except, unlike Glenn, I must succeed. Taking a razor blade that I used for craftwork from a drawer, I rolled up my sleeves and sat sobbing on the bed. I slowly moved the blade across my wrists trying to press hard enough to make a cut. Having a low pain threshold meant every time I felt the sharpness of the blade, I flinched. The desperation and sense of hopelessness made me press harder. I couldn't do it. I tried not to cry too loudly as I turned the light out to go to sleep as it would be difficult to explain to my parents the distraught state I was in. The only indication of what had transpired that night was a little blood and some scratches across my wrists, which I hid by wearing long sleeves for a few weeks. The turmoil in my mind was driving me crazy; I had to talk to someone.

I'd always related well to older women and one of those was Maggie, a solo mum in her late twenties who lived next door with her son and her current boyfriend. Her experience of life as well as her artistic ambitions meant she mixed with all types of people, so I felt it was worth taking the risk of opening up to her.

'I think I'm a homosexual, Maggie,' I divulged cautiously over coffee the next day. There was a sense of relief but mostly shame as I finally allowed those words to come from my lips, at seventeen, labelling myself a criminal and mentally ill.

The most wonderful thing that happened was that her facial expression didn't change; she continued to look at me as though I'd just told her what I'd eaten for breakfast. She listened intently while I unloaded the incidents with Glenn and the man in the black Morris along with the depression and thoughts of suicide.

'Would you take your life?' she asked and from her expression, I knew she'd experienced the emotions that had overwhelmed me. I rolled back my sleeves. Maggie gasped.

'I need help, Maggie. Things are getting out of control and I can't go on like this for much longer.' I was hoping that Maggie, a nurse, would know someone who would give me the professional help I was seeking but I knew I couldn't pay. She was genuinely concerned about my state of mind and could see that I might actually harm myself in some permanent way.

'Would you like me to speak to your parents for you?' she asked.

'No!' I protested immediately. 'They must never know, they wouldn't understand.' My parents' reaction was more than I wanted to think about at this time, but Maggie continued to reason this was the best way to get any help and she'd break the ice with Mum and Dad for me. Finally, I agreed and braced myself while Maggie went next door to make the big announcement to my mother that I was a 'homosexual'. Such an uncomfortable word; like epileptic, alcoholic or addict. A word that indicated that there was something drastically wrong with Tony.

The wait seemed like an eternity. Maggie returned half an hour later reassuring me all would be okay and I should go home. Mum was strong; she took the matter in hand and spoke to my father about my need to see a psychiatrist, although he was never to know the real reason why I needed professional help. Mum made an appointment with a psychiatrist at the North Shore Medical Centre under the guise of being the mother of a very confused teenager who was suffering depression.

In the 1950s and 1960s, behavioural therapy was used to try to 'cure' gay men. In 1966 the *Sydney Morning Herald* published an article that discussed 'a new hope for deviates' and talked about a research program at Prince Henry Hospital. The options for homosexuality were cure or incarcerate[1]. The program used aversion therapy, which involved electric shock treatment on the genitals and arms of homosexual men as they viewed images or words. Each treatment lasted about thirty minutes.

Another treatment was to inject patients with apormorphine which produced nausea and vomiting. Patients receiving apomorphine were often admitted to hospital due to side effects such as dehydration and the need for repeated doses, while those receiving electric shock therapy were treated for weeks on end or in some cases up to two years. Many years later it was revealed that in their enthusiasm, therapists caused permanent damage and even death to some patients.

It wasn't until 1973 that the American Psychiatric Association removed homosexuality from its list of mental disorders and it took another twenty years (until 1993) for the World Health Organization to officially delete homosexuality from its list of diseases. Preparing for my first visit to the psychiatrist in 1968, I was too uninformed to even imagine what my visits might consist of. I just knew I needed help to find out what was wrong with me and get better so I could become 'normal'.

Dr Denzo matched the image of a psychiatrist that I had received through television and the movies. He had a goatee beard and a large, hooked nose perfectly designed for holding his wire rim glasses. He looked at me over the top of them after bending down to take notes. He spoke with a strong Eastern European accent and, occasionally, at the end of some words, made a deep raspy sound, like he was clearing his throat.

'Where's the couch?' was my first question, trying desperately to ease the awkwardness I felt. Dr Denzo steered the hour-long session by asking probing questions and feverishly took pages of notes detailing my responses. What sexual experiences had I had and what was my relationship with my family and parents like? How long had I been thinking of suicide? Did I masturbate? How often? What did I think about? It was embarrassing to talk about the things I'd done but I felt the only way to get help was to be honest, no matter how uncomfortable I might feel. Ten minutes before the end of the consultation, he instinctively looked at his watch and prescribed some medication to ensure I'd remain happy and wouldn't try to do anything foolish again.

Getting into my father's car on the Pacific Highway, the atmosphere was very tense and I saw the displeasure on his face as he made several attempts to discover what was happening. He was obviously wondering if his son had had a nervous breakdown and would be requiring hospitalisation in a mental institution. I knew my therapy wasn't coming cheap and as we weren't a wealthy family, I worried about what the final bill for a total cure might be.

At the conclusion of our sixth session, Dr Denzo looked over the top of his glasses and summed up my condition, gleaned from the extensive notes he'd taken.

In one way it was a relief to hear him say, 'Tony, it's normal to feel some of these feelings, this is a stage you are going through in your life. It's normal to experience some confusion in your teenage years but you're going to be okay.' He told me to finish my friendship with Glenn and talk to someone when I was feeling depressed. I didn't think this advice was worth the hundreds of dollars my parents had spent. Knowing the struggle I had already experienced, it was difficult to believe I could be cured that easily.

When I told Glenn I'd been seeing a psychiatrist and we couldn't be friends any more, he was angry that I had talked with someone about what had happened between us and that we could no longer be friends. My explanations seemed feeble against his anger but, knowing this was an essential part of changing, I remained steadfast. I wasn't going to be a homosexual, and having Glenn so close was too much of a temptation. I couldn't cope with any more of those situations.

Even though I really desired change, there was still an incredible urge to go out and walk at nights, never honestly admitting to myself what was happening but subconsciously wanting the same outcome. I suppose I was experiencing what all the heterosexual guys in my year were experiencing, the awakening of sexual desire, except they were free to express theirs, the opportunities were all too easy and they could openly boast. The awakening of my sexual desire was driving me to self-hatred and secrecy. The late night encounters with strangers created a warped perception of physical contact with a man. There was never any warmth, tenderness or affection, only a quick orgasm in a car or behind some bushes that lasted only minutes or seconds. The most devastating impact was the aftermath of these encounters. Guilt. The next day was always a dark day for me; overwhelmed with feelings of self-loathing and depression.

A homosexual act between consenting adults in private was still a crime, so there was always the underlying fear of being caught by the police. I knew that outcome would be devastating not only for me but also for the family; the stigma would be ten times worse than if I'd made a girl pregnant out of wedlock.

Two incidents remain in my mind, which affected me for over twenty years. The first was with a taxi driver who picked me up on Ryde Road. It wasn't until after I got into the car that I saw how old and fat he was. Even though I told him I wasn't interested and I wanted to get out, he kept reassuring me it would be okay and drove me about ten kilometres to isolated bushland. He turned off the engine and lights and we were immediately plunged into total darkness. Fear gripped me; I knew there was no escape.

'What do you like to do?' he asked, obviously delighted by his catch of such a young man.

'I want to go home, I don't want to do anything,' I said, hoping my lack of cooperation would dampen his forceful attempts but it only seemed to delight him more. He began undressing me, but my struggling and protesting was useless, he was so much stronger. I screamed and protested at the pain. 'Please don't do this to me! Stop it!' But it was no use. There was no-one to hear. How stupid I'd been to allow this to happen. Sitting silently in the passenger seat as we drove to the main street, I was convinced this experience would finally cure me. I felt disgusting, violated, dirty and as if I'd been damaged in some way. How could I explain to anyone I'd been raped? What was I doing out on the street late at night? What was I doing getting into the car? There were no reasonable explanations so I kept it to myself, hoping and praying no permanent physical damage had been done.

That experience didn't teach me the lesson I'd hoped it would. Several months later, a guy in his early thirties picked me up in a station wagon, his rough appearance making me think he was a tradesman of some kind. He asked all the usual questions, 'What are you doing, what do you like?' as he drove me to the local high school and parked out of view in the shadows.

He began to masturbate and tried to kiss me but I drew away. I never really enjoyed kissing a man, it just didn't feel comfortable. He placed his hand firmly behind my head and pushed it down into his groin. No way, I'm certainly not doing that! But he wouldn't let go.

'Go on, suck me off!' he yelled aggressively. It was terrifying but, scared of the consequences of any resistance, I gave into his threats. I gagged with each thrust, hating every moment of what was happening.

'Please, please let me go,' I pleaded. The relief of his orgasm quickly subsided as he yelled at me and pushed me out of the car. I ran and hid behind one of the school buildings. After he'd driven away I walked home via the back streets in case he was still driving around, and promised myself once more that this would never happen again. Why was I so weak, why was I so stupid, why was MY life so difficult? It just wasn't fair. What had I done to deserve this terrible curse?

Another storm was looming on the horizon. My time at school became a nightmare as a gang of a dozen boys in Year 10 decided to target me for harassment. I constantly tried to avoid them, which was difficult. The gang's threats commenced the moment they saw me, so I tried to move around the school campus with a large group.

'We're going to punch your head in, you fucking queer,' they'd shout across the playground. They would stand behind me in the canteen lines and punch me in the head and back, whispering, 'We're going to get you after school. We'll be waiting for you at the gate.' The thought of being attacked by a group of a dozen boys made me ill and for months I lived in fear, leaving classes early, finding different escape routes in order to avoid the possibility of the threatened attack.

A number of years later I discovered some of the group were actually gay, confirming the research that shows some people who internalise or deny their homosexuality often vent anger on other gay people, manifesting their internalised homophobia and self-hatred by becoming serial poofter-bashers and even murdering gay men. Repression will always manifest itself in some unhealthy or destructive behaviour.

I was desperately unhappy and knew it would be impossible to live any longer with this constant torment and stress in my life.

CHAPTER 4
Enter Christianity

By the age of sixteen, the Anglican Church had ceased being a part of my life. Like many people, I could not reconcile the suffering in the world with a loving God. As far as I could see there was nothing substantial to base a belief in God on except occasional answers to prayers I'd prayed in crisis, and if the prayer was answered I quickly discarded it as coincidence. God had certainly never answered the most important prayer, my constant pleading to take away my homosexual feelings, so why should I believe in him? In our white, Anglo-Saxon community there was a strong division between the Catholic and Protestant families, giving me another reason to doubt the existence of God and to view religion as hypocritical.

A political, cultural and sexual revolution was happening in the 1960s when the term 'generation gap' was created. The emerging philosophies were encapsulated in slogans such as 'Make love not war' and Timothy Leary's 'Tune in, turn on, drop out'. Victorian codes of morality and established religion were being challenged and people began experimenting with drugs such as marijuana and LSD. Even though there were drugs at our school, for some reason I could never access them. Being opposed to the Vietnam War, I joined a communist group called Student Underground. Soon after, I discovered that my mail was being opened somewhere in the postal system. One day at the local bowling club, one of the members suggested my father warn me about the dangers of involvement with Student Underground. I was amazed at Dad's questioning about the organisation, as he had no knowledge of my connection with the group. McCarthyism existed in Australia as well and I've often wondered if, somewhere in the deep vaults of the Australian Security Intelligence Organisation (ASIO), a file exists on me … a communist activist?

During my final year at high school in 1968, much of my spare time was spent escaping to places where I felt safe and wasn't noticed as being different. A highlight of the week was going to the Sydney Domain on Sunday afternoons to hear the public speakers. Here I could dress outrageously in my burgundy cord jeans, orange tie-dyed shirt (my own creation), beads and top hat with a single ostrich feather out the side, blending in with the avant-garde. There was always a curious selection of speakers; some were just plain fruitcakes, but Webster was always popular. Webster spoke eloquently about anything and everything, including politics, sex, witchcraft and contemporary issues such as censorship. He was a professed warlock which, at that time, was a brave thing to admit in such a public way, considering witchcraft was still illegal. When witchcraft was the topic for the day, Webster added to the impact by dressing for the part in black with a cape. His teased, reddish, straw-like hair protruded from underneath his pointed witch's hat. Delighting in horrifying his audience, Webster promoted worship of the devil and satanic rites, detailing orgies he'd been involved in and often commenting that the sex was the only reason he was a Satanist.

Webster cleverly worked his audience and used every abusive comment from the crowd to his advantage, until hecklers cowered in defeat. No-one ever matched Webster's wit and tongue.

Ada Green, a spritely little woman in her sixties who reminded me of a little leprechaun, was another interesting identity. Ada was a Christian zealot, complete with tambourine and two sidekicks: old Bill who played the squeezebox, and Elsie who accompanied her with a tambourine. The zest and energy exuding from that little frame was amazing, as she sang triumphantly without amplification, waving her arms excitedly, loudly emphasising each point in her preaching and frequently reaching a crescendo with a volley of speaking in tongues. Ada was such a contrast to Webster because she was totally oblivious to her audience, except when the harassment from the crowd proved too much and, rattling her tambourine erratically and feverishly speaking in tongues, she'd chase the hecklers like a farmer's wife chasing the hens back into the pen. Occasionally, Ada gained a convert from the crowd who she'd lay hands on and pray for but, most of the time, it was someone playing a trick on her. Most people considered her mentally unstable. In the 1960s, Ada Green was an identity in Sydney, like Arthur Stace.

Arthur Stace, known as 'Mr Eternity', had been an alcoholic and petty criminal before his conversion to Christianity, when he felt called to walk the streets of Sydney. In the most beautiful copperplate script, he would write the graffito 'Eternity' on the city footpaths and the steps of public buildings. Normally he couldn't even write his own name legibly but the word 'Eternity' flowed effortlessly from his chalk. He passed away in 1967 but he must have smiled in heaven to see his trademark used as the centrepiece of the fireworks display on the Sydney Harbour Bridge on New Year's Eve in 2000. Amazing how some people's seemingly insignificant lives can have an impact.

Another place of safety for me was the trendy suburb of Paddington with its many art galleries and psychedelic shops that sold hippie paraphernalia, emulating the Haight-Ashbury district of San Francisco.

I began experimenting with spiritualism as I'd always had a fascination with the supernatural and ghosts. I discovered a United Kingdom publication called the *Psychic Weekly* and this fuelled my interest in the occult with its regular articles on ghosts, séances, spirit guides, mediums, ectoplasm and witchcraft. This publication helped me to access other newsletters and discover similar networks in Australia. I became a regular user of the ouija board, pushing glasses and holding hands around tables in dark rooms. The fascination grew to incorporate witchcraft even though my upbringing told me I should avoid it. Delving further into the darker arts, I began to read books on Satanism, finding it intriguing, exciting and frightening all at the same time. It wasn't long before I had an experience that made me rethink the direction I was going in.

Maggie, the next-door neighbour, and I often talked about the occult and held séances. We decided to use some of this power to deal with Maggie's partner, Joe, who'd been playing up on her. We decided to put a curse on him, so while he was asleep Maggie secretly cut off a lock of his hair and, following a ritual from one of our books, placed this on a cake of soap. After saying the Lord's Prayer three times and burying the lock and cake of soap in the backyard, we urinated on them. A chill ran through my body as we summoned the powers of darkness in the light of a full moon. Joe returned home later that night in a rage and bashed Maggie so badly she had to go to hospital. After that experience, we both decided it was safer not to dabble in witchcraft.

I'd maintained contact with some of the people from the Anglican Church and one of those was the minister's daughter, Betty. Betty was annoyingly enthusiastic about an Anglican holiday camp for school children and insisted I should volunteer as well. After much pressure from her, I finally succumbed and applied to be a group leader, thinking it would be a nice break to go on a beach holiday anyway. In preparation for my week at camp, I was instructed in the religious lessons I had to give to my group of ten or so young boys.

There are two streams of Anglicanism: one is 'low church', which is more evangelical and fundamental; the other is 'high church', which focuses on rituals and tradition and is closer to Catholicism (excluding the worship of Mary). This Anglican camp was unashamedly 'low church' and as I prepared my lessons I realised I was required to teach something I knew nothing about. Teaching Sunday school had familiarised me with *Bible* stories and how to apply them to living a good life, but these lessons were different. I had to teach these kids that the most important thing was to accept Jesus as Saviour so as to be saved from their sins and come into a relationship with God. I'd been told that I was a Christian because I'd been christened as a baby but I knew that wasn't true. How could I be a Christian because of something someone else had decided for me? I also believed nothing the church taught. I remember thinking how difficult it was going to be for me to talk about something I neither believed nor had experienced.

The time away in January was a welcome relief from the year of depression, seeing a psychiatrist, and the traumas with Glenn. I enjoyed the activities on the beach, campfires at night, and camp concerts; lots of singing and laughter had to be good medicine. The leaders were a group of fun-loving people and it was not difficult to feel like I belonged. After the campers went to bed, the leaders met for their own *Bible* studies and we sat in a circle and prayed for each other and especially the kids under our care for the week. The leaders' daily connection with God and talking about Jesus as though He was living and not just a historical figure, was foreign to me. Why hadn't I encountered this before?

One night early in the week, when everyone was asleep, I went for a walk. The beach was deserted and eerie, but as the moonlight broke through the clouds, pools of light moved across the sea through to the horizon. The strong wind was picking up dry sand from the dunes and moving it across the hardened, moist sand where the tide had retreated. Away from the activity of the camp, strolling alone on the beach, the issues of the previous year rolled repeatedly in my mind. Why couldn't I change? How did this happen to me? If God was real, then surely He could answer my prayer, change me and extinguish the feelings of guilt that constantly plagued me. I walked down to the edge of the water and into the darkness cried out a prayer of desperation, 'God, if you really are there, and if you're a God of love like they say, please come to me and help. You can have my life, as messed up as it is. I give it to you.' That intense prayer demonstrated how I was desperate for a miracle and not just praying to get out of an awkward situation; I was actually willing to surrender my life to God.

At the first street light I was able to check the time on my watch. I must have been lost in my thoughts and on the beach longer than I realised as it was already nearly midnight. The hour and a half on the beach had seemed like fifteen minutes. Returning to the campsite, I quietly got into bed trying not to wake the other campers.

During that week I hadn't seen any visions, heard any voices or experienced anything I would call supernatural, but something happened. I certainly talked to God more than I ever had before. Returning home from camp, I felt different; the depression that usually hung over me was gone, the inner turmoil stilled and the urge to walk the streets at night and have sex with men ceased. God had answered my prayer. Finally, I was free.

Within days of returning to Sydney, my Higher School Certificate results arrived in the mail. Not good. The year of focusing on my dramas had taken their toll and the only subjects I passed were art, because I was good at pottery, and English. Mum and Dad were very disappointed but I promised that if they allowed me to repeat Year 12, I'd be a good boy, study hard this time and get better results. Of course, everything would be better now I was a Christian—God was on my side.

I returned to church with a passion, attending early morning communion, youth fellowship after the evening service, and teaching Sunday school. Now believing the *Bible* was the inspired word of God, I began reading it daily, and was determined to read it from cover to cover. Every day I prayed and my week was interspersed with *Bible* studies and prayer meetings. I became a religious zealot and quickly earned the titles of '*Bible* basher' and 'God botherer' at school because

I had to talk to everyone about my conversion. I felt indebted to the God who had performed this miracle in my life and to Jesus who had died on the cross so that I could experience forgiveness. Telling others seemed to be the reasonable response and, besides, Jesus had commanded us all to go into the world and share the good news.

In many ways 1969 would be an historic year for me and for the world, it seemed. While I was busy establishing my life as a former homosexual, now heterosexual Christian, an event occurred in New York City that would not affect my life for another thirty-two years. On Friday 27 June 1969, the New York City tactical police force raided a Greenwich Village gay bar, the Stonewall Inn. Raids were not unusual in 1969; they had been happening regularly without much resistance, always resulting in gay men being taken off to be charged at the police station. That night, though, the patrons of the Stonewall Inn protested that enough was enough; they would no longer be victimised or treated like criminals for being who they were. The crowd in the bar fought back, a riot erupted on the streets and the police had to call for reinforcements. The backlash and following nights of protest became known as the Stonewall Riots and birthed the gay rights movement. I'm sure here in Australia we didn't even know it had happened. Had I read about it, I probably would have responded like most Australians of that era, with disgust and horror.

Only three weeks later, one event that I didn't miss, along with over 600 million other people, happened on 20 July. We were all glued to our TV screens and watched with amazement as Neil Armstrong put his left foot on the surface of the moon and declared: 'That's one small step for man, one giant leap for mankind.' When President Kennedy in 1961 in his address to Congress had declared that before this decade is out we will achieve our goal of 'landing a man on the moon and returning him safely to the earth' it had seemed a fanciful dream. Now it was happening in real time before our eyes. The world was changing, and changing at a faster pace than at any other time in history. But

I was a slow learner.

While repeating Year 12, John, who had been brought up as a Baptist after his mother became a Christian at the 1959 Billy Graham crusade in Sydney, became my closest friend. Our combined zeal meant we were a force to be reckoned with; we took control of the school's Christian group and organised early morning prayer meetings and lunchtime *Bible* studies. The existing Christian group was called the Inter School Christian Fellowship (ISCF) but its impact on the student body at my school had previously been non-existent. I directed my energies towards bringing people to God and the numbers of the ISCF meetings grew from a little group of eight Christians, hiding away in a room, to gatherings of 100 students in the school auditorium. We were having a revival. It was exciting to see the impact it was having as many of the students became Christians and began attending the local churches. At the peak of our success, we were attracting ten per cent of the student population to hear the Christian singing groups and speakers we invited to the school.

As John had become my best friend, I felt he could be trusted with the secret of my life. 'I used to be a homosexual but God has set me free,' I told him cautiously, as he drove me home from one of the many Christian groups we attended. He appeared shocked about my disclosure and responded, 'That's great, mate, but I wouldn't go around telling everyone that.' Something told me that even among Christians a degree of secrecy about such matters was necessary, and even though I believed God had changed me, others might not.

My friendship with John meant I became involved with Ryde Baptist Church. The strong *Bible* teaching and emphasis on adult baptism showed me that, even though I'd been christened as a baby, Jesus and His disciples only baptised adults who had made a personal decision to follow Him. If I was going to follow the Lord then I must follow Him into the waters of baptism, I was told. Mum and Dad were having difficulty with my newfound religious zeal because Anglicans aren't supposed to be excited about God—it's meant to be a personal, private thing. My announcement that I was going to be baptised in the Baptist Church horrified them.

After much arguing, Dad issued his ultimatum. 'No son of mine is going to be baptised in a Baptist Church and if you go ahead with it, you can leave this house.'

From my reading of Jesus' words, I knew already that being a Christian would always involve making choices: choices for good or evil, to follow God or follow man, go with the crowd or be prepared to face ridicule. I'd read in Matthew 10 that Jesus said, 'Do not suppose that I have come to bring peace to the earth. I did not come to bring peace but a sword. For I have come to turn a man against his father, a daughter against her mother, and a man's enemies shall be members of his own household. Anyone who loves his father or mother more than me is not worthy of me.' This was the first of many dilemmas I faced where I had to choose between following the family tradition and doing what I believed God wanted me to do. My previous religious upbringing had been irrelevant and now I'd experienced God in such a personal way I had to do something to demonstrate my new faith, so I held my ground. The people in the Baptist Church supported me in my decision and John's family even offered me a place to stay should my parents disown me. I was learning that being a Christian meant making sacrifices and that there would always be hard decisions to make. That's why Jesus said, 'If you are to be disciples then you must take up your cross daily and follow after Me.'

As we approached the day of the baptism, Dad softened. Mum surprised me by coming to the service but Dad went to the bowling club for a drink. I wanted my parents to be happy with the new direction in my life and couldn't understand their opposition. After all, I'd been such a rebellious teenager, making their life a misery, disrupting family life and never doing what I was told. Even though the changes had been positive, my evangelistic zeal gave me the stigma of being a 'religious fanatic', which was far removed from our family's respectable Anglican background. At this stage I had no plans of actually leaving the Anglican Church I just enjoyed fellowship with Christians in any denomination.

My schoolwork definitely improved and I studied subjects at higher levels than previously attempted, this new motivation coming from a desire to serve God and become an Anglican minister. Moore Theological College in Sydney required candidates to reach a tertiary level of education, so the dream of entering the Anglican ministry was shattered when I missed out on university entrance by one subject. I tried to find another way around it but there were no exceptions to the rule.

This situation only confirmed the difficulties I was having with Anglicanism and traditional religion. Why couldn't I be a minister? I believed it was my calling in life—I had the skills, intelligence and motivation. Most of the ministers I knew were either intellectuals who lacked essential communication and people skills, or were doddery old men who made me wonder if they had ever experienced a moment of passion in their entire lives. The language these ministers used was totally irrelevant to people in the 1960s. 'Thou', 'thee' and 'yea' may have been fine in the 1600s but still using these words in the twentieth century only proved how outdated the church was. One of the most annoying traits was that they often used a religious, pious tone of voice (with a frightfully nice English accent) when saying prayers and preaching. It all seemed such an act. Desperate attempts were made to attract and hold young people with coffee groups and folk dances but these always caused conflict. I was tired of the weekly ritual of going to communion and grovelling to God, the prayers and service reminding me over and over again what a wretched sinner I was.

Week after week, I joined in the prayer, with the other parishioners: 'We do not presume to come to this thy table, oh merciful Lord, trusting in our own righteousness but in thy manifold and great mercies.

We are not worthy to gather up the crumbs under thy table, but thou art the same Lord whose nature is always to have mercy.' Of course I was very aware of my failings and the need to draw on God's power to overcome sin and temptation. But the Anglican way seemed like only one side of the coin. I thought Christianity was meant to be a celebration of life but I could see little difference between the Sunday morning service and a funeral. Where was the hope, power and positive change that Christianity was supposed to bring into my life? There had to be churches that were more vibrant and relevant so I searched for life and vitality in other denominations.

The euphoria of my initial conversion was beginning to wane and I found that temptations were becoming harder to resist. I was failing God and knew I had to try harder to be a good Christian. What else could I be missing in my life? So when I heard about the baptism of the Holy Spirit and speaking in tongues, I thought that this would be the final answer. The promised power of the Holy Spirit must be what I was lacking.

In the late 1960s and early 1970s, unusual things were happening in some parts of the Christian world, and in Los Angeles, California, there had been an unprecedented revival known as the 'Jesus Revolution'. Many young people originally involved in the hippie movement had become disillusioned and their search led them into Christianity, giving birth to cults such as the Children of God. They converted in their thousands, and this unique phenomenon prompted *Time* magazine to report on it regularly. In 1971, *Time* stated (with a picture of a psychedelic Jesus on the cover) that, 'Jesus is alive and well and living in the radical spiritual fervour of a growing number of young Americans who have proclaimed an extraordinary religious revolution in his name.'

The traditional churches were having great difficulty accepting the new zealots (sometimes called 'Jesus Freaks') because their dress, language and experience were foreign to those who had known nothing but the staid, protective environment of the established church.

New churches blossomed to accommodate the movement and many of the mega-churches that emerged still exist today in California and other parts of the United States. The 'Jesus People' were giving established religion the greatest shake-up it had had since the Protestant Reformation and, as the movement spread, it gave birth to the Charismatic movement.

There were small stirrings in Sydney as well. On Wednesday nights, a Healing Service had commenced in Saint Andrews Anglican Cathedral. This was a unique event and the Sydney newspapers reported that strange manifestations had been happening such as healings, miracles and speaking in tongues. My interest in the supernatural and my disillusionment with established religion meant I became a regular attendee. The songs were more contemporary and people's experiences of God up-to-date, which created a vibrant atmosphere. Through my network, I was able to encourage about forty new people to join me and attend the services.

After a few months, I experienced the 'baptism of the Holy Spirit' as described in the New Testament. The first disciples spoke in tongues on the Day of Pentecost, at the commencement of the Christian Church, as a sign that Jesus had sent the Holy Spirit to empower them. Speaking in tongues was becoming more widespread in various denominations and became one of the main evidences of the Charismatic movement. After this spiritual experience of speaking in tongues, once again there was a great feeling of relief and power to overcome the temptations that had been increasing. Now I had the same power the early disciples had, I would be able to live a holy life.

The Charismatic movement swept through the traditional churches like a wave in the 1970s, breathing new life and vitality into many decaying congregations. The manifestations of the Spirit were very controversial and some denominations vehemently opposed the revival, even to the point of calling the renewal a work of the devil. More than once other Christians told me that I was demon-possessed because I spoke in tongues. These supernatural experiences were not new, though, and occurred regularly in the Pentecostal churches that sprang up in America and other parts of the world from the early 1900s; the Azusa Street Revival of 1906 being commonly thought of as the birthplace of modern Pentecostalism. When the Pentecostal revival emerged, a wave of persecution followed. As has been the case throughout church history, the established forms of Christianity opposed the new churches, treating them as heretics and cults. Over the decades the radical Pentecostal movement lost its initial zeal and became as conservative as the churches they originally opposed.

When I later began working at Macquarie University as a laboratory assistant, I met some young people who attended a Pentecostal Church at Petersham. Historically it had been the first Assemblies of God church in Sydney, established in 1922 and the pastor known as P B Duncan was a founding father of the denomination. The supernatural tongue-speaking, healing and prophecy expressed during the services fascinated me, so I began attending there as well. The services were different but while I enjoyed the lively clapping and singing of choruses instead of boring outdated hymns, I could see how bound they had become by traditions. Behind the displays one could smell the stale stench of decaying religion.

The Charismatic renewal in Sydney had given birth to other services and numerous small Charismatic prayer meetings, but it was still very early days; mega-churches would not appear for at least another decade or so. The enthusiasm of the participants at this time certainly made up for the lack in numbers.

The largest and most exciting of the new churches was the Christian Faith Centre. Meetings were held in a disused scout hall in Turramurra, on the upper north shore of Sydney. I walked into the service not really knowing what to expect from this radical new group; I'd heard so many things. Everything about Christian Faith Centre was radical. Even though the service was scheduled to commence at 3pm, arriving on time meant you might be unable to get a seat. I remember one Sunday the service commenced early at 2.15pm because the building was already full. The service began without any leader or minister; there were no hymn books but people began singing and it gradually swelled into a crescendo of voices, all singing praise to God. Then, without any obvious signal, the entire congregation progressed into the most melodic heavenly singing I'd ever heard. Directed by some invisible conductor, it sounded like the song of angels as each individual began to sing their unique song of praise with harmonies, melodies, soprano and male voices all joining together producing a glorious anthem. One by one, people stood with hands upraised in worship. I stood in awe, feeling like I was in the very presence of God; it was amazing. In the Anglican Church I was used to hearing the wonderful choral pieces which we rehearsed for hours but this was happening spontaneously. Later I learnt that this was known as 'singing in the Spirit'.

I was sold. How could I remain in the Anglican Church attending dreary services written in a language that was archaic, and sing hymns that made church seem like a funeral service? However, because I had so many close friends at the Anglican Church, I maintained some involvement. Also, despite wanting to leave, I didn't feel Mum and Dad could cope with me rejecting their beloved church.

I didn't have to wait long before the local minister solved my problem. He kicked me out. I hadn't realised how upset the minister was about the number of people in the church and youth group who I'd introduced to the Charismatic movement. They were grateful for their newfound spirituality but he wasn't. It just wasn't Anglican. One Sunday night at youth fellowship, I was chatting casually with some of my friends when the minister appeared in the doorway of the church hall. By the look in his eyes, I could tell something was wrong. He kept me in his gaze as he walked towards me and, putting one arm around my shoulder then around my neck, marched me out of the church hall, while the youth group looked on in astonished silence. None of us had ever seen this man of the cloth seething before. Out of earshot of the youth group, he yelled at me, the familiar pious air in his voice replaced with rage. 'You are not going to take any more people away from my church!'

'I'm not taking people from the church; I'm introducing them to the power of the Holy Spirit,' I countered in a calm manner, knowing we were all better Christians for our extracurricular spiritual activities. This comment only fuelled his anger and he forbade me taking any more people to services elsewhere, finally issuing me with an ultimatum: 'Anglicanism and Pentecostalism don't mix. Decide what you want to be!' That was easy—I never went back.

I had such a strong desire to be obedient to God and live a life that would honour Him. People in these new groups genuinely believed God was very real and we were encouraged to develop a personal relationship with Him on a daily basis. This involved praying and reading our Bibles daily and also expecting to receive special guidance that we might do his work. I'd been praying about being more sensitive to the Holy Spirit's direction in my life and to learn to hear God's voice. I knew this didn't mean hearing voices but learning to listen to an inner prompting about decisions and choices. If I did what God wanted then I knew my life would be blessed—that's what the *Bible* promised me.

One day I was getting ready to go to work at Macquarie University and went to the bathroom to clean my teeth. Suddenly I got the impression that someone was saying to me, 'Quickly, I've provided a lift for you.' This was a strange thought so I dismissed it and continued getting ready. Then it came again. 'Hurry up, I've provided a lift for you.' I began arguing with the sanity of this suggestion. I didn't need a lift, I had my trusty little red Honda 50cc motorbike. Then it came again. I'd asked to be more sensitive to God's guidance but this seemed ridiculous. If the inner voice was saying 'take your *Bible* to work with you today, there is someone I want you to share it with,' then I probably would have packed it in my backpack immediately. The impression became stronger and I decided I'd never learn until I obeyed that inner voice. I remember thinking how crazy this was as I headed out the front door.

'You'll be late for work! Aren't you taking your motorbike?' Mum called out.

'It's okay, I've got a lift,' I replied hesitantly, knowing I would have to come up with some excuse if this didn't come off.

Walking to the front gate, I began to panic about the consequences of what I was doing; I'd be late for work. Then I heard a reassuring voice say, 'Trust me.' It seemed so real, just behind me, I almost turned around to see who'd said it, yet I was aware I'd not heard the words with my ears. Those words seemed to give me faith and, feeling more confident, I walked out onto the footpath expecting something to happen. As I looked to the left, two cars were coming my way. Instinctively I let the first one pass, crossed the road, and put my finger out to hitchhike when the next car pulled up. It was one of the members of the local Anglican Church.

'Where are you going?' he asked.

'Off to work,' I replied.

'I'll drive you there,' he quickly responded.

'No,' I protested, 'It's out of your way.'

'Get in,' he said, unconcerned about driving me the opposite direction to his normal route for work. I thanked him for the offer and thought it best not to mention what had happened minutes before, knowing most people would think I was mad. It seemed Charles was keen to unburden his heart and immediately began sharing some issues of faith and difficulties he was having in his marriage. Was this what God had planned? Considering my age, it seemed strange discussing such personal aspects of Charles's life. As we entered the gates of the university, I told Charles what had transpired that morning and that I had only walked out on the road to hitchhike because of a prompting. 'I've provided a lift for you.' Had this been a divine appointment?

I was elated that, even though I was only nineteen and a Christian of just eighteen months, God had spoken to me in such a clear way and through my obedience, I'd been able to help another person. Surely if I continued to learn sensitivity to the Holy Spirit's leading, God could use me in even greater ways. Serving God would be the ultimate reward but that would only happen if …

CHAPTER 5

Devils in bible college

Ever since I'd become a Christian I'd had the feeling that I was not going to be a pew-hugging believer, but that God had called me to preach and to make a difference in the world. A sense of destiny, you might call it. This meant that I had no other career ambitions. The desire to be a fireman or ballerina man had died during primary school. Dad was concerned about my lack of career focus and kept pressuring me about getting a job with a future. Dad and Mum's generation had known the effects of the Great Depression. I was regularly reminded of Mum's early school days when she would line up behind the rich kids to see who was lucky enough to be given the apple core when the rest had been eaten. The Depression creation of bread and dripping was something we still ate when we arrived home from school ravenous. No wonder that generation only ever wanted their children to have a job with security. I took the job at Macquarie University as a laboratory assistant for two reasons; I was working with two of my Christian friends, and I could save up to go to a bible college.

I was keen to attend Grace Bible College in New Zealand as the basic course only lasted four-and-a-half months compared to being locked away in some boring theological college for three or four years. From my observation, people in theological colleges commenced with enthusiasm and a genuine desire to serve God, but after the period of being cloistered away, emerged totally out of touch with the real world. We often called them theological cemeteries instead of theological seminaries. No-one was going to quench my spirit. It was important that I be trained quickly so I could get out and preach, as evil and unrighteousness was increasing in the world. The preaching I heard frequently focused on the urgency of the time, as Jesus was coming back soon and we had a responsibility to preach salvation to as many people as possible before He returned to earth. Even though the Second Coming of Christ had been predicted for nearly 2000 years, somehow it really seemed close.

I began dating a girl at Christian Faith Centre called Pam. We were so 'spiritual', and attended Christian meetings almost every night of the week, but the only real connection we had was our desire to serve God. Pam had already spent time working in the mission field in Papua New Guinea. Everyone in the church seemed pleased with this match. We were the perfect young Christian couple, always praying together, sharing *Bible* verses and making sure we were never in the vulnerable situation of sexual temptation. Good Christian couples don't engage in sex before marriage. 'Sex is like a fire,' we were told. 'In the fireplace of marriage, it provides warmth and comfort but take it out of that situation and you have a wildfire.' The problem was that, with Pam, I wasn't even smouldering, not a spark. I'd hold her hand and give her a quick goodnight kiss on the lips but that's as far as it went. This was very convenient for me, as I didn't have to deal with my lack of sexual response to females and having Pam by my side also demonstrated that God had really healed me of homosexuality.

During 1970, I put every spare dollar away for my bible college fees. When I finally plucked up the courage to tell my parents, they were predictably horrified. Dad made me promise that when I finished college I'd come back to Sydney and get a 'real job' as he called it. I said yes, but secretly hoped to be 'called' into the mission field when I finished my course.

So at the tender age of nineteen I was planning on serving God for the rest of my life. Pam and I booked a passage on the Northern Star cruise ship to Auckland. I don't know why we didn't fly; I guess it was because I hadn't travelled before and air travel was foreign to us. I'll never forget the farewell, as we had a huge entourage to see us off—about thirty in all, all of my family, Pam's family and friends from church. Tears began to flow as 'Now is the hour, when we must say goodbye' filtered through the speaker system, most of us aware this could be goodbye for a long time, maybe forever. Obedience to God's call would always be paramount.

The trip was terrible. After leaving Sydney Heads my stomach felt like it contained sour milk, but I was determined not to be sick as we believed all sickness was from the devil and should be resisted. Pam was encouraging me to have faith and believe that God could heal me. For days I lived with queasiness, burped with the consistency of a machine gun, and was always on the verge of vomiting. I felt such a failure running out of the dining room on the fifth day, gagging on the lumps of vomit forcefully making their way up my throat. Throwing up was a relief, but not as much as arriving in Auckland Harbour.

Driving onto Grace Bible College campus I felt like bursting into 'The hills are alive with the sound of music' as it was positioned in a beautiful rural setting, with a backdrop of a steep mountain spotted with fluffy white lambs. The college was only eighteen months old but already had successful graduates who'd become pastors and missionaries. The basic philosophy was that in order to serve God, you must firstly be 'called' and secondly receive short-term *Bible* training. After this, God would continue to teach while you served Him. 'We give the training, God gives the exams,' was the motto. I liked the practical philosophy. The first week was exciting, meeting the students who'd come from Australia and all over New Zealand. It was wonderful to think that now I could totally devote myself to *Bible* study and prayer, mundane, worldly things would no longer distract me and the final traces of my homosexuality could be dealt with.

A pattern had developed in my life, of cruising on a spiritual high for six months, then experiencing temptation and failure. About halfway through the course I was beginning to reach the end of a cycle. Masturbation was always the starting point of the downward spiral. Even though the *Bible* didn't specifically condemn masturbation, it was understood that God disapproved. In the Book of Genesis a man called Onan allowed 'his seed to fall on the ground' and the ground opened up and swallowed him. The story is not actually about masturbation; rather that Onan was avoiding his responsibility for maintaining his brother's descendants by having sex with his brother's widow. God had said to Adam and Eve in Genesis, 'Go forth and multiply' and to have sex except for procreation was disobedience to His command. Semen belonged in one place—a vagina—and anything else was self-gratification and sin. To serve God I must be holy and how could I ever expect to serve God with sin in my life? No matter how much I fought it, my mind would insidiously creep back to thoughts of sex with men. Jesus had said that even thinking about lusting after a woman in your mind was the same as actually doing it. I had double the battle to contend with, not just sexual temptation but the evil of homosexuality. Even though I knew it was wrong, I'd try to fantasise about having sex with a woman. Maybe this lesser of two evils might help me change so I'd experience temptation like any 'normal' male.

Not that I fantasised a lot. In fact, I'd developed an incredible strength of mind in this area, knowing I couldn't allow my mind to drift off to thoughts of sex with men. When I did notice an attractive guy, I immediately looked the other way and fought the thought by rebuking the devil, quoting scripture or singing a Christian song. When I masturbated, I did it as quickly as possible so that other fantasies wouldn't take control, and if I managed to do this I'd be okay. Total freedom seemed close, so I kept a record of how many times I masturbated to ensure God's power was stronger than my flesh. Most people would have thought the chart of ticks and crosses in the back of my *Bible* were about some spiritual exercise but to me they represented success or failure. Several times a week was totally unacceptable and even when I reduced the event to once a week I knew God was not pleased. It was like the first slippery step Satan used to take me back to my bad old ways.

The daily program at college was intense: we rose at 6am for a half-hour prayer meeting, then ate breakfast, and lectures went from 8am until 1pm. Then the afternoon was spent in private study and doing chores around the college. Monday night was missionary prayer meeting where we prayed for the world and ex-students, while other nights we were involved with the local churches, assisting in children's after-school *Bible* groups, prayer meetings and *Bible* studies.

Keeping my struggles secret, I thrived in this atmosphere and was a popular student at college. The 'romance' with Pam was suffering and she wasn't getting the attention she'd previously enjoyed as I now had so many other young Christian people to share my time with. The tension between us grew until finally she went to the college principal for counselling. I was called to his office to discuss the situation, where we concluded that while at college we should both concentrate only on our studies. I was a good boy and gave her the Dear John spiel, 'It's best we just be friends. I don't believe God wants us to be together at this time. Maybe after college.' The convenient thing about being a Christian was I could cloud my lack of commitment in spiritual terms.

The college principal lived on campus with his wife and children, had strong feminine traits and wore a toupee. I've never understood why people make such obvious attempts to hide their baldness—their attempts only attract more attention. While studying in the United States the principal and his wife had both discovered wigs, which were very popular amongst Americans in the fifties. In all the years I knew them I never saw their real hair, except for an occasional strand that rebelliously slipped out, like a weed in the crack of a cement path, seeking daylight.

It was obvious I was the principal's favourite; he spent more time with me than with other students and took me on special trips when he preached in different parts of New Zealand. There were times when he did unusual things—like squeeze my knee under the table while we said grace or make comments about how attractive other men in the college were. He was always looking for a response from me, but I just thought he had a bizarre sense of humour. He appeared genuinely concerned about me because of my intense desire to serve God.

My speaking experience had been limited to children's ministry and small *Bible* study groups, but I wanted to preach to crowds of people and be used by God in a greater way. Over the last two years, every time I heard someone preach on serving God I'd respond to the altar calls (the time at the conclusion of the service when people who feel they want to respond to God come forward for prayer) and plead with God to use my life for His glory. Now I was getting close to having that desire fulfilled, or so I thought.

Within weeks of arriving at college I had my first opportunity to practise my preaching skills. Most of the students were petrified about the idea of speaking in front of a congregation but I was champing at the bit. Every weekend small groups left the college to do 'outstation work', which involved travelling to smaller churches around New Zealand and spending the weekend speaking at youth meetings, Sunday school and the Sunday services. Many of these churches, being small, were unable to afford visiting speakers and so the congregations welcomed a different preacher to vary their diet. The majority of these congregations would never grow beyond a small handful of people because the local pastor lacked strong leadership skills as well as the ability to preach inspiring sermons. Lack of finance also meant most of the pastors had to work full-time in some form of secular employment, never able to move beyond their trade in order to devote all their energies to church growth.

As Pentecostal churches are biblically based, the source of our sermons was inspiration from God and the Bible. Once assigned for weekend preaching, we spent time praying, asking God to give us a message that would be particularly relevant to that congregation. During the week we developed the sermon by searching through our Bibles to find relevant verses and praying that God would use the words we spoke to touch the hearts of the people. Some of the students were embarrassingly hopeless speakers, but others of us just needed the chance to practise on these poor, struggling congregations.

My first opportunity to preach was in a tiny church of about twenty people in Rotorua. I was convinced I'd received a message from God on the importance of unity in the congregation. Later I was to learn that it was a relevant message to every small congregation, as the small-ness of their church often meant there were power groups where egos and gossip flourished. I knew from my observation of various preach-ers that, when preaching, there were a number of indicators that demonstrated success. Was the congregation asleep or awake? Awake, good. Now look at the faces and see if they are bored or interested? The real measure of success was the 'altar call'. If people responded by coming to the front of the church during the final song for prayer, I knew I'd successfully communicated what God wanted me to say, and returned to college elated that God had used me. Sometimes it worked and if it didn't I reasoned it was because the congregation was unre-sponsive or hardened to the Spirit of God. Just one sweet, little old lady came to me at the end of that particular service in Rotorua, held my hand and complimented me on how much she enjoyed my sermon— then I found out she was totally deaf.

As college progressed I was having more difficulty with temptation, which left me feeling condemned and a failure, increasing my sense that I was unworthy to serve God. Living in an environment where everyone appeared so holy and righteous made me feel worse and it came to a point where my inability to suppress these thoughts made me depressed. It became increasingly difficult to attend the lectures or prayer meetings, so one day I quietly slipped away from college to try and get some answers from God. I wanted to spend the day alone, so climbed the mountain behind the college and sat staring at the view. After a while I noticed an unusual amount of activity on the college campus, with students and staff scurrying between the several buildings. Initially, it never occurred to me that I was the reason for this activity and that they might be trying to find me. Finally, realising this flurry of activity was caused by my disappearance, I decided to come down and face the music. My welcome was like that of the prodigal son and I was immediately ushered into the principal's office. Apparently the reason people became so anxious was that during the previous year a young male student had disappeared and was found drowned a few days later. Possible suicide was the coroner's report, and I often wondered if his problem had been the same as mine. Thoughts of taking my life were always prevalent at my lowest points of discouragement and failure.

The principal was in a frantic state, knowing the scandal of another possible suicide would be detrimental to the college's reputation. Apologising for the drama I had caused, I sat in his office, pouring my heart out but trying to disguise my problems in terms that wouldn't indicate I was homosexual. 'I'm struggling with sin, trying to overcome temptation, the devil seems to get the victory,' were phrases I used to screen out that one word. The same word described as an abomination in the book of Leviticus and deserving of the death penalty. It wasn't until thirty years later that I discovered that the word homosexual had not appeared in the *Bible* before 1946 and that the word, like the recent invention of metrosexual, only came into existence in 1869. I always read the Revised Standard Version of the Bible, which was the first translation to use the word. It was obvious to the principal that I was hiding something so he kept pressing for more details. Finally, I got the words out. 'I have homosexual thoughts.' It was better to say I had homosexual thoughts than to say I was a homosexual, thus trying to distance myself from the reality of being an abomination to God. Opening my heart, I talked about the struggles I'd been through and the cycles that had occurred since becoming a Christian.

Like the diagnosis of a terminal disease you don't want to hear from a doctor, the principal suggested that maybe I had demons in my life and that exorcism was the only way to be released from the power that was taking over my life. The reason I had not become totally free, he suggested, was that these demons needed to be cast out. There was plenty of evidence in the gospels of Jesus setting people free by casting out devils. It sounded logical to me because I'd tried everything to break the pattern and yet the desires only seemed to leave for a while, always returning like devastating bouts of chronic fatigue. This must be the answer I was looking for; thank God, at last I was going to be free.

The expression on the principal's face changed. 'You're not the only one to have struggles like this,' he said, with what appeared to be a strong sense of empathy. I wondered if he could be talking about himself, but surely a man of God with such a well-known ministry would never experience temptation like I did? It was inconceivable. He must be referring to one of the other students—but I couldn't think who.

Deliverance and casting out demons was a controversial doctrine in the Pentecostal churches in Australia, one which only the most outrageous practised, because it was believed to be impossible for Christians to have demons. Once a person has become a Christian, how can demons continue to take possession? 'If any man be in Christ, he is a new creature: old things are passed away; behold, all things are become new', it said in 2 Corinthians 5:17. During the early weeks at college, Pastor Frank Houston had taught us the doctrine of exorcism and I was beginning to see things from a different perspective. I was hoping the principal would take me through the exorcism and save me the embarrassment of telling another man of God I was a homosexual. Frantic phone calls were made. I thought it strange when I was informed that the principal had arranged for me to be taken to Auckland later that week and have the top deliverance ministers in New Zealand cast the demons out of me. The next few days were torturous and depressing, as I walked around college believing devils were inside of me. Why did I have to wait so long? If I had demons, why didn't they cast them out immediately? How could they leave me like a patient dumped in emergency with an iron stake still through their leg?

I'd heard frightening stories about people screaming, contorting and frothing at the mouth when devils were cast out of them but whatever it took to get rid of these terrible thoughts, I wanted to do it. Word quickly spread around the campus, 'Tony's demon-possessed,' adding to the sense of alienation I was already feeling.

I travelled to Auckland the following weekend with Paul, one of the married students, so that a pastor of a large Pentecostal Church could pray for me after the evening service. The pastor was like a Christian mystic who regularly spoke of his visions, personal encounters with angels and ability to see into the spiritual world. Apparently, during the services, there was a special powerful 'anointing' that made the exorcism easier.

Normally, I'd be excited to be at this church as it was famous for the miracles and the growth experienced during the 'Jesus movement', but I felt very uncomfortable during the service. Tension began to build in me when the service commenced. I feared the demons inside me would possibly take control and make a public spectacle of me. When the preaching came to a close and the pastor asked people to come forward for prayer, it felt like the demons were rising up inside me wanting to come out. I stood sweating and shaking while I watched several people scream and convulse as the pastor yelled, 'Come out, you devil!'

The altar call seemed endless and when the service finally concluded forty-five minutes later, the pastor walked towards me and introduced himself. I felt incredibly privileged that this great man of God was prepared to give me such personal attention. He looked at me sadly and seemed genuinely concerned. I tried to smile and look appreciative but it didn't work; I burst into tears.

The pastor, his assistant and my friend Paul led me up the stairs to the hall above the main auditorium. Cold and empty, our footsteps amplified and echoed as we walked across the polished wooden floor. The only comfort I had at this point was that no-one was going to see me manifesting demons. What was going to happen? How long was this going to take? Was it going to be painful? I was becoming even more anxious. A seat was placed in the middle of this huge hall and as I sat the others walked to different parts of the hall, picking up chairs for themselves and returning to surround me like Indians around a wagon train. I noticed one of the pastors had an old newspaper but I was unsure what it was for.

'The first thing you need to do is confess all your sins,' the pastor said. So I confessed everything I could think of beginning with the sin of homosexuality. 'Now don't pray,' he continued, 'it will stop the demons from coming out.' They began praying and speaking in tongues while I sat passively, waiting for something to happen. Nothing. The assistant pastor, who was being apprenticed, began commanding the demons to manifest themselves and come to the surface. Still nothing. 'Start breathing out, expel the demon, you have to want to get rid of these things.' Filling my lungs with air, I tried to expel more than I'd taken in. I felt something begin to happen, a tingling sensation in my fingers and around my mouth. This must be the demon coming to the surface I thought, not realising these were symptoms of hyperventilation.

The pastors became more excited and began yelling and shouting, louder and louder. 'Come out, come out, you unclean, foul spirit from the pit of hell! You have to obey us, we have the authority of Jesus Christ the Son of God. Name yourself!' Apparently it was important to know the demon's name. When Jesus had difficulty casting a particularly strong demon out of a man, he asked it to name itself. 'Legion,' the demon said, 'for we are many.' Surely then there must be a multitude of demons living in me? The pastor said he could count them as they left. The more they yelled the stronger I felt the sensations, until my hands, fingers and face became contorted and tight and I fell off the seat onto the floor. The pastors became more excited and commanded the spirits to leave me. This continued to build to a crescendo as I began to moan trying to expel the demon. I coughed and at this sign the newspaper was produced and laid on the floor next to me. After thirty minutes or so, I finally coughed up some phlegm and spat it on the conveniently placed newspaper.

Now at a feverish pitch the pastors screamed, 'That's it, come out you devil, you must obey the name of Jesus!' For another twenty minutes I continued to cough and moan, encouraged by the delight of the pastors as they praised God for His power. But this was not the end; apparently I had many devils. The exorcism went on for almost two hours until I was totally exhausted. What a relief it was to hear them finally praying for God's peace to fill me. I thought it was over.

'How do you feel?' the pastor asked when all the activity had died down. I felt a sense of relief but not totally free. 'I think you need more prayer,' he continued. So the next three Sunday nights I travelled to Auckland and endured a similar performance. Over the next three weeks, at the pastors' prompting, I confessed everything I could think of—homosexuality, masturbation, spiritism, witchcraft, stealing a Violet Crumble honeycomb bar at the local shop when I was ten years old—until I was unable to think of another thing. I even had to renounce my father's and grandfather's involvement in the Masonic Lodge because the *Bible* says that 'God visits the sins of the fathers to the third and fourth generations' and the Masonic Lodge was considered a satanic group. All kinds of demons were cast out—every sexual perversion imaginable, necromancy, spirits of fear, deception and insanity—

until finally it seemed they were all gone.

Although this leading pastor was considered to have great spiritual gifts, several years later he had to leave the church under a cloud of accusations of false teaching and having an affair with his secretary. He moved to Australia and began a new church.

I felt greatly relieved returning to bible college on the Monday morning after the final deliverance session and everyone commented that I looked different. Being free meant I could now get on with my calling and serve God with a holy life. This new experience placed me even higher in the popularity stakes at college. No wonder the homosexual desires had kept coming back, it all made sense now—it was those rotten demons. They were gone and I certainly wasn't going to fall back into the old traps of the devil. The rest of college was a breeze and whenever temptation came my way, I just said, 'Devil, I resist you in the name of Jesus, I won't let you in.'

I never spoke publicly about my experience for fear of people's reactions. Also, I still wasn't sexually attracted to women so didn't have the evidence I was totally healed.

After graduation, before returning home, I travelled south with the college registrar and a few students to spend a week with some friends in Wellington. They stayed at Hastings, halfway down the north island, and I was to travel further south. It was late at night and I booked into a local caravan park, planning to hitchhike to Wellington the next morning. For nearly six months, I had been constantly surrounded by Christians and, as the others drove off, I felt alone, vulnerable and restless. I walked into the town to get something to eat, and passed the local cinema. At the time, attending movies was frowned upon in Pentecostal circles, as was dancing, wearing make-up and listening to 'worldly music', but I felt I was fairly safe considering that *Paint Your Wagon* was G-rated. I bought my ticket and sat alone in the middle of the theatre. While the previews were showing, a man in his early thirties sat next to me and we nodded a casual hello to each other as he sat down to watch the movie. I felt a small movement as his leg brushed against mine. I drew my leg away. People do that accidentally, I thought. As the house lights went down for the main feature he moved his leg over again to touch mine. The hot sexual feeling that had been extinguished over the last few months began to rise again, but I didn't want it. My legs began to shake and it was difficult to concentrate on the movie as I fought an internal battle. I'd been delivered, how could this be happening? The demon of homosexuality had been cast out and no longer had control over me. Don't go back, Tony, you've got the power to beat this.

When the movie finished, I got up and shuffled slowly with the crowd out of the theatre. Part of me wanted to run away as quick as possible but another part wanted what was being offered. In the brightness of the foyer I paused, allowing my eyes to become accustomed to the light. I sensed the man was hot on my heels and, looking around, I saw him standing just a few metres away, staring at me. When our eyes met my resistance fell—it was the point of no return I was too familiar with. I'd learnt through many experiences not to play with temptation—if a time factor was involved then I was destined to fall. I was too weak. We said hello and walked out onto the street. I was surprised at the ease at which I was willing to cooperate as we walked away from the theatre together and even more shocked at what came out of my mouth.

'Would you like to come back to my caravan for a coffee?' I asked. It had been nearly twelve months since I'd done anything like this and as we walked to the caravan park, the battle continued in my mind, the thoughts of resisting slowly overtaken by thoughts of yielding.

I couldn't believe the lies I gave to his questions about who I was, why I was here and where I was going. The words I'd often heard, 'the life of the homosexual is a life of deceit', kept playing in my mind. Once inside the caravan I made a cup of coffee and was hoping that if I stalled, somehow, I might become strong enough to say no, just have a conversation, maybe even tell him that Jesus could set him free and he should become a Christian. That would be a wonderful victory. While I was making the coffee, he moved from the galley seat and started kissing the back of my neck. That was all I needed; I was gone. The sex was awkward, amateur and quick—all over, for me, in a matter of minutes. The many thoughts running through my mind ensured I couldn't focus on pleasure. As usual, I wanted to get away from the person immediately; the sense of guilt and failure had settled in.

The man was obviously very dissatisfied and kept pressuring me to let him stay the night but I resisted, making up every excuse I could think of. I was getting worried about being alone with him in the caravan and wondered if I could resist him if he tried to attack me. What a fool I'd been to once again place myself in such a vulnerable situation. Finally, realising that I was totally disinterested, he left.

I had something else to contend with now—the thought that the demons that had been cast out of me would come back in again. Jesus said that if a person who had been delivered allowed the demons to come back, those demons would bring many more with them, so that person's state would be worse than before. I fell into a restless sleep, crying and pleading with God to forgive me. Could it be possible that I'd become demon-possessed again? I really didn't know.

The very next day a bizarre thing happened. At the outskirts of the town I began hitchhiking south, trying to put last night's events behind me. Within minutes a car pulled up – 'I'm off to Wellington,' the man in his early thirties said. 'Perfect, me too,' I replied gratefully, stepping into the car so I could sit back and relax for the rest of the journey. It was important to introduce the fact that I was a Christian into the conversation early to ensure that I wouldn't be tempted. Plus, of course, we were taught that Christians are supposed to talk to as many people about God as they can. When the driver asked what church I attended, I replied the Assemblies of God, and he immediately asked which one. Once he realised I was from Australia he talked openly about his current girlfriend, a nurse, who'd had a secret sexual relationship with a pastor's son. He chuckled often as he detailed the sordid affair and I sat and listened, not letting on that I knew them both. Her family attended the church and the pastor's son was going through bible college. My travelling companion thought the hypocrisy of it was very amusing; the fact that these two were regularly getting off behind everyone's back while the church thought they were models of Christian morality. In the more 'spiritual' church in Auckland I'd heard this particular church spoken of: 'an unclean demon of immorality inhabits the congregation,' I'd been warned. Now it appeared I was hearing this confirmed by a non-Christian total stranger.

The synchronicity of this encounter baffled me for years and made me wonder the purpose of knowing this information. The only conclusion I could come to was that this encounter was a reminder that no secret is safe, everything comes out in the end, and everything happens for a reason.

CHAPTER 6

In the army now

By 1971, the Australian government had been sending troops to the Vietnam War for the previous six years. Australia had followed the lead of the American draft system and in 1964 National Service was introduced with selected twenty-year-olds, based on date of birth, required to give two years' continuous full-time service. It was becoming increasingly obvious that the Vietnam War was a costly mistake with over 1000 troops dying per month. The American and Australian populations were polarised and there were constant protests. The opposition had been growing during the late 1960s and the first visit of an American president to Australia only exacerbated the problem. In 1966 US President Lyndon Johnson came to Australia for talks on Vietnam, cheered on by the Prime Minster, Harold Holt, who'd picked up the Democratic Party's campaign slogan, 'All the way with LBJ.' While President Johnson was riding with the New South Wales Premier Robin Askin through the streets of Sydney, the car was surrounded by Vietnam protesters. Askin told their driver, 'Run the bastards over.' Emotions were running high and large protest rallies occurred around the world. The largest protest to ever happen in Australia occurred when 100,000 people occupied the streets of Melbourne in 1970. As a pacifist in high school I'd opposed the war, but since becoming a Christian my political beliefs had mellowed somewhat. After all, the godless ideology of communism was evil, possibly even the Antichrist,

I'd heard preachers say.

Towards the end of college, I received a letter saying that my birthday, 13 March, was one of the chosen dates for conscription and I was to report for a medical examination in Sydney. At first I was unsure how to respond because becoming a soldier had never been a part of my plans, especially after the experiences of cadets in high school. More importantly, how could I, as a Christian, kill anyone? The idea was horrifying. I wrote to the National Service Board letting them know I was completing theological studies and asked if I was able to postpone national service until I finished college. The reply was swift, informing me that I must return to Australia as soon as the course finished as my name was down for the intake in August. I hoped God would call me to a foreign mission field and that I could continue postponing conscription until the war was over. Failing that, there was always the option of becoming a conscientious objector based on religious grounds, though this option had its limitations. Even though the numbers were growing, only 700 men were granted total exemption from military service and the court battles were long and costly. Opposing the government in such a public way would also be very embarrassing for my parents. Dad had willingly served his country and for me to not fulfil my responsibility as a citizen of Australia would have been too much.

As the college course was coming to an end I made the conscription issue a matter of prayer. Reading through the *Bible* it was unclear what I should do as a Christian. The Old Testament had numerous examples of God's people being involved in war and the great warrior patriarchs leading the nation of Israel into battle. The New Testament was a different story. In the famous Sermon on the Mount, Jesus talked about loving your neighbour and that even hating someone in your heart was the same as murder. Later, in the New Testament, the apostles Peter and Paul both mentioned that Christians should obey the laws of the land and if they were soldiers that they should be good soldiers of Christ. It was always difficult to determine exactly what God wanted me to do in the face of such contradictions.

The more I prayed, the stronger I felt God wanted me to do my national service, and with this conviction came another unusual impression. It was as though God was telling me I'd only be in the army for a short time. It was very confusing, especially trying to understand why God would want me to kill people who were going to hell. Surely I'd been called to save people from that fate.

After my eventful trip to Wellington, I left New Zealand at the beginning of July and returned to Sydney, hoping and praying I wouldn't have any more slip-ups. My family was pleased to see me back on Australian soil and when I attended Christian Faith Centre, people quizzed me about my reaction to being conscripted.

'I believe God wants me to do it,' I replied confidently, 'Maybe the army is my mission field.' I could see that most doubted what I was saying and only saw mission work in non-English-speaking countries as worthy of the term 'mission field'. The next day I had my medical for national service. Thank God it wasn't as humiliating as the times at cadet camp—this time each candidate was examined individually. Secretly I wished I'd made a mistake about what God wanted me to do and was hoping the doctor would discover I had flat feet or something else that would make me unsuitable as a soldier. Guys were going to great lengths to escape national service. I remembered that Student Underground, the communist group I'd belonged to in high school, had produced a small booklet called *How to Escape the Draft*, which offered a range of suggestions. The police raided Bob Gould's leftist bookshop in Goulburn Street and all the copies were seized and destroyed, but not before I'd read the contents. 'Camping it up' was one suggestion—homosexuals were not wanted in the forces—but I knew I couldn't do that. Some guys didn't eat for days and put puncture holes in their forearms, giving the impression that they were addicts. There was also the option of pretending to have some form of mental illness and dribbling a lot during the medical. The list was extensive but I couldn't do any of these things because I believed that if God didn't want me in the army, He would do something about it. As far as I could see, going into the army could only be happening for one reason—to serve God in the forces. I would have preferred being called to Papua New Guinea, Africa or Asia but I'd given my life to God, and His will for my life was what I must yield to.

Several days after the medical, the letter arrived and my heart sank as I read the instructions. Within three days I must report at the recruitment centre and then be transferred to Wagga Wagga for ten weeks of basic training. I would be in the army for the next two years with the possibility of being sent to Vietnam. Again, the impression came to me that I'd only be in the army for a short time.

I spent the few remaining days in Sydney catching up with people in the church and my family, knowing I'd miss them all. After being processed at the recruitment centre, I was loaded onto buses with about two hundred other recruits and driven out of Sydney. It was daunting being with this group of strangers and not knowing what lay ahead. As the bus drove down Wentworth Avenue, we passed my father's workplace and I saw him crossing the road, walking directly towards the bus. Hoping to get his attention I waved and tapped on the window, trying not to make too much of a spectacle of myself in front of all these strangers. He was too busy watching cars whizzing past and so was unable to notice his son gesturing frantically. Although Dad and I were never really close, this was one moment when I craved a connection. A sense of isolation crept over me as one by one familiar sights disappeared behind me.

The main objectives of the ten-week basic training were to bring us to a level of physical fitness and to transform us psychologically. To create a soldier out of a civilian means you must break his will; this ensures he's a person who obeys orders and works together with his fellow soldiers. This was achieved by driving us to physical limits, commanding us to do things that we hated doing and taking us to breaking point. Only people who've experienced extreme group dynamics or pack mentality would understand the impact of this pressure. The first step in the process was to ensure we lost our identity as individuals—the haircuts achieved this successfully. I'd purposely had the shortest haircut of my life before going to training camp, as I wanted to be spared the humiliation of the army barbers giving me one of their butcher jobs—I took pride in my appearance. My first lesson was that, in the army, everyone is treated the same. Anyone who protested ended up with an almost shaved head, so I remained silent, allowing the army barber to successfully destroy a perfectly good haircut.

The next step in de-individualising us was the uniform. I took my place in the queue of one hundred guys waiting for their issue of equipment and uniform. Once inside the building, I noticed the speed with which the recruits were being fitted out. The pants, shirts, socks, underwear, blankets, sheets, et cetera, all in jungle green, were unceremoniously thrown at us, and finally a hat was slammed on our heads. Struggling with the load of an entire wardrobe, I searched for a place among the piles of clothes and half-naked bodies to try on my uniform. Privacy: another thing that had disappeared. The sergeants yelled at anyone who complained about wrong sizes, so I was grateful my uniform was at least a reasonable fit. I knew that tightening the belt would keep my fifteen-centimetres-too-large trousers up.

Emerging from the store we lined up in rows of threes: huge brown duffel bags loaded with summer and winter uniforms on the right shoulder; blankets, linen and pillow precariously balanced on the other side. 'Left, left, left, right, left,' screamed the sergeant in our ears as we struggled down to the barracks like circus performers practising a balancing act. I was allocated to Platoon 17 in D block on the second level of the three-storey barracks, built to accommodate about seventy men on each floor. Some guys had already bonded. Finding a room with a spare bed I began to pack my stuff away and put on my uniform, carefully folding and putting my civilian clothes away to take on my identity as a soldier in the Australian Military Forces. I introduced myself to the three strangers who would be my room-mates for the next ten weeks. They seemed friendly and fairly normal guys and I wondered if any of them felt as scared and disoriented as I did. I doubted that there was anyone else concerned about living in such close quarters with all those men.

Nicknames were quickly allocated to most in the platoon but showed little imagination as they usually ended in 'y' or 'o'. Macko, Johnno, Westy and Chucky; there was no particular pattern to the naming. It could come from your first or last name or the town or suburb you came from. I was unimaginatively named Browny. The next few weeks were an intense program of indoctrination, ensuring we no longer thought of ourselves as individual civilians but as a platoon of soldiers; to think and act as one and always look out for your mate. We were instructed in the precise way to make a bed, the way to dress, how to pack our lockers, the way to act, how to respond, when to go to sleep and when to wake up.

Our sergeant had managed to learn every swear word in the English language and in one sentence of twelve words ensured that at least six were profane. To me as a Christian, the 'fucks', 'shits' and 'cunts' were offensive enough but mentioning Jesus Christ, Mary and God every time with such an aggressive tone made it blasphemous and even more disgusting. I got to the point where I was actually glad to hear him swear mildly. We spent endless hours marching up and down the parade ground while he shouted abuse.

'I'm going to make fuckin' soldiers out of you fuckin' assholes!' The slightest error triggered a barrage of abuse from the sergeant, three inches from your face. Suddenly I was grateful for the training I'd received in the school cadets—at least I knew how to respond to the commands of quick march, halt, about face, eyes left, right and left turn.

We would have mastered the drill much quicker had we not had at least ten guys who'd obviously been born with two left feet.

Getting up at 5.30am for 6am reveille parade was torture, as it was usually below freezing in Wagga Wagga that time of morning. You could feel the crispness of the snow in the biting winds blowing in from Australia's highest peak, Mount Kosciuszko, not far away. Talk about brass monkeys. You could even see the condensation of our breath in the room before getting out on the parade ground. Never a morning person, I wished I could return to my warm bed instead of standing on the cold, dark parade ground, waiting for the sergeant to do a roll call to ensure everyone was out of bed and no-one had gone AWOL.

As the weeks went by, more and more of us became sick until the colds turned into flu and, for some, pneumonia. Reporting to the doctor with an illness was considered weak: you had to be on your deathbed. The sergeant let us know in no uncertain terms that anyone relieved of duties because of illness was a wimp, had let the platoon down, and deserved harsher treatment in order to toughen them up. The hacking coughs every morning and night were horrific. I'll never forget one morning when I stood next to a guy called Johnno. He coughed the most horrendous cough for at least ten minutes until finally between the spasms and gasping for air, he screamed in frustration, 'Get out and walk, you bastard!' The entire platoon cracked up, the comic relief was most welcome. The sergeant, seeing the humour but knowing he had momentarily lost control, quickly snapped, through a wry smile, 'Shut up, you fuckin' bastards, you're on fuckin' parade!'

Frightening stories of Christian guys being bashed because they would not deny their beliefs or join in the activities of the other platoon members filtered through the army camp, some apparently even hospitalised with broken ribs and other injuries. Courage was not my strong point and the thought of being beaten up was terrifying but

I knew I must maintain a strong Christian witness. I consoled myself in the fact that I was fortunate, as I was not one of the thousands of Christians behind the iron and bamboo curtains who, at that time, were tortured for their faith. It didn't take much to stand out from the crowd—I was the only one in the platoon who didn't swear, drink, tell filthy jokes, smoke or have pictures of naked women all over my locker door.

Those pictures of women with their legs apart and huge breasts were so crude. (Of course it wasn't until many years later that I realised my repulsion was not so much righteous indignation but the fact that I was homosexual not heterosexual.) These guys really needed Jesus. I had *Bible* verses and Christian poems behind my locker door, as this was the only bit of individuality allowed. At 8am, after breakfast, our uniforms, rooms and lockers were inspected. Every bed had to be made perfectly and each article of clothing folded exactly as the sergeant had taught us. If there were any flaws then the entire contents of the locker or the meticulously folded blankets were thrown on the floor.

'Make that fuckin' bed again, you fuckin' idiot. That cupboard looks like a fuckin' brothel. Your fuckin' mother isn't here to do your fuckin' housework. Now do the fuckin' thing again!'

During one of these early inspections, when the sergeant looked through my locker, he paused for a moment scanning the *Bible* verses pinned behind my wardrobe door. I froze in the tense silence expecting a barrage of abuse at any moment. What should I do if he asked me to tear them down? Over the sergeant's shoulder, I could see every eye in the room on me, awaiting an outcome.

'Do you believe that stuff, Recruit Venn-Brown?' he snapped in his usual gruff voice.

'Yes, Sergeant,' I snapped back with as much confidence as I could muster, knowing any sign of weakness would be taken advantage of. There was another uneasy pause before the sergeant snapped again.

'Good,' he said, turning on his heels and marching out to terrorise the guys in the next room. I nearly wet myself with relief but felt good that I'd made a stand. Determined to continue with my witness until each guy in the platoon knew I was a Christian, I always carried a little pocket *Bible* with me and took it out to read at every opportunity.

Our platoon consisted of regular soldiers who'd enlisted and those of us who'd been conscripted. The regular soldiers were a motley crew consisting of guys who had been in gaol, men who wanted to get away from the responsibilities of wives and kids, others who couldn't get a job, and a couple who weren't the brightest of boys. Only one or two of the conscripts really wanted to be there and the rest of us resented the fact that the government had stolen two of the best years our lives to fight what was obviously America's un-winnable war. The peer pressure in the platoon was enormous and I was surprised how many guys weakened to conform to the group's attitudes and moral standards. After six weeks of basic training, we were allowed to go into the closest city, Wagga Wagga, for our first weekend leave. Sex had been the topic of conversation every spare moment and it seemed that the objective of each man over the weekend leave was to get drunk and laid as quickly and often as possible. This included single and married men as only a handful took the opportunity to go home and visit their wives and families. The ultimate objective of the weekend, though, was to guarantee that the few guys who had been brave enough to admit they were virgins returned to camp with at least one root under his belt. Not that there were many, but certainly everyone knew who they were crusading for. It was quite tragic to see men who had a good marriage and family at home pressured into sleeping with a hooker or being unfaithful to their wives. I thought the whole exercise was barbarous and was sure that under normal circumstances most of them would have maintained fidelity. Heterosexual males at their worst. The army prepared us for the weekend by showing us a highly educational film on the prevention of sexually transmitted diseases, with demonstrations, to ensure we didn't get the 'clap' as it was called. After all, we want our boys to have fun, but not get sick.

Of course I didn't want any part of the platoon's activities but the rare opportunity of getting out of the camp was not to be missed. Passing through the gates of Kapooka Army Base produced an extraordinary feeling of relief, like being released from prison. My goal was to find a church and have some fellowship with Christians so I went to visit the Assemblies of God Church for the morning service. Even though the congregation was small and traditional, the services were like an oasis in my desert of immorality, profanity and debauchery. A large Scottish family in the church were extremely kind and took pity on me—every weekend from that first day out of camp they invited me home for beautiful home-cooked meals and fellowship. The opportunity to share with other Christians and talk about God without the fear of reprisal was so refreshing.

We had to return to camp by Sunday night and even at a distance from the barracks I heard the laughter as stories were being told of the weekend conquests, some still in the final stages of their alcoholic stupor. Apparently, every goal was achieved. However, I noticed some guys trying to hide their unhappiness—obviously not everyone was pleased with what they had done. It's very difficult to hide guilt. That's how a mother always knows when her children have done something wrong.

'What are you doing?' my mother would say, surprising me after I had quickly scoffed a couple of Adora Cream Wafers.

'Nothing,' was my quick response, attempting to hide the crime.

'You've done something wrong; it's written all over your face!' she'd reply.

And I could never work out how she knew.

Guilt was hanging over some of these men like a dark storm cloud—it can take days to leave, I knew all about that. Through the speaker system, the bugle played the Last Post for lights out at 10pm and, as the final sounds of revelry dissipated, I quietly got into bed, praying God would give me strength to get through the final four weeks of basic training.

The pressure of being in this environment was beginning to affect me—there was never any escape. I was experiencing the same physical and psychological pressures as the rest of the guys in my platoon but on top of that I had other things causing me stress. For the past six months in bible college I'd been living in a totally protected, spiritual and Christian environment, but now I was surrounded by everything I thought of as evil. It made me feel like I'd been transported directly from heaven to hell. It felt like everyone was against me and even though I hadn't been overtly trying to convert anyone in the platoon, I knew I wasn't popular. Most of the guys kept clear of me and only talked to me when it was really necessary, for fear of being preached at. The isolation, threats and oppressive environment became too much, and finally I cracked.

I was having my evening meal with three hundred soldiers in the dining hall but was sitting away from my platoon. Every time I sat with the guys from my platoon they made sure I wasn't included in the conversation, making me feel more like an outsider. If I sat with a stranger, though, we might start a conversation about the activities of the day or, better still, I might get an opportunity to tell them about the difference Jesus Christ had made in my life. Looking down at the sloppy stew mixing with the watery mashed potatoes and peas that had turned yellow from being boiled too long, I began to lose focus. My eyes filled with water. I slowly moved the slop around the plate with my fork and tried to gain my composure but tears began to fall into the plate adding to the watery mess. It was impossible to hold them back. The guys around me looked bewildered as I quickly grabbed my plate and utensils and ran from the mess hall. I moved as fast as possible trying to contain the emotions that were erupting in me, but where could I go? Not back to the barracks where others could see me in this state.

I hurried to the tiny chapel on the base, which was my only place of refuge. Thank God the building was open and no-one was there. Of course, it wasn't Sunday. I sat down on a hard wooden bench and sobbed for over an hour, waiting to be in control enough to return to my room. Just when I thought I'd gained my strength again, another wave of sobbing came over me. I prayed and prayed. 'God, please help me, help me be strong for you and a witness to those around me. You'll have to help me, I don't think I can go on much longer.' Out of the public eye, I was unaware how much noise I was making until I heard the door open at the back of the chapel. Looking up, my eyes slowly focused on the figure moving towards me. It was one of the corporals who trained us in weapon maintenance.

'What's wrong? Are you all right?' His genuine, warm voice was a welcome relief from the aggressive shouting I'd been encountering for weeks. Apparently I'd been crying so loudly it could be heard on the road fifty metres away, so he had come to see what the noise was about. The last thing I wanted was to be discovered as a blithering idiot crying his heart out in a church. In a guarded way, between the sobs, I tried to explain.

'I've just come out of bible college and I'm finding it difficult adjusting to army life,' I replied. I couldn't get much else out as every time I tried to speak, I sobbed even more.

'Would you like to speak to your sergeant or lieutenant? Shall I get someone for you?' he asked in a caring way, but I knew it could be dangerous to reveal too much. He sat with me a while, putting his arm around my shoulder and giving me a reassuring squeeze every time I'd begin to cry again.

'Everything's going to be okay,' he said and just those few words and kind touch were enough to help me gain some strength. Finally, I was able to say, 'I'll be okay, I just need some time alone.' He smiled and patted me on the shoulder as he left the chapel, reassuring me once again that I'd be okay. I thanked him for his kindness but was thinking next time I saw him I'd feel strange knowing he had seen behind my facade.

Feeling stronger by the minute I continued to pray that God would use me to influence the lives of those in my platoon and help them to know God loved them and promised them a better life. Then it came to me, that impression I'd had months earlier, 'You won't be in the army for long.' It was so clear. 'What do you mean?' I responded in my mind. The thought came again, 'You'll only be in the army for a short time.' 'Okay, when will I be out? Give me a date!' I replied, becoming a little annoyed at the vagueness of the impression that had come to me on several occasions now. As soon as I'd said this, the eighteenth of October became clear in my mind. My initial reaction was that I was imagining things, as this was only weeks away, or could I be going crazy with the pressure? Could my mind be playing tricks on me? I tried to think of other dates but no matter how much I tried, only one stayed indelibly in my mind. The eighteenth of October. That's it, God's going to get me out of the army by the eighteenth of October. This new inner knowledge strengthened me and I began to feel better immediately. In fact, I was sure God had really spoken to me. Returning to the barracks, I went to bed early and, facing the wall, prayed. 'I don't know how you're going to do it, God, but I believe you are going to get me out of here by the eighteenth of October. Thank you.'

I was surprised to be called out of the platoon exercises the next day by the sergeant.

'You've got an appointment at the medical block,' he said. I asked what was happening but he said he didn't know. Reporting to the medical centre I waited in the reception area. An officer appeared through the frosted glass door and invited me to come inside, introducing himself as one of the army psychiatrists. Apparently, the corporal who'd spoken to me in the chapel had tracked me down and recommended I have some counselling. The psychiatrist, an avowed atheist, asked me about bible college and my experiences and tried to argue with me about everything I believed. But I remained strong in my faith. I didn't dare tell him God was going to have me out of the army in a few weeks—they have places for people who hear voices.

'Are you happy in the army?' he asked. Maybe this might be the answer to my prayers and I'd be discharged from the army but I was concerned they could have me committed as mentally unstable. I also knew it wouldn't be a good witness to be discharged as a fruitcake or someone who was too weak to cope. Thinking about the implications of my response, I answered very cautiously. 'Not really.' I thought I'd take the risk and asked, 'Can I get a discharge?'

'No!' the officer snapped back. His aggressive approach was very different to my experience with Doctor Denzo three years earlier. The psychiatrist reinforced that I had to learn to cope and if I needed counselling he would arrange it, but I wasn't getting a discharge. Once inside the army, it was virtually impossible to get yourself out. If a person was injured, they'd nurse them back to health in the army hospital. I heard of one soldier who spent twelve of the twenty-four months of his national service in hospital, the big green machine refusing to discharge him. If a soldier committed a crime they locked him up in the army gaol, but no discharge. So I had to go back to the platoon and learn to deal with the pressure.

A regular soldier in our platoon called Mac was harassing one of the young recruits, Ricky. Mac had become one of the platoon heroes. After being placed in various youth corrective centres, Mac finally went to prison. 'Nothing too serious like murder,' he boasted, 'just armed robbery.' I never really understood how his criminal record gave him such status among the guys, but obviously it meant he was special. Agreeing to go into the army and fight in the Vietnam War had reduced his sentence. There was a lovable larrikin quality about him but Mac had taken a fancy to young Ricky and used opportunities to come on to him in front of the other guys. Most of the platoon thought that it was a great sport for Mac to say suggestive things to

Ricky, touch him, and insinuate he was going to fuck him one night.

'I like a bit of boy occasionally,' he frequently said. Of course he did. Mac had been in gaol and even though everyone knew what went on between men in prison, no-one dared challenge the platoon hero with the accusation of being queer—it was just all good fun. The harassment increased to the point where poor Ricky was obviously stressed and unable to sleep at night. I was concerned for Ricky's state of mind; no-one stood up for him and the constant harassment was making him lose his temper, which only encouraged more taunting.

Campaigners for Christ had set up an evangelistic ministry on the base called The Everyman's Welfare Service. They tried to reach out to the soldiers with the Christian message by providing refreshments and a recreational room as an alternative to the well patronised bar. When the lads from my platoon went to have drinks at the bar, I detoured next door for coffee, hoping to find other Christians to talk to. The fact that I had remained steadfast in my beliefs meant I'd gained some respect from a couple of the guys in my platoon and they occasionally came with me to Everyman's, but most nights it was empty. Stan, the Christian officer who managed Everyman's, was pleased to find a zealous evangelistic Christian on the base. When no-one else was there we spent many hours talking about God, the Bible, and occasionally praying together. I thought it best to talk to him about the situation with Ricky and Mac and, sensing my concern, he said he'd speak to someone about it.

The next day at marching practice, Mac was called out to report to the camp commander. That's a relief, I thought, now something's going to be done. The rest of the morning the guys theorised about what was happening to Mac. When he returned, he stared at me with a murderous look in his eye. Immediately his friends gathered around him as he told them what had happened. Apparently, the opening words of the camp commander were, 'We've had a complaint from Recruit Venn-Brown that you have been making homosexual advances towards one of your platoon members.' The final warning was, 'If this doesn't stop immediately you will be discharged from the army and returned to prison.' I knew I was in big trouble. How could the man at the Everyman's be so stupid as to involve me? Why did the camp commander have to mention my name? A wimpy Christian had dobbed in the platoon hero. I feared for my life.

I remembered the impression I'd received, that I was going to get out of the army early. It all made sense now—probably in a coffin. I tried not to show how petrified I was and avoided Mac. As long as our officer and sergeant were around, I knew I was safe, but seeing the looks on the guys' faces and the sniggering whispers confirmed that I was going to have the shit bashed out of me. Over the next few days I was often told, 'We're going to get you.' My protests, explaining I hadn't dobbed Mac in but had only talked to someone about the situation, fell on deaf ears. The possibility of being bashed was terrifying and over the next few nights, expecting a group to come rushing through the door at any moment, I prayed desperately that God would protect me. I thought it was a miracle that I slept safely each night. Within a week the hostility towards me subsided and everything returned to normal—ignoring me.

The eighteenth of October was only two weeks away and even though I could not see how my release from the army was going to happen, I was not going to give up hope—I knew God could perform miracles.

My feet began giving me trouble; first of all a little discomfort that turned into a mild pain, that increased to the point where I was unable to wear army boots any more. The doctor at the army base couldn't find anything wrong, so he arranged for me to see an orthopaedic specialist in Wagga Wagga. Our platoon was about to spend five days in the bush on training manoeuvres and this meant I'd be away from camp on the date I'd been given—the eighteenth of October. Everything around me said it was impossible for this to happen, but I kept believing, reminding God of His promise and refusing to entertain any doubts. Packing my gear to go bush for five days I kept asking God, 'How are you going to do this?' Then the words 'Trust Me' came so clearly. Same as the encouraging words I'd heard when I felt God had provided a lift for me when I was working at Macquarie University. I suddenly felt a boost of faith and knew I WAS going to have a miracle. Our platoon assembled with sleeping gear, backpacks and rifles, and sat for two hours waiting for the transport to arrive. This was unusual as the army always ran like clockwork. I kept praying, buoyant in my faith, believing that somehow, someway, God would soon intervene. When the trucks finally arrived, our sergeant ordered me and two others to wait and load all the platoon gear on the last truck. With the rest of the platoon gone, we spent the next twenty minutes packing the truck with tents and supplies for the five days manoeuvres. While we were packing the final boxes, a sergeant major arrived and asked for Platoon 17.

'They've gone out on manoeuvres, Sergeant Major,' I responded.

'I'm after Recruit Venn-Brown,' he said.

'I'm Recruit Venn-Brown, Sergeant,' I responded, wondering why I'd been singled out of the platoon of seventy men.

'Take your gear and come with me. You have an appointment with a specialist in town tomorrow; we'll send you out to the platoon later.' The split-second timing was amazing—another five minutes and I'd have been in the bush for several days. I was given cleaning duties to do during the day but it was an eerie feeling sleeping alone in barracks usually full of noise and activity.

The next day I was taken to my appointment with the orthopaedic specialist in town, who examined my feet. I had never had problems with my feet before this and I wondered what he was trying to find as he prodded and squeezed my angles and arches.

Two days later the sergeant major arrived at our barracks and announced, 'Pack your stuff, you're going out on civvy street.'

I couldn't believe it. Had I really heard what I thought I'd heard?

'What did you say?' forgetting to address him with the correct title.

He repeated again but slower this time so the statement sunk in. 'You are being discharged from the army, your national service is over.' I tried not to look too excited. He told me to pack up all my gear and I was taken from the platoon barracks and moved to the discharge cells. The date? The seventeenth of October.

I remembered reading that God can bless a person so much it almost seems like a dream. It certainly felt like that being driven through the gates of the army base on the eighteenth. It was so exciting that I'd received such specific guidance and I was extremely grateful for the miracle God had performed. God was more powerful than the Australian Government or the Big Green Machine.

Back in Sydney, I couldn't wait to tell my Christian friends about my amazing miracle. When I arrived for the morning church service everyone was shocked to see me. I was given the opportunity to share a testimony and everyone cheered when I told them the story, going back to the impression I'd received at bible college and detailing the events up to leaving the camp. Surely this incredible experience was a sign that God had something special planned for my life? It was true that with God all things are possible. And with such a powerful God on my side, any problems I had with homosexuality could also be overcome. It was all a matter of faith.

CHAPTER 7

Rehab with a twist

Back in Sydney I had to decide what to do next and, considering I'd had such an incredible experience of divine guidance, I was convinced God was going to call me into the ministry very soon. The *Bible* says that after Jesus was baptised He was sent into the wilderness to fast for forty days, and that during that time was tested by the devil. Overcoming all the temptations put to Him, He came out of the wilderness in the power of the Spirit and commenced His ministry of preaching, healing the sick, performing miracles, and casting out demons. We'd been taught about the importance of fasting at college. Why don't I fast for forty days like Jesus did, I thought, and find out exactly what God wants me to do? I'd learnt that fasting was one way of getting a greater anointing of God's power on your life. I thought the power I would get from this time would also deal with the homosexual thoughts that were beginning to creep back again. I wasn't going to quit fighting this thing.

Kihila was a Christian retreat in the Blue Mountains, which had become a meeting place in the late 1960s and early 1970s for the new Charismatic movement happening in Sydney churches. I knew the owners well as I'd attended most of the conventions there and had spoken at a few youth camps. I thought this would be an ideal place for me to hide away and fast. So within a week of getting out of the army, much to my parents' dismay, I packed my bags and took the train to the Blue Mountains.

I ate my last meal when I arrived at Kihila and was committed to only having water and fruit juices for the next forty days. Most days I spent in a bare room with only a bed and lounge chair and devoted myself to prayer, reading the *Bible* and books about finding God's guidance. Spending so much time alone made me very reflective—I thought about my motives and what might be the real reason I wanted to serve God. Why did I want to do great things for God? Why did I want to be a famous preacher? Was it to gain God's favour and score brownie points? Was it just my selfish ego? After much soul searching all I could see was a life of sacrifice and service ahead of me. God had produced many wonderful changes in my life and I wanted to show my gratitude to Him.

After the second week, my mind occasionally began slipping away from the spiritual issues and that all too familiar restlessness came over me. On about the twentieth day, when night fell, I went for a walk down to the main road. The desire to be with someone was rising again but from where? Was it the devil tempting me or maybe a demonic spirit seeking control again? Or, as I'd just been reading about, a work of the flesh? Whatever it was I knew it had to be overcome. Arriving at the main road, instinctively I began hitchhiking along the highway towards Katoomba. It was a still, eerie night with few cars on the highway so late. Winter always left the mountains later than it did in Sydney; the clouds hung so low over the mountains the reflection of the orange streetlights mixed with the dark grey of the clouds created a mauve ceiling. My eyes followed the cars as they passed, hoping a man would stop and pick me up. After walking half a kilometre, a car pulled up ahead of me so I ran and opened the door.

'Where you off to, mate?' he questioned. The gruffness in his voice indicated he was straight—he was probably a local coal miner or something—but I already knew by experience that the masculine voice occasionally disguised a man who enjoyed sex with men. There was a desperation driving me as I tried all the usual tricks to indicate I wanted sex—sitting with my legs apart, scratching my crotch when he looked over, moving my leg over towards the gear stick so that when he changed gear he touched my knee—but nothing worked. In fact, I was beginning to sense the man was becoming suspicious, so I decided to retreat for safety's sake. The conversation ceased and he dropped me off at Katoomba. What will I do now? I walked up and down the main street of Katoomba for half an hour, hoping that maybe another homosexual man was out on the prowl. It was a fruitless exercise.

Now that I was thirty kilometres from Kihila I walked back to the highway and began hitchhiking again. By this time it was about midnight, traffic was even lighter and drivers were fearful of picking up strangers alone on the road, so I walked for what seemed like forever before a nurse on her way home from night duty picked me up. It soon became clear she had another motive behind her act of kindness when she began hinting that I might like to go home with her. Why was this kind of temptation easy to resist? It was 3am when I finally fell into bed exhausted. Isn't that just like the devil? I thought, tempting you to the point where you finally give in but in the end not delivering the final product. Even though the *Bible* warned me 'beware of the tricks of the devil', it had happened too many times. The next few days were spent repenting, crying, asking God to forgive me and pleading for Him to take these terrible cravings away from me. I'd been fighting this now for two years already; it had to go soon.

After forty days of fasting I was skinnier but I still had no clear indication of what God wanted me to do. My Christian friends in Sydney were impressed that I'd completed the forty-day fast; so few did. I could not tell them about the real struggles I was experiencing as we rarely spoke honestly about our failures, only our victories, a little like compulsive gamblers who always tell you how much they've won but never how much they lost. Being an ex-bible college student, and therefore supposedly more spiritual than the average Christian, made me retreat further into my secretive life of conflict.

All my original feelings about homosexuality had been reinforced since becoming a Christian. I'd become a devoted reader of the *Bible* and had already read from Genesis to Revelation five times. Memorising individual verses and passages was always encouraged as a sign of spiritual maturity so I was able to quote numerous verses from the Old and New Testaments. There were only six verses in the *Bible* that mentioned homosexuality, as far as I knew. Leviticus 18:22, 'You shall not lie with a male as those who lie with a female; it is an abomination,' was one. Leviticus 20:13, 'If a man lies with a male as those who lie with a woman, both of them have committed an abomination and they shall surely be put to death,' another. Then there were the New Testament verses in 1 Corinthians 6:9–10: 'Do you not know that the wicked will not inherit the Kingdom of God? Do not be deceived: Neither the fornicators nor idolaters, nor male prostitutes nor homosexual offenders nor thieves nor greedy nor drunkards nor slanderers nor swindlers will inherit the Kingdom of God'. Having no knowledge of the original languages, historical context or cultural meaning of these passages, I assumed they were all talking about me. I certainly didn't want to be an abomination to God or be ousted from the Kingdom of God—hell was a frightening prospect. Words like 'transgression', 'unrighteousness', 'ungodliness', 'wickedness', 'fornication' and 'sin' reminded me that God had his standards and if I was going to serve him I had to do it from a pure and holy life.

Over the next six months I lived off the money I'd saved while in the army and only took casual jobs such as cleaning. This meant I had the freedom to answer the call as soon as it came. This also meant I could accept invitations to speak at high school Christian lunchtime meetings and also at youth groups and camps.

During January 1972, John, my friend from school, and another friend David, organised a gospel tour into the central west of New South Wales and we travelled for a month singing and preaching in

Charismatic and Pentecostal churches.

In March 1972, my parents wanted to organise a twenty-first birthday party for me but as I didn't drink alcohol or dance, it turned out to be a very low-key affair. Family members were surprised at how subdued all my friends were and how they mostly talked about God. My most treasured gift was a combined gift from my friends; a big, black, leather-bound Dakes *Bible*. It was the most expensive on the market—almost every verse was cross-referenced and at the back included a huge concordance so that I could always find those elusive verses. A great preacher's *Bible*, I thought.

It wasn't long after my birthday that the old habit of walking the streets at night began again—I knew I had to do something. The stress of the constant battle made me feel like I was heading for a nervous breakdown so I rang the pastor at Christian Faith Centre and told him I needed some counselling. I said I was willing to see him immediately. It was a big thing for me to admit I needed help.

'How long have you had this problem?' he said.

'Before I became a Christian,' I admitted with a defeated tone in my voice.

'Well, another night's not going to make any difference then, is it?' he quickly replied, in a way that made me think he'd used that line before. He told me to go to the boys' home for the night and he'd talk with me tomorrow. (The church had organised boys' and girls' homes for young people in the church who needed accommodation.) Poor Mum and Dad were at their wits end seeing me in such a distressed state and tried to find out what was wrong. I couldn't tell them because I knew they wouldn't understand, and besides, I was a Christian and if I told them honestly what was going on then they might think God had failed me. I didn't want that. 'I'll be away for a few days,' I announced as I walked out the door with a few belongings in my bag.

The journey from Hunters Hill to the beach suburb of Narrabeen meant I had to go via Town Hall Station. Sydney was like cities all over the world at that time where a homosexual act between two consenting adults was illegal. Fear of discovery forced most into a life of secrecy and the only place that some men could occasionally connect with other men was at certain well-known public toilets. In order to keep homosexuality in check, plain-clothes policemen often baited gay men by pretending they wanted sex with them, sometimes arresting them after they'd had sex with the accomplice. It was always useless accusing the officer of being a willing partner—we were the criminals, they were upholding the law and cleaning the scourge from society.

The underground male toilets at Town Hall station was a place where the thrill of an encounter could become a prison sentence within seconds with the revealing of a badge or the words 'you're under arrest'. Because of the danger I rarely visited the beat, but somehow that night the threat dissipated once the desire to connect with another male rose to the fore. Alighting from the bus, I immediately walked down the steps to the station toilets. I looked in disbelief at the person I recognised walking up the steps towards me.

'Ben, what are you doing here?' I asked, trying to think what excuse I'd use for being there. Ben was my age with beautiful, blond, curly hair and piercing blue eyes; just gorgeous. I'd worked with him at Macquarie University. Even though I thought he was incredibly attractive, I never even entertained the thought of anything happening between us as, firstly, I thought he was straight and, secondly, I wanted him to become a Christian. Every time I'd talk to him about Jesus, Ben argued to frustrating infinitum just for the sake of argument, and often tried to make me lose my temper by annoying me while I concentrated on my work. He delighted in this game because he knew when I finally lost my temper, he could say I was a bad Christian. 'Christians aren't supposed to get angry,' he'd say with a devilish, tormenting tone. He loved winning arguments and showing up my imperfections and now, face to face in my weakened state, with no other Christian backup, I was completely vulnerable. He seemed to know why I was there and I thought it useless to try and explain that I was only passing through.

'Come with me,' he said, and I followed without question, allowing myself for the first time to really admit to myself how attractive he was. All over my body, cells were now being activated at a feverish pace. So often I'd prayed that God would use me to lead Ben to Christ but now he was leading me, without protest or resistance, to sin. He took me down a narrow lane, about a block away from the station. As we walked down the alley into the darkness, he occasionally looked behind to ensure no-one saw or followed us. Reaching the end, Ben made a quick turn to the right; he'd obviously been here before. Now out of public view, Ben grabbed me and pushed his lips against mine and slowly I felt his warm tongue slide through my lips. Every time a man had tried to kiss me before I had turned my head away, never wanting to do the thing I'd been taught was for a woman; that would be like giving in to homosexuality. With Ben—I surrendered completely. It was so sensual and delightful to have him do these things to me.

All thoughts of guilt and consequences were lost in the overwhelming moment of passion with this stunning man. We quickly fumbled with each other's flies, wanting desperately to touch each other as intimately as possible. Ben seemed delighted that I screamed with relief when I came, and kissed me again. He smiled knowing he'd taken me to a place I'd never experienced before, or was it that he had just had complete power over me? Without speaking we moved back into the street. What could I say anyway? 'That was fantastic,' was an admission I didn't want to make. Saying, 'I'm sorry Ben, that shouldn't have happened,' would have sounded very empty. At a nearby coffee shop I explained the situation I was in and Ben seemed sympathetic.

'It's too late to go to Narrabeen now. Why don't you come and sleep the night at my place?' he suggested. I didn't need much coaxing, despite knowing that tomorrow I would have to face the consequences of my actions. The saying 'May as well be hung for a sheep as for a lamb', crossed my mind. Tonight I wanted to be with Ben. I wanted him to kiss and touch me again—I wanted to experience that beautiful passion just one more time.

Ben's father was the mayor of a wealthy North Shore suburb. The family lived in a beautiful two-storey federation mansion, and even at night I could see the meticulously manicured lawns and well kept gardens. We crept in, quietly went upstairs to his bedroom, stripped down to our underwear and slipped into bed. Ben was very comfortable with this but it was actually the first time I'd spent the night in bed with someone. I was expecting the same experience I'd had in the alley but Ben kissed me gently and whispered, 'Go to sleep, we don't want to wake my parents.' Sleeping with Ben felt wonderful—it was so good just being next to him, with the warmth of his body pressing against mine and his caring arms wrapped securely around me. He held me in a reassuring way as if he knew the turmoil I'd been experiencing. Ben's tenderness and affection was like water on a thirsty land. Inwardly, I knew this was what I was looking for and stayed awake as long as possible to savour every moment and sensation. Even though I'd had sex with various men before, something far deeper had happened that night. I'd made the mistake of letting down my guard emotionally; and yet what I craved was perverted and forbidden. It seemed unfair that the events of the last hour were so natural for Ben but for me, as a good Christian witness of Jesus Christ, I'd failed miserably.

By the morning the glow of allowing a man to touch my emotions and soul was diminishing and the all-too-familiar insidious guilt took over. I said goodbye to Ben knowing I could never face him again and rang the pastor to confess my failure. If only Pastor Paul had seen me last night this terrible thing would never have happened. He told me to come immediately to the church. Within an hour I was in his office telling him the details of how much I'd struggled with homosexuality and my numerous attempts at breaking free. I'd never spoken so openly with Pastor Paul before but I guess this wasn't any great new revelation to him. No matter how hard I tried to hide it, I'm sure he'd always thought I was a homosexual.

'You know you can't keep going back into sin like this, don't you?' he said in a sobering and threatening manner. 'Eventually God will give up on you. The *Bible* teaches that God turns his back on those who consistently sin because they grieve the Holy Spirit. This is probably your last and best chance to overcome this.' I knew the scripture well and as Pastor Paul spoke, the fear of God struck my heart. How could I keep on falling into sin, repent, and expect God to forgive me? Surely His patience was not endless.

'The only way for you to really beat this, Tony, is to go into rehabilitation. Are you prepared to do that?' he said, in a challenging voice. With my head in my hands and too ashamed to look up, I replied, 'Yes, I'm sick of this defeat. Whatever it takes.' There had been times I'd considered this drastic step but always felt that somehow God and I could overcome it together. But the two years of unsuccessful struggle and repeated cycles told me this was the only way. Maybe my last hope.

Paradise was an independent Pentecostal Church in the southern suburbs of Sydney that had gained some fame for its success in rehabilitation. It was pastored by two women, Joyce and Edna, which was highly unusual as most Pentecostal churches banned women preachers because of the teachings of St Paul who said in 1 Timothy 2:11-12: 'A woman should learn in quietness and full submission. I do not permit a woman to teach or have authority over a man, she must be silent.' The fact that Joyce was also divorced was another mark against her in Bible-believing circles. In Matthew 19:5-6 Jesus said, 'For this reason a man will leave his father and mother and be united to his wife, and the two will become one flesh. So they are no longer two, but one. Therefore what God has joined together, let man not separate.' To be divorced was against God's will as far as we knew. No wonder she had to have her own church, no other denomination would have her. Males being given token positions of authority in the church had tempered the strong matriarchal structure somewhat. But in many ways Paradise was a forerunner of what would later be known as a 'lesbian collective'. There was certainly plenty of them among its members.

Paradise was well-known not just as a church but as a rehabilitation centre for drug addicts, prostitutes and homosexuals. One of Joyce and Edna's great trophies was Marion, Queen of the Underworld, who had been a hooker and also heavily involved in crime. Edna had rescued her from the streets of Kings Cross, Sydney's red light area, and after rehabilitation Marion spoke in churches about what she'd done before becoming a Christian. Most congregations found this incredibly exciting because they were so far removed from that type of existence. Even though Jesus was consistently accused of being a friend of prostitutes and sinners, the average church person would never allow themselves to be in an evil red light area, let alone befriend a prostitute.

Paradise had also been successful with a few drug addicts. (I think they were more drug users than addicts but the term drug addicts sounded more dramatic.) It appeared that they had also been able to rehabilitate homosexuals—a couple of guys living at Paradise were almost 'free' and one who had been 'cured' was now engaged to a girl in the church. When I met Nigel he still seemed to have feminine traits and rarely showed any affection towards his fiancée Lynn, but who was I to judge or doubt his miracle? Pastor Paul rang and arranged with Pastor Joyce for me to go down the next day and discuss the possibility of going into the rehabilitation program. Now I had to go home and face Mum and Dad. What would I say? I really felt sorry for them and all the stress I'd been putting them through. I told Mum what was happening but again it was decided it would be best to keep the full details from Dad. When Dad discovered where I was going, he became very concerned. He didn't want me to go because the controversial tactics used by Paradise had been publicised in the Sydney press and it had been branded a cult. I reassured him I would be safe and if there were any difficulties, I promised I'd come home.

Whist in New Zealand I'd met Joyce, the leading pastor, when she came and spoke at the bible college. At the time, I was still in a euphoric state just after my exorcism but in a private meeting whilst sharing my excitement of my new deliverance, she'd implied that the only way a person can really be delivered of homosexuality was through a rehabilitation program. Casting the demons out was just the beginning, she had told me; I also needed to change my way of thinking and that would take time. It was confusing to be getting different counsel from different leaders. It was certainly easier for me to believe that I was over my struggle at that time. According to Joyce, Paradise's system was the only successful program available in Australia, possibly the world. I hadn't wanted to believe her then, but now I felt like she was taking delight in being right and having me just where she wanted me. Once in the program, I remember her warning me more than once that I should have limited contact with my previous Christian friends saying, 'Not all Christians are like Paradise Christians,' insinuating that somehow Paradise Christians were superior. She was very open in her condemnation and considered most Christians shallow. This elitist, arrogant attitude made her unpopular and added to her independence, as you can imagine.

Dad and I drove down the steep, narrow, windy road towards the water and arrived at Paradise. The tyres crunched on the pebbles in the large parking lot, built to accommodate the cars for services held at the mansion. It was a stately two-storey sandstone building that had been converted for the dual purpose of live-in rehabilitation and weekly services. Dad drove off as Joyce greeted me at the door, and led me into her large, tastefully appointed office. When she sat at her desk I could see the idyllic view through the windows behind her of the boats on Port Hacking Bay, artistically framed by over-hanging gum trees. The décor spelt class, with fine furnishings and antiques that matched the historic building. Noting that I was impressed by the surroundings

Joyce quickly stated that Australia's celebrated opera soprano Dame Nellie Melba, also famous for Peach Melba, and Melba toast, had sung from the balcony off her bedroom upstairs.

Joyce wore the uniform she had established as the dress code for the women in Paradise. Clones of Joyce and Edna were everywhere, modestly attired in twin-sets in the most insipid pastels, set off by a small string of pearls, and tartan skirts with the hem no less than three inches below the knee.

I heard the door open behind me and turned around to see a tall, 180 centimetre, ruggedly handsome man. 'This is Patrick,' Joyce said and I rose to feel the strong masculine grip of his handshake engulfing my much smaller hand. I tried not to show that handshake hurt. Patrick wore the Paradise male uniform, which consisted of brown riding boots, bone-coloured moleskins and a plain, light blue country-style shirt. His simple manliness made him very attractive. I wondered if Patrick was an example of a successfully rehabilitated homosexual man, but Joyce assured me, 'Patrick's straight and married to Rachael but he understands what you will be going through.' I wondered how, but becoming a man like Patrick was very appealing. Apparently he was to be my 'minder' and, more importantly, the strong male role model/mentor I'd lacked all my life.

Unknowingly, Paradise had become Australia's first 'ex-gay' program. Ex-gays are Christians who believe God has 'cured' them and that they are no longer homosexual but heterosexual. The program was based on what later became known as 'reparative' or 'conversion therapy', with Christian ministries such as Exodus Global Alliance and Love in Action being two well-known promoters of this type of 'therapy'. Love in Action made the news in May 2005 when an American boy, sixteen-year-old Zach, told his Christian parents that he was gay. Horrified by the news, against his will they planned on sending him to an 'ex-gay' camp called Refuge in Tennessee. In the meantime, he'd shared his concerns about his parents' intentions, and the consequences of being locked up, on his internet blog, suddenly involving a global audience. The cost for Zach's treatment was thousands of dollars, but back in 1972 all I had to do was sign over my unemployment benefit to Paradise and they would take care of the rest.

Like all ex-gay programs, Paradise believed that homosexuality was not innate but caused by a father who was distant and a dominant mother (early sexual abuse was also touted as a cause), and for three decades these ministries have tried to hold back a more educated understanding of sexual orientation. As a distant father and strong mother was directly in conflict with the *Bible's* ideal of the family where the male is the head of the home and the wife is submissive, apparently my upbringing had caused me to be defective in my sexual development. If that was the case then there must be an entire generation of latent homosexuals, as that was very much the culture of my day. Fathers fulfilled the role of provider and most didn't show affection or love beyond a practical way. Just as authority figures such as headmasters and managers believed, distance not closeness was the way to rule. Based on what Paradise believed, I wondered for a moment how useful my relationship with Patrick would be considering we were being dominated by two very strong-willed ladies. Maybe Paradise was a breeding ground for homosexuals.

Joyce interrupted my thoughts, 'To be rehabilitated permanently from homosexuality will take at least twelve months, possibly two years.' My heart sank. Joyce walked me through the rules I was to live by for the coming months of full-time rehab.

'We've found,' Joyce added, 'that homosexual men like bikini underwear.' Any bikini underwear I had would be taken from me and destroyed as it was too sexual. Y-fronts only. (It's strange that today fashion labels such as Calvin Klein have built a market among gay men selling Y-fronts.) In addition, I was not to be alone at any time—if Patrick wasn't with me, someone else would be assigned to look after me. I was to be up promptly at 6 o'clock in the morning, so I didn't lie in bed and masturbate, another downfall of the homosexual. While in the shower Patrick or one of the other counsellors would be standing by to make sure I didn't masturbate. I would work hard all day so that when I went to bed at night, I'd fall asleep immediately. And, finally, ensure that I urinated directly before going to bed so that the pressure on my bladder didn't arouse me and—I was beginning to get the picture—cause me to masturbate. Joyce's bluntness was embarrassing. I later discovered that she delighted in learning if any of the inmates had a bent penis and made sure she brought this up in a counselling session. Patrick took me to the bunkroom I was to share with four other guys and went through my luggage to remove every piece of offensive homosexual clothing, including my new trendy pink shirt and matching socks. Real men don't wear pink. Even in a gaol all your belongings are returned when you're released but I never saw those items of my wardrobe again.

I quickly learnt that Paradise was incredibly creative with minced meat—it was unbelievable, they must have bought it by the truckload. One day it was meat loaf, the next savoury mince, then Bolognaise, and then shepherd's pie. The only deviation from mince was a stew made with the cheapest beef or old boiling fowls. Obviously Paradise was on a tight budget.

I spent the first week adapting to the structure of the daily program. After breakfast I began the day by listening to tapes of the *Bible*, which I listened to while I read the same verses from the *Bible* in front of me. This double reinforcement—the aural and the visual—was to reprogram and renew my mind. The rest of the day was occupied with chores including gardening and maintenance work around the properties, manual labour or working with tools—always male chores that would help me become a 'normal' man. Never cooking—I was told that homosexuals love to cook.

The entire church consisted of about one hundred and fifty people. Approximately twenty 'lived-in' at Paradise while another thirty lived at the other property another fifty or so kilometres away at the secluded beach of Bundeena. Being a bible training centre, Bundeena would be the next stop for me in my rehabilitation program. The remainder of the congregation consisted of locals. All church meetings were compulsory: Sunday morning service was at Bundeena then back to Paradise for the evening service; Monday night was prayer meeting; Wednesday night was family dinner at Paradise; Thursday night was worship night down at Bundeena again; and the Saturday night youth group was also held at Paradise. Not much time left! The basic philosophy was that by living in a totally protected environment, you were able to gain more control and overcome your sin. Once you learnt not to sin then you would be given more freedom, eventually being strong enough to live victoriously in the outside world. I was angry that I'd allowed myself to get to a point where I had to give total control of my life over to other people.

Paradise leaders had developed a warped theology that was based on the Greek word for love, *agape*, which is the highest form of love, the unconditional love of God; different from *eros* (physical) or *phileo* (brotherly) love. According to Paradise theology, loving someone with the *agape* love of God meant you could do anything as long as your intention was for their highest good. Desiring a person's highest good was used to justify humiliation, deprivation, manipulation and sometimes even physical abuse. Seeing one of the girls with a black eye one day, I questioned her on what had happened. She had a rough counselling session apparently—of course it was for her highest good as she had some sense knocked into her. She didn't leave the program. The leaders' authoritative methods and motives were never questioned.

An example of the way they showed their *agape* love involved Sharon, who had come to Paradise just before me. She'd been sexually abused by her stepfather and other family members and was finally thrown out of home by her mother. Her mother saw Sharon as a threat to her marriage and accused her of leading the abusive men on. Sharon had come to Paradise seeking help and a way out of her life of drugs and prostitution. It had taken her at least a week to feel comfortable in the new household, as this was the first time in her life she had been with people who seemed genuinely concerned for her welfare. Fifteen of us sat around the large kitchen table—for Sharon and I it was our first compulsory Wednesday family dinner. At the conclusion of the meal it was time to give a special greeting to the newcomers.

'I'd like to introduce you to Sharon,' Joyce commenced, 'But you really wouldn't like to know Sharon.' What did she mean? I thought. Knowing she now had everyone's undivided attention Joyce continued, 'You see, Sharon is selfish and not a very nice person. She's proud, conceited and a slut. After some time here, if she lets God work in her life, she will change.' Sitting opposite Sharon, I watched her face change from smiling, to shock, to tears and finally to hanging her head, sobbing. She was devastated and so was I, and I wondered why I'd been spared a similar ordeal. That was to come later.

After a few weeks of compliant behaviour, I was allowed to venture out into the real world and get a job that would help pay for my rehabilitation and the next step, training college at Bundeena. Paradise had an arrangement with the human resources manager of the Brownbuilt factory a couple of suburbs away, and selected inmates could get work on the production line making office furniture without being asked too many questions. I was given the stimulating job of putting handles onto steel lockers. But it was a relief to get away from the oppressive environment for eight hours. Another reward for my compliance was a trip to the south coast for a Saturday outing with three other people from the church, to see the sights and spend time being normal. Most of all, though, it was a test of trust. We stopped for lunch at a little town where the main street was called Queen Street and, being the clown I usually was, I ran over to the street sign, leant against the post, and assumed the position of a hooker. One of my companions took a photo, unaware that this bit of frivolity was going to be my downfall.

The next Sunday night a carload of my friends came to see me—the select few who really knew what was going on. We hadn't had any contact for six weeks and I knew they were concerned about me so it was great to see them again. We were standing together casually chatting in the lounge room after the service, surrounded by about sixty other people, when Joyce suddenly stormed into the room. Her dramatic entry ensured that all conversations subsided and heads turned in her direction. I somehow knew I was in trouble as she marched towards me.

'What do you think you're doing?' she screamed, having no regard for the friends around me. In fact, I think she had particularly chosen this time to ensure my humiliation had maximum impact. She knew how guarded and embarrassed I was about letting people know about the real me. I felt ill when I caught a glimpse of the photo in her hand. 'I suppose you think this is funny?' she yelled, waving the photo in the air for all to see and pausing for a moment to ensure that everyone in the room was focused on what was to come. She continued her barrage as she tore the photo to shreds in front of us all. 'So you're a queen, are you? Well, if you want to be queer we can certainly arrange that for you. If I ever catch you doing something like this again I'll get that photo and put it on the noticeboard so the whole church can see. Un—der—stand?' She poked me in the chest with her finger with each syllable for added emphasis.

I tried to speak and defend myself but nothing came out, I was numb. My friends stood in shock, wondering what horribly evil deed I'd done to deserve such a tirade. Explanations were useless. 'You'd better go,' I said quickly, trying to hold back tears. Escaping to the kitchen, I cried like a little child. I remember thinking how infantile my response was, but I couldn't stop sobbing for the next three hours. I knew some people at Paradise felt sorry for me but no-one dared console me or challenge Joyce's tactics. Greg, my roommate, came into the kitchen on the pretext of getting a glass of water and quickly looked around to make sure no-one would see or hear. A simple, 'You'll be okay, mate,' and he'd disappeared again back into the lounge room for safety. As long as I was in the kitchen it was the enemy's camp and siding with me would mean rejection from the others. The *Bible* says that 'rebellion is the sin of witchcraft' and to rebel against the God-given authority of the pastor was considered the same as rebelling against God. And anyway, Joyce was showing me *agape* love because she was dealing with my homosexuality.

I was still shaken from the weekend humiliation when Mum phoned to see how I was going and when I was coming home. I was very noncommittal, as I knew it might be years. The frustration at my lack of disclosure prompted her to exclaim, 'Sometimes, Tony, I wish I never had you!' I understood her frustration, but at this point this was not what I needed to hear and I hung up. I'd never done anything like that to my mother before. As a rebellious teenager there were times when I'd hated my parents, but since becoming a Christian I did really love them. I knew that we frequently didn't understand one another but we were doing the best we could.

The next day was pay-day at the Brownbuilt factory and, feeling fragile and frustrated, I was ready to break out—I'd had enough. A new privilege I'd been given was to catch public transport to and from work so as soon as I picked up my pay envelope, instead of taking it to Paradise and handing it over, I boarded the train to the city. Arriving at Town Hall Station I had five-minute sex with a stranger and then just had to get a drink. I knew there was a homosexual underground some-where in the city, probably at Kings Cross, but I had no idea how to find it. I went to a hotel and drank until I could hardly stand, then put myself back on the train to go home to Paradise, the only place I believed I could get help.

I was still very drunk when I arrived by taxi at 10.30pm with my reduced pay packet. Patrick greeted me at the door with a predictably displeased look and took me to the kitchen for a cup of coffee. We were both sitting in silence when Joyce appeared with Patrick's wife Rachael. Patrick rose to his feet and the three stood over me.

'What have you been doing?' Joyce asked gruffly. I started to cry again and apologised for what I'd done.

'Did you have sex with anyone?' Joyce continued.

'Yes,' I replied.

'Was it good?' she asked, knowing that the guilt I felt ensured I never really enjoyed what I did.

'No.' I knew I was being painted into a corner.

'Well, that was a waste of time and money, wasn't it?' she said gleefully.

'Please let me stay, I've nowhere else to get help,' I pleaded. 'I've got to keep trying.'

'Go to bed, we'll talk in the morning,' was all that was said. I was expecting much more.

The next day I had a shocking hangover and Patrick and Joyce thought it amusing that I couldn't keep breakfast down. Summoned to the office, I was given my schedule for the day. First of all, no work; I was pleased about that. An appointment had been made for me with a doctor at Cronulla at 11am so that I could have a VD (venereal disease) test. This was necessary as there were children at Paradise, I was told, though I wasn't quite sure what that meant. Did it mean that they subscribed to a belief, prevalent at that time, that homosexuals were not really attracted to the same sex but were actually paedophile predators who wanted to molest little boys? I didn't question their reasoning, but as uneducated as I was about sexual things, I really didn't think I could get an STD from masturbating with someone. Although I *had* heard you could pick one up from a toilet seat. Maybe it was just another way of humiliating me and reminding me of how disgusting and dirty I was. The doctor was more reassuring and after questioning me about what actually happened, obviously felt this was an unnecessary degradation. Of course, I was eventually pronounced clean.

After another three months of 'treatment', I lost all desire to fight my homosexuality. I was tired and just wanted to get out. But how? I'd already run away once and my money was kept in trust. I asked to see Joyce and Edna and was granted an audience.

'I'm finding it hard to fight my homosexuality,' I began. 'I've never really known what it is like to be a true homosexual. Maybe if I go out and find out what it's like, I'll learn to really hate my sin and then when I come back I'll have more motivation.' This was only half true. I had lost motivation but I still wanted to be free from homosexuality and was hoping there would be another way other than Paradise. If God was ever going to set me free it wasn't going to be through bullying. Joyce and Edna knew it was impossible to work with someone who'd lost their motivation so agreed I should leave. They reminded me of my future as a homosexual, which included never having a lasting relationship and never finding happiness. 'It's a shallow world of bitchy, dysfunctional, nasty, lonely people,' they said.

I was allowed to make a call and arranged for my sister and brother-in-law to pick me up the next Sunday (they weren't allowed to come immediately— the hope was that I would change my mind) and as with every call I'd made previously, Patrick sat next to me to make sure I said the right things. From that point, people treated me as if I was unclean, except for a couple of friends I'd made. According to 1 Corinthians 5:5, because of my willingness to be a fornicator I was to be 'handed over to Satan, so that the sinful nature might be destroyed and my spirit saved in the day of the Lord.' As someone who had now consciously rejected the grace of God, I was to be treated as an outsider.

When Sunday arrived, I purposely sat at the back of the congregation so I could see when the family arrived in the car park. The service was almost over when I saw Sue, already showing signs of her first pregnancy, and Ian on the veranda and moved quickly to make a fast getaway. Joyce caught the movement out of the corner of her eye and was hot on my heels. Just before I'd reached my sister, Joyce grabbed my arm and held me back; even though she was skinny she had a surprising strength.

'Do you know your brother is one of Sydney's worst homosexuals?' she began. 'He is filthy and disgusting and does …' She told them everything I'd done but exaggerated wildly making every detail sound as sordid as possible. I remember thinking that she made it sound like I did drag and had sex with several men on Saturday night then went to church the next morning, still wiping the make-up from my face. It was incomprehensible to think that she could lie so blatantly in front of me. She knew that I had never even been inside a gay club or bar. Sue and Ian were having trouble hearing such things; so was I. It was important not to cry this time as I was determined to show Joyce she couldn't break me any more. My sister Sue straightened herself up and with the strength and integrity that my older sister possesses, said, 'Well, there's a lot of love in our family, I'm sure we'll work it out.' I was so proud of her. Good on you, Sue, I thought. Joyce persisted in assassinating my character but Sue refused to be intimidated. 'Well, there's a lot of love in our family,' she kept repeating. Ian, a quiet natured man, feeling a little embarrassed at the openness and confrontational nature of the conversation, picked up my bags, indicating it was time to move on. We walked to the car in silence but when I sat in the back seat I breathed a sigh of relief and broke down. Even though it was so good to at last be free of the oppressive environment, I wondered how this might affect my salvation. What if I should die while I'm away from God? I knew I was taking a huge risk.

Travelling home, we didn't talk about what had happened, but instead focused on good things, catching up on developments in the family during my absence of nearly six months. In fact, we never really talked about it until twenty-eight years later! Families such as ours find it difficult to talk about awkward and painful moments, but there came a time when I realised I needed to acknowledge the power of those words 'there's a lot of love in our family' and thank Sue and Ian for rescuing me.

Over the years I've connected with a number of people who were in Paradise at the same time as me or soon after. I was shocked to hear their stories of affairs with fellow inmates and church members. I was obviously a saint in comparison. How could all this have been going on under the surface? Obviously many were only presenting an image of holiness and, fearing rejection or reprisals, never spoke to each other about what was genuinely happening in their lives. Joyce and Edna had a falling out, Paradise finally imploded and, surprisingly, most of the gay men and lesbians went on to live fulfilling lives completely at peace with the sexual orientation that once caused them so much angst. There are a few who still suffer psychologically and as with most of these programs, there are those who suicided; but we will never really be able to count the toll. In that time we put these experiences down to life lessons but had we been living in this litigious era, Paradise would have been sued many times for neglecting its 'duty of care' if not for emotional and psychological abuse. The greatest surprise of all was to hear that Joyce had been living with another woman for over sixteen years and, although never acknowledged publicly, many people see Beryl as her partner. All that time pastoring the church, could Joyce have been venting her internalised homophobia on us, or hoping that through helping others she might indeed resolve the struggle inside herself? Only years with a highly trained therapist could possibly sort that one out.

The saddest thing of all is to know that, more than three decades later, under the banner of Exodus, Focus on the Family, the National Association of Research and Therapy of Homosexuality (NARTH), and Love in Action's Refuge, ex-gay programs continue to use the same methodologies; based on old, discredited philosophies and producing the same destructive results. Young teenagers are sent into these programs by their misguided Christian parents who, believing that they have contributed to their children being gay and that they can be 'cured', are spending thousands of dollars on 'treatment'.

CHAPTER 8

Tony's out

In 1973, there was still very limited understanding of homosexuality. Studies of gay, lesbian and bisexual people involved only those in therapy, thus biasing the resulting conclusions. In 1968, when a survey was done to test the community's views on reviewing the laws that made homosexual acts between consenting adults a crime, only twenty-two per cent said it should no longer be an offence and sixty-four per cent disagreed. Of the sixty-four per cent who disagreed, many made comments such as 'they should be whipped severely' or 'sentenced to long-term imprisonment'. So, to the majority of society, the homosexual was a criminal offender/deviant; to mental health professionals he was sick; and to the church he was a sinner. For those remaining, the most common view was one of pity, 'Oh you poor thing, what a shame,' as if homosexuals had been dealt the genetic death card. No wonder I expected my experience in the homosexual underground to drive me back to God.

After leaving Paradise I packed my *Bible* away. As far as I knew, being a Christian and homosexual at the same time was not an option. There were no 'welcoming' or 'affirming' churches and no-one had heard of the term 'gay Christian'. But what if I liked my new life and didn't want to come back to God or died while out of the Kingdom of God? This thought was frightening. Mum and my sisters were pressuring me to tell Dad the truth about my homosexuality as soon as possible, just in case he found out accidentally what was really happening. What if someone in the close-knit community of Hunters Hill found out and told Dad at the local bowling club? Gossip was rife among the burgeoning upper middle classes. The thought of this disclosure was terrifying and I wasn't looking forward to his reaction; I was sure it would not be one of understanding. How could Dad understand? He was a product of white, middle-class, suburban Anglicanism. I'd seen his responses to news items on the television when there'd been Vietnam War protests or union demonstrations. 'Ratbags!' he'd say in a disgusted tone of voice. Up to that point that was the strongest language I'd ever heard him use. Normally he was such a placid, mild-mannered man. I was the only one who seemed to take him to the limits of his patience. I waited a couple of days to pluck up some courage and think of how to tell him his son was 'one of those': a queer.

I was finding it difficult to eat my evening meal when Dad arrived home from work. It was surprisingly quiet in the house because every-one knew this was the night. I went to the kitchen to wash the dishes, abnormally willing to make my contribution to the domestic chores. The soapsuds were up to my elbows when my sister Sue walked through the kitchen door.

'Go on,' she said firmly, 'you've got to tell him.' She knew I would take the slightest opportunity to back out. The nervousness that had taken away my appetite suddenly increased, my heart began to pound and my mouth became dry. Wiping the soapsuds from my hands I walked into the lounge room. Dad was sitting in 'his' chair reading the evening paper; everyone else had disappeared, retreating to various rooms of refuge, as if seeking shelter from the bomb about to be dropped.

'We have to talk,' was the opening line I'd prepared.

'Yes,' he replied, still perusing the pages of the evening edition of *The Sun* newspaper.

'Can you come to my bedroom? We need to talk in private.' Dad closed his paper, placed it on the chair and followed me to the room and as we sat on the bed together the look on his face told me he realised that the privacy and a trip to my bedroom meant trouble. I wished the news could have been that I'd made a girl pregnant—although catastrophic it would have been better than what I was about to say. I fingered the raised pattern on the orange cotton chenille bedspread I'd chosen to set off the olive green I'd painted the walls. Taking a deep breath, I filled my lungs with as much oxygen as possible.

'There's something I have to tell you. I'd rather not, but Mum thinks it best I'm honest with you.' I thought blaming Mum might take the pressure off me.

'I'm a homosexual.' Once again, there wasn't any sense of pride in my declaration, I was only aware of the shame and embarrassment this would bring to my family, reinforced by the disappointing fact that being the only son meant the family name would not be carried on. Also what did it say about Dad's masculinity and parenting? A queer son was every father's worst fear. Dad's face initially turned bright red, but within seconds all the colour drained away to reveal a grey, pallid complexion. Poor Dad already had experienced a mild stroke and was suffering from hardening of the arteries; the doctor had told Mum that he could die at any time. For a moment, I was convinced he was going to have a heart attack right there on my bed and I'd be held responsible. The fifteen-second pause was an eternity as I watched normal colour slowly return to his face. Up to this point I had never heard my father swear—profanity was never used in the Venn-Brown household.

My father's furious response was, 'You mean you ...' and he proceeded to accuse me of various sex acts. I couldn't believe what my father was saying, he made it sound so disgusting.

'No,' I protested.

'How do you know? ... How long have you felt like this? ... Who else knows?' Simple questions answered with quick statements. Our entire conversation lasted less than five minutes and concluded with Dad's comment, 'You just need to find a good girl, get married, and then you'll be okay. I don't want to hear any more of this nonsense.' I was about to tell him getting married wouldn't solve the problem but he left the room, leaving me once again aware that I wasn't the son he wanted. For the first time I really knew my father's acceptance and love was available only if I was 'normal', married and able to produce grand-children—never as I was. My outing was everything I imagined and worse. My father had responded as some parents still do today, first with rejection, then denial. If only Dad had talked to me more he may have known the terrible struggle I'd gone through, how much I really wanted to be straight and the courage it required to actually tell him. I didn't leave my room all night and for the next few days made myself scarce. Whenever I unavoidably passed Dad in the hallway my eyes dropped to the floor and we passed each other without a word. The topic was never discussed again.

Paradise had kept all my money saying that it was to pay for the treatment that I'd had, and that they wanted to make my new life as difficult as possible. Even though my personal freedom was important, boarding at home was my only option and it wasn't long before Dad had arranged a job for me, working in the warehouse of Patterson Reid and Bruce, a wholesaler of soft goods.

I think Joyce was concerned that I might talk about Paradise's heavy-handed tactics, so she issued a decree to all Christian churches in Sydney stating that all contact with me should cease as I was in a state of rebellion. Unaware that I'd been labelled an apostate, I thought I'd make contact with some of my Christian friends. I drove past the house of my friend from high school, John, and I was excited to see several familiar cars parked outside. I knocked on the door and waited. John answered. I knew my friends would be upset that I had become a 'prac-tising homosexual' but never expected the response I received.

As I walked into the lounge room the familiar smiles and welcoming faces were non-existent; some looked at me sadly and others with anger. David, who I'd done the country gospel tours with, spoke on behalf of the group.

'As long as you are a homosexual and away from God we are not to have anything to do with you; we've handed you over to Satan,' he declared in a pious, arrogant tone. Recently he'd been developing an unnatural English accent, the beginnings of the transformation that eventually led him out of the Pentecostal Church and into the extremes of high-church Anglicanism.

I could see how they justified it biblically but it was still difficult to comprehend that these people, who'd been my closest friends, were now rejecting me—it was so unchristian. I could never imagine treating them that way no matter what they'd done. It seemed that being a homosexual meant I was worse than the average sinner. My feeble objections were met with several verses from the *Bible* to remind me of my no-longer-under-grace state. Realising I was not in a position to quote the Word of God, I left.

David was already becoming a leading light in Charismatic circles in Sydney, but had always found Paradise difficult to break into because of its exclusivity. Now he was ensuring that Joyce's commands were carried to the churches in Sydney and using this opportunity to become better acquainted with them.

Entering the clandestine world of Sydney's homosexual underground posed two problems for me. Firstly, how did one find the bars and clubs and, secondly, how did one get in? I imagined it was much like the speak-easy of the prohibition era where there would be a door, with a small peephole through which one had to give a secret password to gain entry. I was sure Ben would know what to do and would be willing to help me. I phoned him and talked about what had happened since we'd spent that memorable night together.

'You can't change it,' he reminded me again. When I asked him to take me to a bar, his reluctance surprised me, as I thought he would be happy to see a Christian give in to sin. Even though Ben appeared happy to be gay he was disinclined to take me into the scene, believing that once I took that step it was a journey of no return. He wasn't sure he wanted that responsibility. Underneath that confident exterior Ben was secretly dealing with his own demons. His path had been similar to mine and included confusion, depression and attempted suicide. His parents had sent him to a psychiatrist for help, but the practitioner had sex with him on the first and succeeding visits. I finally persuaded him though, and arranged to meet up on Saturday evening.

In 1973, Sydney was not the gay mecca it is today, although there were a few venues known as homosexual haunts. During the 1960s the Rex Hotel and Les Girls in Kings Cross were two such venues. Les Girls was purely an entertainment venue with a predominantly straight audience who gawked at the 'girls'' tits and sniggered behind their hands saying, 'That's amazing, where does he tuck it?' It was a Las Vegas style show with stunning female impersonators, Carlotta being the most well-known, who afterwards established a successful career in other areas of entertainment. Some people naively believed the stars were normal men who just liked dressing up like any actor. Gay men and lesbians could also be seen at the Taxi Club with its smattering of underworld figures, probably because of its twenty-four-hour licence.

By the 1970s the emerging gay community was developing an identity and culture through its own venues, which were exclusively gay but welcoming of straight friends and supporters; often the place to educate people about how much fun and normal homosexuals were. There was Capriccio's, a nightclub and bar up a dark narrow staircase in Oxford Street, Darlinghurst; Enzo's, a wine bar opposite the Paddington Town Hall; and Chez Ivy's in Bondi Junction. These three venues were all on Oxford Street but approximately eight kilometres apart. Adonis's, opposite the infamous Wayside Chapel in Kings Cross, was also a meeting place for gay men and the occasional prostitute who worked in the area.

Ben decided my first experience should be Capriccio's. I was both excited and a little nervous as we climbed the dark narrow stairway to an open room with tables and chairs and a bar down one wall. Capriccio's, because of licensing laws, operated as a restaurant but no-one actually went there to eat. It took some time for my eyes to become accustomed to the dim light and for the figures to become clearer. It was not a large crowd, only forty or so people, and I felt intimidated sitting alone at a table some distance from the bar while Ben went to buy drinks. I was unaccustomed to having other men so obviously look me up and down and I found it unsettling. I was really only interested in one person: Ben. The memory of that one and only night with him was indelibly imprinted on my mind. If only we could have more of those.

Ben knew so many people and, with drinks in hand, moved from one group to another saying 'Hi' and greeting a number of men with a kiss. Finally, he arrived with my beer and a few men he'd collected on his journey back from the bar. After chatting for a while we moved up an even narrower flight of stairs to a similar-sized area with a stage at the front. As soon as we arrived the show began (Ben knew the timetable at Capriccio's well), the curtains opening to reveal a stunning red-headed woman. It wasn't until I finally got to meet Red Leslie that I was convinced she was a man, her deep speaking voice letting me know she wasn't really singing the song, only miming. I was amazed. The only men I'd ever seen dressed up as women had been in English comedies and they were very unattractive.

After the show we moved downstairs again and had a couple more drinks. Ben announced it was time to go, we kissed everyone affectionately goodbye, which was nice, then we made the descent to Oxford Street. I'd survived my first night on the scene—I'd overcome my first major hurdle and was now a little more educated. Although there were things that made me feel at home, like the affectionate kisses, there were other things like the open talk about sex and the obvious cruising that made me feel uncomfortable. I had a lot to learn.

I was disappointed that Ben had given me no indication he was interested in having sex with me again and acted as if nothing had ever happened between us. He waved goodbye as he boarded the bus and I walked down another block to catch mine.

Gay activism was born in Australia in 1970 under the organisation CAMP (Campaign Against Moral Prejudice) and Ben took me to a party at their premises on Darling Street, Balmain. The strong political emphasis was not something I felt comfortable with and I chose to devote my time exploring the social aspects of the homosexual world instead. It wasn't long before there was a split in the organisation and the Gay Liberation movement was established. Gay Lib chose to withdraw from political activism, choosing instead to focus on the inner search, believing that for change to happen in society, homosexuals must first learn to discover self-acceptance. Gay men and women needed to free themselves from the conditioning of a hostile society and become proud of who they were. Gay Lib opened up discussions at Sydney University and their venue in Glebe. It styled the discussions on the consciousness-raising group sessions used by women's lib, and aimed to help gay and lesbian people come to terms with the years of fear, guilt and self-loathing. As one writer said in the *Sydney Gay and Lesbian News*, 'The greatest battle of the homosexual in an oppressive society is within himself, more precisely the image of himself as forced on him by nonhomosexuals.'[2]

One good thing this activism had produced was that I could now use the less offensive words like 'camp' or 'gay', so much nicer than the accusatory term 'homosexual'. The word homosexual had every negative perception of society attached to it.

At a Gay Lib dance at Sydney University, I was forced to face the fact that Ben didn't have the same feelings for me. These feelings had continued to grow the more time I spent with him. I always followed him around like a sad puppy, getting under his feet and waiting for some recognition from my master. His interest in other men made me jealous and my constant companionship destroyed his opportunities to be with someone else. On the balcony, away from the heat of the hall and the loud music, I had to tell him how I felt.

'I don't love you,' he said bluntly, after I told him that he was the only one I wanted to be with. Crying on the balcony I was reminded of Joyce's words: 'Homosexuals never find happiness or have lasting relationships.' I left and went home alone.

Without Ben, it was time to develop my own circle of friends. David was an outrageous queen, with shoulder-length hair, tight-arsed bellbottoms that hung over his ten-centimetre platform shoes, and always with a strappy shoulder bag. After a night of drinking we regularly picked him up from the floor, footpath or gutter and perched him precariously once more on those amazing platforms. He was the first gay man I met who'd been married, thinking this would solve his 'problem'. After the marriage failed, he had left the United Kingdom to live as a gay man, away from the prying eyes of family and friends. David's friend, Chris, was a tizzy little queen, two-thirds the size of David, who minced along trying to keep up behind David's huge strides. Initially, I thought they were a couple.

'No, pet!' David protested, flicking his hair back with his hand, 'I never sleep with my sisters.' It felt like I added balance to the lives of this outrageous couple. David and Chris were wild and their lifestyle self-destructive. 'Live hard, die young' was their philosophy. I often wondered what became of them—it's hard to imagine they survived.

They insisted on taking me to see the film *Cabaret*, with Liza Minelli and Michael York. Of course, they'd already seen the winner of eight Academy Awards several times but I just HAD to see it; one simply cannot call oneself camp if one doesn't know every line and every song, I was told. The first time I went, not knowing the story line, I began to think that something was going on between the rich Baron

Maximilian and Michael York. It's starting to affect you, I thought. You're beginning to be suspicious about everyone's sexuality. Settle down. Then it came to the scene where Liza and Michael have a huge argument over the abortion of the child. In anger Liza yells, 'Screw Maximilian,' and Michael helplessly replies, 'I do.' I wanted to stand up in the cinema and cheer. For me to hear those words, to take what most of us had to keep secret and declare it so publicly on the screen, was such a liberating moment. I went back and saw the movie three more times and, thanks to the drag shows at Capriccio's, and purchasing the soundtrack, I could soon sing the words to all the songs.

Another social activity in the gay scene was a gathering that happened every Sunday at a little coastal township, about eighty kilometres south of Sydney, called Scarborough. For some strange reason that I never did find out, gay men and lesbians invaded the local pub on Sunday afternoons, to drink in the back bar overlooking the ocean and watch drag shows. An occasional highlight was the appearance of 'The Contessa' in full opera regalia. The Contessa was a guy called Graham who, unlike the drag queens that mimed the songs of divas, actually sang famous arias with a shrill falsetto voice.

We were relatively protected, as legislation dictated country hotels and bars could only sell drinks to bona fide travellers on Sundays, so locals were barred. On arrival we always had to sign in and produce our driver's licences to prove we lived out of the legislated radius for Sunday trading. When the police arrived to check the details were correct, word was quickly passed to the back bar and we all sat upright in our seats like good schoolboys as they walked around. Obviously, not all the local residents were pleased about this invasion as, more than once when I emerged from the pub, I discovered my motorbike had been thrown off the cliff at the edge of the car park. Despite this occasional harassment, 'Scarborough on Sundays', as it was known, became an enjoyable regular event for me.

Another new venue called the Barrel, decorated like a German beer house, opened in Kings Cross. It survived during the week as a restaurant, but on Sunday nights the forbidding wooden doors were closed, tables and chairs were stacked back to the walls and the place was transformed by sequins, feathers and Shirley Bassey numbers. The drag shows varied from embarrassingly tragic to outstandingly entertaining and the drag queens correspondingly ranged from sadly ugly to deceptively stunning. They were usually a bitchy, backstabbing bunch, though.

Adonis's provided me with many interesting experiences. The café was also a haven for the local hookers, a place where they could get away from tricks in the brothels and drumming up trade on the streets. I got to know many of the girls on a first name basis and was impressed with their openness and lack of façade. It was refreshing to meet some real people like Sandy and Julie—they were always friendly and grateful for a conversation with someone who wasn't out to get something from them. For the first time I understood why Jesus made mixing with prostitutes a priority.

One night, Sandy seemed very agitated so I sat down and had coffee with her. She mentioned that her 'sitter', Billy, only seventeen and a runaway, had been taken by the police and she was paranoid about working alone. In my naivety, I thought she needed a baby sitter for her child, as many of the girls had children and gay guys often looked after them while they were working the streets. So I offered to help.

Prostitution in the early 1970s was very different to what it is today; the girls had a regular spot on the street and for years maintained their own territory. Walking down a street you'd been on twelve months earlier you'd usually see the same girl working the exact spot. Today, because of heroin abuse and other factors, it's a very different culture and you see different girls on the street weekly, if not daily. Sandy lived in the suburbs, was married with kids and saving money to give her children, the education and life that had eluded her. I never asked how her husband felt about the situation and found it difficult to comprehend the mechanics of such an arrangement. Sandy and I walked down Hughes Street to her flat, where she took me into the kitchen, handed me a large wooden table leg, and explained the role of a sitter. Apparently a sitter's job was to make noises so that clients knew there was someone else in the flat, and to protect the girls if any of the men got out of hand. If there was any trouble, I was to run into the room and dong the client on the head, then we'd take him outside and dump him in the street. The thought of doing this was horrifying—I imagined cracking open a guy's head and being up for murder. I was quite nervous about the situation but I'd offered to help Sandy so I sat in the kitchen and prayed the clients would be good boys. Thank God the night progressed without incident. Sandy paid me almost a day's salary for my services.

Realising I was safe to let into their secret network, Sandy and her hooker partner Julie invited me to a party at the flat. I was excited at being taken into the girls' confidence, but I realised after a while that some of their other guests were detectives. Everything seemed very amicable, they behaved like old chums, and didn't seem to mind the drugs at all. I didn't dare ask what the police were doing at a party in a brothel but figured it was time to remove myself from the environment.

One Wednesday night I walked into Adonis's and found Marion, the ex-hooker from Paradise, sitting at one of the tables. Marion and I had clicked immediately and her down-to-earth input at times had kept me sane during my 'rehab'. It was unbelievable that now here she was in Kings Cross, with one of the young girls from Paradise, in my favourite café.

'What are you doing here?' I screamed, as I ran over and hugged her knowing she would never reject me as the others had. She proceeded to tell me about a lesbian affair she and the other girl were having. It had been going on for months, even while I had been there. Joyce and Edna thought she was out doing some church work that night so she was able to have a secret rendezvous with her lover. Marion made me promise not to tell anyone and I understood her need for secrecy, but it would have been wonderful to blow away Paradise's pious, arrogant attitude with this piece of information.

Several months after my final contact with my Christian friends, I was in Kings Cross with a group on my way to Adonis's. Walking down Darlinghurst Road, I heard singing. Before I'd gone to bible college I'd been involved with a street ministry called Gospel Crusaders and every Saturday night we went out talking to people about Jesus and singing in the hub of Kings Cross. When I turned the corner, I saw David preaching in front of the fountain. David had once let down his guard and shared with me that he had a problem trying to control his masturbation. We'd prayed together that God would give us the strength to overcome this terrible habit. Now, knowing what was behind David's zeal in alienating me, anger rose within me (the few drinks I'd consumed helped, I'm sure) and I walked up and stood at the front. He was preaching about how God can change anyone's life if only they will come to Him. I could tell he was feeling uncomfortable having me in his audience so I waited for the right moment, knowing he would eventually be asking people to receive Jesus into their lives.

'Has Jesus helped you with your problem with masturbation?' I shouted above the other hecklers, making sure everyone heard me. David was speechless. 'Did Jesus stop you from masturbating?' I repeated, feeling even more confident. Hecklers were common on Saturday nights but no-one ever got this close to the truth. Immediately, I was surrounded by some of my Christian friends who tried to silence me. 'How dare you condemn and judge me. Remember Jesus said, "Judge not, lest you be judged",' I concluded in defiance.

David was obviously shaken and people tried to move me away from the crowd but I'd done my work and walked away to catch up with my gay friends who had walked ahead.

Over the last six months my skills of picking up men had become highly developed. It may have been my age, but I usually had a one hundred per cent success rate. New Year's Eve 1973 was one of my greatest conquests. A friendship had grown with Ray (the owner of Adonis's) because I frequented the place so much. He was finding it difficult to get staff to work on New Year's Eve. The extra money sounded good and, having no particular plans, I offered my services. Steve, the English chef at the café, was very cute with a great body. He was in his early twenties and was a stud with the girls. All the boys tried desperately to convert him but no-one even got close. We worked hard that night together in the kitchen, pumping out meals and drinks to the constant stream of New Year revellers who popped into the café.

As the evening progressed, Steve and I decided to join in the festivities and have a few drinks and by 6am we were pretty drunk. Steve had been touching me more than a heterosexual man should touch a gay man, to the point where we were both in flirting mode. There was no mistaking that tell-tale eye contact. With the last meals and drinks out of the way and the kitchen cleaned we left the café and walked out into the early light of morning. Once away from the eyes of the regulars at Adonis's, Steve asked me to come back to his hotel room for a drink. Walking through the debris of the New Year festivities littering the streets of the Cross, I wondered what motivation was behind the invitation. I'll just take it one step at a time, I thought.

The room above the hotel in William Street was sparse; dirty clothes were scattered on the floor and the odour of the used cooking oil that impregnated his clothes filled the room. Steve immediately began undressing and that was the only signal I needed. I broke the world record for getting undressed that morning. Steve grabbed me and threw me onto the bed; he was passionate and aggressive as he rapidly moved his hands over every part of my body, like a man who hadn't had sex for years. It was wild—about the best two people could do when severely drunk. We'd rest a few moments, lying on our backs and laughing at the intensity we'd just experienced, then within minutes we were back into the flurried movements. Finally we collapsed with exhaustion and fell asleep. A few hours later I woke and decided it was best to leave immediately in case Steve had second thoughts about what he'd done. I didn't want to go home, so I staggered around Kings Cross with a throbbing headache and the hot summer sun adding to the intensity of the hangover. Alone again, I began to feel lost and empty as I thought about the previous New Year's Eve, when I'd been with my friends at Christian Faith Centre enjoying a time of singing, worship and prayer, dedicating our lives to the service of God for the coming year. The word spread quickly about my night with Chef; apparently someone had seen us going home together. I was considered a legend but Steve, embarrassed by the taunts of Ray and others, still professed his heterosexuality, and finally left Adonis's to work elsewhere. Maybe the saying is true: 'The only difference between a gay man and a straight man is a can of beer.'

One night at Capriccio's, Lawrence was sitting at one of the tables with some people I knew. Everyone knew Lawrence—he turned heads when he entered a room—but I only admired from a distance as he carried an air of being unobtainable. He was over 180 centimetres tall and stunningly beautiful with long hair cut in a pageboy style. As a fashion designer he made all his own clothes and lived in the trendy suburb of Paddington. I felt nervous when Lawrence was introduced to me and tried to ignore him most of the night; his presence was unsettling and I was afraid of saying the wrong thing and making an idiot of myself. As was our pattern, we moved on to Adonis's for coffee and sat side-by-side in a booth. Lawrence put his hand on my leg. I froze and did nothing to respond except occasionally smile in his direction. This was the last thing I expected to happen—surely he was playing a trick on me. Everyone else was unaware of what was happening under the table and I was finding it difficult to concentrate on the conversation. Lawrence finished his cappuccino quickly, squeezed my leg in a way that said 'let's go' and announced he was going home.

'I think I'll go home, too,' I said, endeavouring to maintain a casual tone in my voice, and followed Lawrence out the door seconds later, leaving my friends bewildered and suspicious at the sudden exit. Sure enough, Lawrence was standing a little further up the street, smiling and awaiting my exit.

'Coming back to my place, aren't you?' he said in a confident tone. Of course, no-one in their right mind would refuse an invitation like that from Lawrence, so we hailed a cab in Macleay Street and within minutes were outside his house in Paddington.

The white two-storey terrace in Elizabeth Street was exquisitely decorated, with everything tastefully coordinated like homes I'd seen only in magazines. Still a little nervous about being with such an attractive man, I waited for Lawrence to make the suggestion of when to retire to the bedroom. I was besotted as he took me by the hand and led me upstairs to his attic. Lawrence was like my Prince Charming and could have played that role easily in any film or play without make-up or even a costume change. Usually after sex, I'd excuse myself and head home to Hunters Hill, still afraid of reprisals from my parents for not sleeping at least a few hours in my own bed, but Lawrence was worth the risk: I wasn't leaving his side for anything.

Lawrence was the first man I saw more than once and we spent several nights together. Within a week I fell hopelessly in love with this beautiful man but doubted that I could keep him. Sure enough, arriving at his house one day, intending to spend the weekend together, I knew something was amiss. I felt Lawrence withdrawing from me. Everything was different, the glow was gone, the warmth replaced by a coldness as Lawrence hastily announced he was already seeing someone else and our romance was over. He said he was sorry but he didn't love me any more.

I was heartbroken and tried to get some consolation from my friends but was told to get over it. Their coldness and lack of sympathy was upsetting—I expected more support. It wasn't that they hadn't experienced a broken heart but they had chosen to harden themselves to what they thought was inevitable.

I'd been in the gay scene for seven months and I'd had enough. The one-night stands with different men left me feeling empty. The unrequited love I had for Ben and my brief romantic encounter with Lawrence confirmed what I'd been told, that homosexual men never find happiness or have lasting relationships. There were things about gay culture I didn't like, such as the insincerity of many people I met and the bitchiness that was an art form. There didn't appear to be many gay men who were masculine, only the stereotypical hairdressers, dancers, window dressers, musicians and arty types who often enjoyed camping it up to the point of being annoyingly offensive. I was fed up with the flapping wrists and screamers and couldn't see myself ever fitting into the scene. Although my Christian friends were currently rejecting me, in the Christian world I had known a much deeper level of friendship. I felt that once I'd gone back to God I would be accepted again.

I had been shown that a homosexual lifestyle would never satisfy me. God had called me to the ministry and I remembered the verse in the *Bible* that said 'the calling of God is irrevocable.' In other words, I could never escape God's calling on my life. God would always have His hand on me and real peace and fulfilment would only be found in loving and serving Him—which meant being straight not gay.

What I didn't realise at the time was that my decision to become straight was going to take me to a dark place, a place of secrets, lies and deception where I would plumb the depths of self-loathing. I'd come out as a homosexual but now, by choosing to be straight, I was actually putting myself back into the closet; by seeking to be free I was creating my own prison.

CHAPTER 9
A miracle?

On 15 December 1973, the board of the American Psychiatric Association unanimously voted to remove homosexuality from its official list of psychiatric disorders and urged the repeal of all laws discriminating against homosexuals. Even if I had known of this complete turn-around amongst mental health professionals, I still would have taken the path back into the church. The belief that 'heterosexuality is normal and homosexuality is an abomination' was just too deeply entrenched in my thinking. Psychiatry was viewed as some form of worldly 'hocus-pocus' in the circles I mixed in and a poor substitute for the healing power of God. It would be years before I realised that my sexual orientation was innate, unchangeable and healthy.

As I was coming out of my brief gay sojourn in January 1974, the Watergate scandal was reaching its height and President Nixon's integrity was on the line. Taped conversations that took place in the Oval Office revealed details about the burglary of the Democratic National Committee's headquarters at the Watergate Hotel that deeply implicated the President, and brought him to the brink of impeachment. Those tapes also revealed his warped view of history and current events. Nixon saw homosexuality as a Communist conspiracy, and that it had also caused the downfall of civilisations. 'You see: homosexuality, dope, immorality in general — these are the enemies of strong societies. That's why the Communists and the left-wingers are pushing the stuff; they're trying to destroy us.' In conversation the same day, President Nixon said, 'I don't want to see this country to go that way. You know what happened to the Greeks. Homosexuality destroyed them. Sure, Aristotle was a homo, we all know that, so was Socrates ... Do you know what happened to the Romans? The last six Roman emperors were fags ...You know what happened to the popes? It's all right that popes were laying the nuns. That's been going on for years — centuries. But when the popes, when the Catholic Church went to hell in — I don't know, three or four centuries ago — it was homosexual, and it had to be cleaned out.' He was not alone in these views. Hitler believed that homosexuality was 'degenerate behavior' which posed a threat to the capacity of the state and the 'masculine character' of the nation; gay men were charged with 'corrupting' public morality and posing a threat to the German birthrate. As many as 600,000 are thought to have perished in Nazi concentration camps. Even today, many people share this bizarre hatred of, and obsession with, gay men and lesbians.

Thoughts of myself as a homosexual, while not as extreme, were still unhealthy and my seven months' experience in the gay world had confirmed almost everything I'd been told. I had no illusions anymore about what it meant to be gay; any mystery that had existed was gone.

The following Saturday night I went to Capriccio's and said goodbye to the people I had known. I wasn't planning on coming back to Oxford Street, living a double life or making myself vulnerable by hanging around the gay scene—I had to make a clean break. 'I've tried it and I don't want to be gay anymore. I'm giving my life back to God,' I boldly stated, genuinely believing that God could and would perform the miracle. As I expected, no-one understood my decision but I thought that in the future, once I was free, there might be an opportunity for me to help them come to God. The next day, on Sunday afternoon, I went to the service at Christian Faith Centre, only to be greeted with caution and suspicion. People smiled and said hello but their acknowledgment lacked warmth. I knew so well the parables Jesus taught about the shepherd going out of his way to find the one lost sheep, and the celebration when the prodigal son returned to his father's house, but I was to get none of that treatment.

Maybe I should have called but I didn't think it necessary—I thought everyone would be thrilled about my decision to come back to God and would know that the only reason I went into the gay world originally was to learn to really hate my sin. I was fully committed to being a Christian and living the life God wanted for me, and now more than ever I wanted to be 'normal'—get married, have children and serve God. When the service concluded I was immediately escorted to the church office for a talk with the pastors.

'What are you doing here?' Pastor Paul asked in a strict tone of voice.

'I've given my life back to God,' I replied with confidence, knowing I would never have been at church otherwise.

'Why did you leave Paradise? Why did you leave without contacting us? Do you really want to be free?' The questions came thick and fast but it was difficult to explain what had really taken place at Paradise because of the recognition its rehabilitation program had received. People genuinely thought they were doing wonderful work. Who'd believe me if I told them about what really went on? I was more concerned about being accepted at Christian Faith Centre than destroying the credibility of Paradise.

'God's patience with you is wearing out; you cannot go on sinning, expecting His forgiveness,' Pastor Paul reminded me again, and continued with guidelines of what I must do. 'You cannot do any ministry in the church until we believe you are free. If you want to stay in the church you must report for counselling once a week and be totally honest about what's happening in your life; no more hiding.' This sounded good—I wanted that sort of accountability anyway, knowing it was the only way to be free. But I couldn't understand why I'd been banned from doing any Christian ministry. Was I really the only imperfect member in the church and everyone else was holy? My spiritual development was placed in Pastor Roger's hands. He was a family man who I respected greatly as he'd studied psychology yet also believed in casting out demons. I promised to meet with him for a couple of hours every Wednesday afternoon and call him immediately should I have any problems.

During the counselling sessions I was able to vent my feelings, but Roger had difficulty understanding and couldn't relate to my struggles. His suggestions of praying and reading the *Bible* to overcome temptation and change my thinking seemed far too simplistic. If it were that easy, I would have been heterosexual years ago. I submitted totally to the leadership and attended all the services and prayer meetings, waiting for the time they were convinced I was really free of homosexuality and I was off probation.

I was still working for Patterson Reid and Bruce in the menswear department. After attending an internal sales course I was chosen out of the group of ten men (females were never given positions as sales representatives) to go out on the road with one of the reps for some experience. Recognising my natural selling ability, the company offered me a position as one of the sales representatives in the central west of New South Wales. Obviously God was blessing me for my obedience, as this meant a promotion, car, increase in salary, expense account and, even better, a move out of Sydney, which would remove me even further from temptation. Surely in the country I was less likely to be confronted with opportunities to have sex with men and this would give me 'time out' in order to prepare me for the ministry. I'd be able to find a little country church and take on some form of lay ministry with the youth or music, even hand out books at the door; anything that would show I had a heart to serve God. It was an opportunity to start afresh without everyone knowing I had a problem with homosexuality. The leaders at Christian Faith Centre thought it would be a good idea I move to the country but I had the feeling that they were relieved to see me work through my problems elsewhere.

Orange (approximately 300 kilometres west of Sydney) was a growing rural city with beautiful parks, wide tree-lined streets and elaborate Victorian architecture. It had many picture-postcard scenes, especially in autumn when the trees turned rich golds and crimsons. Orange was to be my base while I travelled up and down country New South Wales selling fabrics, children's wear and soft furnishings. Within a week I'd found the tiny Assemblies of God Church and had set myself up in a small one-bedroom flat. My new life had begun.

The Assemblies of God Church was a congregation of thirty people that increased to forty for special occasions, originally founded during a revival in the 1920s by a Dutch healing evangelist. I was frequently told stories of the 'good old days' when the local theatre of Orange overflowed every night with Pentecostal believers and supernatural signs. Not so now. The glory had well and truly departed after the evangelist was run out of town under a cloud of questionable connections with a number of women. The shell that was left bore no resemblance to the early days of miracles, healings and growth, now replaced by family power struggles, tradition, hypocrisy and suspicious dealings with the other rival Pentecostal Church in the city.

Most of the church members were related to each other, which created an unhealthy, incestuous air. Mumma Daphne played the piano; Dad Claude was an elder who greeted everyone, handed out the hymn books, and did everything Daphne told him to; their daughter taught Sunday school; and their son-in-law played the organ and ran the Sunday school. Mumma's brother Dick was also an elder of the church, God only knows why. This poor man lacked even basic communication skills and usually only grunted responses. During my five years in the church I never saw him smile, and often joked that he must have been baptised in lemon juice. Apparently his life was a misery at home as his wife was a backslidden Christian who fought with him constantly, to the point of violence. This may have been justified—being married to such an unresponsive person must have been incredibly frustrating. The handful of young people in the church were related to the family and only attended services because they were forced to, having little personal experience of God. One of my goals was to establish a youth ministry in the church and try to bring some new life into the place.

My one ray of hope was the change of pastor the church was about to experience. Very soon, the conservative, old-school Welsh pastor would be replaced by Pastor John and his wife who I knew from my involvement with Pentecostal churches and youth camps in Sydney. The Assemblies of God churches were having great difficulty coming to grips with the new Charismatic movement, especially the renewal happening in some of the traditional churches. The Pentecostals felt that if a new wave of renewal was going to happen, then it should happen within their churches. However, Pastor John, in his early thirties, was part of the new breed that recognised that the Assemblies of God had lost the fire and needed renewal as much as any denomination. His transfer to Orange meant we could join forces and transform this entrenched congregation, bringing life, vibrant worship, relevancy and growth to the church. John was glad of my allegiance and we hit it off immediately.

I enjoyed my work as a sales representative, especially the long country trips to places like Cobar, Bourke, Coonamble and West Wyalong, often commencing my week with a four- to five-hour drive before seeing my first customer. Some of these towns had experienced times of boom during the gold rush or when merino fleece was known as liquid gold or when being a cattle farmer meant being wealthy, but now the rural sector was struggling. Driving down the main street was like arriving on a movie set; time stood still, leaving the towns as tangible testimonies of a more prosperous era. The first time I arrived in Coonamble, I was unpacking my clothing samples to take into the store when I heard the shop doors slam shut one after another down the street. I looked up to see that the men had removed their hats and everyone was standing still with heads bowed. At the end of the main street a man appeared in a black suit with tails and a top hat and long scarf trailing behind; he was followed by a hearse. Apparently when anyone died in Coonamble, every shop shut its doors in respect to the deceased as the funeral procession passed from the church to the local cemetery.

In Cobar, the town where my father was born in 1918, it was not difficult to picture the days I'd heard about when my grandfather was the manager of the Great Cobar Mine and had to attend a meeting of disgruntled miners carrying a pistol in his pocket for protection. The evidence of those days remained—large mounds of waste from the mines and scattered, abandoned, rusty machinery. My great-grandfather was also the Anglican minister at that time, and travelled by horse and sulky to visit his parishioners, sometimes hundreds of miles from Cobar. Visiting these places made the stories come alive. Dodging the kangaroos and emus on the highways was a new experience for a city slicker like me but I was beginning to love my new life in the country.

My sales career was coming along well and every other spare minute I threw myself into church activity, setting up a Christian coffee shop on Friday nights to reach some of the young teenagers hanging around the streets. From the contacts I'd made I was able to establish a youth group of about thirty young people on the Saturday night as well.

Julie, a schoolteacher who'd transferred to Orange, began attending the church. Being of similar age, and desperate for companionship, we began spending time a lot of together. She seemed quite interested in me so occasionally we'd hold hands and be mildly affectionate with each other.

Having coffee after church one Sunday night I drove her home and parked outside her house, then turned off the car lights. I was never attracted to Julie but thought that maybe if I just tried it out the right type of feelings would surface. I leant over and we began to kiss—she was very keen. Our lips moved awkwardly over each other's and our tongues connected. It was difficult to determine what it was doing for her, she seemed to be enjoying it, but nothing was happening for me. All I could think of was how repulsive and unnatural it felt—so unlike the fireworks I'd experienced with Ben. Why did it feel so dead? Obviously I had a lot more work to do before normal heterosexual feelings would begin to surface. I quickly stopped kissing her and suggested she'd better go inside. After all, we were good, Christian young people and we didn't want to put ourselves in a vulnerable situation of temptation. What a convenient excuse. I wonder if other Christian girls have woken up to why their soft and sensitive Christian boyfriends can be so self-controlled.

Then Helen arrived in the church like a breath of fresh air. She was young (eighteen), attractive and a very keen Christian. Helen was a product of many influences; the daughter of a migrant family ('new Australians' as they were known) who had been raised in a country town near the Victorian border. Helen's parents had known great hardship during the war, as the Germans had invaded their little town near Minsk and burnt the village to the ground along with Helen's grandmother who was too frail to escape. With their two young children Helen's parents were taken to Germany and forced into hard labour growing vegetables for the German army. After the war they were given the opportunity of returning to the village or coming to Australia. They saw no reason to return to their native Russia, so decided to begin a new life in Australia. They arrived in Australia with only a couple of suitcases, and were sent to a small country town where Boris worked as a railway fettler and Nadia in the fruit cannery. The family grew to seven children and once the kids had grown up and began to leave for city life, Helen's parents moved to Orange to become a part of the large Slavic Pentecostal community.

Helen's parents' English skills were limited, which meant she'd always assisted them in banking, making phone calls, accompanying them to doctors' visits, et cetera, and this responsibility produced a confidence and strength that was immediately noticeable. Underneath the confident exterior, though, was a surprising lack of self-esteem, the result of being a 'new Australian'. Being a part of one of the three migrant families in a small country town made Helen feel she was different and inferior. Over the years she told me stories of the lengths she went to trying to gain the acceptance of her friends and be like everyone else. Having seven young mouths to feed, her Mum never bought milk, cheese, butter, cakes or biscuits—instead they made their own, grew their vegetables, and sewed the children's clothes. All was provided by the land in the same way they had known back in Russia. When Helen brought her friends home from school she tried to disguise the peasant lifestyle by doing things like shaping the butter her Mum had made into a block so that it resembled the supermarket brands, thus giving the impression they were a normal Australian family. It wasn't until many years later, after a visit to her parents' homeland to meet her relatives, that she learnt to be proud of her heritage and appreciate the simple lifestyle of her parents.

Helen came to join her parents in Orange after spending twelve months at a church in New Zealand pastored by her brother-in-law, where she'd seen a revival among the hippies and surfies of New Plymouth. Helen was a fine young Christian girl with a vibrant faith. I noticed her the moment she walked into the church; when you have such a small congregation, visitors are always made to feel welcome.

Helen wanted to go to an English-speaking church instead of the Slavic Pentecostal Church her parents attended. Coming from such a lively congregation in New Zealand to arrive at the Orange Assemblies of God must have been a culture shock. There was always a great pressure in the churches for singles to get married, and that morning most people in the church had already decided Helen was the one for me. European mamas are fearless, embarrassing matchmakers and Helen's mother was keen to invite this nice, young Christian man around for lunch to get to know her daughter and her family. I'd always been a fussy eater, being brought up on the Australian diet of greens, spuds, grills and roasts, but Helen's mum was determined to introduce me to Russian cuisine. My first meal in a European household with Mama's delicacies of piroshki, holopsi, pelmenny and borsch converted me.

Still reeling from the main course, the table was cleared and again covered, this time with sweet delights. 'Try this, sweetie,' the plump little woman said as she placed homemade pastries, cakes and biscuits in front of me. Even though I felt bloated, I knew it was useless to resist this determined Russian Babushka.

'You must eat, darlink, you're too skinny.' Groans of protest came from Helen and her brother and sisters. 'Leave him alone, Mum!' But it was futile, she always won.

From that day I became an adopted member of the family and called Helen's parents 'Mum' and 'Dad'—it seemed the natural thing to do as they were so loving and hospitable. Being with Helen was extremely comfortable and we became instant companions, but I knew she was going to be more than a friend. It felt like destiny.

We spent most of our spare time together and when I returned from my sales trips, not completely happy with Helen's wardrobe, I replenished it with new dresses, jeans and tops I was able to purchase wholesale. She began to help me in my youth work at the Friday night coffee shop and we attended every church activity together. Knowing I was called to serve God, it was important that my future wife also felt called. Helen was ideal; a woman who wanted to serve God as much as I did. I decided she'd been brought to me, she was the miracle I needed to completely free me of homosexuality. I'd never felt this way about a woman before. I thought about her often and genuinely cared for her. This must be love, I thought. God has finally answered my prayers, and I was glad I hadn't given up the struggle. Sometimes when I was with Helen I actually got sexually aroused a little but I felt that if God had been so good as to give me Helen and normal heterosexual responses then the worst thing I could do would be to blow it by having sex before marriage.

The three weeks since Helen and I met had been fantastic and I already felt like a new person. After closing down the coffee shop on Saturday night we dropped the young people home and parked outside the Orange railway station, a strange place for such a significant event. By May, Orange was already into winter and the clouds had settled on the town producing a thick fog, common at that time of year. Occasionally a glow appeared down the street, and eventually two headlights would emerge through the mist only to fade away into a red glow in the distance. I turned to Helen and held her hand.

'I've never asked anyone this question before,' I said cautiously and seriously, aware of the implications of what I was about to say. I took a deep breath as I said, 'Will you marry me?' I don't know who was more shocked I'd said such a thing—Helen or I. I'd thought about this since the moment we'd met and this seemed like the right time to pop the question. I didn't want to wait any longer.

'You've got to give me more time!' she replied, catching her breath. 'I thought you were going to ask me to be your girlfriend.'

'I feel it's the right thing and it's God's will for us to be together,' I replied, knowing it was paramount for two Christian young people to find God's chosen partner. 'Why don't we pray and see what God wants?' I suggested. In the haste of my proposal I'd failed to mention the all-important word—love. At that point in my life I loved Helen with as much love as a gay man is capable of giving a woman and would never have asked her to marry me unless I felt that. Not the kind of love that makes you lose your appetite, talk on the telephone for hours or sends you into emotional ecstasy, but it was a love. I continued to persuade her, 'Why don't we see if God will confirm if we should be together? If we both feel the same way about each other in three weeks, your parents are happy and the pastor agrees it's a good idea, then we can be sure this is God's will.' It was always necessary to get two or three confirmations that something was the will of God. It was difficult for Helen to argue with such spiritual terminology.

Pastor John and his wife were thrilled when we shared the news with them. John's wife was an enthusiastic matchmaker who often mentioned couples she'd been instrumental in bringing together. Now we just had to get the approval of our families.

The three weeks passed quickly and we planned to have dinner with Helen's parents when I returned from my weekly sales trip on the Thursday night. My nervousness made it difficult to eat my borsch that night, even though I'd come to love the delicious beetroot and meat soup. I played with the dollop of sour cream on top, rehearsing in my mind the approach I planned to use. I knew Helen had said nothing to her parents but they could tell something was in the air because conversation was unnaturally awkward. I couldn't remember the last time I was so nervous. What would be their reaction to my request? I knew it was a big ask, I'd just turned twenty-three and Helen was about to turn nineteen and we'd known each other less than two months. When the meal finished I asked Babushka and Dedushka to come into the lounge room and the rest of the family were allocated the chores of clearing the table and cleaning up. Helen had made sure of that. I straightened myself up in the chair and tried to make eye contact with them.

'Helen and I believe God wants us to be together and we want to get married,' I said in a wavering voice, knowing it was essential to mention God. This was harder than I thought it would be. 'And I wanted to ask if you will give us permission to get married.' They both gasped as the shock hit.

'My little Helen is so young, we've seen so little of her, only just come from New Zealand, don't want to lose her!' Dedushka protested in his broken English. Babushka was backing him up, saying she was too young and it was too soon. I didn't really want this reaction but couldn't tell them how incredibly significant this was—that Tony Venn-Brown actually wanted to marry a woman. We talked further about how we wanted to serve God together. Having a second son-in-law who was going to be a preacher would be something I knew would please them. Helen's parents were beautiful, not hostile or aggressive; just shocked that this had happened so quickly.

'When do you want to get married?' Babushka asked and I knew the walls of resistance were beginning to crumble.

'We don't want to wait, just four months to arrange everything,' I replied, having never really discussed final dates with Helen. This seemed to please Dedushka. He suggested, in his simple way, that it was better to get married as soon as possible instead of 'having big accident'. What a vote of confidence in my masculinity. Like a salesman waiting for the buying signal I knew it was time for the close. 'So you are saying it's okay then?' They looked at each other, smiled and nodded and I jumped over and hugged them both. We discussed some marriage plans and a tentative date was set in four months, enough time to organise a wedding. Helen and I arranged to go to Sydney the week after to buy a ring and announce the news to my family, as I'd neglected to tell them about what was happening.

There was also one more important thing to do. Helen must know about my past. Honesty had to be an important foundation to our relationship and even though I had never made my homosexuality public, I had to tell her in case some insensitive person disclosed that information at an inappropriate time. How was I going to tell her? This might change everything. Maybe she would reject me? Would she be able to trust me once I told her or would she always be suspicious? It was a risk I had to take. Considering the way I was feeling since I'd met her, I never expected homosexual thoughts to be a problem again. I really thought that now I had feelings for a woman, and after marriage, I would be able to channel my sexual energy in a 'normal' way, then the desire to have sex with men would no longer exist. Sort of like letting a plant die by not watering it any more. It was a sound biblical and simple process—kill sin, grow righteousness; homosexual plant dies, heterosexual plant flourishes. Surely Helen believed as I did that God's power is stronger than anything else?

After the next Sunday service, we were sitting in the car outside her parents' house saying good night.

'Helen, there's something I need to tell you before we get married.' She looked at me strangely, aware an introduction like that meant something seriously important was about to be revealed. 'I used to be a homosexual,' I said carefully. 'What do you mean?' she said, as she moved away from me a little. She sat in amazement as I told my story of struggle, psychiatrists, rehabilitation and exorcism, ensuring that the details were not too graphic. She questioned me briefly about my experiences, as she'd never met a homosexual before, and asked me how I knew I was free.

'It says in 2 Corinthians 5:17, "If any man be in Christ he is a new creation, old things have passed away, behold all things have become new". I've always believed that scripture but since meeting you I really believe this is now true in my life.' I quickly reassured her. 'God has healed me and it's a wonderful miracle we are experiencing together.'

I began to cry and, taking my hand, Helen said reassuringly, 'I feel privileged to be the one who God has chosen to complete this miracle in your life.' We both felt God's blessing on us as we hugged, kissed and prayed together. It was a wonderful relief to know that Helen would accept me with my past. But of course she would … she was a Christian and forgiveness of the past is the foundation. We both knew the verse that says, 'As far as the east is from the west so has he removed our sin from us,' and were naive enough to believe we would live happily ever after.

With this hurdle behind me I was even more ecstatic and I organised for us to go to Sydney the following weekend, meet my family, buy a ring and get together with Pastor Paul in Sydney to discuss wedding arrangements. The next Friday afternoon, we packed the car after work, Helen sat beside me on the bench seat so we could hold hands during the trip, and we left Orange for the three-hour drive to Sydney. I had already told Mum that I was bringing Helen down with me and I had a special surprise. I couldn't wait to make the announcement to the family; I was sure they'd be excited. The closer we got to Hunters Hill the more restless Helen became. So occasionally I'd squeeze her hand reassuringly to let her know it was going to be okay. When we arrived outside the family home we left the luggage in the car and raced inside. Everyone was home, my sisters had come for a family meal with their husbands, and Dad had skipped the drink with his mates after work. As the family processed down the long hallway that ran the length of the house towards us, I introduced Helen with a grin like a Cheshire cat.

'I'd like you to meet Helen.' I couldn't wait another minute. 'My fiancée.'

There were shrieks and hugs from my sisters.

'I had a feeling you were going to do something like this!' my sister Sue said, knowing it was typical of me to spring surprises. Helen was quickly ushered in and I went out to get the luggage from the car. When I returned the family was bombarding Helen with questions. When did we meet? How did Helen's parents feel? Were we sure we wanted to get married so quickly? Where would we get married? While I was getting Helen's room ready, Dad took her aside. 'Are you sure you know what you're doing, luv?' He had many concerns about my stability and sense of responsibility, and was perhaps even fearful that I was not the sort of man who should be marrying such a sweet, innocent girl. Helen assured him we were very much in love and that she was happy. The family celebrated with champagne and welcomed Helen into the family.

I'd decided it was best to get married in Sydney because most of my friends and family lived there. Also, my two sisters had been married locally so we had all the contacts needed to arrange a wedding. Helen went along with everything I wanted and if she disagreed I'd usually talk her around. The next day we went for our appointment with the pastors of Christian Faith Centre. It seemed right to me that Pastor Paul should marry us as this had been my home church. I thought he'd be happy about the news but when we arrived he looked concerned, and Helen and I were immediately separated. Helen was taken away with one of the female pastors and I stayed alone with Pastor Paul.

'Do you really trust yourself?' were his opening words. I reassured him that I felt free enough to get married. Sometimes I'd had homosexual thoughts, I told him, but it was only temptation. Surely the fact that I was sexually attracted to Helen meant God had healed me? I knew nothing of Alfred Kinsey's scale or his research that found that nearly forty-six per cent of his male subjects had 'reacted' sexually to persons of both sexes and nearly forty per cent had at least one homosexual experience. We were still unaware that there was already an entire generation who had attempted what I was planning on doing. In the other room, the female pastor questioned Helen as to whether she knew about my past and what she might be getting herself into. Having never met these people before she was taken aback by their intrusion into our personal lives and defended me all the way. After our separate chats, Pastor Paul eventually decided to marry us on the condition we were willing to come for pre-marriage counselling. Even though this meant more trips to Sydney, we agreed. Anyway, we would have to come to Sydney regularly to make wedding arrangements. I found his lack of faith in me quite unsettling. Why didn't he trust me or more importantly have faith in God? Hadn't we prayed for this miracle? It seemed hypocritical to me that after hearing all his preaching about finding God's will for your life and taking steps of faith, that he should doubt that this was God's will. Would I have to live with this constant doubt and disbelief from others as well as dealing with my own fears? I was glad that at least Pastor John back in Orange had faith in God and me.

The next four months were a whirlwind as we made regular trips to

Sydney to organise the wedding ceremony, suits, reception, flowers, et cetera, as well as pre-marriage counselling with Pastor Paul. The family's previous experience with wedding plans was invaluable; Dad booked the bowling club for the reception, Stewarts'—the local caterers—gave us a brochure on their selection of wedding menus, and Mrs Gladys Jones, who specialised in floral arrangements for weddings and funerals, gave us a good price.

Helen and I experienced many ups and downs as we dealt with the pressure of the deadline and tried to get to know each other. She was strong-willed and so was I. I didn't consider the fact that we were still relative strangers a major problem because I believed that if God had brought us together, it was for life, and we'd have the rest of our lives to get to know each other more intimately. There were a couple of times when Helen began getting cold feet, saying things were moving too quickly and she wanted to back out, but there was too much pressure to turn back now. My convincing arguments always centred on God's will for our lives and that it was normal to feel this way before getting married. I was afraid of losing Helen; she meant more to me than she knew.

The night before the wedding I stayed with my sister Cathie and her husband Graham at Gladesville, and Helen stayed with my parents. There were no bucks' or hens' nights; Christians didn't do such debauched things. The day arrived, the third of August 1974. Those who knew me closely understood the significance of the day. They, more than anyone else, knew this was not going to be an ordinary wedding, but a testimony that God can heal homosexuals and make them heterosexual and that now I would truly be an ex-gay. I'd been forgiven my past failings and now I was really free to serve Him without any fear of the possibility of dishonouring His name. There were nearly two hundred who attended the service at Christian Faith Centre, now based in a converted office building next to the railway at St Leonards in North Sydney. It was a solemn and memorable moment as I looked into Helen's eyes and we prepared to make our vows. Her face, framed by the traditional Russian headdress her family had given her, was glowing. With great sincerity, reverence and gratitude, knowing the vow I was making was before all my family and friends but especially God, I tried to fight back the tears as I promised to love, honour and cherish her, and that the only thing to ever separate us would be death. This was my promise for life.

The farewell at the reception was especially emotional. Moving around the circle, the goodbyes to friends and family were occasionally interspersed with a brief conversation with those in the know about 'the miracle'. It wouldn't be long now before I could really demonstrate just how much God had changed me. Helen and I drove off in the graffitied car with cans rattling behind us to the motel for the first night of the honeymoon.

At the motel, which we'd especially chosen for its views of the city lights, three men got into the lift with us, and once they realised we were on our honeymoon, made crude remarks. I was embarrassed by their comments and thought how disgusting it was that they should talk about my wife and I like that. Now with the reality of my miracle only moments away, questions began to run through my mind. Should we do it the first night? Should we do it immediately? Do we get undressed separately? Should I undress her? Should I wait until we were in bed? I'd never had sex with a woman before. Of course these questions would never have entered the mind of any normal, full-blooded, testosterone-driven heterosexual male. I imagined most men would be like a stud bull on heat.

My parents had given us a bottle of champagne and even though as Christians we were not drinkers, the opportunity to get a little tipsy and ease the stress was certainly welcome. Mum had been a little over enthusiastic in her suggestion that I take it, saying, 'It will help you relax, dear.' Maybe my parents thought that I needed to be plied with alcohol to do the deed. Helen went to the bathroom while I opened the champagne and I had already nearly finished my first glass when she came out of the bathroom in the nightie she'd especially bought for the night. Sexy, revealing, sensual … apparently. I'd already softened the mood of the room with minimal lighting and was standing looking out the window at the lights spread out like fairyland in front of us. Suddenly I realised I could have sex whenever I want to—it was legal and I didn't have to feel guilty any more—what a relief. Handing Helen her champagne we began to kiss and within seconds I'd undressed and we were under the sheets in bed. It felt good making love to the person I'd promised to spend the rest of my life with but most of all there was a great sense of relief to know that I was able to satisfy her. She seemed to be happy. All thoughts of having sex with men were gone as our bodies entwined. As we fell asleep in each other's arms, I had a wonderful sense of feeling safe and secure, like a weary soldier arriving home to be with his loved ones knowing the war was won and the battle over.

We had planned a honeymoon in New Zealand and the flight was to depart at 9 o'clock the next morning. We'd only slept a few hours as the night had been spent talking and making love. We drove my car to my parents' house so Dad could drive us out to the airport. Of course I was strutting like a rooster in a chicken yard with my head held high, and for the first time in my life I felt like a real man.

We travelled around the north island of New Zealand, staying with Helen's sister and brother-in-law who were pastoring the Assemblies of God Church in New Plymouth, and friends of mine from bible college. It wasn't really much of a honeymoon for poor Helen; she wanted to spend time alone with me, but I was too much of a people person and wanted to catch up with friends and show off my new bride. Others thought the way I had organised the honeymoon strange, but I didn't fully realise it was supposed to be about having lots of sex and time together; I thought it was having a nice holiday. Even though I had changed some of my behaviours and was now a married ex-gay, my mind in many ways still thought like a gay man. It was the way I was wired and difficult for me to comprehend fully my role as a heterosexual husband. During our trip we had a couple of huge arguments, Helen realising that she was not going to get the attention and devotion she expected. The honeymoon was going to be the first of many things that she would learn to take in her stride; constantly having to take second place to other things I considered important in my life. I loved her but I loved serving God more—surely that's the way it was meant to be.

CHAPTER 10
Married life

Coming home to Orange as Mr and Mrs Venn-Brown felt pretty special and although much of my week I travelled around the country areas for work, I took every opportunity to drive back home to be with Helen. As a married couple our commitment to church life remained the same, with both of us involved in operating the youth group, attending *Bible* studies, teaching in Sunday school, and leading the singing during the Sunday services and prayer meetings. Church life and serving God were our top priorities. Behind the scenes, though, Helen and I experienced a volatile time adjusting to married life; there was much to learn about blending our two lives into one. The strength and independence Helen had gained from taking responsibilities for her parents conflicted with my ideas of how a Christian marriage should function. According to the Apostle Paul, I was the final decision maker. He wrote in Ephesians 5:22, 'Wives submit to your husbands as to the Lord.' I was the head of the house and Helen should submit to my authority. I'd regularly remind her of her role by quoting the appropriate verses during our arguments and what I had learnt whilst at Paradise, that 'rebellion against God's ordained authority is just like witchcraft'. When all else failed I'd just say the words 'submit woman', which were meant to end the discussion but for some strange reason seemed to fuel the fire.

Another major area of conflict was the amount of time we spent alone together. Or should I say didn't spend together. Work and the hectic life on the weekends meant there was little time for us, except in bed at night. Whenever Helen complained, I reminded her that we were called to serve God and that meant we'd have to make sacrifices. I knew the day would come when we'd be in the ministry on a full-time basis, which would mean even greater demands on our time, so it was important we got this right at the beginning of our marriage. We worked hard trying to resolve the conflicts, knowing that love and harmony in our marriage was our Christian testimony to others. The most important thing was to keep our marriage together—divorce was like the unforgivable sin and meant I would never be ordained in the Assemblies of God. The *Bible* says, 'If a man cannot manage his own household how can he manage the household of God.' Preachers and pastors were meant to be above everyone else; people found it hard to forgive any evidence of human failings so we tried to hide our conflicts as much as possible.

Helen and I loved children and often borrowed the pastor's young-sters to spoil them by buying them clothes and taking them to the movies or the circus when it came to town. We'd decided to start our family after twelve months of marriage, as that was enough time to work through our major difficulties and be settled in our relationship. Helen fell pregnant immediately after she went off the pill. It was so exciting to think I was going to be a dad—the ultimate reward of God's transformation and public proof of my manhood. I felt so blessed. My excitement was short-lived.

I was on a sales trip west of Orange on my way to the isolated town Bourke, and after showing my clothing samples at the local store in Nyngan, I booked into the local motel. Nights in motel rooms were lonely with not much to do except paperwork or watch television, so I'd take my *Bible* and other books to read. This particular night I decided to eat early and walked down the one flight of stairs to the motel restaurant as soon as it opened at 6pm. Eating alone was rarely an enjoyable experience so I took *The Greening of America* by Charles A. Reich with me. I was re-reading it, trying to get insight into current thinking and culture. The restaurant was empty and the waitress with her pink uniform, blue hair and a pencil behind her ear, greeted me. 'Sit anywhere you like, luv.' So I moved to a table by the window to enjoy a break in the monotony by watching the occasional road train and cattle truck pass along the highway. The restaurant was awkwardly quiet and the silence was broken by the piercingly loud clunks of the waitress's heels as she moved across the wooden floor to drop the plastic-coated menu on my table. A bit of music, a TV, or even a radio playing in the background, would have helped. She returned to the counter giving me a few moments to peruse the menu and then strolled back to the table, removed the pencil from behind her ear and simultaneously threw out her left hip, putting her weight on her right leg. There was never a great variety to choose from in country restaurants; twenty items including the entrees and dessert was the usual and main courses came with chips and salad except the daily roast. After ordering my T-bone steak, cooked medium, the waitress disappeared through the saloon-style kitchen doors that swung backwards and forwards several times before coming to rest on their hinges. I heard every word as she gave the cook my order.

I'd nearly read three pages of my book when an attractive guy, about my age, entered the restaurant. It's automatic to look up when someone enters a country restaurant, the tinkle of the bell above the door breaking the silence always elicits a Pavlovian response. We acknowledged each other with a nod, and then he sat two tables away. Strangely, instead of facing the door as I was, he decided to sit looking directly at me. Being the only people in the restaurant with him facing me the way he did made me uncomfortable, like being in a lift with a person facing you directly instead of the door. Every time I looked up, I caught him looking at me.

As soon as our eyes met, I quickly dropped mine to continue reading again. Why was he looking at me like that all the time? Within moments I was feeling that familiar stirring that had laid relatively dormant for well over a year. No, I'll be all right, I reassured myself. I've got the strength to resist temptation.

It was a relief to hear the waitress's clunking heels behind me and to know that my meal would be delivered first. But as soon as the waitress turned her back to return to the kitchen, he called from his table, 'Do you mind if I join you?'

'No, of course not,' I replied too quickly, knowing it was always better to eat with company and much easier to finish the cat and mouse game we'd been playing with our glances.

There were no real indicators by the way he was dressed or spoke that he was gay. Martin was also a sales representative, which made conversation easy, as we had common things to talk about immediately and we laughed about the eccentricities of buyers we had dealings with in the Central West. The conversation turned to my life in Sydney and Martin was very inquisitive about the places I'd frequented and what I did with my spare time. He suggested the names of a couple of venues I knew to be gay but I pretended I didn't know them.

The temptation wasn't fierce at this stage; I was able to control it. No, Tony, you're married now, God has healed you, you can resist. I talked about my wife and being involved in the church, attempting to throw Martin off his now-obvious quest but it didn't seem to be working. A couple of times during the meal I felt his leg bump mine under the table. It was hard to imagine that this could be happening in such a remote place and in this tacky little motel restaurant that hadn't changed its décor since the early 1960s. Martin continued to use a number of methods to indicate his intentions and I began to blush and tremble as my resolve slowly melted away.

'Like to come to my room for a coffee?' Martin said in a casual manner but with a knowing smile on his face, after the waitress presented us with our individual bills. If he hadn't asked that question,

I might not have taken the next step, but in my aroused state it was a difficult invitation to refuse. Curiosity, the need for company and also the belief that I had the strength to say no were all active at that moment. In my mind, I began justifying my affirmative response. I'm just going for coffee and if he tries anything I'll leave, I thought, not willing to acknowledge the odds would be against me. Maybe I'll be able to witness to him and tell him how I used to be a homosexual but God has healed me.

Following Martin into his room I noticed little had been disturbed and the budget accommodation meant there was no seating except for the double bed.

'Coffee?' Martin asked, as he turned on the television and the jug in two automatic movements while I sat on the edge of the bed trying to steady my trembling legs with my hands, hoping he wouldn't notice. What was happening? How could I be experiencing this temptation, hadn't God healed me? Why was this old life of mine so unwilling to completely die?

'I'll just go for a leak,' Martin said, unzipping his fly seductively in front of me as he walked into the bathroom. I knew the safest thing to do was to excuse myself and leave now, but I couldn't. The mirror on the wardrobe meant I could see into the bathroom and even seeing him standing with his back towards me was taking me down that familiar, slippery path where each moment locked me into an inevitable outcome. He turned, smiled, and made sure I saw him slowly put his half-erect penis back in his pants.

He poured the coffees and, after handing me mine, placed his on the bedside table. Martin lay back on the bed, sitting uncomfortably close and pulled his legs up so that his knee was touching my thigh, the weight of his body on the bed drew me closer. At this point I knew I wasn't going to succeed in overcoming the temptations I'd been trying to fight for the last hour.

We talked for another three minutes while Martin continued to 'accidentally' rub his leg up against mine. It was difficult to concentrate on the conversation.

Martin gazed hypnotically into my eyes as he moved his hand onto my leg and began rubbing. I froze as his hand moved over to my crotch. For a brief moment, the thought crossed my mind that now was the last opportunity to stop this journey back into sin. How good it would have felt, had I stopped this activity midstream. So much was racing through my mind. Why was I so weak? Where was the power of Jesus to fight this sin? All too easily I yielded as Martin stood in front of me and dropped his pants. We didn't even get undressed and it was over within a matter of minutes.

'You've come,' Martin commented disappointedly, which was fine as he'd been the seducer; I didn't approach him, he came on to me and I wasn't there to make him happy. Quickly pulling up my pants I made for the door. 'Don't you want to stay for a while?' he said.

'No, thanks. I have an early start tomorrow.' I replied quickly, feeling angry that I'd allowed myself to be seduced and desperate to get out of the room as quickly as possible.

The bracing, cold winter air hit me as soon as I walked outside, reinforcing the feelings that engulfed me. I've failed, failed again. My lonely motel room three doors away offered little comfort as I fell on the bed and buried my head in the pillow. I prayed, confessed, and pleaded with God to forgive me. I wanted to cry but the tears wouldn't come, only a gnawing wretched pain inside and the guilt I'd been free of for over a year. I'd sinned against God before but now I'd also sinned against the woman I'd promised to be faithful to and thrown God's miracle back in His face. How could I have been so wretched?

The next day I was supposed to call on clients on the way home but couldn't; I was too distressed and feeling ill. All I wanted to do was get home, but at the same time I didn't want to go home. I drove for hundreds of kilometres along a road without a bend or twist, just one straight line stretching to the horizon. The monotony of the journey allowed my mind to race down torturous mazes of confusion and self-hatred. Like a continuous video my mind replayed the events of the previous evening, and the consequences of my failure began to mingle with the memories. Why hadn't God saved me from that situation? He knew how much I never wanted to do that again. Was I that evil? The ministry, Helen, my unborn child. God, what happened to my miracle? Thoughts and questions spinning constantly, and only one conclusion—I've failed. I was a pathetic excuse for a Christian and I knew no-one would understand that I really didn't want it to happen.

The closer I got to Orange, the lower I sank. I imagined turning into the path of an oncoming cattle truck just metres before we met, then I would never have to deal with the consequences of the previous night. I asked God to kill me; in times of desperation it seemed like the only solution. It was a far better option to be dead and plead God's forgiveness in heaven than serve Him on earth and possibly bring shame to His name.

I wanted so much to cry and show God I was truly repentant, but the tears wouldn't come. Maybe I'd become too hardened to sin or I'd grieved the Holy Spirit and God had forsaken me. During the five-hour drive I'd thought of a number of options. Option one: pretend that nothing happened and keep trying to do the right thing; I was sure it wouldn't happen again. Option two: tell Helen and face the consequences. Option three: tell the pastor and get counselling. I didn't have the courage to face Helen with the truth so I chose to see the pastor and tell him what happened. A wave of nausea suddenly came over me as I parked outside the church manse.

Pastor John and his wife were always pleased to see me as Helen and I were their constant supporters. I'd often arrive with groceries or clothes for the kids that I'd obtained wholesale or the end-of-season samples of the children's wear I sold. It was obvious to them both that something wasn't right as we were running out of conversation.

I knew the pastor's wife couldn't be trusted with the information I desperately wanted to unload as she had a reputation for being a shocking gossip and knew everything going on in our church as well as in the Assemblies of God in New South Wales and beyond. Pastor John was the person I felt confident would never betray my trust. There would be serious consequences from my confession, such as not being allowed to minister in the church, and my plans to be in full-time ministry would be delayed once again. This was not what I really wanted but how could I serve God and hide my sin?

'John, can I talk to you alone for a moment?' I finally said. We walked out to the front porch and I kept walking to the car just to make sure we were out of earshot of his wife. 'Something terrible happened last night when I was out in Nyngan,' I said, the words so difficult to get out. 'I've fallen,' I continued. Fallen was the nicest possible way of saying I'd committed adultery.

John stood by the car in silence for a few moments and then asked the question I was hoping I wouldn't have to answer. 'Was it with a man or a woman?' I knew he would be happier if it was a woman. It was difficult to look him in the eyes so I kept my gaze on the ground.

'A man,' I replied, 'but I didn't initiate it, he came on to me.' I continued giving the details of the previous night. John was motionless while I spoke, suspended, and lost in those two words 'a man'. I knew what I was saying was shocking to him, but his eventual response astounded me.

'I guess it just goes to show that none of us are exempt from temptation and falling,' he said, after taking a deep breath. I was relieved to have my humanity acknowledged but it still didn't seem right.

'What should I do then?' I asked, waiting for some further counsel and direction. After another long pause I asked if, when and how I should tell Helen.

'I suggest you don't say anything to Helen.' Now, this was not what I was expecting to hear. It was wrong. I knew there had to be consequences for my actions and God didn't want us to just sweep it under the carpet. Like most Pentecostal pastors I knew, John had only two resources at his disposal; the *Bible* and his life experience and that was about it. No counselling training, no understanding of psychology or sexual orientation, so how could I expect him to come up with anything more? Maybe this was God's way of giving me another chance because I was willing to be honest.

Leaving John's house, I drove home with a feeling of relief but also troubled that things were going to be left unresolved with Helen. At the time I followed Pastor John's advice but knew one day I would have to confess, as all marriages whether Christian or non-Christian are built on honesty and trust. I thought the best thing to do was to get a job that didn't take me away from home; the lonely nights spent in motel rooms were something I wanted to avoid, and I feared a repeat of the Nyngan experience. I applied for a position at the local travel agency and was amazed that I was chosen above other applicants, considering I had no experience in the travel industry. It seemed like God had provided another miracle for me. The feeling of excitement quickly faded when this new position turned out to be very difficult, requiring weekend roster work that conflicted with the church program. The salary was very basic and even though I would be enti-tled to travel discounts after twelve months, the meagre wage meant we could never afford even discounted travel. The ideal situation would be for the church to employ me as a youth pastor but that wasn't going to happen. Within a few months I was back out on the road again as a sales representative. I hoped the break had made me a little stronger, but I quickly found myself in a place of temptation again. It seemed like the only place I was safe was at home with Helen—my life would be much easier that way as this protective environment would limit my opportunities and ensure I remain an ex-gay.

Among some Christian churches in the mid 1970s there was an emphasis on a New Testament type of lifestyle; living together and 'sharing all things in common' as the early church had done in the Acts of the Apostles. This was supposed to be a demonstration to the world of the love Christians had for each other and God, as Jesus had said, 'They will know you are my disciples by your love.' That is, not by the words you speak but by the life you live.

With another couple, Robert and Toni, and two single guys, Bryson and Michael, Helen and I rented a beautiful, rambling five-bedroom house on the outskirts of Orange, endeavouring to set up our own little Christian community. Living in a community would not only be an expression of our commitment to each other as Christians but the openness and accountability would also provide me the protection I needed to live a holy life.

Set among a cherry orchard opposite the golf course, the glorious Victorian mansion was ideal, and provided us with the opportunity to live in community. The ballroom became a meeting place for church celebrations and youth activities. We opened our lives to each other as we learnt to share our finances and the everyday chores of cleaning, cooking and maintenance. Everything we did was to serve each other. Once the practical was taken care of we developed a more spiritual life in our community by always spending time in prayer after meals, opening up our house as a place of hospitality to serve visiting preachers and others in need of short-term accommodation, and instituting a weekly community meeting to maintain honesty and openness. Initially it was fun and exciting but we quickly discovered it was much easier to love people you only saw for a few hours every Sunday in church than to live with them under the one roof.

Mostly it was Helen who found the lifestyle difficult as it meant I spent even less time with her, and we often argued about the importance of living in community and losing our identity as a couple. I thought she was being selfish demanding we have more time alone; after all, wasn't the community a mini-expression of the Kingdom of God and shouldn't we be prepared to sacrifice for the sake of the

Kingdom? I wasn't backing down.

Helen and I were having a rare night alone while the other members of the household were at various church meetings. The phone rang. I left the warmth of the lounge room and rushed down the cold hall to answer it. The enormous house and its high ceilings made it difficult to heat and the only comfortable rooms in winter were the kitchen and lounge room. I didn't recognise the male voice immediately on the other end as he said, 'Is that you, Tony?'

'Yes,' I responded.

'This is Martin, the sales rep. We met in Nyngan.' Suddenly the temperature in the hallway dropped ten degrees. 'I was calling to let you know I'm in Orange tonight and wondered if we could catch up?'

'No, thanks,' I quickly replied.

'When are you going out west again? I thought we might coordinate our trips together.' I kept my answers brief, knowing Helen could possibly still hear the conversation. He went on to explain that he looked up my name in the phone book. How stupid of me to have given my real name, I thought. But then I'd never intended for us to have sex that night in Nyngan and given no indication we would even see each other once more. Leaning against the wall with the receiver pressed tightly to my ear, Martin attempted to make conversation from my monosyllabic responses as thoughts cascaded through my mind about the possibility of being exposed or even blackmailed. I'd obviously been on his mind over the last few months, while I'd tried to erase every memory of him.

'So you don't want to see me again?' he said.

'No, thanks, I'm not interested,' I replied in a quivering voice, and hung up. I stood by the phone shaking. That was too close for comfort; what if Helen had answered the phone? Would he call again? Was my secret safe? If he'd found me in the phone book and called me at home, what would he do next? He seemed pretty persistent. Would he arrive on our doorstep? Stalk me? The possibilities were frightening; I no longer felt safe.

I needed time to compose myself. I couldn't return to the lounge room in the stressed state I was in so went to the kitchen, made a cup of coffee and tried to stop trembling.

'Who was that?' Helen called out from the lounge room.

'Wrong number,' I replied, trying to hide the quiver in my voice.

'But you said you weren't interested,' Helen called back. She sensed something was wrong and when I entered the room with my coffee her eyes followed me to my seat. She wasn't satisfied and questioned again, 'Who was it on the phone?'

'Some crazy guy I met travelling, who wanted to meet up again,' I blurted out, realising my stories were already conflicting and shocked at the amount of information I was giving to arouse her curiosity even further. I didn't turn around, knowing she'd see the deception in my eyes. Maybe this was the time to tell Helen what had really happened and ask her forgiveness? No, I was too shaken and too afraid. The rest of the night we sat in silence watching television, as I waited for my heart to stop pounding in my chest. Something had happened and Helen knew it.

There were many times Helen knew something was wrong and when her intuition became too much she'd challenge me, but I'd always deny it. My protests of innocence and accusations of her being over sensitive usually settled things down, but she knew. As many women do in that situation she'd deny her intuition or hope her fears were unfounded, but she always knew. In bed that night, instead of cuddling up to Helen as I usually did, I rolled over with my back to her, watching the shadows of the trees being tossed by the wind outside move across the lace curtains. It was difficult to sleep. I thanked God that I'd not been discovered and asked him once again to forgive me for the terrible thing I'd done. 'With your help, Jesus, it will never happen again, I want to live a holy life and please you,' I prayed silently over and over again, never really feeling like it was over but hoping this was the lesson I needed to keep me on the straight path. I had to keep hoping. If I lost hope then I'd lose everything. I was sure this was God's way of scaring the living daylights out of me so that I would never do anything like that again. Maybe God had His own aversion therapy program to cure me.

It was now the dead of winter and it had been threatening to snow all day. I'd purposely arranged my itinerary so I was only doing day trips out of Orange and I could return every night to be with Helen, knowing she'd be giving birth within days. In the early hours of 1 July 1976, the labour pains began, so we put the final few items quickly in her prepacked bag and drove to Orange Base Hospital. When Helen was settled, I rang the families to let them know things were underway. The adrenaline rush was amazing. We'd planned and waited for this moment for so long and now it was happening. It was still a relatively new concept for husbands to participate in the birth of their children, but as I'd always had a weak stomach I decided to stay outside. It wasn't long before I was called to give Helen some comfort and rub her back. I was lousy at massages. The last few hours of night passed quickly, the contractions got closer and closer and my plan was to leave before things got too messy; it wouldn't be good to faint in the labour ward. The nurses were no longer running in and out and told me it wouldn't be long.

'Let me know when it's time to leave,' I kept reminding them.

'You'll be fine,' the nurses kept repeating, which made me feel more and more uncomfortable. I felt they had an agenda to make sure I was there all the way through. One of the nurses kept calling the doctor to keep him updated but he hadn't arrived. Helen groaned and sweated while I mopped her forehead, assuring her everything would be okay. Then one big almighty push and it was over.

'It's a girl,' the nurse said, with a glowing smile on her face, even though she'd announced the sex of more babies than she could count. I looked at that tiny little six-pound bundle of purity that Helen and I had created and began to cry. I couldn't believe it. This was my little girl, my daughter, and she was so beautiful. My little Rebekah held her head up with such strength, her eyes wide open, looking everywhere, so alive and vibrant already. This was the way she would always be.

Only people who have experienced a birth know the magic of that moment; it has a touch of the miraculous about it. And no words can adequately describe the feelings parents experience knowing the two of you have, from something so microscopic, created a miniature human being. Everyone should experience a birth and also a death. Those moments when a spirit becomes a life in human form or leaves the body to return to spirit again, can be incredible. Nothing surpasses a birth, especially of your own child.

The doctor finally arrived, rushed into the room, grabbed Becky, and frantically checked her over. During the initial stages of Helen's pregnancy the doctor had advised us to terminate, as Helen had fallen pregnant a month after her rubella injection. The doctor swore he told her to wait three months before falling pregnant but we knew she would not have mixed up such a significant fact. There was a strong possibility our baby would be born deformed or with brain damage, we were told. Helen had called me in tears when she returned from the surgery. She was carrying a life inside her and we already felt strongly connected to our little one from the day we knew Helen was pregnant; there was no way we could terminate. We'd prayed hard. Now we waited in faith as the doctor prodded and poked, testing sight, hearing and reactions.

'She's fine,' he said, with a relieved smile on his face. Helen and I knew she'd be okay. The incredible feeling of joy, relief, excitement and pride was overwhelming. Our little Rebekah was a miracle of our very own making.

The fresh winter air was bracing as I walked out of the heated hospital towards the car park. It had just begun to snow so I stopped and looked up to feel each snowflake as it settled then melted on my face. For a moment, everything in my world could not have been more perfect. My heart was so full of gratitude to God for what He'd given me. I knew I didn't deserve such a wonderful gift that would constantly remind me of God's grace. Something was different, I felt different, and my world had changed. I went home and after calling everyone I could think of, cooked myself a big breakfast; I had to keep my strength up now I was a father. The smile stayed on my face for days.

No matter how ecstatic that moment seemed to me, my world was not really perfect. It was the same for thousands of men and women before and after me, desperately trying to do the right thing, and hoping we would finally become who we were pretending to be. Pressured by our families, societies and churches that, in numerous ways, sent messages that told us this is the only way you'll be accepted. Having sex with our partners, loving our children, attending school and family functions, giving everything we could to complete the dream—trying desperately to deny the truth that deep down inside we were not who we appeared to be.

When I finally found the courage to face the truth, that truth would break my little Becky's heart.

CHAPTER 11
Preacher on the road

The responsibility of parenting the little life we had brought into the world was a bit overwhelming and Helen and I often jumped out of bed in the middle of the night just to make sure our darling was still breathing. Helen blossomed as a mother and confidently took on all her new maternal responsibilities. Maybe this blossoming was the result of her busyness and the rewards of motherhood that had filled the void I was unable to. Our little Rebekah brought a new dimension of love into my life and I had no difficulty slipping into the role of being a proud and doting father. It seemed that everyone loved our little girl— she was very responsive and full of life, always smiling and gurgling at any prompting.

When Helen was able to return to work I began making plans to get into the ministry. The strong sense of destiny that had taken me to bible college and motivated me to overcome my homosexual problem had only increased. I wanted to serve God and help others come to know Him. During the years since I'd finished bible college I kept faith in the belief that one day I would go into the ministry on a full-time basis and do something great for Him. Pastor John and I talked about the possibility of the church employing me part-time as a youth pastor and teaching scripture in the primary and secondary schools of Orange. In this protected environment I felt sure there would be no more difficulties with homosexuality, and working part-time as the youth pastor would be the next step in achieving my goal of serving God on a full-time basis.

I loved the idea of having more time to help people, counsel, organise youth programs and preach in the church. Although Helen would have loved to spend more time with Becky, she agreed to continue working so we'd meet our financial commitments, believing God would bless us for the sacrifices we made. Even though I was planning on working several days for the church, the board approved a salary of fifty dollars for one day's work.

When Becky turned one we decided it was time to have another child; we wanted two at least. Helen fell pregnant immediately again. At the same time things went horribly wrong in the church. The family power base that had existed for decades lost its control and I became the target of their abuse and anger. Even though John was the pastor, in their eyes I represented the changes they weren't happy with, by creating a more vibrant service, using the new chorus style songs instead of the old hymns. The new Christians that had come into the church through our evangelistic efforts didn't fit the mould or wear the right clothes, and occasionally swore. The traditionalists made my life a misery by ignoring Helen and I at every opportunity, gossiping behind our backs and constantly blocking every effort to bring about change.

Whenever I tried to introduce one of the new lively songs, Mumma Daphne slowed the tempo down on the piano making it impossible to sing. One Sunday morning, while leading the service, I began to jig around to the music (sometimes called the Pentecostal hop)—horrified, Claude stood up and publicly abused me. It was beyond my comprehension that Christian people could be so petty, vindictive and malicious. It was bad enough for one human being to do that to another but in my mind that kind of behaviour in the church was inexcusable. Church life was becoming increasingly unpleasant, more like a battlefield, and the constant conflict of ideologies meant the church was on the brink of splitting. It was not an uncommon phenomenon at the time for Pentecostal churches to split over doctrinal issues or personality clashes. John didn't want to have the stigma and embarrassment of a church split as a part of his history. We tried everything to keep the peace but others in the church were fed up with John placating the old school and his ineffective attempts to keep the church on an even keel. Unwittingly, Helen and I ended up in the middle of the conflict. It was a great relief when finally the family left, taking their supporters with them, and started their own church, reducing our already small congregation of nearly eighty to about forty.

My preaching had improved with the few opportunities I was given; people often responded for healing or prayer and occasionally people became Christians at the end of my preaching. I was thrilled that the youth group also continued to grow and we were able to have such a positive impact on these young lives. Some of the remaining church members felt John's time pastoring at Orange was finished and that he should move on. Some secretly came and asked if I would apply for the leadership of the church, saying they would back up me up. They suggested that as I was getting more results obviously God was anointing me to lead the church, and that John was restricting my ministry as he was threatened by my success. It was getting very nasty; the church had seen enough trouble and dissension. Causing another split in the Orange Assemblies of God was a reputation I didn't need or want.

As I prayed for guidance I had a strong feeling that it was time to move on from Orange and that God wanted me to launch out into a new ministry as a travelling evangelist. It was difficult to share this with anyone—what I was planning to do was crazy. Just who did I think I was? My preaching experience was minimal, we had no way of supporting ourselves financially and Helen was pregnant with our second child. How would we survive? It was pure madness.

I'd read so many times about Jesus teaching his disciples to live by faith, that is, he sent them out to preach and told them not to take anything with them but trust God to provide all their needs. If God was really calling us to step out to serve Him then He would provide, that's what the *Bible* promised, and all we had to do was have faith. Helen had to be convinced that this was God's path for us to take but I felt sure God would speak to her as well. It would mean leaving her family behind and the security we had known, so I asked her to pray for what God wanted us to do. There were moments of doubt and fear for both of us but especially for Helen as she had only known what it was like to receive a weekly salary, not to have to trust God on a daily basis for everything.

Even though she always knew we'd eventually be in the full-time Christian service, I think she was hoping it would be pastoring a church somewhere with the security of a full-time wage. We began making plans to leave and gathered together as much money as possible, by selling furniture, wedding presents we'd packed away, everything. Amazingly, we somehow managed to get enough money together to buy a second-hand seven-and-a-half metre caravan and a Ford station wagon to tow it. Helen was trying to be brave but I remember her crying as we packed up our last few wedding presents and anything that would not fit into the caravan to take to the local auctioneer, who gave us a pittance for them. During the final months at the church, some of our friends lost respect for John and were considering leaving or getting a new pastor. John blamed us, believing we were behind the new dissension even though I assured him we had not done anything to cause these problems. Five years of faithfully giving ten per cent of our salaries and more, loyally supporting John and his wife through difficult times, clothing their kids and providing hours of service were quickly forgotten, and the tension between us increased to the point where they refused to even organise a farewell. Seeing how unjust this was the members pressured John and reluctantly, at the last minute, he announced we'd be given a farewell social, where people would make a financial contribution through a special 'love offering' to help us get on our way. No-one knew Helen and I had already invested everything we had in the car and caravan, leaving us with only enough to live on for a week, so the three hundred and thirty dollars from the offering was a welcome gift. Already God was showing us we needn't worry and that our needs would be met.

There was a real atmosphere of anticipation and faith in our car as we towed our caravan out of Orange that early, crisp May morning of 1978, and our little Becky in her car seat behind me clapped her hands gleefully as she sang along to our contemporary Christian music tapes. It was a journey into the unknown with only the money from the 'love offering' and two invitations to preach. But we knew two things: one, God had called us and, two, He would look after us. There was also a sense of great relief at escaping the bickering, gossip and fighting in the church.

It took me a while to get used to towing the monstrosity behind us and the caravan swayed from side to side as we drove north towards Dubbo. Even though Helen had three months left she'd been putting on a lot of weight and was 'great with child' as the *Bible* says Mary was before that first Christmas night when she rode on a donkey to give birth in a stable. What we were doing seemed so biblical, like so many characters in the *Bible* who had left family and homelands; forsaking security to embark on a journey of faith and fulfil a destiny, obedient to the voice of God. Struggling for the tenth time to hold the caravan on the road when a large truck overtook us, I remembered Helen had often suggested a holiday in a caravan to which I always protested, 'You'll never catch me towing a caravan let alone holidaying in one!' I chuckled and reminded Helen of the words I'd spoken and how careful we should be about the statements we make. Never say never.

Our first stop was Port Macquarie, a beautiful seaside town and holiday resort on the mid north coast of New South Wales, about five hours' drive north of Sydney. I'd met the minister of the local Anglican

Church when we were co-speakers at a Charismatic convention in the central west, and after hearing me preach and talk about my plans of becoming an itinerant preacher he'd invited me to spend two months working with his congregation. The Port Macquarie Anglican Church had come into the Charismatic movement a few years previously but the rector had limited experience of spiritual gifts (spiritual gifts are mentioned in 1 Corinthians 12, where the apostle Paul speaks of nine supernatural gifts that were given to individuals, such as healing, working miracles, speaking in tongues, interpreting those messages in tongues and also speaking words of prophecy). My role was to work with the various departments of the parish and especially build up the Sunday night Charismatic service.

I'll never forget the first Sunday night with a little Charismatic group of about a dozen strong women and a few weak men. It was chaos. After singing a nice worshipful song, one lady screamed out a prophecy, another spoke out loud in tongues, and another collapsed on the floor. Apparently this was the usual Sunday night performance. I'd never seen anything like it. It was obvious why the group hadn't grown beyond a small handful of people—any visitor would have thought they were a bunch of lunatics.

The next weekend we read in the *Sydney Morning Herald* that there had been a protest march (later to become the famous Sydney Gay & Lesbian Mardi Gras) of about 1000 people that had ended in a riot. The march had been organised to coincide with International Gay Solidarity Day, to protest against the legalised discrimination of gays and lesbians: permission had been granted but this was later revoked, and the march broken up by the police. All fifty-three people arrested had their names published in the press, leading to many people being outed to their friends and places of employment, and many of those arrested lost their jobs. Reading a story like that made me glad that I was now an ex-gay and could put the whole thing out of my mind to get on with God's work.

Over the next few weeks I began a series of talks on spiritual gifts and the power of God to heal, and tried to bring some balance to the services. Word about the good *Bible* teaching and the new atmosphere began to spread and before long the hall began to fill with people every Sunday night. After I preached, people always responded at the conclusion of the service by coming to the front of the meeting to give their lives to God, then I'd pray for the sick. Some healings were instantaneous and people demonstrated their new ability to walk unaided or bend over without any pain for the first time in years. Others returned the next Sunday night with glowing testimonies of how they no longer required medication. Some had been healed of back problems, others skin disorders, deafness and so on. So much was happening it was difficult to keep track of it all. Some people began travelling from the surrounding areas because they'd heard of the little revival happening at the historic Church of England on the hill. When our two months ended, our final night was a great celebration as the group had now grown to about one hundred and fifty people. The many lives that had been changed and the infectious enthusiasm of the people was something I'd never seen in Pentecostal churches. This was the type of Christianity I wanted to be involved with, one that was having a positive impact on people and causing them to experience a new dimension of living.

We'd planned everything so the baby would be born in Port Macquarie and then Helen would have two weeks to rest before moving on to our second appointment at the Assemblies of God Church in Tamworth. Unfortunately, babies don't always follow plans. Helen was getting larger, being two weeks overdue, and the doctor was getting concerned. Against the doctor's advice we packed the van and took off on the day's journey of about five hundred kilometres over the Great Dividing Range to Tamworth as we had to go to our next engagement. Helen looked so uncomfortable and I tried to make her journey easier, but every time the caravan rocked and swayed she braced herself against the lunging and jolting with pillows. Helen hardly complained, she took it all in her stride.

What a relief to complete that stressful journey. In Tamworth we set ourselves up in the local caravan park then visited the hospital to let the staff know we could be coming in at any moment. The staff were very reassuring and at 11pm we dragged ourselves home and fell into bed exhausted. At 6am, Helen's contractions started, waking me up from what I had hoped would be a sleep-in. Trying to remain calm, I packed Becky, Helen, and the suitcase into the car and drove to the hospital. What happened next was to become of the greatest regrets of my life.

By the time we arrived at the hospital, Helen's contractions had increased and she was in a great deal of pain. I wanted to be with her again as I had been with the birth of Becky, but little Becky hadn't had breakfast. I had to leave Helen alone in the hospital to have the baby. Helen pleaded with me to stay but there was no-one to look after Becky—I reassured her that I'd return as soon as possible. Back at the caravan park I ran out to the public phone booth every twenty minutes to call the hospital for updates on Helen's progress, hoping and praying she would be okay. Finally, the news came that I was once again the father of a beautiful girl. The baby was fine but because she was so big the birth had been difficult and the doctor had to do some surgery on Helen. I returned to the caravan and in the cramped space of the galley kitchen, held Becky as tightly as I could. I began to cry for the sheer relief, sadness that Helen was alone and for the joy of having a new daughter. Between my sobs I tried to explain to my little two-year-old how happy we all were that she now had a little sister. She'd never seen her father cry and placed her tiny hands on each side of my face and in her sweet little voice said, 'Don't cry, Daddy. Jesus will look after us, don't cry.'

Hannah was born 15 August 1978 in the late morning. We chose biblical names and used biblical spelling for our daughters, a common practice in Pentecostal churches. Helen was so relieved to see us she immediately burst into tears and Becky looked confused as she tried to understand why we cried so much now she had a little sister. The nurse wheeled Hannah's crib out of the baby's room and placed her next to Helen. Even though she was a healthy baby, the extended time in the womb meant the skin on her face was peeling, and there was a big bump on her head from the difficult birth, but I thought she was beautiful. Hannah just slept and hardly cried—almost as if she sensed that we needed to have a good child.

Over the next few days Helen was definitely neglected because church meetings were already booked. The situation became increasingly difficult as I tried to look after my little two-year-old and work in the church, and visit Helen. Our families were miles away and we felt so alone. To make matters worse the matron in the maternity ward was a sour old woman who was abrupt and very intimidating and ran the maternity ward by bullying staff and patients. The only explanation I could come up with for the bizarre behaviour was that she must have been a bitter spinster, determined that no-one would enjoy the joys she had missed out on. I arrived one night to find Helen in tears. Apparently the matron had come to dress Helen's stitches and didn't even bother to pull a screen around the bed; when Helen requested some privacy, the matron abused her. 'Don't be ridiculous, dear, this is a maternity ward, we've all seen it,' she said in a condescending and demeaning tone. Helen couldn't wait to get out of the place and even though she would have had more rest in the hospital thought it better to come home and hobble to the laundry and amenities block in the caravan park. I was grateful to have her home again and knew I could never survive as a solo parent.

The month of ministry in Tamworth went well and even though the results were not as dramatic as Port Macquarie, the pastor was pleased to see some new people coming to the church. Then a group of Christians in Bellingen heard about my preaching and invited us over to spend a month working with them. Bellingen would have to be one of the most pleasant places to live in Australia, a place the hippies had discovered in the 1960s and 70s. The lush rainforests and rolling green hills were smattered with communes and everything alternative. The small group of enthusiastic, freshly saved Christians would also have been idyllic to pastor, so the invitation to lead the church was a temptation: but something inside me said no. As we finished the agreed month of ministry in Bellingen, we received an invitation to another church.

The Lord's Prayer says, 'Give us this DAY our daily bread' and it seemed this was to be our experience; just one day at a time. We were often down to our last few cents and then a miracle would occur. Someone would arrive with a meal they 'just felt they should bring around to us' or someone would give us a donation not knowing we only had a few dollars left for food or petrol. It would have been wrong of us to let people know about our material needs—then we'd be looking to people for our supply instead of God. If we believed God would meet our needs then He was the only one to talk to about them, and it was up to Him how He provided for us.

Of the miracles that happened, many were connected with our monthly payments. In one instance, we'd parked our caravan in the backyard of a doctor who attended the church I was preaching at. After dinner he asked me to join him in the surgery. I thought he wanted some personal counselling but instead he pulled out a chequebook from his drawer, wrote out a cheque and handed it to me. I always found it a little embarrassing to receive money in such a direct way and could never understand how televangelists could so brashly and unashamedly beg for money to feed their extravagant lifestyles. I graciously thanked him for the gift, folded the cheque and placed it in my pocket. Back in the caravan, I pulled the cheque out of my pocket and placed it on the table in front of Helen and we looked at each other in amazement at the amount: one hundred and seventy-five dollars exactly. I couldn't believe it, it was the precise amount needed for the car payment we had to pay the following day. Helen and I both knew we didn't have the money and had wondered how God was going to provide this time so we rejoiced that once again He was our faithful provider. Miracles like this happened constantly and even though at times it was stressful, we learnt to rest, trust and have faith. God would always come through, often at the last minute, and we never went without a meal or missed payments on our car and caravan. It was a constant test of our belief and faith, but they say where God guides He always provides.

There was never an oversupply or abundance but we learnt as a family to be grateful for everything we had no matter how small. I remember Hannah's first birthday when Helen and I walked up and down the toy aisle of Kmart, trying to find something to buy for her birthday. After buying the groceries we only had a dollar to spend and were upset when the only thing we could find to give our daughter for her first birthday was a one-dollar giggle stick. Every time Hannah moved it up and down it made a ridiculous squeaking noise. We finally consoled ourselves with the fact that the stupid little thing did make her chuckle every time she moved it and heard the noise. Refusing to let go of it, it actually went to bed with her as well. I'm sure she sensed the significance of that gift as this was the only time we'd ever spent every cent we possessed on our daughter's birthday present. It's all relative, really.

We continued to travel around New South Wales and up into Queensland, moving from church to church, preaching, often not knowing where we would be the next week but confident it would always work out. My preaching kept improving and some weeks I would speak up to twenty different times at services, ladies' meetings, youth groups and schools; every opportunity. We spent two months pioneering a new church in Gunnedah, near Tamworth, supported by a wealthy family of poultry farmers. They were very generous and promised us a weekly wage. We were over the moon—a weekly salary!

We'd maintained contact with people in the Port Macquarie area and I'd been feeling for some time that Helen and I should establish a Pentecostal Church there. I knew this might cause difficulties because of our previous involvement with the Anglican Church, and possibly some members of that congregation might want to join us. My intention was not to steal someone else's 'sheep', but to grow a congregation of new converts along with some of the Charismatics who hadn't made a commitment to any particular denomination. Confident we could work in harmony, I arranged a meeting with the local Anglican minister to ensure there was no possible misunderstanding. I thought he'd be happy about it, but I was so wrong! He abused me, telling me that he had already had a revelation that revival was going to come to Port Macquarie through him, and that my presence in the area would divide the churches. He never spoke to me again despite my numerous attempts to heal the fractured relationship.

Ethically the thing to do was to cease all contact with the friends we'd made in the Anglican Church so that we could never be accused of 'sheep-stealing'. The minister preached against me from the pulpit saying we had come to cause division and the devil had sent us to break up the work God was doing through him, even naming us as having the spirit of Antichrist. Helen and I were stunned and disappointed that our intentions had been totally misunderstood and we were being alienated from the people we'd grown close to. Why couldn't he see the value of us working together instead of being so insecure and defensive? After all, weren't we working for the same Kingdom of God? They were just different expressions of Christianity and I certainly was not the kind of person who would be running around telling people to leave their church and come to mine. That was unthinkable, I had more integrity than that.

It wasn't until twenty-five years later that I discovered we had more in common than just our desire to serve God. This man had also tried to find a path to 'normality' and acceptance by getting married and having children. Considering that he was twenty years older than me, he had little real choice. During his late teenage years in the 1950s, homosexuality was considered such a problem that the NSW Police Commissioner called it 'Australia's greatest menace, and fastest-growing crime.' Over a two-year period, 150 men were arrested and sentenced to up to eight years' imprisonment with hard labour. The struggle to suppress one's true identity with the resulting internalised self-hatred, in my experience, eventually comes out in some kind of unhealthy behaviour. Self-hatred can easily be projected onto others, especially those who remind you of yourself.

Helen and I decided the most honourable thing to do would be to move about twenty minutes' drive down the coast to a little retirement community of nearly three thousand people called Laurieton. God had called us to the area so we weren't going to be put off by the hostility and initial dramas.

How do you start a church without a congregation, premises or funds? We just had to ask God to keep the miracles coming, and they did. A couple from a church in Tamworth heard about what we were doing and gave us their holiday house to live in, free of charge. We sold the caravan that had been our home for over twelve months and, after paying out the loans, the balance of four hundred dollars went into a bank account in the name of Camden Haven New Life Centre. I hired the School of Arts hall for twenty dollars and placed an advertisement in the local weekly newspaper announcing the inaugural service at our centre. 'GOD HEALS AND CHANGES LIVES" I boldly stated in the ad. Most of the little township was horrified that something as weird as a Pentecostal Church should invade its quiet, respectable community. 'We don't need another church,' was a common response, 'We have our Anglican and Catholic Churches.' But these were attended by only a handful of people and did nothing to appeal to people who weren't already churchgoers. Our presence challenged that conservative community, and within weeks rumours spread that a weird cult had come to brainwash them and take over. Mind you, they had reason to be concerned. Only months earlier, in November 1978, the 'Jonestown Massacre' had occurred, when 914 people including 276 children died in a mass murder/suicide ordered by the Reverend Jim Jones. Jim Jones had moved his Christian cult, the People's Temple Christian Church, from San Francisco to Guyana in South America and by means of teachings on conspiracy theories and twisting *Bible* verses had convinced his followers they were creating a utopia which required their unquestioning loyalty to him, even if it meant death. We were all still reeling from the impact of this tragedy, that something which had begun with such good intentions could have ended so disastrously. It was certainly not an ideal time to come into this little village with a vision to begin something unconventional.

The Camden Haven area was a popular holiday spot with magnificent, long sandy beaches, glorious mountains rich in rainforests and one of the most moderate climates in Australia. It made us feel a little guilty that we'd been called to serve God in such a picturesque place in contrast to the people we knew who'd made huge sacrifices and worked under difficult circumstances in third world countries. Our first service had an atmosphere of excitement and anticipation. We were conscious the birth of a new church was special and about a dozen people attended, including myself, Helen, and the girls. The majestic School of Arts, built for the needs of a past generation, still maintained much of its former glory. The floors, ceiling and walls of rich red cedar were originally felled from the local forests, and created a marvellous acoustic affect.

When I strummed my twelve-string guitar and our tiny congregation sang, the sound reverberated around us making us sound like a choir of hundreds. After communion, I preached and we took up an offering. There was enough to cover expenses and a little over for us to buy food and fill the car with petrol. Camden Haven New Life

Centre was now on the map and I'd started my second church.

What happened over the next twelve months was nothing short of amazing as our church grew, mostly with new Christians plus a few people from other churches who wanted a more lively service. At the conclusion of every service I gave people the opportunity to give their lives to God—lives were being transformed, people were being healed and marriages restored. It was like a mini-revival. Our services were always vibrant as the enthusiasm of the new converts was infectious, but the most exciting converts in the church were from the counter-culture and hippie movement. Our congregation members were very evangelistic and keen to share their faith, and were always picking up the hippie hitchhikers and telling them about Jesus. When the hippies gave their lives to God they stopped doing drugs, got work, no longer received social security payments, and settled down in our church. Some of the hippies were sole parents, their children had only known a nomadic life and had received no regular schooling nor enjoyed a normal family life. Their stories of rape, sexual abuse, abortions and addiction often horrified me, so it was wonderful to see the dramatic changes that happened for them in the supportive, loving environment we'd created. Camden Haven New Life Centre was a place of healing.

Summer holidays were the best times. Laurieton's population tripled with visitors taking their annual Christmas break and our services swelled to two hundred, the congregation spilling out the doors. Our church was very welcoming and hospitable so visitors took stories back to their churches in Melbourne and Sydney about the exciting things happening in Camden Haven New Life Centre. Within twelve months, the church had grown to a strong core membership of one hundred, which wasn't bad for a little fishing village of three thousand—just over three per cent of the population. If we were in a large city, three per cent of the population would have been a church in the thousands—a mega-church. At that stage, the Assemblies of God had not pioneered a church for nearly twenty years, so we were unique.

In the midst of all the excitement I couldn't foresee the dramatic event that was about to change our idyllic situation.

Helen typed the printed material for the church bulletins, *Bible* study notes and Sunday school materials, then I'd photocopy it at the local printers, which was proving expensive, so I organised a bank loan to purchase our own photocopier. A small group in the church were unhappy about this decision as they felt I had put the church under financial pressure. I knew this wasn't true as the regular offerings each week were able to cover our small salary and church expenses with enough left over to pay off the loan payments. I hadn't appointed a church board as the majority of the church were new Christians and I was waiting to see who were really committed and for it to be evident who had leadership skills before I appointed anyone. In hindsight, I see what a big mistake this was, as being the sole decision-maker left me open to accusations. Accountability around the finances had been created by making sure two people counted every offering, recording each amount. I would never do anything inappropriate with church funds and, of course, I was always accountable to the leaders of the denomination.

Like many small communities, gossip had controlled the village for years, destroying relationships and families, and alienating people—now it was ravaging our congregation. Lincoln, a person I'd considered would become one of the church's future leaders, visited all the other members to speak against me. It seemed that he wanted to take over and start his own church, so he tried to get as many on side as possible. I was in a no-win situation. I didn't know exactly who was being fed the gossip and if I went around visiting all the members, trying to get information, it would look like I was being manipulative or vindictive. I thought the best thing to do was to lie low; I was sure people wouldn't believe the lies and accusations Lincoln was making.

People I'd prayed for, counselled and supported through difficult times were now turning against me, and one by one saying God had spoken to them and they were leaving the church, having been won over by the other group—the betrayal was difficult to handle. Within two weeks our vibrant congregation dwindled to a few, now disillusioned, faithfuls. Twelve months of hard work and sacrifice disappeared; we were almost back to square one. Helen and I were devastated but one of the most difficult things to deal with was the impact this had on the new Christians, who couldn't understand how Christians could be so slanderous and malicious. (I was having difficulty with it myself.) Weren't we all working for the Kingdom of God? Why the division? Why would they want to work against us? Some returned to the church many months later, a little wiser, but others never survived the split, lost faith and returned to their previous destructive lifestyles.

Even though some leaders within the denomination encouraged us to count our losses and pull out, but we couldn't do that because God had called us to work there. There was no way we'd leave just because of this setback. I always loved reading books like the Reverend Robert Schuller's *Tough Times Don't Last But Tough People Do*, and this was to ever be my philosophy—never quit. It had certainly been my policy with homosexuality. God would tell us when to move on and how could I desert the faithful handful who remained loyal? To leave would be admitting the devil had won. We needed comforting, it was like losing family and it took us quite some time to feel like that experience was behind us. Gradually we built up the numbers again and over the next four years commenced two other churches in the area.

Those five years were great times of learning about myself and people, and how to make things happen. I realised I was too accommodating and compromising. In a word, I was too 'nice' and needed to be stronger in my leadership. It seemed that my naive belief that Christians were different to other people was unreal—some could be as vicious, deceptive and as power hungry as anyone outside the church. But I always looked for the best in people.

At the time, I wondered if the church split was the judgement of

God because I hadn't been able to completely overcome my attraction to men. It was always there lurking in the background. I was excited by watching surfie guys at the beach changing out of their wetsuits or by well-formed, tanned men lying on the beach in their Speedos. The opportunity to fantasise was everywhere but as soon as I was aroused I'd try and think of something else, then rebuke the devil for tempting me. I didn't always win the battles though; occasionally I'd slip up. These incidents were never planned, they just happened. At times, just like a junkie needs a fix, I'd find myself desperately craving sex with a man. The battle to resist was torturous, the aftermath depressing, but no-one could know about the struggle inside me. I was the pastor, the one who should have it all together. If people knew what temptations I really felt they could lose faith; I had to maintain the image and keep silently fighting on. The problem was obviously not with God, it must be me. When was I finally going to be free of that kind of temptation?

Unknowingly my suppression and hatred of my sexual orientation was creating an obsession that would become an addiction. The closet can be psychologically destructive and often produces pathological behaviour. Another element that was creating this dark thing in my life was denial. Like most people who claim to be ex-gay, I felt justified that my marriage and children identified me as healed and heterosexual and then denied what was really happening by saying that every Christian experiences temptation—there was nothing abnormal about me at all.

After four years in the Camden Haven area, I began to get an impression that became stronger and stronger. I should leave Camden Haven, go to Sydney and commence a new evangelistic ministry. The experiences of living by faith, itinerant ministry and pioneering four churches had been preparation for something greater. It was all in God's plan. How? Why? Will it work? All questions that came into my mind that I really didn't need answers to. We'd lived by faith for so long that I knew if we just followed the promptings of the Holy Spirit everything would be okay. God always looked after us.

Announcing our new direction was difficult as I was the only pastor most of the church had known. Eventually, people realised we all had to do what God wanted, so we made arrangements for another pastor from Newcastle to take over the church and planned to move to Sydney. Once again, there was no financial support, nowhere to live, only three invitations to preach and no money in the bank. As a preacher of faith I'd often told the story of the night Jesus came to the disciples during a storm on the Sea of Galilee, walking on the water. The disciples at first thought it was a ghost. Peter called out, 'If that's you, Lord, call me out to you on the water.' Jesus said, 'Come on then.' Peter got out of the boat and started to walk on the water to Jesus. Now, once again, God was calling us to step out of the comfort and security we had known and walk by faith.

CHAPTER 12
Dreams come true

Miracles always happened for us in the area of accommodation: the homes we lived in at Orange, the caravan, the rent-free holiday house in Laurieton for twelve months, the town house in Port Macquarie. The beautiful, architect-designed, two-storey home we rented at Lakeside Village, Laurieton, could have been featured in any interior design magazine. All had been just perfect and came to us at the right time. My father called a few weeks before we left Laurieton to let us know the Hunters Hill Bowling Club had a cottage that had been freshly painted and carpeted and would be available the week before we had planned to move to Sydney. We were amazed that the rent was to be only eighty dollars per week—in that affluent suburb and location they could have asked much more and got it. It was one block from the primary school my sisters and I had attended and two blocks from my Mum and Dad's. We'd always worked weekends and out of Sydney, which meant our girls had spent little time with their grandparents, but now they would be so close. Hunters Hill would have been my first choice but I never thought we could afford to live there. How silly of me to limit God. The timing, rent and position could not have been more perfect; yes, we were on the right track.

Leaving the people we had come to love so much was very difficult and services over the last few weeks had many teary moments. We left and moved to Sydney just before the Christmas break of 1982.

A number of churches in Sydney were experiencing growth and this would be an opportunity to build a strong base of ministry, although I received no encouragement from the leaders of the denomination.

Now I would devote myself to being an evangelist instead of pastoring churches and launch an independent ministry called Every Believer Evangelism, preaching the gospel in churches and crusades but also training Christians to share their faith. I believed this unique concept would work. Few shared my enthusiasm or vision. 'How will you survive?' was the common question. I couldn't believe their lack of faith. Concerned ministers reminded me of all the people who'd previously tried to be full-time evangelists in Australia and failed—most of them were now the leaders of the denomination, and were very good preachers, pastoring the largest churches. I sensed that in the minds of some leaders I was acting too presumptuously and a little arrogantly to expect I could succeed where they had failed.

Historically, the main difficulties of itinerant ministry had been the lack of financial support and the strain on the family and marriage. Within a year or so, those who'd attempted to be full-time evangelists always retreated to the security of a regular salary and pastoring a church. There were currently no full-time evangelists in Pentecostal churches in Australia but I was determined to change that, seeing my role as a groundbreaker who would open the way for others to follow. To me, the lack of support or encouragement didn't matter, as everything we'd accomplished over the last five years had been done without any assistance from the denomination. I had such a strong conviction that we were obeying God's will. God was our source, not the Assemblies of God.

The largest church in Sydney, Christian Life Centre (later to become Hillsong City Campus), was pastored by Frank Houston who allowed me to use an office in the church premises in Goulburn Street, Darlinghurst. Helen and the girls made this their home church. Frank had been the superintendent of New Zealand Assemblies of God and my lecturer on demonology at Grace Bible College. Being an evangelist at heart he was very supportive of what I was trying to do. Frank and his wife Hazel had many years' experience in the ministry, and he was taking a strong leadership role in Australia as well as pioneering new churches. (Unfortunately, years later, his son Brian Houston, now the national president of the Assemblies of God, had to stand his father down from ministry for a serious moral failure dating back to his early days of ministry in New Zealand.)

I'd always had a strong teaching element to my preaching and every opportunity that came to preach opened another door. It wasn't long before I found myself with advance bookings, first one month ahead, then two, then three and more. News about my ministry also spread to churches in Queensland, South Australia and Victoria, so that I began flying interstate to speak as well. It's amazing that even though I prayed, believed and expected success, I was still surprised when it actually happened. Every Believer Evangelism, as a ministry, was evolving and gaining credibility and I was acquiring a reputation as a preacher. Usually, I'd preach motivating messages at the morning service encouraging the church to reach out to people who needed God, and at the evening service I'd preach messages to the unconverted, the 'lost', the 'unsaved'. (I cringe now at those terms, they are so judgemental and separatist.) Then, on Monday and Tuesday nights, I'd present my seminars training people in one-on-one evangelism.

Even though my preaching ministry was well received by churches around Australia, I sensed resistance from a couple of the leaders of the denomination. Apparently, now that I was having such success in the ministry, Pastor John from the Orange church had decided he should tell some people about my confession of eight years ago. For him to now decide to talk about my moral failure was not only a reflection of his inability to deal maturely with the situation, but was also a breach of trust.

As my ministry increased in popularity, an area that became extremely effective for me was speaking at youth groups and camps, so the leaders of the Assemblies of God approached me to unite the youth groups of the churches all over Sydney with large-scale events. Initially, I was reluctant to take this on because my organisation Every Believer Evangelism had become a growing concern, but I was also aware of the enormous need of youth. For many years, the Sydney Assemblies of God youth met for a combined meeting every few months with just over one hundred attending, mostly second-generation Christians who'd been brought up in the church. The youth of the churches were unwilling to work together and there were hostilities over a variety of issues, as well as power struggles between the most significant churches, each group thinking they should take the leadership and do it better. I could circumvent these issues because I was an independent preacher with no particular loyalties to an individual church, so I decided to take it on, get it established, then hand over the leadership to someone else. Once this was successfully underway I could then give my total focus to Every Believer Evangelism.

To achieve my goal, I had to get as many young people on side as possible so I worked hard, building relationships and encouraging youth leaders in the city to get involved and work together, knowing that a combined, large visible presence was much more powerful than just their little group meetings in the suburbs. I tried to impart a large vision: one I knew they had never seen before. The mission, should they choose to accept, was to create a lively, contemporary rally that would present Christianity in a way that was relevant to youth in the largest entertainment venues Sydney had to offer. What I was planning on doing was radical and I needed sound and production people as well as contemporary Christian musicians. The existing name of the Assemblies of God youth, Christ's Ambassadors (or CAs for short), had to be changed. Who'd go to a youth rally called Christ's Ambassadors? I knew I wouldn't. After much arguing and persistence, the name Youth Alive became the name of the organisation, but as we prepared for our first event, other problems began to develop.

Within Pentecostal churches, most people had been taught that rock music was from the devil and some sensationalist preachers, like Gary Greenwald, even said that some rock musicians used backward masking to hide demonic, subliminal messages that could be heard when songs were played in reverse. Greenwald claimed that back-masked messages propelled listeners into sex and drug use. *The White Album* by the Beatles was said to contain backwards messages such as the repeated words, 'Number nine, number nine, number nine …' in the song 'Revolution 9', which backwards supposedly became 'turn me on, dead man, turn me on, dead man …'. Probably the most well-known example of alleged back-masking was Led Zeppelin's song 'Stairway to Heaven.' If a particular portion of the song is played backwards, then supposedly the phrase, 'Here's to my sweet Satan,' can be heard. Those who had the sense to investigate the claims discovered that, given a randomly generated series of syllables, it would be easy to find a two-syllable pair that could be liberally interpreted as 'Satan'. It was possible that any person with some creative interpretation skills could play virtually any song backwards and uncover 'Satanic messages', especially if you were a Christian preacher and rock music was taking away your young people. Christian youth were being encouraged to forsake the rock stars and burn their records. Foolishly, in this highly-charged, controversial environment, I wanted to introduce Christian rock music at Youth Alive rallies.

On 23 February 1985, Youth Alive's first event began with a day of evangelistic outreach at Manly, one of the major beach suburbs of Sydney, consisting of a concert in the mall using a variety of Christian bands and singers, drama and dance. Several hundred Christian youth showed up and people spoke excitedly about the innovative program we'd put together—Sydney had never seen anything like this before. We talked to many people on the streets about having a relationship with God—even a few of the local street kids prayed to receive Christ into their lives. The day climaxed with a youth concert in a nearby basketball stadium. The entire event had been a great risk but the evening rally was to be the greatest test.

The excitement increased as the audience in the stadium grew to five hundred people (an unheard-of figure among the youth of Pentecostal churches) but I could also sense tension building when certain groups arrived. They were so straight-laced and boring it was understandable that their youth groups were small. Their youth leaders fostered a defensive siege mentality, and their only objective was to protect their young people from the temptations of the world, not to reach out to young people in need outside the church. Even if they had attempted such a radical thing I doubt they would have related or been able to communicate with them anyway. They were fearful their Christian youth might find out how much fun you could have enjoying life—if they discovered it, they'd defect from Christianity. The program was about to commence. I prayed together with the performers at the back of the stage for God's blessing and most of all that we would somehow be able to communicate to young people how much God loved them.

The hall was in darkness … Wah, wah, wah, wah, a sole electric guitar whined and screamed … then the drums kicked in … Boom, boom, boom … lights flashed and we were underway. I loved it, but others didn't. Some of the youth leaders became restless, you could feel the tension rising in the air as they muttered to each other about the music, lights and atmosphere. One of the leaders stood up, gathered his little flock of young people together, and walked out. I was standing at the back of the stadium watching the band when another youth leader moved towards me, his eyes flashing with rage.

'What do you think you're doing?' he shouted, trying to make himself heard above the Christian rock band. 'You can't win people to Christ with this type of music, it's satanic!' I tried to settle him down and reassure him that it would be okay.

'Just wait and see,' I said, but he wouldn't listen, returned to his group sitting near the front and marched them out defiantly. I couldn't believe what was happening. I was called out to the car park where another leader was so upset he had gathered his group and was praying against us. Apparently I was doing the work of the devil. As the program continued, even more walked out, arguing with me as they departed. I was trying desperately to keep cool and calm, wishing my spot in the program would hurry up so I would have some people left to preach to. At the conclusion of the one-and-a-half hour program, when I was scheduled to preach, we had lost at least a third of the crowd.

I preached like a man possessed that night, possessed with a mission. A mission to reach out to young people, to let them know God loved them; they could have hope, healing and the power to change their lives. A mission to also let young Christian people know that they did not have to be dull and boring, looking and acting like they belonged to a former generation, totally out of step with the rest of the world. I was also angry. Angry that the youth leaders had judged what we were doing, judged the Christian rock musicians who were using their talents for God's Kingdom. I was disgusted by their religious, sancti-monious, pious attitude—it was the greatest barrier to God's love touching the world. As my message ended I needed God to perform a miracle. After all we had done and been through we had to see results. Preaching into the glare of the spotlights only heightened the feeling that came over me several times. Is anyone out there? Is anyone listen-ing? I could barely make out the sea of faces as I asked people to come to the front and ask God to come into their lives. There was a long deathly silence that was occasionally broken with a nervous cough from somewhere in the stadium. No-one moved. I waited and asked again. 'Who would like to give their life to Jesus tonight?' Still nothing. One more time, I had to have results from all the work we'd put in.

Then I heard a chair move, a rustling at the back of the hall, and a big biker in leathers moved quickly towards the front out of the darkness, the sound of his boots on the wooden floor echoed throughout the building. I had never seen anyone come to the front at that speed before and for a moment thought he may have been angry about my Christian preaching and was coming to attack me. He stopped directly in front of me. 'Have you come to give your life to God?' I asked hesitantly.

'Yes,' he replied in a strong, confident voice that could be heard throughout the entire auditorium. The crowd burst into spontaneous applause as I jumped off the stage to shake his hand. One person, but it had been worth it for just one. I nearly cried at the sense of relief. Then I heard other footsteps as another came down the front, then another, then another, until within minutes there were twenty young people standing with me. Some were crying, others smiling. All young people who previously had little or no experience of God but wanted to make changes in their lives. Afterwards, when we talked and prayed with each of them, we discovered most had come from difficult situations and were in great need. Mission accomplished, and the foundation laid that Youth Live would always be about reaching out to young people in a contemporary and relevant way.

The high of that night lasted for days, and I assumed the results of our first Youth Alive outreach would speak for themselves. Sometimes I was so naive. The Assemblies of God Executive Committee requested I meet with them immediately because the youth leaders who'd walked out had complained about the concert. We'd achieved at our first youth rally something many had wanted for years and I knew the methods we used were essential for the continued success of Youth Alive. I was not going to compromise but would stand my ground—a new position for me.

Waiting outside the meeting was daunting as I had never been in trouble with the Executive before. It felt like I was a naughty little schoolboy waiting outside the principal's office, about to be disciplined for some misdemeanour. The door opened and I was asked to enter. I knew all the men on the Executive, most on a first-name basis. I showed others respect by calling them 'pastor'. None of them was under forty, all attired in their outdated, conservative suits. Their greetings were formal and cool and their faces told me we had some serious business to deal with. I was still grinning ear-to-ear from the excitement of the previous Saturday night. The seating arrangement was ridiculously intimidating—a solitary seat faced the dozen men. Images of a firing squad flashed through my mind.

'Mmmmmmm, we've had numerous complaints about your rally on Saturday night,' was the superintendent's opening comment, spoken in a slow, deep tone to reinforce the seriousness of the statement. I listened as they detailed the reports they'd been given about the worldly music, seductive dance and dark atmosphere, just like a rock concert. We had used rock music to share the Christian message, we had used flashing lights and created a rock concert atmosphere, we had used a contemporary dance sequence to communicate a powerful message, the Christian youth had danced exuberantly. It had been intentional—to communicate in a medium and language young people understood. I denied nothing.

Today it seems so ridiculous that this was so controversial—now this is the normal Sunday service format in almost every growing Assemblies of God, Hillsong and Pentecostal Churches around the world. I knew there were a couple of men in this group who supported the changes I had to make, but in this arena with their peers they made no comment. As a group, it seemed the Executive were asking me to go back to the old way of running a youth service, maybe a middle-of-the-road approach to please everybody, they suggested, be less controversial. They were concerned that by using contemporary means and rock music to communicate with young people, we were lowering our standards and using worldly methods.

'Yes,' I finally responded after listening to their criticisms, 'We have lowered our standards. In fact we have lowered them so much we were actually able to reach twenty young people for God.' There was silence in the room. Knowing Youth Alive's success depended on developing what we'd started, I gave them my ultimatum.

'Here are the options, gentlemen.' (Even I was shocked by the assertiveness of my statement.) 'If you're not happy with what I'm doing with the youth groups of Sydney then I'll resign now. If you want me to continue then you'll have to leave me to do what I feel is right to reach young people. I'm not going to come in here after every rally and have to justify our program. You'll just have to trust me.' I smiled and made eye contact with everyone in the room.

They backed down immediately and from that time on I was never pressured or questioned by them again; they allowed me to fulfil Youth Alive's vision of presenting the Christian message in a contemporary mode. The numbers increased at each event, the word spread around Sydney and other denominational churches wanted to join us, so we decided to take over Sydney Town Hall for our last rally for the year. Once again, this was groundbreaking for the Assemblies of God. We had no money to fund such an event, but believed God would provide. When we inquired about a booking, apparently the only night the Sydney Town Hall wasn't booked was the exact night we wanted. We took it as a sign from God that it had been kept for us. We had enough funds for the deposit so we paid that and worked on the preparations to produce the best program yet. It seemed like a big step of faith but if I'd waited for the funds to be in the bank before I did anything, I'd still be in Orange working part-time in the church.

When I walked into the Sydney Town Hall on the afternoon of 7 December 1985 to see how the preparations were going, it looked huge. I'd attended concerts there throughout my schooling and remembered it was large but now it looked so much bigger—and I was responsible for filling it. There were a couple of brief moments of doubt as I wondered if we could draw a crowd big enough. The largest crowd we'd had to date was around 800, but for tonight to be a success we needed over 2000. We opened the doors half an hour before 7pm and the few people who trickled in only accentuated the emptiness of the building. More arrived, and then a steady stream of young people flooded through the doors and took up their positions in different parts of the ground floor. During the last five minutes the ground floor and balcony were packed. The atmosphere was electric, as most of these young people had never been to a Christian event of this size before. The crowd shouted and applauded as the evening's program commenced. I felt both humbled and excited walking out on the stage at the end of the evening; it was a wonderful privilege to be speaking to this crowd of over 2000 young people. In my mind, I'd rehearsed my message over and over again knowing it would look ridiculous to come out on stage with preaching notes—it was important to speak from the heart. Preaching with passion and conviction, I spoke about the power of God's love to heal, forgive and change anyone who was willing to acknowledge their need of Him. To say 'I don't need God' seemed a ridiculous statement to me as I was constantly aware of my need for God's love, forgiveness and power. The response was more than I had hoped for. Over two hundred young people came forward at my invitation to give their lives to God. A stillness came over the crowd as we realised the significance of what was happening. Certainly a new chapter was beginning in the history of youth outreach that would have an impact for years to come.

Even though we had our critics, their murmurs were quickly silenced by the reports from youth leaders all over Sydney whose youth groups had received a fresh burst of enthusiasm and growth. Youth Alive was well and truly established; there would be no going back. It continued to grow at each rally and within twelve months I was preaching to five thousand young people in the Hordern Pavilion at the Sydney Showground. The dream I had of taking over the big entertainment venues was being fulfilled and in the future we would create large youth choirs, launch music careers and mobilise Christian young people for evangelism within Australia and to needy countries overseas as well.

At youth camps, I often had a following of aspiring young preachers who saw me as a role model and mentor and although there was never anything sexual, there was an attraction I didn't want to acknowledge. Sometimes these guys would ask for counselling, sharing openly their problems with temptation, but all I could do was tell them what the *Bible* said and encourage them to overcome temptation. Even though the formula of prayer, reading the *Bible* and resisting all sexual thoughts wasn't completely working for me, I genuinely believed it was the only way and I hoped they could find the answers in God. I wasn't going to quit so it was easy to encourage them to keep trying.

Such a person was Georgio, an attractive young man in his mid twenties from an Italian background, with beautiful olive skin and strong, black, curly hair. His eyes glistened when he smiled and his company was always enjoyable. The bond between us was growing. He'd always seek me out at youth events, neither of us acknowledging that there was a covert attraction developing underneath the friendship. I knew it was dangerous but found myself thinking about him often. Speaking at a youth camp for one of the large city churches, Georgio and I had the opportunity to spend more time together.

It was nearly midnight, and I was walking around the camp grounds making sure no young couples were involved in hanky-panky, and chasing the last few stragglers off to bed. Approaching the men's shower block I saw Georgio coming towards me out of the shadows. He looked so handsome as he smiled at me. My heart began to race as I realised the danger of this late-night encounter. I'd previously successfully subdued the feelings I had when we were together but in this situation late at night, alone in the dark, there was an energy drawing us to each other. We talked as we walked down to the oval. Georgio had to be feeling the same stirrings I was but it was too risky, wrong and forbidden. The light of the full moon cut through the darkness as we walked through the trees out onto the oval. Every cell in my body was tingling as I noticed the moonlight highlighting the features of his body, face, and especially his eyes. The conversation suddenly ended and we looked at each other. I put my arms around him and we embraced. It was not an unusual thing in Pentecostal circles for men to hug, but not like this; I could feel Georgio's hardness pressing against mine. Unable to resist any longer, I moved my hand down to his crotch. Our expressions of intimacy were very restrained and within seconds thoughts about the implications of what was happening overcame the strong desire I felt. What was I doing? This would destroy my ministry, my marriage, everything I'd worked for! This was wrong. Inside me I wanted to hold him longer, to do more, to kiss, but I pulled away. I told Georgio we must not carry this on any further and it would be best that we return to our separate huts. Walking away in different directions it was difficult to find any excuse for what had just taken place.

Georgio disappeared into the darkness and the impact of what had just happened dropped like a bomb on my psyche. Oh my God, what have I done? It was bad enough I'd had sex with other men, but now with a Christian? The thought of doing such a thing was horrifying. Georgio was a young, vulnerable Christian and I'd violated a trust. The consequences were enormous but, more importantly, this was the worst type of evil.

There was such heaviness upon me and speaking at the meeting the next morning was difficult. It was not easy to look at the faces of the young people knowing I was such a hypocrite, and when it came time for communion I knew no-one else in that room was more acutely aware of their need of cleansing from sin than me. How could I call myself a man of God? Most people probably didn't notice me desperately trying to manufacture a façade of normality, pretending nothing was wrong. Georgio was sitting at the back of the auditorium and I tried to avoid eye contact with him; he looked disturbed, tormented and angry. There'd been other times when I'd continued my ministry under the heaviness of guilt but this morning shame and remorse weighed too heavily and there were several times I nearly stopped the proceedings. If he told his youth leader or pastor it would mean the end of my ministry.

I knew I had to take responsibility for what I had done and apologise to Georgio, so when the morning service finished I waited for the crowd to disperse and followed Georgio outside.

'Can I see you a moment?' I asked cautiously. He followed me as I walked to a place away from the crowd so no-one could hear our conversation. A safe distance from prying eyes I turned to Georgio; the beautiful shine was gone, replaced by anger. I didn't want him to be angry with me, I was genuinely sorry.

'I have to ask you to forgive me, Georgio, for last night. It should never have happened and I've done the wrong thing by you. I'm so sorry,' I said quietly, hoping he could see how much I meant those words. The anger in his voice cut me even further as he questioned me about my homosexuality. I tried to be as honest as possible but was afraid to tell him the whole story, unsure of what he might do with the truth. How could I tell him of the temptations I experienced and sometimes gave in to? He'd looked up to me, I was a preacher, a man of God and a person with all the answers. He told me he'd fooled around with a couple of guys but didn't feel he was gay.

'It's up to you what you do about this, Georgio, but I am genuinely sorry,' I said, apologising once more and reassuring him it would never occur again. I knew our friendship was over and the warmth we'd experienced gone. My admission of guilt and pleas for forgiveness had little impact on Georgio. I saw how troubled he was, and even though he was a twenty-five-year-old adult, I'd betrayed a trust and crossed a boundary that could possibly damage him forever. He disappeared from the camp early: part of me wanted him to go to someone for help and another part feared the consequences of him sharing our secret.

After camp, I tried to put the incident out of my mind believing this was a warning from God—another close call. How could I keep failing and expect God to protect me?

Then the phone call came.

Two days after the weekend I was in my office working through some administration and could still feel the effects of the weekend, when the phone rang.

'Good morning, Tony, this is Pastor Chris.' My heart sunk: Georgio's pastor. It was not unusual to receive a call from Pastor Chris as I'd preached regularly in his church, but by the overwhelming nausea I was feeling I knew deep down inside this was not a social call. 'Hello,' was all I said, my voice already beginning to tremble. Pastor Chris broke the silence, 'Georgio came to see me this morning, I think we need to talk as soon as possible.'

'Yes, I'll be over right away.' Knowing this was something that couldn't be put off, I drove to the church in Sydney's outer suburbs. Thoughts and prayers raced through my mind. Thinking about the consequences made me feel sick; this was going to be the end. The outcome would be horrendous, all my hard-earned success gone and there'd be a scandal. I prayed and told God that I was willing to take whatever the consequences might be. Part of me wanted the battle to be over and the secrecy to finish.

Pastor Chris looked very solemn as he greeted me at the door and led me into his office. This was worse than I thought; two other pastors were waiting inside. Apparently Georgio had become depressed after the weekend and during counselling confessed what had happened. Strangely enough I was relieved he'd gone for help. The last thing I wanted was to be a destructive influence, and I knew Georgio could possibly lose his faith over the experience and I didn't want to be responsible for that. The pastors asked me if anything like this had happened before and about my homosexual past. Fear gripped my heart. Already there was too much at stake to be completely honest, too much to lose and too many people would get hurt, and even though I'd said to God I would take the consequences, the strong need for survival kicked in. I told them that there were times when I'd experienced temptation but I was always able to overcome it. My experience with Georgio was a slip-up.

'We can see how much God is blessing your ministry and we feel this has been an attack of the devil, to try and destroy it,' Pastor Chris said. They had obviously already worked out a strategy depending on how I responded.

'We want to handle this wisely. We'll look after Georgio, we don't want you to see him any more,' (I was happy with that, I couldn't face him anyway), 'and if you have any more problems we want you to feel totally free to come and talk with one of us. Now let's pray for you.' It was a relief to lay down some of the guilt I felt and have someone pray with me, specifically naming my problems. I was always praying for everyone else, always giving but finding little time to receive and now, for the first time, I understood the benefit of Catholic confession. You can walk away feeling like you've dusted off your clothes.

That was it. All sorted out in less than an hour and no more repercussions. Believing that God was gracious and forgiving towards me I was grateful that He had saved me the humiliation of a scandal. He was giving me another chance—but in terms of God's grace, this was strike two. Immediately, a warning sounded in my mind —'three strikes and you're out'.

The strange thing was, Pastor Chris was extremely effeminate, and I'd heard the rumour that a member of the church had caught him in a compromising position with a young man in his church. Maybe this incident with me was too close to home; he understood exactly how frightening it was to be discovered, and so had let me off. During my years as a preacher it was not uncommon to hear gossip about others over late night suppers whilst winding down from the evening service. Most of the time I was unwilling to accept there was any truth in these rumours and made sure I didn't repeat them. There must have been stories circulating about me as well but, of course, I never heard them. It was easier for us all to talk behind people's backs rather than face them with the truth. After leaving the ministry I found that people were willing to be much more open and honest with me and that much of what I'd heard was valid and not just idle gossip. Over time I've come to have a greater appreciation for the proverb, 'Where there's smoke there's fire.'

My response to this incident was to throw myself into the ministry. It was difficult to tell whether that drive was to compensate for my failings in the hope that, somehow, my good deeds would balance out the times I'd failed God, or if I was trying to be so busy I didn't have time to be tempted. Of course being so active also meant my mind was totally occupied with the work of God and therefore thoughts of my failures remained buried. Probably a combination of the three and underneath all was still the genuine desire to serve God and His people. I still believed that, one day, I'd be set free for good. I couldn't give up.

It was time to find someone else to take on Youth Alive and so I approached Mark, an experienced youth leader, who was managing a Christian organisation in New Zealand. As I'd been supporting myself through Every Believer Evangelism, Youth Alive had no salary to offer him and he declined. Pat Mesiti, the youth pastor of an Italian congregation in Sydney, had been my enthusiastic assistant, so he was my next choice. Pat did a tremendous job and under his dynamic leadership, Youth Alive continued to grow, opening up opportunities for him to preach around Australia and overseas. Seeing the potential in Pat, Brian Houston, the senior pastor of Hillsong Church, invited him to join their team. Basing himself at the large church in Sydney, Pat became a very popular speaker and sold thousands of tapes, videos and books on youth topics, as well as speaking regularly at multi-level marketing conferences for companies like Amway.

It hurt me when I heard, not long after I had fallen off the radar so to speak, that Pat had taken on the title of 'founder' of Youth Alive

NSW. My teenage daughters were finding it difficult enough to come to terms with what had happened to their dad, but hearing Pat regularly acknowledged for what their father had done caused them even more pain. My sense of pride and achievement in founding a successful youth organisation, eventually growing to events of 20,000 or more people, was now, along with many other things, also to be taken from me.

However, Pat would eventually discover himself what it's like to have your humanity become public knowledge, with all the pain and grief this brings to your family. In 2002, Pat was stood down from all ministry in the Assemblies of God because of misconduct, the result of a sexual addiction. I'm sure he was unaware how blessed he was to have a pastor like Brian Houston support him and his family in counselling and other ways. This support meant Pat could focus on getting his life and marriage back on track in order to be restored to the ministry. Sadly, even with that support, Pat's marriage didn't survive. Phil Pringle, the Senior Pastor of another mega-church in Sydney, willingly took Pat's healing and rehabilitation in hand. In his new church home and with his new wife Andrea, Pat was re-instated as a preacher on Sunday 19 February 2006 and serves God with a new awareness and humility.

The Christian Church—a place of love, forgiveness and restoration—proved to be so for Pat. His repentance opened doors and people came to his rescue. Why hadn't it worked like that for me? I wondered. Was my sin so unforgivable?

CHAPTER 13

Popularity

The strong impression I'd had back in Laurieton in 1983 that I should go to Sydney and start an evangelistic ministry that was strategic for evangelism in Australia, was now quickly becoming a reality. Every Believer Evangelism's profile increased each year as I devoured every book I could on evangelism and developed new and innovative ways to train people on how to share their faith.

Even though the invitations to preach kept rolling in, it became evident that I had to put more structure into the information I was giving out and market it more strategically. Pentecostal churches professed to being evangelistic, but evangelism was usually left to the preacher at Sunday night services to preach a message relevant to the unchurched. This was very different to the methods of the New Testament church where every Christian was empowered to speak about the resurrected Jesus.

My first step was to develop a four-hour seminar on effective witnessing that taught people basic communication skills, how to over-come the fears of speaking about their Christian experience and dealing with misconceptions about evangelism. I'd usually do this over two nights after preaching to the Sunday congregation or on a Saturday.

As word spread about the results people were gaining from the seminar, it wasn't long before I found myself being invited to the largest congregations around Australia. For me it was important to not only work with the large congregations but also encourage those who were pioneering the numerous new churches that were springing up, such as Brian and Bobby Houston's Hillsong Church. In 1983, Brian moved out of his father's church in the city with a vision to establish a church in the north-western suburbs of Sydney. No-one at that time dreamed that the outreach church would quickly outgrow the mother congregation, except maybe Brian and Bobby. Like his father, Brian was very supportive of my ministry and I preached for him at least once a year and watched the attendance grow from an initial forty-five to today's congregation of 19,000, whilst also establishing branches around the world. Through its phenomenal growth, its worship style, and the music of, firstly, Geoff Bullock and, later, Darlene Zschech, Hillsong gained both national and international recognition.

When the Prime Minister of Australia, John Howard, opened the 3500-seat convention centre in 2002, and the National Treasurer Peter Costello attended special events, Hillsong suddenly became the focus of media attention. Many people in Australia saw this as the beginnings of a duplication of America's Religious Right (a mixing of religion and politics) but for the church it was really more about the recognition the nation's leader would bring. Originally dismissed as being little better than a cult, the Assemblies of God had been the Cinderella of the Protestant family until the tide turned and they were gaining more members each year than the traditional churches were losing.

Having a Prime Minister and national political leaders in the service, was a major coup for the church in terms of recognition and credibility, but who was using whom? It may have seemed like a good idea at the time, but after that Hillsong's Pastor Brian Houston had to regularly remind the media, 'One thing we are not is a political movement …The Assemblies of God in Australia does not have a political vision and we don't have a political agenda. I think people need to understand the difference between the church being very involved in politics and individual Christians being involved in politics. There is a big difference.'[3]

In 1985, I began training weekends that I called Adventure in Evangelism. These started in Sydney—weekend programs of intense training for people who felt called to the ministry of evangelism whether it be street ministry, door-to-door evangelism or youth evangelism. Wanting to ensure that people got much more than just theoretical information, I'd always take the group out onto the streets of Sydney to sing, preach and talk to interested passers-by. This was always the highlight of the weekend and it was not unusual for us to pray on the streets with up to fifty people to receive Jesus into their lives. From this experience, many people returned to their churches inspired and set up evangelistic teams in their local community to try to achieve the same results. Initially, people travelled from different parts of Australia to attend Adventure in Evangelism and by 1989 I was devoting the first two months of the year to reproducing the same program in seven major cities around Australia.

In June 1989, I developed another four-hour seminar I called The Confidence Builder, having observed that most Christians found it difficult to articulate their faith beyond just talking about how Jesus changed their lives. The Confidence Builder trained them to talk about their beliefs from a scientific and logical basis, focusing on the authenticity of the scriptures, the divinity of Jesus Christ and the resurrection. My extensive experience and increasing knowledge in evangelism meant I gained credibility as an expert. Invitations came from bible colleges around the country to train their students, sometimes giving me the entire student body for a week of lectures. Conferences for pastors and leaders were becoming increasingly popular and I found myself frequently joining the line-up of popular speakers. At these conferences I worked hard to challenge the status quo, inspiring the ministers to reach out beyond the walls of the church to people who needed God's power in their lives. I encouraged them to present

Christianity in a relevant way and to reject all forms of religiosity. It wasn't long before I was booked eighteen months in advance, and the hectic schedule meant I was travelling over 80,000 kilometres a year by air around Australia. The opportunities to preach overseas in Malaysia, Singapore, Thailand, the Philippines, Papua New Guinea, the United States, the United Kingdom, Europe and Africa began to make the schedule even more hectic. Eventually, I was away from home six months of the year. The possibilities seemed endless and everything I attempted turned to gold. In order to give out so much I knew that I had to make sure I was receiving as well, so I took invitations to attend international conferences such as Billy Graham's Congress on World Evangelism in Amsterdam, the Lausanne Congress on World Evangelism in the Philippines, and other conferences in the United States. These events were always fascinating as I was able to gain a global perspective of the church—the 10,000 people that attended these events came from almost every nation of the world.

Back home in Australia, many issues were facing Pentecostal churches in the 1980s. Pharisaism, the same thing Jesus encountered in his day from religious leaders, was alive and well. 'Religion Versus Christianity' was probably my most famous sermon. At least half of Jesus' ministry was involved in challenging the religious leaders of his day (the Pharisees), who had created an incredibly binding matrix of rules and regulations that enslaved the Jewish people in an oppressive religion. Rules about where they could go, whom they could mix with, what they could and couldn't eat and the perceived external signs of piety. It was a religion of isolationism and elitism, do's and don'ts. Jesus' simple message of love for all people threatened the Pharisees and they abhorred his willingness to mix with publicans, tax collectors (the most despised people of His day), prostitutes and sinners. Jesus challenged the power and control these leaders had over the people, which kept them bound in fear and guilt. Jesus, the great rule breaker, was scathing in his condemnation of their false piety. In Matthew 23:23–28 he said,

'Woe unto you, scribes and Pharisees, hypocrites! for ye pay tithe of mint and anise and cummin, and have omitted the weightier matters of the law, judgment, mercy, and faith: these ought ye to have done, and not to leave the other undone. Ye blind guides, which strain at a gnat, and swallow a camel. Woe unto you, scribes and Pharisees, hypocrites! for ye make clean the outside of the cup and of the platter, but within they are full of extortion and excess. Thou blind Pharisee, cleanse first that which is within the cup and platter, that the outside of them may be clean also. Woe unto you, scribes and Pharisees, hypocrites! for ye are like unto whited sepulchres, which indeed appear beautiful outward, but are within full of dead men's bones, and of all uncleanness. Even so ye also outwardly appear righteous unto men, but within ye are full of hypocrisy and iniquity.'

I could see plenty of frightening modern-day similarities in the Assemblies of God and other denominations. Some people were so legalistic, more focused on standards in the church than reaching out to people in need. I was amazed that history was repeating itself and that for many the church was a church of law not love, using personal interpretations of *Bible* verses to make people follow rules and regulations. A major theme of mine was to encourage the church to abandon the siege mentality and reach people beyond their walls. Some among the leadership of our denomination were defensive, and maintained a self-righteous, sanctimonious attitude that lacked the spirit of humility. They held onto archaic, outdated beliefs that only reinforced unchurched people's perception that the church was out of step with modern society. Such a red-neck mentality—but I was one of the new breed.

The church's rigidity and inability to deal with change or adapt culturally saw our national conferences becoming the scene of hostile debates between the conservative and non-traditional viewpoints. These issues usually seethed under the surface in local congregations only to explode at the conference, threatening to divide the entire denomination. I found the denominational party politics and lobbying offensive, and was often in the firing-line because of my desire to be relevant to the current generation, preaching freedom instead of rules.

In the US it was much worse, and the growing Religious Right was a warning to us about just how far it was possible to move from the essence of the gospel—even with the best of intentions. Christian leaders such as Jerry Falwell, founder of the Moral Majority, an evangelical Christian political lobbying organisation, frequently made statements that seemed devoid of God's love. 'Homosexuality is Satan's diabolical attack upon the family that will not only have a corrupting influence upon our next generation, but it will also bring down the wrath of God upon America,' he said, and, 'AIDS is not just God's punishment for homosexuals; it is God's punishment for the society that tolerates homosexuals ... Make no mistakes my friend, this is a battle between good and evil. And the consequences for America are clear: the judgment of Almighty God on our nation ... If you and I do not speak up now, this homosexual steamroller will literally crush all decent men, women, and children who get in its way...' That was Jerry Falwell.[4]

Believing they were doing God's work, James Dobson, Pat Robertson and others particularly targeted gay men and lesbians as an evil that should be opposed at all costs. By using emotive language, misrepresenting research, and misquoting individuals in order to strengthen their case, they stirred up fear, suspicion and hatred. The term 'the homosexual agenda' was frequently used to imply an insidious conspiracy was at work. '[Homosexuals] want to come into churches and disrupt church services and throw blood all around and try to give people AIDS and spit in the face of ministers,' Pat Robertson said on his Christian television show *The 700 Club*. But it wasn't just the 'gay agenda' that Pat was warning Christians to beware of, it was also women who were not prepared to submit to their husbands. 'The feminist agenda is not about equal rights for women. It is about a socialist, anti-family political movement that encourages women to leave their husbands, kill their children, practice witchcraft, destroy capitalism and become lesbians,' Robertson admonished his supporters in a fund-raising letter.

At that time in Australia, religious leaders like the Reverend Fred Nile spoke vehemently against sin, and wanted the rest of society to live by his 'Christian' standards. Moving from the ministry into politics, he was opposed to the increasingly visible gay community, demonstrating at the Gay and Lesbian Mardi Gras parade with a group of Christians and praying that God would pour down rain on the parade. He also crusaded to stop legislation to decriminalise homosexuality. Fuelled by the hysteria caused by the AIDS epidemic in the mid 1980s and the 'Grim Reaper' television campaign, Fred called for all gay men to be quarantined. Like his American counterparts, he warned Australia that God would judge our nation, like Sodom and Gomorrah, if Australia didn't uphold biblical standards. Even though secretly struggling and suppressing my homosexuality, I could never imagine the Jesus I had read about in the New Testament going to a parade to protest with a sign that said, 'God hates fags.' The only people Jesus condemned were the religious people of his day for their self-righteous attitude and hypocrisy, and I made sure hatred and condemnation of groups or individuals had no place in my preaching—there was too much positive stuff to talk about.

I'd been involved in churches and Christian circles long enough to see the inconsistencies. Thirty years ago, dancing was banned because it was the work of the devil and because many pagan cultures used dance in their rituals. Rock music was also considered demonic. Now at Christian youth concerts and in Pentecostal churches every Sunday, people dance with enthusiasm to Christian artists and music. The church had been wrong but it had changed.

One of the most laughable concepts from thirty years ago was the church's attitude towards young men with long hair. There is a verse in the Book of Revelation that mentions, in symbolic language, that 'demons came out of the pit with faces of men and hair like women' and I remember being taught at bible college that men with long hair were under demonic power and demonstrating rebellion.

People who had been divorced or remarried were forbidden from entering the ministry because of the interpretation of several scriptures—even if they were the innocent parties. Women who wore make-up were thought of as harlots or called Jezebels. I remember hearing a pastor proudly state that he had said to a girl who had smudged her make-up after crying at an altar call: 'God's wiped half of it off, dear, now you go and wash off the rest.' There was also a time when women couldn't wear slacks or jeans because they were men's clothing and in Deuteronomy 22:5 it says, 'The woman shall not wear anything that pertaineth to a man, neither shall a man put on a woman's garment: for all that do so are an abomination to the Lord thy God.' Women's liberation was frowned upon as a work of the devil, a rebellion against divine order, and women were taught to submit to their husbands often in the most oppressive situations. For years in Australia, the Pentecostal Church was a totally patriarchal system that denied women the right to speak or preach because the Apostle Paul, in his first letter to Timothy 2:11-12, said, 'Let the women learn in silence with all subjection. But I suffer not a woman to teach nor to usurp authority over the man, but to be in silence.' They could teach in Sunday schools and run their women's meetings but were never allowed in the domain of the Sunday pulpit. That was a man's job. Today, many pastors' wives and other women have been ordained and preach regularly, their contribution celebrated and valued. But they are still waiting to be elected to a position on the National Executive.

Along with many great things the church has done there is also a list that caused the destruction of vibrant, rich cultures through their missionary efforts. I saw enough during my missionary travels to developing countries in Asia and Africa; Western Christianity has a lot to answer for there. History shows us that the church actually opposed the abolition of slavery, the legalisation of interracial marriages, backed with *Bible* verses.

Travelling so regularly I was in the fortunate position to gain a national and global perspective and understood that another issue faced the Pentecostal Church in the late 1980s—the fact that the growth experienced earlier in the decade had plateaued. The significant and unprecedented growth in a number of churches meant the pastors of those churches held regular conferences to show other pastors how it was done and train them in the principles of church growth. For some these conferences were very helpful but for others very cruel. It made many pastors and church leaders feel like failures because they couldn't reproduce the successes of the handful of mega-churches.

Analysing the growth these churches experienced, I could see it had usually been caused by one or two factors. Firstly, every one of the leading churches had a pastor with a charismatic personality or strong gift of leadership—there was no way in the world the average pastor could reproduce what these men had achieved. I'm not saying they were useless or ungifted but they didn't have what it takes to build a large church, no matter how much they tried to duplicate what they were taught. Not everyone has what it takes to be a CEO of a large corporation.

Secondly, the research revealed what I had been saying all along, that what helped build the mega-churches was the migration of Charismatic Christians from the traditional churches into the Pentecostal stream. When the Charismatic movement hit Australia in the 1970s, many mainstream Christians genuinely believed that they would see their own denominations renewed. But by the 1980s, reality had hit home; they were fighting a losing battle, weighed down by centuries of tradition. The Charismatics left in their droves and went to the vibrant Pentecostal churches where they could freely express their previously suppressed sense of spirituality. A number of pastors in major cities around Australia were patting themselves on the back because of the dramatic growth in their churches, but in real terms it was not genuine growth, only a relocation of the 'sheep' from one pen to another.

Speaking openly about this made me unpopular in some circles as it challenged the egos of some of the mega-church pastors. Saying things like, 'Jesus said, "Go into all the world and preach the gospel" not "Go into all the world and shuffle the sheep,"' disputed the validity of their large congregations. During my travels I'd been exposed to various church growth models. I'd seen the revival in the Korean Church and in 1985 visited the largest church in the world with half a million people in the one congregation. Many other countries such as South America and parts of Africa also enjoyed amazing revivals, the churches growing consistently in their thousands. I wanted to do something to waken people out of the parochial mentality and limiting concepts engulfing the Australian Pentecostal churches. In 1990 I planned a church study tour to the United States and took a group of ministers to visit significant churches which were experiencing consistent, real growth. My objective was to expose them to a variety of models and assist them in identifying principles that could be de-Americanised and applied to the Australian culture.

Our main destination was Willow Creek Community Church in Chicago, a church I'd visited the previous year that was particularly exciting, as it had mushroomed to several thousand within a couple of years using some radically new approaches. In essence, they were doing exactly what I'd been encouraging the church to do back in Australia, and had successfully grown by reaching out to the unchurched, providing a non-threatening environment in which people could engage with Christianity. Judgemental words such as 'unsaved', 'non-Christian' and 'the lost' were removed, and to demonstrate acceptance at that time even provided ashtrays for their guests in the foyer. When it came time for the offering to be taken up, guests were told, 'Please don't give, you're our guest.' Such a radical concept, as most people thought the church was after their money. They had also developed a program to help each individual find their unique gift, then provided an opportunity for them to express that. An astounding ninety per cent of the church's 10,000-strong congregation were involved in some type of service such as helping the poor, assisting people through the trauma of divorce, supporting sole parents, counselling, music, youth work, drama and administration. This was in stark contrast to the majority of larger churches in Australia at that time where ninety per cent were mere 'service attenders', happy to be entertained each Sunday, as opposed to 'service givers'. The pastors and leaders returned with new vision and insight. The impact of this tour was felt in many churches, and the pastor of Willow Creek Community Church, Bill Hybles, was invited to Australia to be the leading speaker at the Assemblies of God National Conference. This was a radical step, being the first time a non-Pentecostal preacher was asked to speak, but he would be invited again to preach at the 2006 Hillsong Conference.

By 1990, I was able to have even more influence through my appointment to the Lausanne Committee for World Evangelism in Australia, which had previously been unwelcoming of Pentecostals. I was involved in creating a conference locally and also asked to be one of the presenters to speak on 'The Work of the Holy Spirit in Evangelism'. While Bill Hybles was in Australia he decided to come back and hold special conferences in Sydney and Brisbane and requested that I join him as one of the speakers. The year 1991 was looking exceptionally good—I was also planning a special pastors' conference on evangelism and taking a second group of leaders to the United States.

We had moved to the Central Coast in 1988. As a family we felt very connected with Central Coast Christian Life Centre and the ministry team led by Pastor Kevin Brett. It was so good to feel we were part of a family church again. Kevin allowed me to set up my offices in the church building and became one of the members of the board of my organisation, Every Believer Evangelism. The schedule was becoming increasingly hectic but it seemed there was so much to be done. I was doing crazy things like arriving home from the United States at 7am and then commencing a ten-day crusade that night at 7pm, or finishing preaching one night in Melbourne then driving through the night to preach at a pastors meeting in Adelaide the next morning. Being highly motivated, I could function on little sleep and while at home I often worked through to the early hours in the morning in the office catching up on planning and organising. In my absence, Helen managed Every Believer Evangelism. Her professional approach and thoroughness contributed to its success; actually, I could never have done it without her as she did much more than was ever required, believing we were both called to serve God in this way. Of course I missed Helen and the girls but there was always that inner satisfaction that I was making a significant contribution to the church and it was as though every member of the family felt called to make sacrifices.

People often asked me, 'How do you do it?' My reply was often 'quality time', as we made sure we enjoyed every moment we had as a family. Many families and couples take each other for granted because they are together all the time, but not us. Flying into Sydney on a morning flight I'd usually arrive home mid-morning after the hour's drive to the Central Coast. Once home, the first thing I did was to unpack my bag, which made me feel like I was really home. Then Helen and I would go the office to clear up any administration, she would update me on developments that had taken place while I was away or we'd have lunch together. I couldn't wait to see my girls and always made sure I was at the school gate to greet them. When Daddy came home the whole routine went into chaos, our plans were always spontaneous. We'd go to the beach, go shopping, take a walk together, play in the park, visit friends, eat ice creams at Terrigal late at night, watch the sunset, have water fights in the garden— whatever we did it was always together. The girls couldn't wait to tell me stories about their adventures or a special achievement at school.

Helen was an amazing mother and wife, and ensured our house was a sanctuary. When I arrived home, Helen had mowed the lawns, washed the cars and done all the gardening, so I only had one thing left to do—spend time with the family. Her dedication was remarkable and I always felt she should be canonised as a living saint. I knew she made more sacrifices than I did.

Every year we took a four-week break over Christmas and spent at least some of that time on the sunny Gold Coast—the friends I'd made there when I was preaching made it their mission to help us relax and enjoy ourselves. We'd arrive totally exhausted from the year's ministry and after days on the beach, nights eating out with our friends, and visits to amusement parks, we would always return home refreshed and invigorated, ready to commence another year of service. I'll be forever grateful to those people and what they did for us.

Watching the unfolding events of high profile US Christianity during 1986 and 1987 was like watching episodes of *Dynasty*, *Dallas* and *Days of Our Lives* rolled into one. It began in 1986 with Jimmy Swaggart, feeling almost invincible, I guess, with his Baton Rouge empire and estimated $150 million per year ministry, revealing that fellow Assemblies of God minister Marvin Gorman had engaged in an extramarital affair with a parishioner. Marvin Gorman was defrocked by the Assemblies of God. Through his worldwide television ministry, Swaggart continued to decry the evils of pornography, prostitution and homosexuality, saying he was committed to creating a nation of righteousness and a holy church. In March 1987, it was revealed that Televangelist Jim Bakker had an affair with Jessica Hahn, a former church secretary, and that Bakker had given her US $265,000 of the ministry's money to keep quiet. In an interview on CNN with Larry King, Swaggart said that Bakker was a 'cancer on the Body of Christ.' Gorman wanted revenge, and hired a private detective to follow

Swaggart; the investigator photographed Swaggart exiting a motel after having been with a prostitute. Gorman confronted Swaggart and told him he would have to come clean. After failing to do so, Gorman took the photographs to the Assemblies of God headquarters in Springfield, Missouri. Jimmy Swaggart, rejecting the two-year preaching ban (the same punishment he'd supported for Gorman), declared: 'If I do not return to the pulpit this weekend, millions of people will go to hell.' For his refusal to abide by their decision, Swaggart was defrocked by the Assemblies of God.

The story finally hit the news on 20 February 1988 and the next day, on his television show, Swaggart tearfully confessed, 'I have sinned,' without, however, saying specifically what he had done. I tried to avoid watching TV that day as each newsbreak played that scene repeatedly—it made me ill, as it was a frightening reminder of the consequences of moral failure. Swaggart preached against the Assemblies of God for its 'unforgiving' stance, and the sordid saga continued with Swaggart getting caught again and facing law suits from Marvin Gorman. Swaggart came into the spotlight again in 2004 during a televised sermon from his church in Louisiana. Speaking against gay marriage, Swaggart said, 'I get amazed. I can't look at it but about ten seconds, at these politicians dancing around this, dancing around this — I'm trying to find a correct name for it — this utter, absolute, asinine, idiotic stupidity of men marrying men. I've never seen a man in my life I wanted to marry. And I'm gonna be blunt and plain; if one ever looks at me like that, I'm gonna kill him and tell God he died.' His comments brought cheers, applause and laughter from his audience.

Those two years of scandal shocked the Christian world and made me, and many other preachers with a secret, I'm sure, a little nervous. Would I find myself one day in this situation and suffer the terrible humiliation of exposure? I hoped and prayed not, but it was a sobering warning.

My ex-gay façade meant my homosexual feelings were hidden,

suppressed, submerged, like nuclear waste slowly bubbling and seething, threatening to leak out of its tomb. Travelling so much caused problems for me so whenever I had the opportunity I'd take someone with me to reduce the possibility of any slip-ups. Temptation was forever close at hand. Every gay man understands the concept of 'gaydar': a gay radar that makes you notice the look from a man in a shopping centre, on the beach, at the airport, or catch the eye of an attractive man walking down the street with his wife. Fantasising about having sex with men was a luxury I knew I could never allow myself. To fantasise could bring me undone and would indicate I was giving in totally to the sin, so I became very disciplined and resisted most temptation that came my way. But not all.

I was in the United Kingdom for the first time and wanted to spend a few days relaxing in London, seeing the sights such as the Tower of London, the Tower Bridge, Buckingham Palace, the Thames, St Paul's and Piccadilly Circus. Returning to my accommodation after a day of sightseeing, I sat on the tube observing the glazed stare of commuters journeying home like caged animals. Then there was one of those moments. I connected with the young guy sitting almost opposite me who looked to be in his early thirties, rugged in appearance with very strong facial features, sandy-coloured, wavy hair, neatly parted on the right side. His masculine, handsome looks made it difficult for me not to look at him. He was a combination of many of the men I had been attracted to: Tom Selleck, Robert Redford, even Glenn from my high school days. There was nothing about him to indicate he was gay—the blue jeans, American-style checked shirt and brown boat shoes all said straight.

I caught him looking at me and our eyes met for a brief second. I dropped my gaze to the floor, then at the backpack resting on my lap, the door, another passenger, the advertising on the wall, the coloured map of the tube system, anything to take my attention away from this magnetic attraction happening in the London Underground. I tried to catch a glimpse out of the corner of my eye to see if he was still looking at me. As soon as he realised I'd seen him looking, he looked the other way, but then slowly and casually returned to me again. This continued for at least four stations and during those brief seconds, something powerful happened. I was mesmerised by his attractiveness.

An older man who'd developed a bulge around the stomach (something that usually appears on men after forty) sat next to him. His clothes were more conservative and his thinning hair gave me the impression that he was a man who thought and dressed much older than he actually was.

Occasionally the two men chatted. Were they together? A couple of times the older man caught me looking and the tension was building. As we approached our fifth station the handsome being began to get agitated, as if he had to do something urgently. The train pulled into the station and he looked me directly in the eye then smiled as he and the other gentleman got up to leave. It was a look that said, 'Yes, everything that you are thinking is right and my answer to you is yes, come with me.' I watched as he weaved his way through the commuters to the door. The attraction was overwhelming and I wanted to follow him but there were too many unanswered questions. This handsome man with whom I'd been connecting for the last ten minutes was about to walk out of my life forever. He allowed the older man to move out first and turned around to look at me one more time. That smile. It was outrageous behaviour but I was on my feet immediately.

I just made it through the doors in time as they slammed shut behind me and stood on the platform trying to find him in the crowd moving en masse up the escalators. What was I doing? Who was this person? Where would this lead? Where was I? I was shocked by my impulsiveness. I should get on the next train, I thought. Then I saw him about six metres in front of me, looking around to see if I'd followed. We caught each other's gaze again and smiled. He'd waited behind, letting the older man move ahead of him, so I pushed through the crowd to get closer as he stepped onto the escalator.

I'm sure the longest escalators in the world are the ones that take you from the bowels of the London tube to the streets above. Most commuters were walking hurriedly up the left side of the escalator but he waited on the right allowing me time to catch up. I walked up the few steps and was able to slip in right behind him. I could feel my heart pounding as we took that slow journey up to the street. We were now only inches from each other and the sexual energy like a force field around him was totally disarming.

Cautiously I moved my hand up the black rubber railing until I 'accidentally' bumped his and left it there. He then moved his hand over mine and gave it a gentle, reassuring squeeze. That touch sent electric shocks throughout my entire body. Like two statues, we stood motionless, our eyes fixed on the approaching exit as we ascended to the street.

His friend was waiting at the top of the escalator so I moved back and watched as they crossed the road then turned down the next street on the left. Suddenly it hit me. Where are you, Tony? I had no idea even what station I was at. I quickly looked around for some landmarks I could recognise when I returned and raced to the corner of the street to follow them. The street was poorly lit and immediately reminded of the old English war movies I'd watched as a kid on the movie matinees, during school holidays. There was a little fog in the air and the darkness of the buildings added to the feel of an old black and white film. It seemed like any minute I would hear the air raid sirens whine through the heavy London air. I could make out the two figures walking about thirty metres in front of me, every now and then appearing in the pool of light made by the street lamps. They were not walking together; my man was obviously dawdling behind and regularly looked back to make sure I was following.

My head was spinning. Part of me was fighting, saying go back to the station and hop on the train, and the other wanted to be with this beautiful man. For a moment, I even thought there was the possibility that this was a setup and I was being baited into a situation where I could be raped by these two. I knew what I was doing was wrong, crazy, even dangerous, but I couldn't stop it.

Three-storey terraces flanked either side of the street and in the darkness it appeared to be a fairly affluent suburb. The two men crossed to the right side of the road and I continued to walk on the left, trying to appear like I was casually strolling home. They stopped at one of the terraces and the older man took out his keys and opened the door as I passed the house. Slowing my pace down, I kept looking back, watching for some kind of signal from my handsome tempter. A quick glance over his shoulder, a smile and he was gone. As soon as the door closed behind them, I stopped dead in my tracks. What do I do now? I was alone in the dark London street without any idea of where I was.

I slowly walked back and forth in front of the house several times looking for some indication as to what my next step should be, hoping this wasn't the conclusion of my encounter with this man who had so quickly captivated me. This was my opportunity to overcome temptation, walk back to the station and go home, chalking up another victory over sin. I was about to do that when the curtains drew back, his handsome face appeared, rather stressed, and he signalled with his fingers to wait ten minutes. I moved away from the light, and quickly looked around to make sure no-one could see me acting suspiciously.

The ten minutes became twenty before he appeared again, this time from the level below the street. Looking up to the storeys above he whispered quietly that his friend was asleep upstairs and that he wanted me to climb over the wrought-iron fence to the three metre drop below.

'Can't you let me in through the front door?' I whispered back.

'No,' he said, 'he will hear,' pointing to the upper levels. Through the faint voice I could hear a southern American accent. Ooooh my Lawd, I thought, as he carefully guided me over the wrought iron spikes. Sliding down the other side, I felt the strength in his arms as he broke my fall. Without a word he held me and kissed me immediately. We both giggled at the insanity of what was happening then he took my hand and led me inside the basement bedroom. We introduced ourselves, a mere formality. so far away from home I felt safe to use my real name and he introduced himself as Hank.

I felt unusually at ease with Hank, like we'd been lovers for years but never lost the passion. Usually I felt that what I was doing was an abomination but not this time. It was such a bizarre feeling to be immediately close to a total stranger. I enjoyed every moment of attention and devotion from this incredibly handsome, masculine and loving man. Then, looking over his shoulder, I saw a *Bible* on the bedside table. He must be a Christian, I thought; there was no other explanation for a *Bible* next to the bed. I wondered how he could be so casual about the sin we'd just committed.

'Are you a Christian?' I asked hesitantly. He replied with a confident, 'Yes', which I found very disturbing. I'd never admit to such a thing in this kind of situation. We talked for over an hour. He was a choir director, married with two young children, who was involved in a music ministry and visiting All Souls Langham Place, a famous stronghold of Anglican evangelicalism. The older guy upstairs was a soloist who sang frequently at Billy Graham crusades. How could this have happened? I thought. I feared telling my story despite the fact that here was a person who would understand the struggles and torment I went through. Hank was having an affair with another young man in his church who was also married and they often went on camping trips together. Hank seemed resigned to the fact. I couldn't understand how he could so willingly live a double life as a Christian. I was always fighting it; I could never purposely deceive my wife and to have an affair on the side was unthinkable. I never divulged that I was a preacher, only that I was also married. I related to everything he was saying and wanted to stay the night, to talk with someone who'd understand my struggles and sleep in his arms, to connect, but knew I couldn't. I postponed my departure as long as possible, Hank always encouraging me to stay a little longer. It was nearly midnight and, unsure of the train timetable, I thought I'd better leave. Hank's strong arms lifted me over the high fencing and we giggled like girls once again about the events that had transpired since the moment our eyes met only a few hours earlier on the train.

I walked back to the station with a spring in my step, feeling really elated—so different from the guilt that usually rushed in and tormented me. Something wonderful had just happened. Even at that time it was hard to identify but it was the tenderness and warmth of Hank's affection and the connection of our hearts—it wasn't just the sex. I wondered for the first time if, in a different place and time, I might not be saying goodbye to Hank but staying with him forever. Something was slowly changing inside me.

The internet is an amazing place. Eighteen years later, out of curiosity, I googled Hank's name and sure enough there he was, several entries actually, with his photo in a line-up of ministers. Still a pastor in a church, (I won't say which one), carrying a few extra pounds, but it wasn't hard to recall the handsome face of eighteen years ago, now a little plump. I remembered his strong curly hair but was that now a toupee? Was he still married? Was he still having that affair? Had he resolved the issues we'd talk about holding each other so affectionately in the cellar bedroom? Those two hours of my life, I've never forgotten. Had he? A carefully worded email that didn't arouse suspicion from others might uncover some answers, but alas, no reply. One more email with some additional details to jog his memory but still nothing. It made me sad, not that Hank hadn't replied but that he might possibly leave this world without knowing the freedom that comes from being completely honest with yourself and others.

In 1987, Exodus International (now Exodus Global Alliance) was established in Australia—a branch of the ministry that was founded in America in 1976 to help homosexuals be healed of their same sex attraction. Michael Bussee and Gary Cooper were involved in establishing the ministry but after travelling all over the US together, preaching the message that they were ex-gays, they finally admitted in 1979 that they were unable to change and had actually fallen in love with each other. Their marriages, often used as proof that ex-gays are now heterosexual, were not real, so they separated from their wives and married each other in 1982. It's difficult to track the failure rate of Exodus style ministries. Thousands come and go with only a small number declaring publicly that they are now 'free'. One of these was John Paulk, a former leader of Focus on the Family's Love Won Out conference and former chairman of the board for Exodus International North America. Paulk and his ex-lesbian wife Anne became the faces promoting Exodus ministries in major daily newspaper full-page ads. They also appeared in the cover story 'Gay for Life?' in *Newsweek* in 1998 when the publication covered Exodus and the ex-gay movement. *Time* magazine also ran a story but reported that it could not locate a single ex-girlfriend of John Paulk's 'former lesbian' wife, Anne. In fact, the magazine reported that John conceded that her ties to women in college were 'more emotional than sexual'. In September 2000, Paulk was discovered in a Washington, DC, gay bar, and accused of flirting with male patrons. Activist and author Wayne Besen took a photo of Paulk leaving the bar and put it on the cover of his book exposing the ex-gay myth *Anything but Straight*. A more recent exposure was Michael Johnston, another prominent ex-gay and founder of Kerusso Ministries. In August 2003, it was reported that Michael Johnston had been meeting other men online under the assumed name of 'Sean'. This was verified through interviews with at least two of Johnston's sexual partners. Furthermore, Johnston was HIV-positive, a fact that he did not reveal to his sexual contacts till much later, which was extremely irresponsible of him. Johnston had starred in a television commercial in 1998, promoting the programs of the ex-gay ministries. In his ad, he said he had 'walked away from homosexuality through the power of Jesus Christ.' Not only had individuals fallen by the way, entire groups have come and gone. The ex-gay ministry Courage UK, formed in 1990 with a stated aim 'to heal homosexuals'. In 2001 the group's founder, Jeremy Marks, did a complete turnaround when he stated, 'While recognising the social pressure to become 'normal' (i.e. hetero-sexual), fifteen years experience has revealed that God's primary concern is not to change the sexual orientation of his gay and lesbian disciples, but to help them find wholeness in Christ—becoming secure, assured of his love and acceptance, set apart to follow Jesus faithfully and responsible in building relationships with one another.'

Like John Paulk and other ex-gays, I had the outward evidence of being heterosexual. I was married with two children and careful about how I dressed, moved and spoke, thinking I was hiding all the clues about my true identity. 'By acting you become' is part of the ex-gay philosophy and I was doing all I could to maintain the cover-up. When temptations became increasingly intense, though, I often thought that I might find help through Exodus but it was too risky to open up my life in that way. Besides there were too many other important things to do with my life than to be a travelling freak show talking about my former life as a homosexual and how God had set me free.

CHAPTER 14

The trap is set

In many ways 1991 was looking awesome, my calendar fully booked, ventures planned overseas and in Australia, new and exciting projects in the pipeline; I knew it would be my best year yet. But something was drastically different to previous years. I usually commenced the year with such enthusiasm and anticipation after our four-week break, but the invitation to spend ten days speaking to one thousand young people at a youth convention in Papua New Guinea in January was too tempting. Returning to Sydney mid January was the first time I was aware I was lacking something. I was tired of the travel, tired of the emotional demands of the ministry and extremely tired of fighting the constant battle in my mind. I think at some time I'd stopped battling and just resigned myself to keeping things in check but I couldn't tell exactly when that happened. Concerned about my mental and emotional health, I knew that if I wasn't careful I could find myself burning out with the demanding schedule that lay ahead.

The year commenced with the six weeks of Adventure in Evangelism conferences around Australia. I completed the first three weeks in Sydney, Tasmania and Victoria, then flew to Brisbane to do it all again. I'd been asked to fly up early so I could spend a few days in Pastor Jim Williams's bible college at Garden City Assemblies of God, Mount Gravatt, in Brisbane. Invitations like this were hard to say no to as these students were the leaders of tomorrow, and the opportunity to share my concepts on evangelism and church growth with them would bear great fruit in the future. I'd preached for Pastor Jim in Hamilton when he was the superintendent of the Assemblies of God in New Zealand. After moving to Australia, allegations of sexual misconduct rose against Jim, dating from the time when I had been in New Zealand. The Australian leadership of the Assemblies of God decided that he should stand down from ministry for a couple of years, then be later allowed to continue as a minister. I always found Jim and his wife Betty to be warm and natural people. After the five hours of lectures I returned to my motel to relax. The motel room was a luxury—not luxurious, just a luxury for me. I'd spent years travelling, staying in pastors' homes in the junk room or spare bedroom, or being accommodated with members of the church who wanted to keep me up all night whingeing about the church's difficulties or pouring out their own personal problems believing I had the answers. Churches were always trying to save money on accommodation. I found it quite draining not having privacy, unable to run my own schedule, watch television or eat when I wanted to. So often I was 'peopled out' and grateful of some time alone to do what I wanted. That night was one of my rare nights off. Before dining I watched the evening news and remembered being grounded at the Amsterdam airport on my way to Africa when the Gulf War began with the Iraqi invasion of Kuwait on 2 August 1990. Now I was watching President George H W Bush announce that 'Kuwait is liberated.'

It was a beautifully warm, balmy Brisbane night. I loved the tropics, especially at night, and always felt I'd been created to live in that climate. Walking out of the air-conditioned airport terminals in Asia and having that wall of heat hit me always made me feel like I was home. After finishing my meal at the motel restaurant, I thought I'd make the most of my night off. No-one to pick my brains, no-one to tell me how difficult their life was, no-one to complain about their church or pastor. It was great. I'd hired a car to drive up to the Sunshine

Coast on the weekend to present the Adventure in Evangelism training camp so I drove into the city—I was always attracted by the bright lights and activity—and drove around for a while thinking about what to do to pass the time. I was feeling restless and uneasy. I wanted company, but not with Christians.

I decided to drive over to one of the trendy new inner Brisbane suburbs for some coffee and cake. I parked at Albert Park overlooking Brisbane city to look down at the buildings and the bridges spanning the Brisbane River as it wound its way past the city and out through the suburbs. When I got out of the air-conditioned car I immediately felt the warmth of the summer's night and smelt the beautiful, sweet aromas of tropical trees in flower. Occasionally there was a rustle in the large Moreton Bay fig trees, then a fruit bat would fly out, screeching, as it moved on to its next feed. In the midst of this quiet park and the stillness of the night, there was another type of activity.

As I'd driven up the hill I'd noticed a number of men strolling alone along the streets and realised I had arrived at a Brisbane 'beat' (cutely called 'cottaging' or 'kite flying' in the UK, and 'tearooms' in the US). Beats were a leftover from the days when homosexuality was a crime and men had to find places to meet each other secretly. As society has become more accepting, the use of these places is diminishing, except for people who are forced to be secretive because they belong to some religious group or are married, as I was. This practice was hazardous enough but I would never have taken the risk of going to a gay venue, firstly because of denial, but secondly there was always the danger of being recognised, as indeed happened to the ex-gay crusader John Paulk. The possibility of being discovered or exposed by someone who knew me from the church was a constant threat. Every week I preached in front of thousands of people who knew me by face and name, but to me they were a mass of unrecognisable people. Total strangers often approached me at airports, shopping centres or in the streets and told me how much they enjoyed my preaching and what an impact it had made on their lives. I knew it was a risk going to beats—among those thousands there had to be some guys who occasionally struggled unsuccessfully with their sexual identity, just as I did. But at least if someone I knew saw me at a beat, I could always say, 'I was just going to the toilet.' Over the last twelve months my visits to beats had become more frequent because my ability to resist was weakened.

Beats could be dangerous places. The state of Queensland was much more conservative than New South Wales and had only decriminalised homosexuality the year before, in 1990. There was the constant threat of police harassment and gay-bashers; even murders had occurred at these places. Over the years I'd encountered most of the dangers the beat held. I'd been robbed and bashed (resulting in broken ribs) by a bunch of straight guys who thought it immense sport to attack a gay man who could offer little resistance. It was impossible for me to report these crimes and so they would not have been added to the almost unbelievable statistic that over eighty per cent of lesbians and gay men have experienced some form of harassment or violence because of their sexual orientation. I took the attacks as warnings from God. The *Bible* says God can look into your heart and know your motives, so He must have known that in my heart I really didn't want this. Why didn't He do anything? Was it a lack of faith on my part? Was it the devil tempting me or just my own inner sinful, fleshly desires? I just couldn't make sense of it all.

Walking along the road at the edge of the park, there was no battle. My focus was on having a brief encounter and the relief I'd feel after being with a man. The beat was incredibly active. As I walked across the road towards Albert Park, there were more men then I'd originally thought, scuttling about in the shadows like cockroaches coming out after dark. There were at least twenty of them, some together as couples but most strolling alone. Cars drove by slowly, parking, then taking off again, backwards and forwards, over and over again in an endless parade.

I knew there would be the usual collection of gay, straight, bisexual and married men all in various states of transition or curiosity. Some old, balding and overweight, and some young guys who were seething masses of pulsing hormones capable of having sex several times a night—and often doing so.

Recently I'd begun going to the gym, put on some muscle and lost five kilos, so now I was feeling, even at thirty-nine, relatively attractive. I scanned for any signs of trouble and at the same time looked out for the man I wanted to be with. Playing the cruising game I walked past man after man, smiling at those I found attractive, pausing for a brief moment to look around for any response and ignoring the advances of those I found unattractive. I walked the entire length of the park and back again without any success. Sometimes this outcome meant I was able to retreat with some sense of empowerment because I had over-come temptation, but mostly it was because there was nothing attractive on offer. I wasn't in a hurry tonight so I cruised up and down for another twenty minutes making attempts at connection and wishing my luck would change.

He stood out immediately.

He was in his late twenties or early thirties, sitting among the shadows on the edge of the low sandstone fence surrounding the park. His blue jeans were well-worn but pressed so the crease was clearly visible and the light, white Indian cotton shirt, opened halfway down his chest, hung loosely on his body. His face was long, with strong, sharp features; his tan made him look healthy, and contrasted with the white shirt. I could see he was slim and tall, even though he was sitting down, but there was one thing that stood out more than anything. His eyes. They were an unusual deep, dark brown. Even under the shadowy light that filtered through the trees, they were striking. The combination of all these features made me think he must have been a model and how lucky people are to be born so attractive—so attractive, in fact, that I didn't even bother to make an approach. Why would anyone that gorgeous want to be with me? At least half a dozen men were cruising him at the same time, like bees to a honey pot. Watching the antics of his possible partners, I really didn't think any of them had a chance.

I sat down on the fence about six metres away to observe the activity. One after another they filed past, smiling and trying to gain his attention, but to no avail; he was a professional at rejection. That cold, stoic stare said it all. They soon moved on to other prey realising their quest was hopeless. As the last one moved away, he rose to his feet. I'd totally misjudged his height, as he was well over 180 centimetres tall, probably more like 190 centimetres. Such a striking man—the term 'tall, dark and handsome' had been created especially for him. I expected him to pass as he walked towards the street but instead he sat a little away from me on the fence then initiated conversation.

'God, I hate these places, don't you?' The comment took me aback as I thought all gay men liked beats; surely I was the only one who hated them. But then again, I wasn't totally gay.

'Yes,' I quickly replied. There was a brief silence because I really didn't know what to say next. His attractiveness was alarming and I didn't want to say anything to embarrass myself or sound stupid. Sensing my awkwardness he broke the silence.

'So, do you live in Brisbane?' That was easy to answer. 'No, I'm here on business,' I replied.

'So what type of work you do?'

'I'm a sales representative,' I answered hesitatingly, drawing on my past to create a false identity. My mind raced ahead trying to form the rest of the story, should he ask more questions. No more small talk, he got straight to the point.

'Do you have somewhere to go?' he asked in a confident manner, as if it was a foregone conclusion I wanted to be with him.

'Yes, would you like to come back to my motel at Mount Gravatt?'

'Can you drive me back to the city afterwards?' he asked, knowing full well that I would have driven to the other side of the city to be with him. His huge strides made it difficult for me to keep up as we walked to the car and I tried my best to make it look like I wasn't running. I opened the door for him and then walked around the front of the car. Getting into the driver's side I noticed he'd wedged himself into the corner of the door and the passenger seat and sat with his legs apart in an inviting, seductive manner.

'I'm Jason,' he said in a natural tone, so comfortable with the protocols of picking up strangers.

'Oh, I'm sorry,' I said, giggling apologetically, realising we hadn't even introduced ourselves. 'I'm Tony,' I said, forgetting to use a false name.

As we drove to the motel all I could think of was how lucky I was to be going home with this amazingly handsome man and the fact I was in a motel for the night and not staying with a pastor. I turned towards him as I asked questions to catch glimpses of the many things about him I was finding attractive, and as he replied he'd lean over and place his hand on my leg. This must be what it's like to have a boyfriend, I thought, as we made our way to the motel.

When I saw Jason in the full light of the motel room I remember thinking that if ever I was to be with a man then he was the type of person I'd like to be with. The strong fluorescent lighting made it awkwardly bright so I quickly moved around to adjust the bedside lamps to create a softer, more intimate ambience. I offered him a cup of coffee. The electric jug clicked as it reached its boil and I turned to pour the water into the cups when he stood behind me, put his arms around me and began kissing me gently on the back of the neck. I melted into the mould created by his body.

His touch was electrifying. I turned around to face him and we began to kiss. First a gentle touch on the lips, then another, and another, passionate but still with an intoxicating softness. Placing one hand behind my head, he kissed me softly on the cheek and forehead. Cupping my face in his hands, he kissed me again, occasionally pulling away to smile at me while his eyes wandered around my face. I savoured the warm energy running through my body, weakening me with each kiss and touch. After five minutes of kissing, Jason moved his hands towards my shirt collar. One button and a touch of my chest, then a kiss, then another button, a touch and a kiss. I was thirty-nine and never had a man touched me this way before. It was wonderful.

It took him another five minutes to remove my shirt and all that I could think was, Oh my God, this is magnificent. I was in the arms of a beautiful man whose only desire was to show me tenderness and affection, my pleasure bringing him delight. With my shirt off he began to touch my back with his fingertips, ever so slowly back and forth then around my neck and down my arms. Feelings of euphoria over-whelmed me. He was a master. This procedure was foreign to me so I repeated Jason's ritual. First the lips, then the touch, then the hands around the face, then the buttons and then the touch again until finally we were holding each other. His body was slim, with not an ounce of fat—a swimmer's build with toned muscle, but not overdone. He was the master so I paused, waiting for him to take the next step. Closing his eyes he kissed me again and I felt the back of his fingers moving down my stomach to the top of my trousers, the tension building making me feel like I was about to explode. Like a movie in slow motion, he removed every piece of clothing, occasionally stopping and kissing me again and again, until I stood naked before him. It was obvious he delighted in seeing me in this state of ecstasy and having such power over me.

Never taking his eyes from me for a moment he gently guided me onto the bed, pulled back the bedspread and lowered me onto the crisp white, laundered sheets. Stepping back from the bed, holding me in his gaze, he slowly undid his jeans and let them drop to the floor. He left his white briefs on, leaving that last piece for me to remove, somehow knowing the pleasure that would give me. He then lay beside me and we continued to touch and kiss for what seemed like hours—him on top of me, me on top of him—our bodies tangled together like a vine.

He gave me a quick peck on the cheek and pulled away, picked up his jeans and pulled out a condom. I began to feel nervous. I never felt comfortable about this kind of activity—the rape of the past had proved to me that this was something I'd never do. Jason sensed my awkwardness and that I was a novice, and took over completely. He placed the condom on me and moved into position. I groaned, screamed and came within a matter of seconds. No wonder, I'd been on the brink so many times during the last hour. He chuckled at my lack of self-control.

'What did you go and do that for?' he said, slapping me playfully on the chest. I burst into laughter at the sheer relief from the sexual tension and said, 'I'm sorry.' The amusement quickly passed when Jason noticed the condom had broken.

'You should be okay,' he said in a reassuring manner, but for a brief moment I saw the concern on his face. 'You are negative, aren't you?' he continued. I reassured him that I was but I had no way of knowing that—all part of my denial about what was really happening in my life. I was actually in a high risk group, the bisexual and married gay men who never self-identified as gay and therefore had not really sought out information on safe sex practices. As far as I knew, all activity that I'd been involved in was safe, but I'd never been tested for sexually transmitted diseases; not since that time Joyce at Paradise sent me to the doctor at Cronulla. Jason showered while I made another coffee (the previous one now cold in the cups) and I wondered why this gorgeous man was so devoted to my pleasure. With towels wrapped around ourselves, we laid on the bed and talked. Normally, by this time, I'd be dressed and suggesting I give him a lift home. Jason began to reveal the events of his life.

He'd been out as a gay man for twelve years, done everything, and was really 'over the scene' as he put it. Tragedy after tragedy had happened, the most recent being the bust-up with his boyfriend

Charles in the Blue Mountains after a five-year relationship. Jason had packed up and left everything he'd worked for after discovering his boyfriend was having an affair and arrived in Brisbane with only a suitcase and a few dollars. The first few nights had been spent sleeping in a park. He had just got a job at an amusement parlour in Brisbane Mall and was trying to put his life back together again. Hearing about his difficult life saddened me and I wished that somehow we'd not met like this because he was so in need of God. In other circumstances I'd be suggesting he pray and ask Jesus into his life, but the hypocrisy of the last hour meant I couldn't even contemplate that.

I sympathised with him about these difficulties and made up quick fabrications to any questions about where I lived, what I did.

'I'd better go now. I have to start work early in the morning,' Jason said, getting up to dress. 'I'd like to see you again. Do you come to Brisbane often?' I wasn't ready for that. I had a policy. What I was doing was bad enough but to see someone a second time would be classed as having an affair or giving up the fight with homosexuality. 'Can I see you again?' he repeated.

'I don't think that's a good idea,' I replied, surprised by his eagerness. Undeterred by my comment, he took the notepad and pen next to the phone and wrote down his name and telephone number.

'There you are, just in case you're in Brisbane again sometime and you'd like to catch up,' he said, placing the piece of paper by the bed.

Jason was reluctant to let me know exactly where he lived so I dropped him off near the park again and drove back to the motel. Lying alone in the bed, I couldn't help wondering why this attractive man was so giving and wanted to see me again. Once again by having time to connect beyond quick sex, I'd experienced one of the most wonderful nights of my life. It was difficult to put thoughts of him out of my mind. They'll be gone by the time I'm speaking at the conference, I thought, unaware that night had changed my life forever.

Clearing the room the next morning I noticed the note still beside the bed and picked it up. I paused and thought about the consequences of keeping Jason's details, then folded it neatly and placed it in the back of my wallet, planning to discard it before I returned to Sydney.

After packing the car I drove north to the Sunshine Coast for the weekend conference. The previous evening had left me in a state of euphoria and on the highway my thoughts drifted back to the sensational feelings I had when I was with Jason. I had to get a grip on my thinking there was a full weekend of ministry ahead of me and how could I expect God to work through me having thoughts like that in my mind? This time, asking for forgiveness as I usually did would have been very hollow. I couldn't say I hated what I'd just done. Before every conference session I prayed before speaking, publicly acknowledging I had nothing to give, I was just an empty vessel for God to use if He chose.

The weekend conference seemed to progress well and people were excited about taking what they had learnt back to their local churches. I'd presented the training material so many times I could have done it with my eyes closed. To the outsider it seemed like nothing was amiss but inside me something had changed and I found myself falling in and out of the blissful feeling left over from that momentous night. Maybe I could see him again, just one more time, before going back to Sydney? Surely that wouldn't hurt. Not to have sex but just see him and have a coffee or something. There was something fascinating and intriguing about this man and I wanted to know more about him. After the Saturday night meeting I removed the neatly folded piece of paper concealed in the back of my wallet and found an isolated public telephone booth. I tried several times to call but there was never an answer. Just in case I was able to contact Jason, I rescheduled my flight to Sydney so I could have some time with him. I knew Brisbane fairly well from my frequent visits and remembered Jason mentioned managing an amusement parlour in the city mall. It was worth a try to see if I could track him down as I remembered seeing a couple of similar establishments when I'd shopped there previously. I felt a nervous excitement as I drove back to Brisbane, hopeful but aware that I was playing a very, very dangerous game.

The amusement parlour was exactly where I pictured it and the entrance was cluttered with rough young teenagers who looked suspiciously like they could break out in gang warfare at any minute. I know I looked out of place in the long room—a mass of lights, game machines and electronic noises with every piece of spare floor space utilised. This parlour seemed particularly rough. I found it hard to picture Jason working in such an environment, as he carried such an air of class and style.

I recognised him by his height and the back of his head and stood waiting for him to turn around. He was standing in the change booth counting money and turned around to serve a waiting teenager when he looked up and saw me. He smiled as I waited for the youngster to move out of the way.

'What are you doing here?' he asked, appearing to be genuinely excited to see me but also shocked at my successful detective work— maybe even worried I would become a stalker.

'I had a few hours before my flight so I thought I'd come and see if I could find you,' sounded like a reasonable excuse.

'I'll be finished in half an hour. Can you wait?' he said enthusiastically, his cheeky grin giving warmth to his words.

'I'll meet you out the front in half an hour but I have to catch my plane in two hours.' That was a long half hour. I filled the time walking around the shops and I arrived five minutes early just in case, but waited another ten. Walking away from the amusement parlour I wanted to embrace him, kiss him, hold his hand, touch him or do something that gave us a physical connection but we were in Brisbane Mall and that kind of behaviour would have been outrageous, even dangerous. We moved quickly to a coffee shop in the middle of the mall and sat down.

Jason leant back in his chair and stretched out his long legs so that we touched under the table. Every so often he'd slip his hand under the table and stroke my leg. I was trying to act cool but I think Jason knew how difficult this was for me. Being affectionate to a man in private was rare to me but in a public place was unthinkable. Talking over coffee for the next hour I became more relaxed and was soon joining Jason in taking every opportunity to touch. He'd touch the sugar bowl and I'd reach out and stroke his hand, pretending to move it, always smiling at each other and occasionally snickering at the secretive game we were playing in public.

The conversation made time fly and too quickly it was time to go to the airport. I could have rescheduled my flight again but I was beginning to get the uncomfortable feeling that I was being pulled into quicksand. We walked to the car park together. Out of the public eye, in the underground car park, we held each other, kissing with the passion of lovers who'd been separated for months. We hurried to the car for more privacy.

In the rental car, Jason's kissing became more and more aggressive, so unlike the tenderness of our first night. Passion, abandonment and intensity were new sensations for me and there was an element of desperation in our five minutes in the car. We were both surprised how intense we were feeling and both let out a 'Phew' as we extricated ourselves from each other.

'I have to go,' I said, realising that the more I became involved with this man the greater the risk of exposure and even possible blackmail. If he discovered who I really was, would he use it against me? I didn't really know who Jason was or what he was about. 'I'll call in a few days and let you know when I'll be in Brisbane again, okay?' Jason smiled, he was familiar with the emotions two men can experience and knew that what had happened was too strong to keep us apart.

I arrived back in Sydney, then spent the one-hour drive to the Central Coast collecting myself and trying to organise my emotions in order to face Helen, the girls and the demands of the busy week before me. Pulling into the drive I honked the horn as usual and the girls came running out onto the decking and down the steps to greet me.

'Daddy, Daddy, Daddy!' Becky and Hannah screamed. It was a ritual they'd developed over the years to welcome me home and after hugging and kissing, helped me to the house with my luggage. I was unusually happy and light. 'Let's go out for Chinese,' I suggested, trying to act as normal as possible, aware of Helen's finely tuned 'woman's intuition'. Over dinner I let the girls talk about their weekend, but it was difficult to focus with such mixed emotions. Guilt, excitement and infatuation—all were present in the back of my mind.

I had made sure the small piece of paper in my wallet was discarded and Jason's number memorised so I wouldn't be discovered. I also wrote it down in a disused page of my diary just in case I forgot it. Already I was changing and becoming incredibly deceptive. Preaching in Melbourne the next week, Jason and I spoke daily on the phone, mostly about him, as I didn't want to weave too large a web of deceit about myself. He told me about the daily bashings by his older brother, the ex-lover who betrayed him and married his sister because he wanted to have children, the unfaithfulness of his partner, Charles. His twelve years' experience as a gay man was extraordinary and the more I heard the more fascinated I became. The stories were endless and I wanted to be the one to bring healing to his life, and say, 'It's going to be all right, I'll be the one you can really trust and love. I want to make life better for you.' It was halfway through the week before the realisation hit me—I'd fallen in love. I was thinking of Jason constantly, planning my times to call, and looking forward to being together in Brisbane within a week.

This is going to drive me crazy, I thought, feeling like a stupid little teenager in love. Even entertaining the thought of seeing Jason again was an enormous risk. I felt like I was standing on the edge of a precipice. He was still unaware of my true identity—I'd maintained the story of being a sales representative, living in Sydney and now on a business trip in Melbourne. In my mind, the thought of maintaining a secret affair was out of the question, so I planned to see Jason just once, maybe twice more, then it had to finish. I flew to Brisbane for another weekend of ministry. I'd already rescheduled the itinerary so that I could spend a couple of hours with Jason. He'd given me the details to find the new flat he'd moved into and the excitement and anticipation of seeing him again increased as the weekend got closer.

Brian, Jason's flatmate, let me in. I felt like I knew Brian already from the times I'd called to find Jason wasn't home and we'd spent a few moments in idle conversation about the weather, work or some other easy topic, just to be friendly. The flat was sparsely furnished with tacky second-hand furniture and had the type of wooden parquetry floor usually found in the red brick home units built in the 1960s. Attempts had been made at decorating, obviously on a budget, by covering the worn lounge with an Indian-print fabric, and a purple, two-dollar, rice paper light fitting hung from the ceiling. The few pieces of second-hand furniture consisted of a walnut sideboard; a teak bookcase with its array of carefully arranged ornaments; a glass and wrought-iron coffee table with cookery and fashion magazines fanned out on its surface, revealing an eclectic selection of reading material; and a white portable television with a twisted coat hanger for an aerial. Nothing matched.

'He's sleeping,' Brian said, as he opened the door of Jason's room. Jason slept on a mattress on the floor and as I quickly took in the surroundings I noticed the second-hand theme had been carried through to the bedroom. There was a tiny, black plastic radio/cassette player by the bed with two cassettes on the floor, out of their cases. Apart from the cassettes everything else in the room was neat and tidy, even the clothes on the clothes rack had been pressed and hung in order. Shirts, trousers, T-shirts, jackets, had all been placed systematically in categories of item and colour. Brian closed the door behind me.

Jason didn't stir as I lay on the mattress beside him. Seeing him asleep for the first time I thought he looked angelic. It was an opportunity to explore every detail of his face. I touched his forehead gently, not wanting to disturb him but also wishing he'd open his eyes and acknowledge my presence. Lying next to him with one arm propping up my head, I smiled when he stirred and watched his eyes partially open. The half smile on his contorted face suggested he was pleased to see me even though his lids closed again. He moved forward, and with a warm moist kiss, made me feel like I'd arrived home.

'Hello, darling, sorry I'm not well. I have a terrible headache,' he said, slowly returning to the pillow and pulling me closer to his side.

'That's all right, you sleep,' I responded, glad of the opportunity to just be there to look at him.

I couldn't remember a man ever calling me darling and immediately, on hearing those words, feelings of warmth melted inside me. I knew that meant I was special to him. While Jason slept for the next hour I moved away enough to see his face and explored the smooth skin, the neatly trimmed eyebrows, the perfectly shaped ears, the flawless line of his nose, the dark hair with the slightest introduction of grey, the small tuft of hair on his chest and the splattering of freckles on his shoulders and back. Occasionally I leant over, kissing him on the forehead or stroking the side of his face as I kept my vigil. Every now and then he took hold of my hand, kissed the back of it then pulled it up under his chin or next to his face. I could have stayed there forever but time was our enemy.

After an hour I got a little impatient, knowing I must leave. 'Jason,' I said, gently shaking him, 'let's have some lunch, I have to go soon.' This comment was enough to encourage an effort at waking and within seconds he was on his feet. I watched his naked body as he emerged from the sheets and put on his black Chinese silk robe. He leant over, took me by the hand into the lounge room and disappeared into the kitchen.

Our conversation revolved around general things in our lives while

Jason made a snack. Sometimes it became difficult to keep up the smokescreen of my story, remember the details I'd previously given, and come up with new facts that would ensure it held together. I endeavoured to do the impossible—eat Sao crackers without spilling a crumb while we continued to talk. No, Jason talked and I listened. I was quickly learning that Jason always had a drama story. Jason was a talker and often the only way to be involved in the conversation was to interrupt him mid-sentence with a comment.

'There's something I need to tell you,' was my successful interruption, feeling the need to be more open with him. 'I want to be honest with you about my life. I'm married and have two children.' Jason didn't seem at all put off by my confession and went on to question me about how long I'd been married and how old my children were. I gave him the particulars, and observed his reactions to see if he could handle the entire story. The opportunity of blackmail was still a possibility.

'Would you leave your wife for me?' he asked.

What a ridiculous question, I thought. It was so casual, the way Jason had asked, as if he'd said, 'Would you like to go for a walk in the park?' How could he think it was even a possibility? The question was utterly absurd and I was sure he would never have asked it if he knew the full story. I answered it anyway. 'No, I love my wife and children.'

Jason didn't appear upset with my answer and said nothing more, almost like it had been a test. It was time to leave. No sex. Just that one question reverberating in my mind, like the numbing, repetitive gong of a cathedral bell. 'Would you … ?'

CHAPTER 15

Turmoil

I had a lot of serious thinking to do when I returned to Sydney after the weekend of ministry and seeing Jason for the second time. No longer could I pretend I wasn't attracted to men, or continue believing one day it would all go away, or fool myself that I was a fine upstanding Christian preacher. It was useless trying to put it out of my mind; the denial had gone on long enough and it was time to be honest with myself.

With Jason's question in the back of my mind, I reviewed my life, remembering the initial sexual experiences, the self-loathing, the depression and thoughts of suicide, the times of confession, asking for forgiveness, repenting and making endless promises I couldn't keep. I recalled believing so many times that God had delivered me from homosexuality only to discover it was always hiding under the surface; the feelings of discouragement and disappointment at my failure, then finding the strength to pick myself up to fight it once again. Imagining I was an ex-gay but never really being bold enough to declare it, knowing in essence I had only changed some behaviours, not my sexual orientation. Like peddling on a stationary bike for twenty-two years; when I got off, I was still gay.

Overwhelming memories that when put together made a pathetic collage of false hope. Falling in love with a man now the final outcome. Had I failed God or had God failed me?

It became very clear how I'd compartmentalised my 'problem'. The ministry and my desire to serve God took centre stage, while behind the scenes I secretly fought a battle to match my image. I knew most people would judge me as a hypocrite, liar and deceiver and never understand the constant internal struggle. In my mind, I could continue to serve God as long as I kept fighting, knowing that every Christian has struggles with sin and temptation. Surely I was no different to any other Christian? Not perfect, just forgiven.

Could I serve God and be in love with a man, or continue to preach and have an affair with Jason on the side? Could I stand up in front of crowds of people declaring God's power delivers from every sin and temptation? The answer to all these questions was a resounding 'No'. I could no longer preach because now, for the first time in my life, I wanted love, affection, closeness and intimacy with a man. Everything I'd unconsciously craved for was epitomised in Jason and to continue preaching would have been hypocritical, leaving me only one choice … accept the fact that I was a gay man and that for some reason even though God was all powerful He was not ever going to change that. The choice was not to be homosexual or straight. The choice was to stop living a lie and begin living the truth.

That decision would bring the entire belief system that had been the foundation of my life into question. Accepting this would open up a floodgate of questions I knew I could not answer. For the last twenty-two years, I'd believed in a God that could heal the sick, make the blind see and even raise the dead, but for some reason was powerless or unwilling to answer my simple prayer for change.

A week later, I was back in Brisbane on my way to preach at Toowoomba, about three hundred kilometres west. I'd hired a car again to have time alone to think and to make sure I was able to catch up with Jason on the way back to Brisbane airport. A contemporary version of the Messiah played on the cassette player and the strong, vibrant tones of the artists made the old classics come alive. 'Behold the lamb of God', 'He was despised and rejected', 'I know that my redeemer liveth', 'The trumpet shall sound' and 'The hallelujah chorus' were all having a new impact on me in my raw, agonised emotional state. I played it over and over again while I struggled with my dilemma—what do I do?

Being willing to accept the truth of who I really was could only result in horrific consequences—the loss of everything I held dear and had laboured so hard for. I thought of all the years of sacrifice that had taken me to a place of national prominence and an even more greater future. Being honest meant I would lose it all: my marriage, daughters, ministry, business, career, reputation and friends. So many people would be hurt and, I knew, there was no-one in my world, not even one of them, who would ever understand or support my decision. One after another, the consequences of choosing to be real knocked me like waves in a thunderous surf as I drove through the tablelands towards the mountains in front of me.

What about my darling girls? They might reject me forever or Helen may forbid them to see me. I couldn't imagine they would react any other way. How could they ever love a man who had turned his back on God and was a homosexual? The outcome was both frightening and heart-breaking. I was angry, so angry at being forced to make such a decision. It just wasn't fair. I longed for someone, somewhere, to understand and comfort me. I wept as the cassette moved onto the next track 'Every valley shall be exalted, and mountains made low and the crooked made straight.' No matter what the price, I could no longer live a lie.

I entered Jason's flat with a different attitude that Monday morning. During our times together and on every call, I had always tried to make him laugh and lift him out of the difficulties he was going through. Jason could tell something was wrong. He walked into the kitchen to make a drink but I called him back.

'I have to tell you something,' I said, pulling him over to sit with me on the lounge, knowing how ludicrous my words would sound.

'You know you asked me if I'd leave my wife and family for you? Well, I've made my decision. I love you, Jason, I want to be with you. I'm planning to leave Helen and the girls.' He was silent, obviously shocked by the radical move that only a week ago I'd so strongly opposed. I wanted Jason to embrace me and say the words I desperately needed to hear, 'I love you, too, we'll work through this together,' but that never came.

'There's more I have to tell you. I want to be totally honest with you,' I continued to confess, feeling I could now trust him with this information. 'I'm a preacher, not a sales representative, and the reason I travel so much is because I'm an evangelist. I've fought my homosexuality all my life and I don't want to anymore. I want to be with you.'

Jason chuckled. 'You're not the first priest I've had an affair with!' he said. This was not what I needed to hear and I wanted to correct his misinterpretation of who I really was. I was not a priest, nor was I going to have an affair, but clarifying these issues was unimportant at this stage. For a moment Jason's face registered regret that he'd asked the question a week earlier. I wanted understanding and empathy but he seemed to back away a little as he spoke.

'I'll need time,' he said, 'twelve months. It's too quick.'

'That's perfect,' I replied having already thought out a strategy, 'I need twelve months to get things set up for Helen and the girls so they have support and as little trauma as possible. I'll get things organised and then just disappear into the woodwork. People will never know what happened; they will think I've had a breakdown or something.' We talked more about what we would have to do to make this happen and I could see that he was actually considering a future together—it was a dream come true.

Time spent with Jason always went quickly and this hour seemed like only minutes. Driving off to the airport I felt great relief and excitement.

The next few weeks were a nightmare of roller-coaster emotions. One minute I'd feel the exhilarating pinnacle of being in love only to plummet into the depths of grief. Being with Helen and the girls was torment, as I was constantly reminded of what I would lose and that the moments of joy together, even sharing breakfast, would be no more. When feelings of grief overwhelmed me, I'd make a quick exit outside or into the bedroom in order to stop the tears and gain composure, knowing I could never let them see the emotions that were tearing me apart.

I spoke to Jason at every available opportunity. Some nights I called after preaching, or I'd find excuses to go to the shops so I could ring from a public phone booth, or from the airport, always trying to fit calls into his schedule, knowing he could never call me. Sometimes I'd write letters or send cards that spoke longingly about our future together, telling him how much he meant to me. (Years later these letters would be instrumental in bringing his memory back after six months' hospitalisation for a brain tumour.)

It was 7pm on a Friday night and I was leaving the next morning to fly out to preach for Pastor Phil Hills at Richmond Temple in Melbourne, another one of the thriving congregations of the Assemblies of God. Helen and I had spent the last twelve hours in the office ploughing through administration and putting the final touches to the promotion of our second church study tour for pastors and leaders to the United States, which already looked likely to be a greater success than the previous one. The girls had called several times asking when we'd be home, so Helen made a quick call before leaving the office to let them know we were going to Pizza Hut for dinner. The girls were waiting excitedly in the driveway, dancing and acting silly, as usual.

At the restaurant we sat down and ordered. Nothing ever changed; Hannah wanted ham and pineapple pizza; Bek ate Supreme with us, no anchovies or olives; Coke for the girls and one glass of Riesling each for Helen and me. Never more than one glass. It was halfway through the meal when I lost control. Looking around at my wonderful family, thinking about the pain I'd cause and how much I'd miss them, the suppressed grief of the last few weeks burst like a dam, refusing to be bottled up any longer.

Helen and the girls looked at me in a confused but sympathetic way as I began to sob and placed my head in my hands, embarrassed at this public display. Helen glanced around quickly to see if other diners had noticed. She took a firm hold of my hand and the girls inquired, 'Are you all right, Daddy? Don't cry!'

'You've all made such tremendous sacrifices for the ministry, and I'm not going to ask it of you any more,' I said, between the gasps. 'I'm planning on finishing up in about twelve months. I can't do this any more, it's too much for all of us,' I continued, trying not to sob too loudly. God only knows why I said that, but how else could I explain this unprecedented display of emotion? What I'd said was half-true but it wasn't something I'd intended revealing. Helen and the girls were worried that I was on the verge of a nervous breakdown. Nothing more was said but everyone knew something was wrong—drastically wrong. Helen had suspected for a while that something wasn't right and, during the heat of a recent argument, confronted me with the words, 'You're planning on leaving us, aren't you?' A woman's sixth sense is rarely, if ever, wrong.

My plan was to set up Every Believer Evangelism to be self-sufficient, thus creating an income to support Helen and the girls—an insane plan in hindsight. Now I was beginning to wonder if I could actually make it through the twelve months.

When I returned from Melbourne, I threw myself into the never-ending administration in the office. On Friday afternoon, Helen and I were trying to get as much accomplished as possible because the following week we'd both be at the Assemblies of God National Conference in Sydney. Needing a break from the office, I suggested that I do the banking. Finding a discreet phone box, I tried unsuccessfully to call Jason and when I returned an hour later, Helen was gone. This was not unusual as she was always running around organising printing, mail-outs, et cetera. During the week I'd written a letter to Jason telling him again how much I loved him and how I couldn't wait for us to be together. I'd kept it at the back of my diary to await its final edit. With no-one to interrupt me, I thought I'd put the final touches to it, then post it, but it was gone from its hiding place. I panicked and searched frantically, exploring every possible place in my briefcase. What could have happened to it? All this pressure, I'm losing my memory, I thought, I'm sure it was here. Where could I have put it? My mind was in a confused state when Helen appeared at the door with the letter in her hand.

'What does this mean? What are you planning on doing? What about us?' she yelled repeatedly, waving the evidence in front of me. The look of anger, horror and betrayal on her face was frightening. 'I don't know,' was the only response I could come up with, knowing being honest with myself had been difficult enough, and being truthful with her was impossible at this time. I shielded myself behind the desk thinking she would hit me at any moment when, suddenly, she passed out and collapsed on the office floor. I quickly moved around to revive her, patting her on the face and hands. Should I get a doctor? How would I explain this? Repercussions, consequences and solutions ran through my mind in a matter of seconds. After a couple of minutes, Helen regained consciousness and acting like a mad woman, immediately pulled away from me, her eyes flashing with rage. I tried desperately to calm her but my empty words were useless. Within seconds she was out of the office and I followed her as she disappeared down the stairs to her car. I watched, terrified, as the wheels spun out on the gravel and her car sped off down the road. I ran upstairs to the office to call Jason. Thank God he was home.

'Something's happened,' I said immediately after his 'hello'. 'Helen's found a letter I'd written to you.'

'What did it say?' Jason's responded immediately, and when I repeated the phrases about my love for him and our future together, he only said one word, 'Fuck!'

'I've got to go, Jason. I'll call you later, okay?' My head was spinning as I drove home wondering what I'd encounter. Helen wasn't home.

'Where's Mummy?' the girls inquired. I assured them she'd be home soon but feared she'd had an accident, or driven off one of the coastal cliffs. I knew she was capable of anything in her hysterical state. 'We had an argument,' I said, trying to prepare the girls for the worst. For a moment, in my mind, I saw myself with a dead wife, living as a sole parent.

Rebekah and Hannah knew a quarrel was nothing unusual and even though Helen and I usually kept our disagreements out of sight, they had witnessed more than one hostile argument. I made frantic phone calls to the places I thought she might have gone but couldn't track her down.

Even though I knew I didn't deserve to have any prayers answered, I prayed with all my heart she'd be okay and was greatly relieved when she arrived home two hours later.

It was good I'd told the girls we'd had an argument as they were on their best behaviour thinking that Mum's tears, silence and irrational behaviour resulted from our 'domestic'. The rest of the evening Helen and I gave each other a wide berth while the girls played quietly in their rooms. We didn't speak to each other during the night and sleep was spasmodic. We were in the same bed but miles apart. In the morning I took the opportunity to get out of the house and prepare Sunday's sermon at the office.

Now my cover was blown, I planned to leave as soon as possible, but knew it would take a few days to organise. What a hypocrite you are, I thought to myself as I attempted to gather my thoughts for the sermon. This would be my last opportunity to preach, my final words to the church must be significant so I spent hours thinking about the sermon, which also ensured I was out of the house as long as possible. When I arrived home later that afternoon, Helen and I agreed to make home as normal as possible, for the girls' sake, and refused to talk any more about what my plans till after the weekend.

At church the next morning we greeted and hugged our friends before the service, endeavouring to demonstrate that everything was normal. Internally, we were both in chaos but only the most perceptive would have noticed anything unusual. I had a strong feeling, though, that Helen had spoken to someone. Our friends maybe, or the Pastor? Of course there was a double standard in what I was about to do but, surely, if there was anyone who knew I had tried everything it was God Himself. He wouldn't condemn me for the message I was about to preach. I knew that what I was going to preach wasn't coming from anger or reaction but from a desire to sincerely share what was in my heart. This was not a totally new message as I'd been challenging Pentecostal congregations for some time to begin to show love in a practical way and become involved in social action. Probably for the very first time in my life I was going to boldly speak the truth without fear of opposition or offending the congregation; that didn't matter any more.

I'd been deeply challenged recently, reading of the life of Mother Teresa and the wonderful ministry she'd established in Calcutta and other parts of the world. Her selfless life of sacrifice for the poor, the suffering and dying, was an inspiration and the message I was about to preach had been burning inside me for months. I walked to the platform and placed my sparse notes on the podium, along with my *Bible* and quotations from Mother Teresa. I rarely used extensive notes and delivered my sermons with naturalness and ease, devoid of religious vocabulary (one of the things that contributed to my popularity). People often commented that I was a very 'real' preacher, which made me wonder whether they thought other preachers were fake or 'plastic'.

I began by reading the parable in Matthew 25:31-46 where Jesus spoke of the last days, and used the analogy of a king gathering the nations together to separate them like sheep and goats. Those on his right were welcomed as the king said, 'I was hungry and you fed me, I was thirsty and you gave me drink, I was naked and you clothed me, I was in prison and you visited me.' The people responded, 'When did we see you hungry, or thirsty, or naked or in prison?' The king replied, 'When you did it to any one of my people, no matter how unimportant they seemed, you did it to me.' Those on the left he condemned. 'I was hungry and you didn't feed me, I was thirsty and you didn't give me drink, I was naked and you didn't clothe me, I was in prison and you didn't visit me.' The people responded, 'When did we fail to help you, when were you hungry, thirsty, naked or in prison?' The king replied, 'Whenever you failed to help any of my people, no matter how unimportant they seemed, you failed to do it for me.'

I continued to elaborate on the parable, relating it to the life of Mother Teresa, who founded the Missionaries of Charity in India and walked the streets of Calcutta gathering the lepers, beggars and dying. Pariahs at the bottom of India's caste system, they had no hope of ever being able to change their lot in life. She fed and clothed the people considered unclean and untouchable, showing them the love of God and creating a place of peace for their last days on earth. How far removed this was from the church we knew in Australia and the western world. Over the years I'd seen the church build so many barriers that kept out those in genuine need because they didn't reach the Christian standards. If it did reach out it was always conditional, expecting people to become Christians before they would be helped. The early days of soup kitchens and evangelical efforts of social work meant the homeless and destitute had to listen to the preaching of the gospel before they got their meal and bed. With conviction and passion, I poured out my heart.

I spoke of the need to cease separating people into who was saved or unsaved, who was condemned or redeemed. To no longer judge people by the church's standards and reach out in genuine love to people, asking nothing in return. To break down the walls that divided the church from the world and begin reflecting the true love of God, inclusive of all humankind. It was time to dismantle all the religious rules and regulations that gave Christians a sense of self-righteousness and value each human life as equal in the sight of God. I didn't even consider that I was actually challenging them to love me.

Occasionally I broke down as I implored the church to change. What I was saying was uncomfortable but most people knew I was telling the truth. I could see the responsiveness on the faces and hear the occasional 'Amens' from those with whom my message struck a chord. Concluding the sermon with a prayer, I felt that, during all my years of preaching, I had never felt more like I had spoken from the heart of God.

The next week, Helen and I went to the Assemblies of God National Conference in Sydney. Normally, I would have been looking forward to meeting up with my many friends who'd travelled from every part of Australia for the conference. My one goal this time, though, was to arrange a meeting with the leaders of the denomination and resign from the ministry, without giving all the details for my resignation. Helen had threatened she would expose me if I didn't resign but I also knew I would never preach again. It was over, but I needed time to sort things out. This life of intentional deception was new to me and reinforced in my mind what a bad person I was.

The Assemblies of God had experienced its strongest decade of growth under the leadership of Pastor Andrew Evans so the conference was the largest to date with over 2000 pastors and leaders. Using a secular venue like the Darling Harbour Convention Centre instead of church premises was also something new and progressive. Helen and I endeavoured to maintain obscurity by arriving late at the sessions, leaving early, and sitting at the rear of the auditorium. The attempt to keep a low profile was impossible. No matter how much I tried to hide it, everything about me told people something was drastically wrong, and when people questioned me, saying, 'I'm burnt out, I'm having a breakdown,' was a reasonable and believable response. God knows that was true, the pressure was enormous. I'd arranged to meet with two of my board members and friends Kevin Brett and Paul De Jong, after the evening service, along with the Superintendent of the Assemblies of God, Pastor Andrew Evans and the Assistant Superintendent Pastor, Phil Hills. Helen vanished with Maree, Paul's wife.

Pastor Andrew was a stocky man in his fifties whose build reminded me of my father. He was respected for his wisdom and ability to hold the denomination together when opposing factions threatened to divide it down the middle. His church at that time was one of the largest in Australia and he'd often invited me to preach, a privilege extended only to select preachers. I had a great deal of admiration for Pastor Andrew and was grateful for his support.

Pastor Andrew would later leave the ministry and become a politician, the Honourable Andrew Evans, the founder of the Family First Party when he was elected to the South Australian Legislative Council in 2002. The Family First Party entered federal politics in 2004 with the election of Senator Steve Fielding to the Australian Senate. There was much conjecture about the connections between the party and the Assemblies of God as well as whether we were seeing the birth of a Religious Right in Australia.

Pastor Andrew Evans once said the party's vision was 'to have a social conservative party. Jesus is our hero, he's our saviour, and we worship and love him, but in politics, it's no good me getting up and preaching about my faith, that's the church's role.' In the same interview on the 'Religion Report' on ABC radio, he also said 'we're a family party based on Christian principles, but we're not church-based.' From what I knew of Andrew, I found it hard to see him in the role of aggressive, Bible-bashing, gay hating, moralist. I'd only seen him as a loving, compassionate and gentle man.

Trying to get Pastor Andrew and the other three men away from the crowds at the conclusion of the service seemed to take forever. Very aware of how Jimmy Swaggart had arrogantly refused to stop preaching, I wanted these leaders to know that I was not going to do any fighting and that it was more honourable to offer my resignation than to force the executive to revoke my ordination. I knew how devastating my news would be to Pastor Andrew as I took the small, laminated minister's credential out of my wallet and handed it to him. Trying to maintain some sense of dignity and with what little integrity I had left, I said, 'I don't want you to have to ask for this. I'm giving you this to acknowledge my resignation from the ministry.' My words were already beginning to betray me and exposing more than I wanted at this stage. It was obvious, from the look on everyone's face, that no matter how much I'd tried to keep things under wraps, all were aware of the seriousness of what was about to transpire. But how much did they know? Pastor Andrew looked concerned and a little helpless, and for a moment I saw his fear about a possible scandal for the Assemblies of God in Australia.

A strong, cold wind blustered across the water as the five of us walked over the Darling Harbour bridge to my hotel room for our meeting. Our attempts at conversation failed miserably and we soon resigned ourselves to walking the next ten minutes in silence. I wondered whatever had possessed me to put myself in such a situation.

'I think you all know why I've asked you here tonight. I'm resigning from the ministry. I want to do the right thing and tell you what's been happening.' I began the story in clouded terms about working so hard, feeling burnt out, my loss of conviction and no longer wanting to preach.

'There's more, isn't there?' Paul said, but I quickly protested that there was nothing more to know. With determination in their eyes and a strength in their voices I'd never heard before, one by one they pressured me for more information. I knew for sure now that Helen had talked, and it was absurd to hold back any longer and deliberately lie to my friends.

I looked down at the floor, not wanting to see the reaction in their eyes. 'I've been having an affair with a man,' I stopped, holding my gaze on the floor, waiting for a response, but there was only silence. My opening words began an avalanche of confession. 'I began having homosexual experiences when I was a teenager,' I continued, 'and it was my homosexuality that brought me to God. I really believed He could change me.'

For the next thirty minutes I detailed my futile attempts to change my sexual orientation; the thoughts of suicide; the numerous times I'd sought help; the exorcisms; the ex-gay program; the failure in Orange and confessing to Pastor John; the meeting with the pastors after the incident with Georgio; the encounters that were becoming more frequent; everything, until there was nothing left to tell. The four men sat in astonished silence without interrupting or questioning as I poured out my life, each one having been so close to me but obviously never really knowing me.

'What about this man, where is he?' was the first question, concerned I'm sure that it was someone in a church I'd preached at. Assuring them it was no-one in the church and wanting to protect Jason, I maintained secrecy about his identity and whereabouts. They began to speak of him as if he was the devil himself, sent to tempt me away from a life of righteousness. 'What are you planning to do?' was the next question. 'I don't know,' I replied, focusing my attention on the two dark stains on the green carpet in front of me, wishing somehow I could be lifted out of that room to be with Jason.

'I love Jason,' I said defiantly, my anger rising as I heard them speak judgementally about a person they didn't actually know. But I was also thinking that there might be some truth in their belief that the devil was using Jason to destroy the work God had given me to do. It seemed like my life had been one continuous fight with the devil.

Each pleaded with me not to leave Helen and to continue fighting my homosexual desires, reminding me of the consequences of such a decision. Hell was the final outcome. It was nearly midnight when Pastor Andrew finished by saying, 'Well, we believe that God's power is greater than sin and if you truly repent and confess then God can set you free.'

Pastor Phil then added, 'It's been proven that habits can be changed in twenty-one days. You just need to be determined, you can change this.' Obviously they were all out of their depth. Pastor Andrew was telling me God would perform a miracle if I let Him, and Pastor Phil was giving me a trite little personal development tip from Robert Schuller's self-help book. The words were clichéd and empty to me.

Fuck, didn't you listen to anything I just said in the last thirty minutes? I thought, Jason's language already in my internal dialogue. I've repented and done everything possible to try and change. The four men prayed for me, asking God to heal, save and forgive me. I wasn't praying, I knew it was useless. I'd spent the last twenty-two years doing that.

Helen returned soon after the men departed and we said nothing as she retired to the bedroom. I lay on the lounge and attempted to turn my mind off by watching the meaningless, second-rate shows and infomercials on all-night television, but all I could think of was Jason and wondering how I was going to get out of this incredible mess.

The next day I took Helen to a doctor, as we'd been living at breaking point for several days now and the stress was affecting her blood pressure. I found a surgery at a north shore shopping centre and we sat in the reception room, flicking through the glossy women's magazines, waiting for the first available female doctor. When Helen emerged from the consultation room, the doctor scowled at me as she gave me the prescription for Helen's Valium. I was shocked at the obvious contempt but knew I deserved it.

Late in the afternoon, we drove back to Terrigal. It was a silent journey. I couldn't think of anything to say, as any subject except the pressing issue would have been trivial. As we drove, I tried to think of strategies to sort out the mess I'd created.

Helen and I decided it was best to leave the girls with the friends they'd been staying with. When we arrived home we immediately retreated to opposite ends of the house, she to the kitchen and me to the bedroom to unpack the suitcases. Jason was all I could think about. I so wanted to be with the man I loved. It was driving me crazy thinking about him and the situation I'd created. I finished unpacking the suitcase, then immediately began packing it again. I couldn't stay another minute. Helen came into the bedroom as I was closing the lid.

'What are you doing?' she asked.

'I've got to go, I need time to think. Time alone. I'll be gone for a few days. I'll call you,' I said, as I pushed past her.

'You're going to be with him. You're not coming back, are you?' she screamed. The look of abandonment on her face was dreadful.

The first part of her accusation was right. I had to get to Brisbane so I could be with Jason. I desperately needed to see him, be with him and talk to him. I needed Jason's support and I needed it now. As I drove down the freeway again to Sydney, I thought it strange, considering all that had happened in the last few days. I no longer cried or felt guilty. There was just a constant overwhelming feeling of stress and pain. At the airport I parked in the short-term car park. I knew there'd only be one Brisbane flight at such a late hour so I ran into the Ansett terminal in case I needed to use my Golden Wing status. The last flight to Brisbane had left ten minutes before and the attendant, seeing how stressed I was, suggested I try the other airline. At this time, Australia had a two-airline agreement and the flights always left within minutes of each other. I ran to the other terminal but missed the Qantas flight by five minutes. I was so used to turning to God and praying in times of trouble, but now it was as though God was stopping me. As if the two spiritual worlds were at war and I was in the middle of the battle. Nothing seemed logical or rational any more. It felt like at any minute I would lose my mind; my life was out of control.

I decided to sleep in the car then catch the first flight out in the morning. Not yet ready for sleep, I drove back into the city. The only place I considered going was Oxford Street, the gay centre of Sydney. It had been over twenty years since I'd visited any establishments there and I thought it would be a place of refuge. A telephone booth was outside the Oxford Hotel and I rummaged through my wallet for change. It was just after ten o'clock. I dialled the well-memorised number and waited for Jason to answer, desperately hoping he was home. It had been impossible to ring him for several days. It rang out but I tried again—just in case he was home but sleeping. Finally, after twenty rings he answered.

'It's me,' I responded after his 'hello'. 'I need to talk with you,' I said and commenced relaying the events of the past twenty-four hours, telling him about my confession of everything to the leaders of the denomination and that I'd just missed the flights to Brisbane by minutes. 'My days as a preacher are over, I'll catch the first flight tomorrow and we can spend a few days together. It looks like we'll be together sooner than we planned.'

'No,' Jason responded quickly, 'I don't want you to come up now.'

What was he saying? It didn't make sense. I pleaded and begged, trying to make him understand the seriousness of the situation and how desperate I was. 'No, I don't want you to come up, it's too soon,' he kept saying. He was unsympathetic and I wondered how he could be so callous, insensitive and unfeeling.

'Jason,' I said, confused by the illogical rejection from the man I loved, 'I've told them everything, Jason, there's no turning back now. Please let me come up to Brisbane!' His 'no' was so definite. 'Jason, this is probably the worst situation of my life and if you can't be there for me now, in my greatest time of need, what hope is there for our future?' Still the resounding 'no'. Jason's rejection in my moment of helplessness angered me. There was only one course of action left: to threaten him with an ultimatum. 'If you can't be there for me, Jason, I'm going to have to say goodbye now, and if it's goodbye, it's goodbye for good. No more letters or phone calls, Jason, it's finished.' I felt helpless, I had so little bargaining power.

My ultimatum only strengthened his resolve. 'No, you can't come up,' was his final comment.

'Goodbye, Jason. I do love you,' was all I could say, trying not to cry pathetically. I slowly placed the receiver back into its holder.

For a moment everything stopped. Colours bleached from my vision. The noise of the traffic and street became silence like the white noise of space. Like I'd just been knocked unconscious in the boxing ring and my body, in slow motion, was on its way to the floor. Locked in this moment, I stood motionless in the phone booth for what seemed like five minutes, feeling like I was about to pass out; wanting to cry, scream, anything to ease the intense mixture of hopelessness and anger. Finally, jolted by an abusive comment from someone wanting to use the phone, I mumbled an apology and moved aside. What would I do now? The ministry was gone, my marriage irreconcilable and any possibility of a future with Jason had disappeared as well. It seemed like the war was over and I was defeated. The devil had won.

The first open door was the Oxford Hotel at Taylor Square. Taking in the scene around me, I moved through the crowd towards the bar, ordered a glass of wine and wondered if I could ever feel at home in a place like this. It was dark, the dance music pumped through the sound system, men chatted, others kissed and embraced, many stood alone looking hungrily for someone to be with for the night. If only things had worked out with Jason, I thought, then I'd be happy. I don't want to be a gay man—alone. Suddenly I realised I was the only one in the entire bar of two hundred men who was drinking wine so I skolled it down and ordered a beer. The mixture of drinks and my lack of tolerance to alcohol had a quick effect. My head spun as I stumbled onto the street.

I began walking. Nowhere in particular, just walking; walking and thinking. Thinking over and over again and wondering how I could get this thing I called my life back into any sort of order. Amongst the confusion came a moment of clarity as I thought about what I was losing. I'd made a terrible mistake to think that Jason would bring me happiness. How stupid I'd been to trade Helen, the girls, my ministry and even salvation, for Jason. Jason had been the devil's bait and I'd taken it hook, line and sinker.

I remembered that two of my friends, who were the leaders of Youth Alive in Victoria and Queensland, were staying in a hotel in nearby Kings Cross and hoped they would have returned from the evening meeting at the conference and be able to help me. Staggering down Darlinghurst Road, I ignored the comments from the young hookers leaning against the sandstone walls of East Sydney Technical College. My friends were horrified to see me drunk, reeking of alcohol and cigarette smoke.

I sobbed, 'I want to come back to God and work things out with Helen and the girls if they'll have me.' I pleaded with who I thought were two of my closest friends. 'Through all our years of friendship I've never asked anything of you before. I've fought this thing all my life and I'm going to give it one more go. So I ask you please, never let me go, I need your support.'

The feeling of total hopelessness was overwhelming. I collapsed on the lounge and asked if Paul could come and pick me up. Paul arrived within minutes and when I saw the warmth of his smile and his look of concern, I fell into his arms.

'I'm so sorry, I'm so sorry, I'm so sorry,' I cried repeatedly. The only thing in my mind was the pain I'd caused so many people. How could this terrible mess ever be made right?

Paul drove me to his house on the north shore and his wife, Maree, met us at the door, her kind face reflecting the pain and helplessness we all felt. I was to see that expression repeatedly on many faces over the next weeks and months. Falling into the bed she'd made for me on the lounge, the combination of exhaustion and alcohol quickly put me to sleep.

In the morning, everyone's program was disrupted. The conference was in full swing and Paul and Maree had already made necessary phone calls to re-adjust their schedules. I asked Paul if he'd arrange a meeting with my friends, as I wanted to tell them what had happened face-to-face. During the lunch break at the conference, ten people travelled in a convoy of two cars to the meeting in Paul's lounge room. Even though they lived in Melbourne, Brisbane and Adelaide, we saw each other regularly and were bonded by age, outlook and our desire to serve God. We were much more than peers, these were my dear and closest friends, like brothers who deserved to hear the truth from me and I needed to ask their forgiveness for bringing shame on the ministry.

Amidst my admissions of sin and failure, I told them of my willing-ness to work towards restoration and asked for their support to help me through the difficulties. I saw the strange reaction my confession brought to some in the room. Most looked overwhelmed but I also saw discomfort, even fear, on the faces of others. Possibly I wasn't the only one in that room who'd committed adultery or had struggled with a sexual addiction. My confession was too close to the bone, as they saw the possible outcome of what they had successfully concealed to date. In different circumstances, it may have been them in my seat. But of course, their fall would have been less repulsive, being hetero-sexual. After my confession, they laid hands on me, praying God would heal me, each one promising their support to help me through this crisis.

Having put Pastor Andrew through such a harrowing experience two nights before, I felt he also needed an explanation for my decision. I told him I wanted to change, get things right with my family and that I'd already said goodbye to Jason. He looked relieved but I also sensed doubt.

'If you're genuine in your repentance, there must be a public confession,' Pastor Andrew said. A public confession was designed to test the sincerity of a fallen minister's repentance, and had the added benefit of putting the fear of God in the congregation should anyone think of going astray. The thought of standing in front of a congregation and publicly confessing my sin was the most horrific thing I could imagine. Immediately that awful, humiliating image of Jimmy Swaggart weeping on national television came into my mind. But at this stage, I was willing to do anything to make amends. I was completely broken and if the leaders of the denomination had said to me, 'Walk off that cliff,' I would have done it. There was nothing left in me to resist.

CHAPTER 16

Damage control

Driving back to Terrigal on the freeway for the third time in as many days—passing through the towering sandstone cuttings, bushland and over the bridges—gave me time to continue my personal stocktake. Already I was missing Jason terribly.

Helen and I had spoken on the phone about my turnaround and she, like many others, felt God had answered her prayers. It was impossible to think how I could ever make it up to her for the suffering I'd caused and what lay ahead. Could my daughters ever respect me again? The terrible consequences I'd been afraid of were slowly looming as very real probabilities but I could only tackle one thing at a time.

My welcome home was subdued. Helen and I discussed the details of what to do over the next few days and how to approach things with our girls. Exhausted, Helen and I retired unusually early, around nine o'clock. We dressed for bed and I put on the flannelette nightshirt Helen had made me; every year for the last six she had managed to produce a new one to keep me warm on winter nights, practical but certainly not sexy. Our usual custom of a kiss and cuddle once under the blankets was dispensed with and I lay facing the window on the left-hand side of the bed with my back to Helen. It wasn't that I didn't want to touch or hold her, but that I felt I had no right to. Being alone together in the silence was uncomfortable.

The quietness of the night was occasionally broken by the sound of a car speeding down the hill in front of our house. The light of an almost full moon illuminated our bedroom, shining through the slats of the vertical blinds, creating shadow lines across the bed. Lying awake in the brightness, feeling the familiarity of being in bed with Helen, away now from all the activity, I was overcome by a feeling of utter failure. I thought about what I'd done to Helen and the girls, the people who might lose faith because of my transgression, the humiliation of everyone knowing my sin, the way I'd discredited the ministry and how unworthy I was of anyone's love, even God's. What could I have been thinking, believing Jason and I could have had a life together? How could I have been so stupid and deceived? I was a failure as a husband, father and servant of God.

My eyes filled with tears until the room swam and became a pool of light and indistinguishable features. I began crying until my entire body shook uncontrollably. Helen turned around from her reclusive position, lost in her own thoughts, to hold me. She'd never seen me cry like this or ever seen a man so broken. Her touch was meant to be comforting but it only increased my pain. I wanted to pull away. The shouting, yelling, and screaming I deserved never came—there was no hatred, no anger or resentment, only her forgiveness and amazing unconditional love.

Finally, the words Helen so rightly deserved to hear came out. 'I'm sorry, I'm sorry, I'm sorry, I'm sorry, I'm so sorry.' I repeated them over and over again. 'I'm sorry, I'm so sorry.' It was all I could say between the sobbing. I knew, though, that no matter how many times I said it, it would never repair the damage or take away the pain. 'I've made such a mess of our lives,' I said as she pulled me even closer. Over the last twenty-four hours I'd confessed to several people but neglected the one person who needed more than anyone to hear those words. How selfish of me to once again be engrossed in what was happening to me. I could not begin to imagine the hell she was going through: the pain, sense of betrayal, anger and confusion. She would be questioning her own womanhood, even wondering what she could have done to counteract what had happened or if she had possibly contributed to my straying.

Her words were simple yet powerful, 'I forgive you.' I slept, in the arms of a woman who showed me a sacrificial love I'd never thought possible in a human being. Helen's resilience was one of her great qualities, but that night I became aware of something emanating from her spirit that was truly divine. Helen was still holding me as I woke to the morning sun lighting the sky and our bedroom, but consciousness only brought weeping again.

Over the next few days, seeing various friends from the coast who came to visit, looking at me with sympathetic eyes, not knowing what to say or do, only reduced me to tears again. News of me having a 'moral fall' was spreading like wildfire and Helen protected me from as many inquiring phone calls as possible as we made preparations for the Sunday morning confession. A phone call came from a pastor I knew in Perth. I was naturally guarded as he questioned me about what had happened, then he mentioned Jason's name, age and the fact that he lived in Brisbane. Only four men knew those details and all had sworn secrecy for my sake and the family's protection. Someone had blabbed and I was angry at the betrayal of confidence I'd been promised. I doubted now that there was any chance of keeping the more personal details quiet. Even though I was only well-known in Christian circles, I knew the media's anti-Christian bias; their thirst for sensationalism would be all they'd need to make a mockery of me. With a couple of sordid details it would not be difficult to turn me into Australia's Jimmy Swaggart or Jimmy Bakker. The nightmare was becoming worse.

Helen went to pick up the girls from our friend's house where they'd been staying and brought them home.

'We need to have a family conference,' I said, as we all sat down in the lounge room together. They were incredibly difficult words for a father to tell his children, especially to these girls who loved, respected and admired their father so much. I clouded my dialogue in general terms.

'Sometimes we make mistakes. I made a promise to your mother when we got married and I've broken it.' I didn't mention a person or give any indication of my homosexuality, knowing that awful disclosure was for a more appropriate time in the future—hopefully never. I told them about the events and changes that would take place, hoping they'd be able to survive the ordeal with as little damage as possible. Their expression told me the meagre explanation was totally inadequate, and only added to their confusion, as they were unable to ask the questions our little meeting had raised in their minds. One last confession to make—to our home church congregation on Sunday.

After dinner on Saturday night, knowing that tomorrow would possibly be the darkest day of my life, I had to do something to escape the pressure and get out of the house.

'I'm going for a walk. I'll be back in about an hour,' I said, trying to ignore the fear on Helen's face. Will he return home, will he kill himself, will he call Jason, or will he have sex with a man again? She knew that in my state of mind there was a very real possibility of any of these happening. I walked passed the shops, down on the beach then up to the top of the bluff called the Skillion, a rock formation with a sheer drop of several hundred feet. I'd left the street lights behind but standing in the darkness on the cliff's edge there was enough light to make out the white froth of the wild surf breaking on the rock ledge below, and thought of the people who'd taken their lives there. Sitting on the edge of the cliff I cursed the day I was born. I cursed my homosexuality I'd tried to change all my life but had now destroyed me. All I would have to do was stand up, take a running leap and it would be finished in a manner of seconds; the final thud on the rocks would end my suffering. I knew the Catholic church taught that suicide was a mortal sin which meant going straight to hell but I was hoping that my God was a bit more understanding and forgiving. For half an hour

I weighed up the outcomes of either jumping or facing the consequences. My death would be a cowardly act relieving me of my pain but would only create more heartache for my family. Surely they'd suffered enough. As I walked back home I wondered if I had the courage to do what must be done tomorrow.

A public confession was a rare occurrence, the worst fear of any Pentecostal minister, and was intended to be the first step towards healing and restoration. Jimmy Swaggart's humiliating public confession was the only one I'd seen. Many had questioned his sincerity and the authenticity of the tears since he was about to be exposed anyway but I knew that tomorrow would not be an act for me. Like everything we do in Pentecostal churches there is always a biblical precedent and the public confession was no exception. When speaking of those that ministered in the church the Apostle Paul said, in 1 Timothy 5:20, 'Those who sin are to be rebuked publicly so that others may take warning.' I was told to skip the exact details of what happened and give a general confession of moral failure, acknowledging I'd sinned, then repent before the congregation and resign from the ministry. That day will remain in my memory forever. It was the day that, despite already losing so much, I handed over my last possession—my self-respect. I publicly humiliated my wife, my children and myself. Something died inside me that day.

After the confession a few close friends joined us for lunch. I must have looked so pathetic as I could do little except walk around like a zombie, disappearing frequently into the bedroom to lie down, the feeling of nausea causing me to bump into furniture on the way. The weeping began again that Sunday night as we lay in bed. There was no way of shutting off the thoughts of my downfall and also the loss of Jason. I knew I shouldn't be thinking of him but I was missing him so much. The emotional drain took its toll and daily I sank lower into an abyss of self-loathing and depression. For the next three weeks, I cried myself to sleep every night. Waking in the morning brought another wave of grief that usually lasted about thirty minutes while I tried to gather the courage to get out of bed, place my feet on the floor and face the challenges of the day. I wondered at times if it would ever stop and I felt like I was teetering on the edge of a complete emotional breakdown.

Initially, my friend Paul called me at least once a day to see how I was and to offer encouragement and support. He genuinely listened and I could be totally honest with him without receiving rebuke or religious platitudes. He'd asked me every day, 'Did you call Jason?' knowing this was a continuous threat. One day I had to say, 'Yes, … just to see how he was going,' I said, trying to justify my weakness. I knew Paul's strong words were what I needed to get me back on track.

Because of the success of Every Believer Evangelism, for the first time in our lives, Helen and I had been able to save $5000 towards a deposit for our first home, but we desperately needed a break to try and recuperate. The ten days in Phuket, Thailand, were wonderful and we enjoyed lazing around the pool, watching the sun set over the horizon silhouetted by the palms, eating lots of seafood and satays on the warm tropical nights, sightseeing and shopping. For Helen and I it was like a second honeymoon, only this time it was like a real one—it was just the two of us. But then we had to come home and face reality.

After returning to Australia, over the months, I had to face the difficult fact that my friends in the ministry I'd pleaded with to help and support me had completely deserted me. I never heard from them again. Certainly no personal visits, and not even phone calls, or letters. Being cut off so rapidly and exactly was something that was very difficult to deal with and it was confusing to determine why. I tried to develop answers to justify why the people who I thought were closer to me in many ways than my family were now treating me as if I no longer existed. I began with the good excuses. Maybe they are too busy with their own churches and ministries. I knew how busy it gets. Possibly they were giving me some space, or was it that they were personally finding the whole thing too difficult to deal with? There were other possible reasons I had to face as well. Was it that I'd fallen in love with a man instead of a woman? Or they had their own secret sins and being with me was too much of a reminder of the consequences they might soon face? It could have been what I knew to be true, that like most Pentecostal ministers, they were homophobic. Maybe their biggest fear was that any association with me might encourage people to think they were secretly homosexual as well. Over time I was to discover this was always a bit of a litmus test. Almost without exception, those who could spend time with me and treat me with respect despite my homosexuality were the people with no issues who were comfortable with their sexuality, while those who were aggressive or rejected me had deep personal secrets and issues to resolve.

Thoughts of Jason and the temptation to call him finally began to subside. Now, I was faced with trips to the unemployment office. I stood in the queue with third- and fourth-generation welfare recipients, being asked questions such as, 'What work have you been doing?', 'What skills and experience have you got?' and 'Why did you leave the ministry?' and other personal questions by someone who was half my age and who could never comprehend what it was like to try and pick up the pieces of your life and begin again at forty.

I began seeing a Christian psychologist to gain some professional help. Being a Christian psychologist, he was holding on to the belief that there was some cause for my homosexuality such as being sexually abused as a child or that there were problems with my relationship with my parents. After digging and digging for several sessions and finding nothing he told me that I must have suppressed the cause. At $100 a session and with no income it eventually got too much financially and emotionally, so I accepted his diagnosis that I was actually bisexual with a homosexual addiction and left to try and sort it out for myself. I was doing everything that a committed Christian should do, trying to get my life back on track: reading my Bible, praying daily, fighting any thoughts that came into my mind, but the most difficult thing to deal with was the looks on people's faces when I went to church on Sundays. It was often like living the humiliation over and over again.

Through the grapevine, I heard that an official decree had been circulated around Australia saying, 'Due to a moral lapse, the National Executive has revoked Tony Venn-Brown's credential. The withdrawal is permanent.' I couldn't understand how the National Executive could withdraw my credential as I had actually already resigned. Wasn't that what I was doing when I handed Pastor Andrew my preacher's licence months earlier? The wording to me only created further humiliation.

I'd heard nothing directly from the National Executive so on 18 June 1991, I wrote a lengthy letter communicating my disappointment at how things were being handled:

> Dear Andrew and the National Executive,
> This is a very sad letter that I feel I must write. Nine weeks have passed since I confessed to you and Pastor Phil, resigning as a minister of the Assemblies of God. What have those days been like? The worst days of my life.
>
> The initial experiences left me devastated. I have totally confessed my sin to my Board of Trustees and also to you and Phil so there are no more secrets, nothing more to tell, you know everything. There are very few ministers that have wiped the slate that clean but I knew it was my only hope of change.
>
> To tell Helen face to face of my deception and betrayal was demoralising as was telling my girls their father was an adulterer, knowing they would also suffer the stigma of my sin but the worst of all was to stand before the congregation and confess to them. Words could never describe the emotions that preceded and followed the event.
>
> For days afterwards I was in a state of shock and for three weeks I

wept constantly through the day. A phone call, someone touching me, anything triggered it off. For many days my Christian experience was hanging in the balance and it wouldn't have taken much to push me over the edge, a phone call from the previous relationship, hearing the gossip regarding my fall, knowing the confidence I had given people by confessing to them was betrayed. By God's grace I am still a Christian.

Losing all the years of hard work building Every Believer Evangelism was devastating. Being obedient to God's will over the years has meant great sacrifice for me but especially for Helen and the girls, not out of a sense of guilt or not trying to buy God's approval but because I genuinely wanted to serve the church. You are well aware of all that has meant and now after fifteen years of serving God what have we got? Nothing. We lost the ministry, our car, our means of employment, we don't own a home, and all our savings are gone.

I wanted to let you know some of the things we've been through in the last nine weeks and ask what the Assemblies of God is going to do to help us. I waited for a letter or phone call but nothing came. Your silence has spoken volumes to me. You said you were committed to my restoration but your actions say another thing. Tell me you hate me, you never want to see me again, tell me you love me but please don't be silent.

People within our denomination and other friends of mine have asked the embarrassing question. 'What's the Assemblies of God doing for you?' What could I say? The truth is, nothing. I understand you are angry and hurt but so am I. Every feeling you have about the situation I have also, but in a far greater way, because it's my fault. I'm responsible.

What about Helen? For the past seven years she's lived the life of a solo parent, coping with the pressures of managing the family and office while I was away preaching in Assemblies of God churches. She's the innocent victim in all this. Reject me if you want to but she doesn't deserve to be ignored this way.

You've missed some precious opportunities to bond Helen and I,
Rebekah and Hannah into the Assemblies of God family. The initial
weeks of incredible vulnerability when we desperately needed love and
acceptance, not rejection and judgement are gone now and we're left
feeling like you've failed us.

I tried to do everything the right way by confessing to you, to the
church. I've forsaken the relationship, I'm seeing a Christian psychol-
ogist, I go to church, pray and read my Bible everyday. I haven't run
away, I do want to change.

Please don't write this letter off as the ravings of a bitter ex-evan-
gelist, please do something to help us.
Sincerely in Christ,
Tony Venn-Brown

I was sure I'd get a response from my letter so I waited. But after a
couple of weeks and no letter, I called and spoke briefly to Pastor
Andrew. A letter arrived the next week:

8 July 1991
Dear Tony
Greetings in the Name of the Lord.

I apologise for not writing to you concerning the decision of the
National Executive.

I shared with the brethren about my meeting with you and your
confession of immorality of a serious nature over an extended period of
time and the meeting resolved that 'in view of the self confessed repeat-
ed acts of moral failure over an extended period of many years, Tony
Venn-Brown's ministerial credentials be revoked immediately and that
we do not recommend his return to the ministry.' I explained to the
Executive that this was your desire, also having clearly expressed to us
that you saw no future for yourself as a minister of the gospel but only

desired to be rehabilitated with your family and as a Christian. And so on that basis, and also the disciplinary statement made by the conference in 1983, where repeated acts of immorality almost surely meant that such behaviour would make it very difficult for a candidate who has a problem for many years to ever take responsibility as a preacher of the gospel.

This may seem difficult for you Tony, and I mentioned on the phone, the 'may' was placed in this statement indicating that, with God all things are possible, but as we see things now, we all felt that maybe the ministry was not something for you.

May God bless you.

> *Your brother in Christ.*
> *Pastor Andrew Evans*
> *General Superintendent*

I couldn't believe the final words on the page in front of me. I knew much of what I'd read was true but it was difficult to comprehend that I was being totally wiped. The realisation that I would never preach again finally hit home. If these men didn't believe there was any hope for me, or that I would ever preach again then why was I putting my family and myself through so much pain, why was I trying to change? Helen stood with me in the lounge room waiting to see what the letter contained. Something snapped inside me and I began to hyperventilate. I tried to speak but nothing came out. I wanted to scream but I'd lost my power of speech. Helen stood helplessly as I paced up and down the room, grunting and making noises like a madman, sat on the lounge, read the letter again, screwed it up, unscrewed it, read it again, screwed it up again, then ran out of the house and drove off with tyres screeching. Anger surged though me as I thought about the hypocrisy of these men making me go through all this and then turning around to say they didn't believe I could ever change. I was condemned to living with the fear of falling back into homosexuality. Where was the redemption or power of God in that? They preached the power of God from the pulpit but were saying another thing to me in this letter. It seemed that they had no faith in my becoming an ex-gay so there was no hope.

I desperately needed someone to talk to but Paul, my single support mechanism, had gone to start Christian Life Centre in Auckland. Sydney was the only place I could think of going. I wanted to lash out and do something to relieve the frustration and anger inside me. I drove to a gay sauna called Ken's that I'd visited a few times when the frustration got too much, a place for quick sex. After undressing in the change room, I placed the towel around me and walked down the stairs into the darkness. The few times I'd visited a sauna, the smells, darkness, oppressive dampness of the steam room and occasional groans of men reaching orgasm were never really pleasant experiences for me. I felt uncomfortable walking up and down the corridors, passing men standing in the doorways of cubicles. As attractive as some of these men were, thoughts of Jason came into my mind—he was still the only man I really wanted even though he'd rejected me. It was difficult to know what I really wanted in the sauna but I knew it was much more than sex. Yes, I needed relief from the pressure, but more importantly I needed a man to connect with, to hold me and touch me or to talk to.

I walked upstairs to the TV lounge. Watching the programs allowed my mind to turn off so that within minutes I'd dozed off. I woke suddenly when another man sat next to me on the lounge. I hadn't planned on sleeping that long and discovered it was nearly 4am. I knew Helen would be distraught and it was time to return home and face the music. It was 5am and the sky was already turning a light grey when I arrived back at Terrigal. I'd decided not to lie about where I'd been or what I'd done. I just wasn't going to talk about it. I was exhausted and needed some rest. I drove quietly into the carport and closed the car door softly, not knowing what reaction I was going to encounter.

At the front door I could see through the window that Helen had fallen asleep in her dressing gown on the lounge. My heart sank at the thought of facing her and so I quietly tried to open the door but the tiny squeak of the unoiled hinge woke her. Helen looked at me and in her eyes there was no anger only compassion and love. She'd read the letter I'd screwed up and thrown away and understood how betrayed I felt. Even though I'd said, on the night of my confession to Pastor Andrew and the others, that I didn't want to preach again, deep down inside that sense of destiny told me that true forgiveness can restore all. Helen understood how important that hope was to me.

Helen's spirit of forgiveness was overwhelming as she smiled and said, 'You must be tired, go and hop into bed and I'll bring you in a cup of coffee.' The place of power she came from, the strength she showed, told me she was not a victim. She was a woman who would not condemn but would desperately do everything possible to save our marriage. Her only other words were 'try to sleep' as she gave me the coffee then got into the other side of the bed to get a couple more hours rest before the girls woke.

Things were never the same again. Even though I was living with my family, I felt totally detached, like something had been severed and could never be reconnected. The man Rebekah and Hannah had known as a devoted, loving father ceased to exist.

Sensing I had given up hope, Helen and the girls made every effort to encourage me, often leaving little notes around the house.

To Daddy,
We love you so much and I really want to thank you for all the hard work you have put into your new job so that we, as a family, can survive. Even though things aren't always great, the best thing is we can forgive and forget. Lots of love Bek XXX.

To Dad,

How are ya? Love ya heaps and heaps and heaps and heaps and heaps (I'd better stop there or there won't be anymore room left to write anything else) etc etc. Hang in there Daddykins, you're doin' a great job. Luv Han.

Dear Precious.

I love you forever. I'll always be here for you. Thanks for looking after us. Much love and kisses.

Your Wifee. XXXX OOOOO.

The notes and expressions of love and support were wonderful but we were fighting a losing battle. All the love and forgiveness they could give would never change the fact that the man they had known was no more. We had all been trying desperately to resurrect a memory.

I'd been able to get a job as a sales representative with a famous Australian landscape photographer and was involved in selling his limited edition prints and organising exhibitions. Realising that there was no hope of ever returning to the ministry, making the effort to be Christian seemed like a façade, but I gave God an ultimatum.

'You've got three months to do a miracle. If you haven't changed me so I'm no longer attracted to men then I'll leave and stop wasting our lives.' I knew deep down what the outcome would be but over the last twenty-two years I'd seen many examples of divine intervention and hoped there might just be an easier way of dealing with the inevitable. For the second time, I was at the point where I could no longer live a lie; this time I would not be swayed again.

I'd seen what had happened to preachers who'd stepped out of the ministry because of immorality or marriage breakdown. I'd even helped a couple of them, like my friend Steve, whose wife had left him. The humiliation and rejection led to hurt and anger, then eventually bitterness and resentment destroyed them like a terminal cancer, eating away at all that had been good in their hearts. It was tragic to watch them become isolated and gather around them others who would feed their negative energy.

I had enough to deal with during the months ahead and, unless checked, those destructive emotions would eventually destroy me also. The next moment in my life was a defining one. One that I've often looked back on and when people have asked me how did you find such peace or how come you still have your sanity, I tell them of this moment when I knew the power of forgiveness would release me to create a better future. I'd read so much about how to let go and now was my opportunity to find it in a profound way myself. Unforgiveness is taking the poison you intended for another. Forgiveness is setting the prisoner free only to realise you were the prisoner. With a conscious act of my will I decided to forgive all my friends who had let me down and the denomination I felt had betrayed me. By letting all that go, I knew I would be free to move on.

It was abnormal for Helen and I to be home the next Sunday night—we were usually at church, but friends had taken the girls. We sat in separate lounges; the Sunday night movie had just begun when the phone rang. I went into the kitchen and answered by reciting our telephone number.

'Hi, it's Jason.' That was all he said. It was all he had to say. The impact was instantaneous and I stood stunned, the emotions of fear and joy I'd felt nine months ago returned in a moment. Jason continued, 'I've just got back from working on Heron Island and I'm staying with my parents in the Hunter Valley. I thought I'd give you a call to see how you are. Can you talk now?'

'No.' I wanted to say much more but it was too risky.

Realising Helen could be listening nearby he suggested, 'Would you like me to give you my number and you can call me?'

'Yes,' I said, quickly grabbing pen and paper.

Our conversation was brief and I tried desperately to make it sound like a normal chat with a friend, knowing Helen's keen hearing would pick up every word.

I folded the piece of paper with Jason's number, put it in my pocket and walked back into the lounge room trying to think of what I'd say if Helen questioned me. When she asked who it was I said it was my friend Chris from Melbourne; getting suspicious, she asked why the conversation was so short.

'Chris had to go, I'm going to call him tomorrow.' Helen didn't pursue it any further, but I knew she felt the energy. Once again she'd lost me.

CHAPTER 17

It's time

Sleep was difficult during that night; the sound of Jason's voice had swiftly ignited the emotions I'd thought were successfully extinguished. I lay awake thinking about him and the very thing I'd given up on— the possibility of us being together. Even with only a few hours' sleep I was unusually sparky the next morning and, attempting to conceal my excitement, left for work early. I stopped at the first public phone box a safe distance from home and rang Jason. It felt awful lying and being devious again but I was already convinced there was no future for Helen and me, it was a lost cause. I just needed the courage to do something about it. Jason answered and we talked briefly, amid moments of cautious silence, summarising events since we'd last spoken. He seemed warm, open and relaxed.

I asked the question I could no longer contain, 'When can I see you, Jason?'

'When are you free?' he replied, the tone of his voice telling me he preferred sooner rather than later.

'I'll leave now, where shall we meet?' I said, then he gave me details of where to get together.

Driving the one-and-a-half hours north to see Jason for the first time in nine months created further exhilaration and anticipation. Even though I'd been thinking of him less and less and had been able to fight the temptation of calling him, he often surfaced in my mind, only to be banished along with any thought that might lead me away from Helen, the girls, and God. It was amazing that he'd actually contacted me after all this time.

Maybe Jason had realised what a mistake he'd made letting go of our love so easily. But I had to be cautious, considering the way he'd treated me when I needed his support so desperately. His influence on me could not be good—it had been less than twenty-four hours since we renewed contact and already I was doing reckless things.

Jason was waiting outside the local post office, his grooming and style impossible to ignore—a striking contrast to the simple country men strolling along the main street in their dirty jeans and checked flannelette shirts. I tried not to show my eagerness as I walked towards him. Jason looked his usual cool self, always in control. We walked about twenty metres along the street to a small café, that served a limited menu of sandwiches, light snacks and cappuccinos made with instant coffee on plastic, imitation-lace tablecloths.

We caught up on our nine months of separation. Apparently, soon after our last phone call, Jason got a job in the Whitsundays, at Heron Island Resort, and was quickly promoted to head of housekeeping. He talked about the dramas with the staff on the island then moved on to the present conflicts happening at home. All his stories revealed his belief that it was always everyone else in the wrong, never Jason. After an hour, his stories began to lose their impetus so I shared briefly the personal hell I'd gone through. Jason gave me little sympathy and seemed to lack any understanding of what had actually occurred.

'Can you drop me home? You can come and see where I'm living,' Jason suggested, after we'd paid the bill. I was keen to be with Jason out of the gaze of the public eye.

Jason's parents were obviously house-proud people who'd spent many hours gardening and painting the weatherboard house to its best, demonstrating the kind of devotion that can only be given by time-rich retirees. They were horse breeders and Jason lived in a flat above a converted barn about forty metres from the rear of the house. We stopped to pat the horses that had come up to the fence near the house. His love for the animals was obvious as he told me of his favourites.

Jason was a meticulous housekeeper and the converted barn reflected, as the Brisbane flat had, his efforts at interior decorating on a budget. Everything was strategically placed, demonstrating an eye for balance; something tall here balanced by something short there. Everything purposefully placed, the ashtray emptied and spotless, all the result of years spent working in five-star hotels. Alone at last, the reserve I'd intended to display disappeared and I moved towards Jason to kiss him.

'Let's take things slowly,' he said, pushing me away. I was amazed at his self-control. It was so frustrating as we'd only had sex once (or was it twice? The trauma had blocked my memory somewhat) and I wanted some physical contact. 'Let's just start seeing each other again if you like,' he commented casually. I knew Jason enjoyed my company and something about the love that I gave, he wanted, but I was also aware I needed to know him better. Could I trust him or would he let me down again?

The thoughts that had formulated in my mind over the last three months were reinforced by the little contact I had with Jason. I am a gay man, I always have been and always will be and I must cease this ridiculous charade of heterosexuality. Helen deserved a husband who would love her completely and I was having difficulty being a devoted father to my girls. They would be better off without me—we were stuck in the quagmire of grief and trauma, incapable of finding new purpose and direction. For six months I'd tried to regain what was lost in our marriage, the three-month ultimatum to God had passed, so now there were no more alternatives. After a month, Jason moved to Newcastle and with my decision firmly fixed in my heart and mind we met up another time. Jason no longer dominated my choices and if he wanted to come with me to Sydney then I considered it a bonus.

'I've accepted the fact I'm a gay man. That's the way I must live so I'm leaving the family. It wouldn't be fair on Helen and the girls to stay on the Central Coast so I'm moving to Sydney. I'm not leaving for you, Jason, I'm leaving because it's the right thing to do. Are you interested in moving to Sydney with me?'

Jason initially, in his guarded way, showed a mild interest at the possibility but within minutes the façade disappeared and he showed eagerness to take the chance.

'I'm leaving in four weeks; will you be ready?' I said, finding momentary assertiveness. Jason was grateful for the opportunity to leave Newcastle and willing to return to the place he'd sworn never to live in again, Sydney. We set the date. I planned to leave after coordinating an exhibition on the Gold Coast for the photographer I worked for.

Once again, I made the most of every moment with the girls, sitting on the lounge with them, holding and kissing them, telling them how much I loved them. They were oblivious to the concealed messages in my renewed affection. There was no guarantee I could ever do this again after what was soon to happen. We were now doing activities as a family for the last time: our final Christmas together, playing I Spy, driving along the Great Western Highway to see Helen's parents in Orange, meals at our favourite restaurants and even shopping for groceries. They never noticed the times my eyes filled with tears.

I was incapable of any more confrontation in my life, and I felt my only course of action was to disappear without any speeches, explanations, arguments or goodbyes. I knew it was a cowardly act of desertion and wished I had the guts to tell them, but any courage I had left would be needed to follow through on my decision.

On 12 February 1992, I'd been given the day off work to compensate for the last fortnight of twelve-hour days, managing the exhibition. This was the perfect opportunity; Helen would be at her part-time job and the girls at school. I'd have time to pack and disappear. I purposely got out of bed early to make sure we had our last breakfast together as a family. During those final moments I thought about how fortunate I'd been to have so many wonderful years with them, sixteen magnificent years to be precise, excluding the last difficult one.

'Daddy really loves you,' I said, kissing the girls goodbye, holding them tightly a little longer in order to feel their love. I wanted their last image of me to be positive and even though I no longer believed in the power of prayer, prayed that somehow they would survive what was ahead of them.

Helen's car disappeared down the road and I stood for a few moments, frozen, knowing my next steps meant no turning back. I shook my head to waken myself from the downward spiral my thoughts were taking me. Moving quickly into the bedroom, I pulled out the suitcases I'd packed weekly as a preacher and crammed as much of my wardrobe in as I could. Knowing my family would have enough to deal with after my disappearance without haggling over furniture and the few possessions we owned, I planned to leave everything at home. There was one possession I wanted to take though—the sound system I loved so that I could listen to my collection of CDs. Packing the car, it seemed pathetic that all I had to show for forty years of life, sixteen years of marriage and thirteen years of ministry, were two suit- cases of clothes and a stereo system. I knew that these missing articles would be the signal that I had left for good and confirmed by the hastily penned note I'd left on the kitchen bench.

As I backed out of the carport and down the asphalt drive, it was bizarre to feel such extreme emotions at once. Yes, it was sad to leave, but at the same time I was beginning a new life and that was exciting. Knowing this could destroy Helen and the girls was an awesome responsibility, yet realising I'd no longer have to fight or pretend anymore brought relief. In that moment I became aware of the enor- mous pressure I'd put myself under all those years trying to be ex-gay.

When I arrived in Newcastle, Jason was ready to leave and we crammed his luggage into the car. During the journey we listened to music and talked about mundane things, but Jason never asked me how I felt or acknowledged in any way the gravity of what I'd just done. Driving south past the turn-off to Terrigal brought an eerie feeling, knowing that my desertion would have been discovered by now. I pictured Helen in a state of hysteria. The shock for her would have been equivalent to the day she discovered the letter or the day of my confession, if not worse. After doing everything possible to bring healing, the battle was lost and she was alone.

In Sydney, we booked into a caravan park in Ryde and paid a week's rent, so that we had time to find suitable accommodation. I felt proud and also a little awkward looking for a flat with Jason, knowing the real estate agents were probably thinking we were a gay couple. Jason had limited funds but I had some money from a tax refund. After viewing some very ordinary premises, we decided on a flat on the Great Western Highway at Ryde, next to the swimming pool.

I remembered these flats being built in the fifties because during the summer months of primary school I'd attended swimming lessons there. The exterior red terracotta brick had dated badly and the interior was worse. The attempts to improve the pokey little home unit had failed and the original features of pink and grey tiles in the bathroom, burnt orange laminex in the kitchen and the badly stained brown and gold loop carpet dominated the decor. The original conifer trees had flourished around the building, now blocking out most of the light but never the noise from the semitrailers changing down gears to stop at the traffic lights directly in front.

The first contact with the girls had been by phone when I plucked up the courage to finally call a week later. Initially I tried to maintain secrecy about where I was and who I was with but eventually felt safe enough to give then my home number so they could call me when they wanted to speak with me. After several months, the girls would come down to spend a day with me or I'd drive up the coast and take them out for a meal. It was difficult seeing them as I felt guilty and it reminded me of what I'd done to them. They'd finally found out I was gay just after I had left, when they overheard Helen and me having an argument one day when I had driven up to see them. Initially, they responded differently; Rebekah flying off in a rage, and Hannah accepting without question, each dealing with it in her own way. Now that everything was out in the open, I admired their willingness to try to re-adjust to seeing me with a man and hearing me talk about different experiences in my life.

Helen, in true Christian spirit, encouraged the girls by saying that, 'No matter what has happened, he is still your father.' I never saw any anger or hatred towards me for what had happened, the girls still loved their Dad, encouraged by the positive attitude of their mother. I knew I was blessed, especially as so many men in my situation had their wives retaliate and turn on them, even ensuring that they had limited access to their kids by falsely stating in court that the children would be in moral danger.

Like most people in my situation any relationship I'd had with God ceased to exist. There are several options to deal with faith in the 'dark night of the soul', that experience of loneliness and desolation when all that you've believed seems to be completely invalid and nothing makes sense anymore. Meaning has gone and the light goes out. One option is to totally reject the previous belief system and think of yourself as having been previously deceived. Another is to re-define the belief system and embrace new understandings, eventually developing something that contains elements of the old but looks quite different. Some choose a completely new religion such as Buddhism, New Age or Islam. Every time I thought of Christianity, or people tried to talk to me about it, my head ached and I broke out in a cold sweat, almost like a panic attack. I chose a fourth option, which was the only way I was able to cope with the enormous dissonance in my mind—I shut down my belief system entirely. There were too many questions I couldn't answer. Had I been deceiving myself for twenty-two years, believing there was a God? What about Jesus? Was He the Son of God and was His death on the cross for the sins of the whole world? What about heaven and hell? Did they really exist? Was I going to hell? Was there really a devil? Was Christianity the only true religion? Speaking in tongues—was it real? Were those healings faked? Would there be a second coming? Was the *Bible* really the inspired Word of God? The questions just went on and on, I could have created a list a mile long and knew I would probably never know the answers, yet I'd preached about them with such certainty and passion. One thing was undeniable. During those twenty-two years as a Christian I had seen and experienced something that you could call God. I had no other explanation for it except coincidence, but trying to explain away twenty-two years of coincidences was ridiculous. Now, I just didn't and couldn't think about it. No-one in my new world as a gay man knew about my former life as a leader in the Assemblies of God. I kept it quiet, I was too ashamed of my past. Funny how the tables had turned; I was out and proud about my sexuality but in denial and ashamed of my religious beliefs.

Jason began working in a nearby budget motel as a housekeeper, commencing early every morning to clean the guest rooms. I started work for Nathan, who'd been my production director in Youth Alive. Nathan, with his business partner Harold, had established a successful chain of furniture stores selling package deals of budget furniture. I began in sales and the plan was that eventually I'd take over managing one of the stores. It didn't take me long to realise that behind the scenes, because of its quick success, much of the business systems were in disarray. During my first five weeks I'd been moved to three different stores with three different systems and was trying to come to grips with new products and prices.

I enjoyed selling and my commission increased weekly. After my day off, I went to work as usual and was told to ring Nathan immediately, as my pay wasn't in the box with everyone else's.

'Nathan, my pay isn't here,' I said, after he answered the phone.

'Yes,' he said, 'we are going to have to let you go.'

I didn't understand. 'Sorry, what do you mean, let me go?' I was incredulous that for the first time in my life I was getting the sack.

'Well, you're just not performing,' was the feeble excuse.

'What do you mean?' I asked again still horrified that Nathan would be speaking to me in this way. 'I'm learning to sell a new product and every week my commission has increased.'

'Well, we don't think you're management material.' I couldn't believe what was happening. I had to pay child support and living expenses. Unemployment would put me in a desperate situation.

'Nathan, you and I both know that's not true. You've moved me around three different stores in the last five weeks, there's a lot to learn. We built Youth Alive together; you of all people know what I am capable of doing. Please don't do this to me!' Every excuse he gave for getting rid of me I met with an answer that destroyed the credibility of his accusations; I knew I'd done nothing to deserve being given the sack.

Finally, he came to the real reason. 'Tony, you're too gay.' What did that mean? I hadn't flaunted my homosexuality or come onto anyone, staff or clients. That would have been completely inappropriate. Not wanting to discuss my sexuality over the phone, standing in the middle of the store, I told Nathan I was coming out to the central office to see him.

As I drove to the headquarters in the western suburbs I tried to think of anything I might have done that would justify being sacked but came up with nothing. Afraid of a public demonstration, Nathan quickly took me into the office and closed the door. 'I don't understand this, Nathan. I know I haven't done anything that deserves this. I've worked hard at learning your products and systems. Five weeks and you sack me?' He listed the reasons again but I had the facts to discredit every statement. 'Nathan, I have the family support and bills to pay. I'll happily forgo the position of manager, please let me work as a sales person and I'll make the extra money through commission,' I pleaded.

He finally came to the real reason again. 'You're too gay.' Of course, he had known that already (all of the Assemblies of God world in Australia knew it). I couldn't understand what that had to do with the situation except that his business partner, Harold, was a Christian who'd been fighting his homosexuality unsuccessfully for years. He often suffered depression and had developed a pattern of being a Christian for a while, then going back out into the world again, only to return to the safety of the church, a confused mess.

Maybe I'd made a mistake caring for Harold and offering help. Did Nathan see me as a threat to Harold and his relationship? It was an unusually close friendship; in many ways they acted like a couple. It was difficult to tell who loved whom the most. Nathan was a twenty-seven-year-old, handsome, beautifully proportioned, married man, and the kind a gay man might become very attached to. Perhaps someone in the church had told Nathan he shouldn't be helping me now because I'd rejected God? Possibly they thought that having a sinner like me as an employee meant God would curse their business. Maybe Nathan even imagined that I was sleeping with Harold but even if I had found him attractive, I still wouldn't have 'fished off the company wharf' or slept with the boss; always the wise policy to follow. No matter how many times I ran what I knew around in my mind, I couldn't come up with any logical answers.

There was nothing I could say to change his mind and I left with the words 'you're too gay' running over and over in my head. How would I pay my bills or deal with the difficulty of being an ex-preach-er trying to find work again? I was angry that once again a Christian had treated me unfairly and rejected me because I was gay..

The Anti-Discrimination Act had been passed in New South Wales in 1977 and I knew it was unlawful to discriminate on the grounds of race, sex, marital status, disability, age and homosexuality. Even though I was shaken, I was determined not to be put down any more so I went to the Anti-Discrimination Board hoping to restore a level of dignity and right the wrong that had been done. I relayed the details to the counsellor who told me it would be difficult to state a case, as everything had been said behind closed doors. I had no witnesses and the fact that Nathan had a gay man as a business partner would work against me. He was as confused about the situation as I was but knew I'd been genuinely wronged.

'I don't think we've got a strong case,' the counsellor said, 'but I'll file a complaint if you like.' The Anti-Discrimination Board made several phone calls to negotiate but Nathan was always in a meeting and never returned the calls. The case was closed.

Occasionally I found Harold cruising in gay bars and I'd remind him that as a Christian he shouldn't be frequenting such places and suggest he leave immediately. I went on to become the leading sales consultant for Australia's second largest telecommunications company and then established my own successful professional coaching company. Nathan and Harold? Nathan left his lovely wife Deb, and Harold sadly is still on that same cycle of conflict and self-loathing, last I heard.

Life at home was becoming increasingly difficult. Jason was always sick with headaches, aches and pains in his body, and constantly tired, often commenting he felt like an old man not a thirty-year-old. We never went out as a couple. The nights we were home together we watched television till ten thirty and then retired to the bedroom to have ritualistic sex. The initial passion of our first sexual encounter had stayed in my mind for twelve months but was never experienced again. Jason stopped working at the motel after a huge argument and was now the night auditor at the Southern Cross Hotel in the city. Occasionally he'd go out with colleagues from the hotel but I was never invited; he said he needed time to himself. Most shifts he finished at eleven at night so I'd drive in to the city to pick him up and when we arrived home, we lay in bed and talked. Well, he talked, and I listened. Jason vented his frustrations about the politics and bitching in the hotel, always speaking as if he hated it. But I knew he thrived on the drama. One night he talked non-stop for one-and-a-half hours while I lay listening to the garbage, uneducated about the reasons for his sleeplessness and incessant, high energy conversation. Jason was able to sleep in but I had to get up and go to my new job with only a few hours' sleep. Some nights he stayed at the hotel overnight but when I rang to see how his day had been he could never be contacted. I was too afraid to challenge him, too afraid of losing him and afraid of his violent reactions.

I'd learnt a great deal about Jason over the last four months. First of all he loved to gamble and at times his entire salary was gone betting on the horses, dogs or pokies. Like a true gambler, Jason boasted about his wonderful wins and never talked about his losses, but I knew when he had lost—there was no mistaking that melancholic, dark manner. Occasionally money disappeared from my wallet and one weekend I'd left my wage envelope in my drawer only to find it gone the next day. Jason came up with the feeble excuse that he'd left our front door open and had seen some stranger stalking around the units. I knew it was a lie but felt powerless to challenge the ludicrous excuses and mismatching stories I was hearing. The dream I had when we moved to Sydney of no longer living a life of guilt, torment and frustration was quickly being transformed into a nightmare. But I'd chosen this path and no matter how difficult it was I had to make it work.

Jason was not only sick physically but emotionally as well, with many unresolved issues. When his ex-lover of five years, Charles, was found dead, gassed in his car, he showed little remorse or grief; yet they'd spent many happy years together. Jason was cynical about relationships and only used the words 'I love you' half a dozen times during our time together. I told him almost daily how much I loved him, which was usually met with a snide remark, such as, 'You'll feel different when we break up.' I couldn't understand how he could say that; I wasn't leaving but Jason had fallen in love and been hurt too many times to believe that anyone, especially gay men, could be together forever. I felt sorry for Jason considering the difficult life he'd lived, and put his outbursts and moodiness down to stress and the fact he was sick all the time. His violent eruptions frightened me and I did everything possible to keep the stress levels down and ensure he was never pushed over the edge. I'd already experienced the results. Violence and anger were foreign to me as I'd never seen my parents exchange harsh words and I'd never been involved in a fight.

It was now six months into our relationship and I'd been working for a training company assisting the chronically unemployed. It was emotionally draining trying to motivate people who had spent years on government unemployment benefits and encourage them to get back into the workforce. Driving home one Thursday afternoon I was thinking how nice it was going to be to have only one more day of work before the weekend break. At our front door, I stopped a moment, as I often did, to take a deep breath, release the stress of the day and prepare myself for what I might find inside. Living with Jason was like living with a time bomb and I never knew whether I would get a smile and a welcome home, or have to walk on eggshells all night. When I opened the door he was sitting on the lounge watching television. The response I got from my greeting told me I needed to be careful—very careful.

While cooking dinner I tried to make conversation and lighten the heavy atmosphere but unfortunately some comment I made pulled the trigger and Jason came raging towards me in the kitchen, punched me in the face and dragged me like a rag doll into the lounge room. He was much stronger than me and, having never been taught to defend myself, I felt the safest thing was not to respond and wait for his anger to subside. At first the glass felt cold as he repeatedly pushed my face against the sliding door and screamed, 'I'm going to put your fucking head through this window!' I knew resisting would only anger him more and was terrified that at any second I was going feel the glass break through my face. That look of horror snapped Jason out of his rage and he pushed me to the floor and stormed off to the bedroom. Still feeling the numbness in my face from the first blow, I took my keys and left the flat, knowing staying at that moment would be total madness.

The only place I could think of going was to see Greg and Peter who lived in Newtown. Greg was a temptation I'd failed to resist in my final days as a preacher when he worked in the Golden Wing Lounge at Sydney airport. For weeks he'd cruised me while I waited for my flight, constantly smiling, tidying up the magazines on the table in front of me or asking me if I'd like another drink. The sexual energy between us was intense and after several weeks I'd weakened and called the number he had secretly written on the napkin under my drink. I remembered Greg mentioning he worked part-time in an antique shop and by process of elimination had tracked him down when I moved to Sydney. Greg was the only gay man I knew in Sydney, so he'd invited me to join his friends at the Newtown Hotel on Friday nights. He felt he had a mission: to introduce me to gay life. My finances were in a desperate state; when I joined them I knew I could only afford two schooners of beer so always avoided shouts and found myself drinking warm beer most of the night trying to make the two drinks last. Greg and his flatmate, Peter, were now my only friends.

Greg greeted me at the door and I followed him down the long hallway of the semidetached cottage to Peter, who sat among a proliferation of antiques in the lounge room. 'How's Jason?' they both asked. 'Good,' I said, quickly moving onto another subject hoping they wouldn't really notice how distressed I was. I never told anyone what was happening at home because I wanted people to like Jason. When it had got embarrassingly late and I couldn't ignore their yawns any longer, I said goodbye and left. With nowhere else to go I thought I'd risk home again; hopefully Jason was asleep or out.

The unit was in darkness. I figured the lounge room was a safer place than the bedroom (I didn't want to venture in there to see if he was home). Turning on the television, I made sure the volume was on low, not wanting to waken the beast should he be in the bedroom, and sat on the lounge. I heard faint rustling noises from the bedroom and within seconds I could feel Jason's presence standing behind me in the doorway. I maintained my gaze on the television, not wanting to acknowledge him and still angry that the man I loved so much had hit me once again. Jason came and sat down gently beside me. I knew by his slow movements that he was already remorseful about what had happened; for tonight I was possibly safe.

'Sorry I hit you,' were his opening words, 'you see, I got some bad news today.' I continued to stare at the television, knowing that whatever the news was, it would be a poor excuse for the violent act on the most important man in his life. 'Because I've been so sick I went to the doctor and he did some tests. I got the results today; I'm HIV-positive.'

Suddenly all my anger was gone. What could I say to a statement like that? I couldn't find any words. We sat in silence, our eyes fixed on the screen, not knowing what to say next. Questions raced through my mind, one a second. I'd had limited education about AIDS and HIV but I knew that for the last six months the only time we practised safe sex was the first night we'd met in Brisbane and even then the condom broke.

Even though I knew I was now at risk my only real concern was Jason.

'What does this mean? Does this mean you're going to …?' I couldn't say the word. Did this mean I was destined to nurse Jason to his death? The thought was too horrifying. Suddenly every dream of happiness together vanished. Jason talked about T-cell count and used other terminology I was unfamiliar with and was too frightened to ask him to explain. There were questions that needed to be asked like,

'When? How? With whom?' Jason got up and walked to the bedroom then I turned off the television and followed. Holding him while we fell asleep I wondered how I would ever cope with what lay ahead of me. Many times I'd felt I couldn't take any more, and now this. If I was a Christian then I could have asked for God's strength to help me through or even for a miracle of healing for Jason, but I knew who we were and what we did was an abomination to God. Even if I did cry out for help I doubted if He'd even bother listening.

The next day at work, it was difficult to function as my thoughts constantly went back to Jason and the consequences of his diagnosis. I called to see how he was going only to have hostility returned. 'I don't want to talk about it,' he said, and hung up.

When I returned home that night Jason was still at work and even though he'd sworn me to secrecy about his status I was desperate to talk to someone—if it didn't happen soon I'd go insane. It would have been useless ringing any of my Christian friends; I'd only be reminded that AIDS was God's judgement on homosexuals and I needed to repent. I flicked through the White Pages directory to find the AIDS hotline and rang the number.

'Hello, this is Terry.' Already the tone in his voice told me he cared and was there to help. 'You don't have to give me your name,' he offered immediately, 'but would you mind giving me your postcode for our research purposes.' I told him of what had transpired during the last couple of days and how badly I needed to talk to someone and find out what I needed to do. Terry listened sympathetically and asked, 'But how are you going?'

His question shifted the conversation to my pain. 'I'll be okay,' I said, between the tears that now flowed freely. 'But I'm worried about Jason.'

Terry, a volunteer, then told me of all the support I could access as the partner of an HIV-positive man. 'If you need grocery shopping done, we can send someone to do it; they'll also help with housework. If you need food at any time, we have a pantry of groceries we can get to you. There is counselling available for both you and Jason with a qualified psychologist and dental assistance …'

As he continued with the long list of support available, I found it difficult to believe that a stranger, an anonymous voice on the other end of the telephone, was offering everything I'd need for the dark days ahead. When I put the receiver down, I sat and reflected on what had just happened. Previously, in my time of crisis, my close friends in the ministry, whom I'd pleaded with for help, had not even bothered to contact me. The denomination that I'd served sacrificially for thirteen years had been totally unresponsive, even oblivious to the trauma and needs of our family, and offered no support at all. The contrast with this moment made me see hypocrisy like I'd never seen it before. The 'evil' ones were reaching out and genuinely caring and helping me, the 'righteous' ones had offered me nothing but judgement and rejection.

Over the next few weeks Jason continued to distance himself while I tried to deal with the possible loss of my lover. Two weeks later, I plucked up the courage and made an appointment at the Albion Street AIDS Clinic. The female doctor was warm and genuine as she took me through the gruelling two-hour interview, asking me every question imaginable about my sexual activities. In 1992 there was still much to learn about the devastating disease, and medical researchers were trying to gain as much data as possible to understand the various possible means of infection. I was naive about many things; my interview lasted an extra half hour because the doctor needed to explain terms like 'toy' and 'water sports', Even though these were not exclusively homosexual practices, they were foreign to me.

Already having some understanding about what had brought me to the clinic, the doctor finally asked that question I usually brushed off quickly. 'So, how are YOU going?' she asked slowly and deliberately. Instead of my usual instant, conditioned response, 'Don't worry about me, I'm fine,' I made the mistake of pausing for a moment. The suppressed emotions of the last couple of weeks gushed forth along with the embarrassing details of my life with Jason, including the violent episodes, although I assured her there was always a valid reason for his behaviour. 'Have you heard of the co-dependent or drama triangle?' she asked. The drama triangle is a psychological model of human interaction in transactional analysis created by Stephen Karpman to help understand the dynamics behind some unhealthy relationships. Drawing a triangle on a piece of paper in front of me, in one corner she wrote the word 'rescuer', in another 'victim', and in the final one, 'persecutor'. Pointing her pen back to the 'rescuer' corner she began to describe typical behaviours and thinking. It wasn't difficult to understand that she was indicating this was me, and I remembered my first thoughts of Jason being, 'Oh you poor guy, life has been so hard, let me help you.' Next she moved the pen to the 'victim' corner. 'Jason in a nutshell,' I thought. Nothing went right for him and I'd often wondered why he seemed to have more bad luck than the average person. She drew an arching line showing how I had moved from rescuer and was now standing with Jason in his corner. Moving Jason now to the third 'persecutor' corner, I saw where that left me. I was now the victim taking Jason's verbal and physical abuse as the true martyr I was. Just as in that moment twelve months before when I chose to forgive those who'd abandoned me, I was once again experiencing a defining moment in my life. It would take me years to fully integrate that understanding; that pattern felt so natural because I had replayed it over and over for as long as I could remember.

Sitting in the waiting room two weeks later for my results, it was disturbing to see the emaciated young men around me, their skeletal features and weak dry coughs hinting at Jason's and possibly my future. Many gay men understand the terror of the moment of entering the doctor's surgery, sitting down and looking for some indication on the face of the doctor as to what the verdict might be, considering at that time it would be a death sentence. I breathed a sigh of relief when the doctor announced the results were negative, but there was still a three-month window period when the virus could be raging through my body. I would have to return and go through the terrible ordeal again. I decided I'd rather not know and never returned. After all, once Jason was gone what would be worth living for? And I had already decided that I'd take my own life when I reached fifty.

Things were never the same again with Jason. The more I tried to reach out the further he moved away and by October he'd announced he was leaving. I believed him when he said he needed time alone and that maybe we might get back together in the future. I later found out he'd had several affairs when we were together. He'd been seeing another staff member at the Southern Cross Hotel, for the last two months we were together.

Knowing Jason would see my tears as weakness, I tried to hide the grief I was feeling. That Saturday morning was a warm, cloudless early November day with spring transitioning into summer. As I helped Jason to the car with his luggage I caught him, for the briefest moment, showing his sense of loss. He stopped for a few seconds in the lounge room before walking out the door for the last time and I saw the tears as his eyes became glazed, then quickly returned to the hardness. Driving to the new flat he'd taken with staff from the hotel, I asked him, 'Jason, have you ever cried over us and what we've been through?', knowing I had possibly shed enough tears for both of us. For a second again his eyes filled with tears, then he looked away and I knew that despite all the hurt, betrayal and drama, there had been some love and now, for a moment, possibly even regret. Strangely, Wendy Matthews' song, 'The Day You Went Away' played its haunting melody on the car radio as we drove, and the words 'and I thought that it would rain, the day you went away' continued the rest of the day in my head.

There was a sense of relief as I kissed Jason goodbye at the door of his new flat, but the pain stayed with me for months.

Within weeks of Jason and I separating Queen Elizabeth II in her speech, marking the fortieth anniversary of her Accession to the throne said, '1992 is not a year on which I shall look back with undiluted pleasure. In the words of one of my more sympathetic correspondents, it has turned out to be an *annus horribilis.*' She was speaking about the devastating impact of several events: the fire in Windsor Castle just four days before, Prince Andrew and Sarah separating, pictures of a topless Sarah being kissed by her friend, John Bryan, on the front page of the tabloids, the Queen's daughter, Anne, divorcing her husband, and Charles and Diana's impending separation. Had the Queen used more common language instead of Latin she would have said '1992 was fucked,' to which *this* queen would have said, 'Amen.'

CHAPTER 18
Evolution

It's painful waiting for a broken heart to heal. There is no timetable, only a process. Living alone for the first time in my life only added to my misery. I dreaded coming home at nights, often referring to the flat as 'the dungeon' because the large trees around the property and the small windows meant it was always gloomy. Up until that point, I'd never known love as intense as my love for Jason and now, for a second time, he was gone.

The last two years had been horrific and I wondered, now Jason was gone, if I would find someone to share my life with or be free of misery again. Was I destined to live in darkness for the rest of my life? Possibly this was God's judgement on me for being gay and for turning my back on Him. It seemed unfair that at forty-two I had to begin a new life in a new culture, no longer with youthful looks; having to learn the protocols of cruising in a bar and trying to find my place within the many subcultures of the gay community. Even though my time with Jason was difficult, it meant I hadn't had to face the daunting challenges of adjusting to life as a single gay man in Sydney. Now alone, I was embarking on a new journey, a personal evolution to really find my identity as a gay man. What would that mean? What would that look like? How would I behave? What would my standards be? What type of friends did I want to make? I knew I had to discover these answers and more for myself.

Carolyn was a godsend. We worked together assisting long-term unemployed people back into the workforce and clicked immediately. Her bright, bubbly personality made me laugh again. I'd often take her with me to the Newtown Hotel and when it closed at midnight, we'd walk down a few blocks to the Imperial Hotel (home of the movie and musical *Priscilla Queen of the Desert*), watch the drag shows then dance until the early hours of the morning. Even though we spent time together in the gay scene, you could never have called her a 'fag hag'; she certainly didn't fit the image those words created in my mind.

Analysing the ten months I'd been going to the Newtown Hotel, I realised the people I'd met would never be significant friends. Every Friday night we'd said little more than 'How are you, how was your week?', commented on the various cute boys in the bar and bitched about the ugly, tragic ones. I didn't know their last names or telephone numbers, we never spoke during the week or had any significant conversations that I could remember. I determined that things would be different for me in 1993 and that one goal was to find a circle of real friends, people I could connect with.

New friendships came, beginning at a dinner party at Stefan and Chris's tasteful little cottage in the inner west. Stefan and Chris were interesting characters I'd met through a church in Sydney. They'd been partners for several years but after becoming Christians no longer slept together. I thought it strange that these two men who were so obviously a couple and cared deeply for each other no longer expressed it physically. After becoming Christians they continued their contact with their many gay friends, and joining them around the table with a dozen men from very varied backgrounds was fascinating. Out of the bar environment, the sexual agenda ceased to exist. I felt connected and over dinner enjoyed listening as they recalled humorous events of their global travels, accompanied by raucous laughter, then moving to serious issues relating to gay politics and the gay community. That evening was a catalyst to further dinner invitations, picnics, parties and introductions to genuine gay guys and straight couples who loved gay people and knew how to have fun.

At the Newtown Hotel, my Friday night drinking partners described Oxford Street as shallow and pretentious. I often thought the real reason behind their condemnations was not that they had a genuine desire to be people of depth but that they were ageing gay men who were unable to cope with the youthful look of the clubs. My new friends introduced me to the venues Jason had mentioned so many times: DCM's, The Midnight Shift, The Oxford, The Flinders, The Albury and others.

I'd maintained contact with Jason, not wanting to completely wipe him from my life, believing there might still be a possibility our relationship could be revived. He moved back with his parents in the Hunter Valley; when we next talked he was less guarded so I invited him to stay with me for a weekend. I'd begun teaching sales to marketing diploma students at the local tertiary college and had classes to take on Friday nights. Jason arrived just in time for me to lend him the car then I went to teach my evening classes. After a restless night waiting for him to come home he called about ten o'clock, announcing he'd gone home with someone but he'd be back at my place for lunch. Jason arrived with the new guy in tow, so I quickly made comparisons and immediately wondered why Jason preferred to spend the night with this man instead of me. He was going prematurely bald and carrying extra weight around the waist but I smiled politely when introduced to Doug. After making coffee, Jason motioned for me to join him in the bedroom, 'Can Doug join us for dinner?' he asked, knowing I had never learnt to say no.

Peter, my friend from Newtown, joined us for dinner, and Jason and Doug sat opposite us on the lounge. Jason didn't take his hands off Doug for a moment—he was getting more affection in one night than I'd received in our months together. The sight infuriated me so the need to prepare the meal in the kitchen was a welcome relief; I was afraid I might explode at any moment. Jason followed me.

'Jason, you obviously want to be with Doug so after dinner tonight why don't you take your things and stay the rest of the weekend with him?' I said, thinking I was saving him making that request later. Immediately, he stormed out of the kitchen to the bedroom then appeared within seconds with his bags packed, his face filled with rage.

'How dare you do that!' he kept screaming, his pride hurt that I'd actually showed some internal strength and taken control. He grabbed his man and headed for the door but his anger had reached boiling point and he came at me, punching me in the face. I cowered and dropped to the floor, trying to protect myself while the other two watched helplessly as Jason hit me again and again, both too afraid to intervene. Having vented his anger and knowing he'd embarrassed himself, Jason stormed out of the flat. Doug followed close behind him with an apologetic look and a weak smile on his face.

'Get out of my life! I never want to see you again!' I screamed, nursing my head and face. The bruises and black eye I received that night made me determined to have nothing more to do with this man as long as I lived. Goodbye, Jason—or so I thought.

One thing bothered me about some of my new friendships. Among the fun and frivolity there was a deeply established, cynical attitude regarding finding real love and the possibility of longevity in gay relationships. My friends' previous experiences of falling in love, then being hurt or betrayed had hardened them, and every time they met someone new they immediately sabotaged the relationship, deciding it was only a matter of time before that person would prove false.

Predictably they always got what they expected, the self-fulfilling prophecy always coming to pass.

This attitude made me grateful I'd come out later in life. My values were very much established, and I knew how I would treat other people and how to respond to life's difficulties in a positive manner. Once again I resolved never to become cynical, bitter or twisted and that no matter what happened, I would always leave myself open to the possibility of finding love.

In 1994, I volunteered to work with the AIDS Council of New South Wales (ACON), on a project that involved going into bars, talking with guys about safe sex and gauging attitudes in our community. It was enjoyable and rewarding giving something positive back to the gay community. Maybe there was still a bit of the evangelist in me wanting to do some outreach work. During the eighteen months of volunteer work I met Dean and Tim who became two of my closest friends and discovered that a great way to connect and meet genuine people was to do some volunteer work.

One night was particularly significant. After moving around the bar of the Oxford Hotel, handing out pamphlets, I noticed a guy standing alone in the shadows leaning against the pillar and began a conversation with him about the project we were involved in. I was surprised by his guarded, even antagonistic attitude; he told me fifteen of his friends had died of AIDS. As he spoke above the background noise of the bar, tears filled his eyes though he tried to maintain his composure, never allowing them to fall down his cheeks. It was difficult for me to comprehend the impact of attending the funerals of fifteen of your closest friends—the only significant funerals I'd been to had been my father's and grandmother's. (Another guy I met said he stopped attending funerals after the twentieth; he just couldn't deal with it any longer.)

There was anger in his eyes as he asked, 'Why me, why am I still here?' Of course no-one had the answer to that question but I realised I was encountering, for the first time, something I'd only heard about: 'survivor guilt'. Survivor guilt had been documented as a common phenomenon among Jews who'd survived the Holocaust, and was also evident among some gay men after the initial devastation of the AIDS epidemic. I made a clumsy effort to empathise with him saying that there were many times I'd wished I wasn't gay and if science developed a pill to make homosexuals heterosexual, then I'd probably take it; most of my good memories were from my life as a 'straight' man.

Expecting him to agree about the difficulties of living a life with a sexual orientation we didn't choose, his positive response came as a surprise.

'I'm happy being gay', he said, 'I wouldn't change it for anything. I'd much rather be gay than heterosexual.' I couldn't understand how this man, who'd suffered the loss of so much, wouldn't want to change what I perceived as the source of his suffering, that is, his sexual orientation. I realised that I had accepted my sexuality reluctantly, only because I'd felt I had no other option and obviously, subconsciously at least, in many ways I was still unhappy about being gay. 'Wouldn't it be wonderful,' I thought, 'to be able to think like this guy and actually love, accept and even embrace every part of me?'

In my quest to find a partner, two things occurred with regular monotony. First, I'd meet a cute guy at a bar or nightclub. We'd have a wonderful night together, talk about our lives, even spend the weekend in each others company, going to the beach, dinner or meeting up with other friends. We'd always conclude our time together by saying what a wonderful time we'd had, exchange phone numbers and plan to meet during the week for a meal.

We'd meet again but I'd immediately sense a coldness. What we'd experienced on the weekend had faded fast for him, though not for me. I was planning more ... a future even. Sometime during the meal a seriousness would settle on the table. It usually began the same way.

'Tony, I think you're a really nice person,' then came the pause, 'but I'm not ready for a relationship; I just want to be your friend.' After a series of these I developed my own predictable response, 'Yes, I know I'm a nice person; actually, I'm a very good person and I have lots of friends. I was hoping for more than friendship with you. I really don't have the time to develop any more friendships. Sorry.' Short, blunt, maybe even cutting, but at least I was being honest.

Looking for someone to make me feel complete, these guys had sensed an energy, even a desperation, that was not attractive but actually made them run a million miles an hour in the opposite direction. I wanted someone to take on the role of making me happy for the rest of my life—a pretty tall order for someone you've just met.

There was Brian, twenty-seven, cute, straight-looking in his jeans and checked flannelette shirt, who picked me up one night at the Newtown Hotel; there was Adrian, the gorgeous blond from Queensland with pecs to die for; Ben, the thirty-year-old chef who'd just arrived from London and picked me up while I was buying a barbecued chicken in Oxford Street one night; Grant, who cruised me at the ATM in Crown Street, and within minutes we were having sex in the attic bedroom of his terrace two blocks away. Then of course there was Rod the actor who bicycled past me at the beach in his very tight-fitting Lycra shorts, buns like boulders, who decided it was time for some further exercise in the bushes; Bobbie the bisexual who kept coming back for more, not sure what he really wanted; then there was … I think I'll stop there. In background conversations I occasionally heard the word 'slut'. Such a harsh word, I thought; that could never refer to me—'active' or 'popular' were much nicer.

The second type of experience I kept having was whenever a relationship did move beyond the one-night stand it was always with someone needy, with a story to tell, who I wanted to help, encourage and support. Either they'd been abused, been a sex worker and had developed a manipulative, deceptive personality or they had been abused by a previous lover and were still getting over it. Oh, you poor thing, I would think, life's been so cruel. Come to me and I'll make you all better—I'll rescue you.

Piers, twenty-five, one of three adopted children, was a Christian who'd tried desperately, like so many, to change his sexual orientation by attending an ex-gay program called 'Living Waters' at Hillsong Waterloo. The church leadership eventually closed the program down as it was highly unsuccessful in making gays straight. Too many had returned to their former life, too many participants were sleeping with each other on the side and others had attempted suicides. One participant told me he attempted to kill himself three times after his relentless prayers and efforts to think like a straight man failed. Michael Buse, who was involved in the early days of Exodus said that a man they had been working with became so distraught trying to change that he slashed his genitals with a razor and poured Drano on his wounds.

Piers was a dropout from the several Living Waters programs and a seething mass of unresolved conflicts. We met at Stefan and Chris's Christmas party, Piers collapsing on the lounge next to me announcing he wanted to leave and go home with me immediately. His enthusiasm was flattering. I welcomed the attention and that night was the beginning of the twelve months of our on-and-off relationship. We'd get close and then Piers would back off, no longer wanting what was obviously so natural to him. After six months we eventually rented a unit together. Piers had sex on tap but, even though we were lovers, we never spent an entire night in bed together—he always retired to his bedroom to sleep alone. Sleeping together in each other's arms, to Piers, was a total admission he was gay and our acts of love were often discarded as moments of weakness, even depravity. Piers's depression often lasted days as he sank into guilt, condemnation and self-contempt.

Arriving home from work one night, I noticed Piers was acting strangely. His cousin's death that day had pushed him a little too far and he was on the phone to a counsellor, trying to find out how many Valium pills and how much alcohol he had to take in order to kill himself. He'd planned it so he would be on the verge of unconsciousness when I arrived home. I'd intended going out after work but I'd changed my plans at the last minute and come home. Piers slipped in and out of consciousness and through his incoherent ramblings I finally worked out he'd taken thirty Valiums.

There was little resistance as I drove him to the emergency ward of the Royal Prince Alfred hospital. When Piers left my life I was greatly relieved, and when we met up five years later sadly he had gone through a failed engagement with a girl, had a number of gay relationships, and still hated who he was and what he did.

Sydney's Gay and Lesbian Mardi Gras Party is famous the world over for being the largest gay event in the southern hemisphere. I'd wanted to go in previous years and now I had friends who enjoyed partying. They were keen to organise a ticket for me and everything I needed to ensure my first Mardi Gras was a night to remember. After the launch of the festival, in the first week of February 1994, the excitement built day by day and the night before the parade and party I could hardly sleep, feeling like a little kid on Christmas night wanting Santa to come so he could wake up early and open the presents.

Few people understand totally the significance of Mardi Gras and other Pride celebrations. Many look at the externals of the night of partying and indulgence and make negative judgements about gay people, but for us it's an opportunity to celebrate our journey of self-acceptance and more. It's a journey many heterosexual people find difficult to understand as they have never had to hide their sexuality or feared the reactions of others for being who they are.

Can you imagine a heterosexual in their teenage years, having to say to friends and family, 'I have something to tell you. I hope you'll still love me. I'm ... I'm ... heterosexual'? They'll never have to hide their heterosexuality in order to be accepted, or walk down the street and have someone yell abuse at them because they are straight. They may experience discrimination at other levels but never because of their sexuality. For most gay people their journey has involved pain, loss of jobs, rejection by families or friends, misunderstanding and prejudice. Much depends on the area or country in which you live. The suburb I live in, gay guys and lesbians walk hand in hand with their partners down the street and no-one takes a second look—they may actually get a smile for the public expression of affection heterosexuals take for granted. Move out two suburbs and they would probably be verbally abused or if they lived in a rural setting may even experience the threat of physical violence or death.

One tragic example of this is the case of Matthew Shepard, a gay, eighteen-year-old Wyoming college student who, in October 1998, after being brutally beaten, was left to hang on a fence for four days in temperatures below zero before he died. At least five Muslim countries, among them Iran, still hang juveniles if they are caught in any same sex activity. We were horrified to see the photo of Mahmoud Asgari, believed to be sixteen or seventeen, and Ayaz Marhoni, eighteen, with nooses around their necks and who were publicly executed in Iran on 19 July 2005 for the 'crime' of homosexuality. They admitted (probably under torture) to having gay sex but claimed in their defence that most young boys had sex with each other and that they were not aware that homosexuality was punishable by death. Gay and human rights groups say Iran's record is particularly shocking, having executed possibly thousands of gay men since the Islamic revolution. Unlike these horrific stories of violence and death, we have survived, so we celebrate in an environment that allows us to do what we want and be who we are without fear of ridicule, physical attack or verbal abuse.

The party was beyond my expectations and everywhere I looked there were the visual delights of costumes, colours, sequins, beautiful bodies and outrageousness. I tried to keep up with my group of friends as we made our way through the crowd of over twenty thousand people, through the three huge dance pavilions, finally reaching the Royal Hall of Industries. We gathered around the third pillar on the left hand side of the hall, towards the front stage, next to the enormous speakers; our meeting spot for that night and many years after.

I stood on the edge of the dance floor, watching the thousands of bodies dancing in rhythm, feeling the thud, thud, thud from the speakers behind me, my eyes following the orchestrated lights and lasers. The enchanting, hypnotic vision was only interrupted occasionally by people jostling to leave or enter the dance floor.

I decided to go for a walk, knowing my friends would remain at the meeting place until I returned. The Hordern Pavilion was even more spectacular than the Hall of Industries, the green laser lights piercing through the darkness, creating geometric patterns, bouncing off the numerous mirror balls and dancing with the music. I mounted the stage to join the other dancers and moved to the front to watch the crowds below. As my eyes passed over the multitude partying everything merged—the lights, the music. Everyone danced in unison—it was as though they were dancing for me, dancing in celebration. A tingle of excitement ran through my body, and for a moment I felt like I was being welcomed home. This is my tribe.

Then I looked at where I was standing and suddenly realised I was in the exact spot I'd stood four years earlier, preaching to five thousand young Christian people at a Youth Alive Rally. Hundreds had given their lives to Christ that night after I'd spoken, but now even though I was standing in the same place I was in a totally different world. The contrast was unbelievably confronting. That moment immediately triggered the suppressed Christian belief system and it came rushing to the surface with the hundreds of questions that still needed an answer. The doubts, fears and confusion that had plagued me for twenty-two years quickly followed, and for an instant I felt like I could lose my mind. It was as though my mind was being thumped against one wall then the next as my thoughts switched between past memories and my present reality. I had to remove myself from the moment; the two extremes were still totally incompatible and needed to be looked at in a different time and place. It was the strength of mind I'd previously developed that took over. I must have looked very strange walking gingerly backwards from the front of the stage, one step at a time until I'd manoeuvred past the dancers with glow sticks and cute muscle boys in their dance shorts, to the steps at the back of the stage. Every one of them was totally unaware of the clash of two belief systems and lifestyles I'd experienced in those thirty seconds. Within minutes I was again on the dance floor enjoying one of the most memorable nights of my life.

The victim in me was still very much alive and it was as though a label was stuck on my forehead attracting needy men. Enter Garth. Garth was a spunky twenty-eight-year-old gym bunny, a stocky 176 centimetres, who often tilted his head like a little puppy, using his soulful eyes to gain attention or approval. He was an extrovert, often to the point of being offensive and annoying—just a bit too cocky. Night after night we glanced at each other moving from one torture machine to another at City Gym and then after numerous smiles over many nights, finally ventured into a conversation.

The more time we spent together the closer we became until everyone presumed we were a couple. It was pretty obvious; we gymmed together three nights a week, beached on the weekends, went nightclubbing on Friday and Saturday nights and Garth slept over on the weekends. I watched, with a sense of confidence, the futile 'pick-up' attempts of other guys, knowing at the end of the evening Garth would be going home with me. I didn't look at other men because I only wanted to be with Garth; Garth didn't look at other men for fear of hurting me, which reinforced my belief it was only a matter of time before the love we had for each other would eventually become a romantic love.

Garth told me on numerous occasions that we'd never be lovers but I kept waiting, knowing what we had was already beyond any friendship I'd known and was everything a couple wanted: honesty, trust, communication and more. Garth had just come out of a five-year relationship with David and had determined his next boyfriend would be his ideal sexual partner—that wasn't me. We slept together for twelve months but never had sex.

I continued to give Garth my love, companionship, and encouragement in his career development, bought him a suit to wear to interviews and became his taxi service, but the frustration of unrequited love was eating away at my sense of self-worth. What's wrong with me, why doesn't he find me attractive? My friends listened patiently to my regular complaints about the Garth saga and occasionally offered advice. Several times I tried to extricate myself from the relationship but his grip on me was like the tentacles of an octopus and every effort found us back together again in increasingly destructive co-dependency. We both needed each other; Garth needed attention to validate his worthiness and I needed Garth to give me a sense of completeness.

Sunday afternoons were spent at the Beresford Hotel in Darlinghurst, which had become the meeting place for our gang of thirty or so friends, to catch up on all the events of the weekend. I was dancing around from the pool tables to the bar, to the dance floor, when I saw one of my friends from the AIDS Council of NSW standing by the bar. I had great respect for Paul. He'd been the director of the AIDS Council in New Zealand and I'd always known him as a man of passion and mission who wanted to make a difference.

'Hi, Paul,' I said, beginning a conversation that once again quickly moved to the difficulties I was having with Garth. 'Oh, well, I'm so busy. I've got so many friends to see, I'd better go,' I concluded in a flippant way, after pouring out my woes, ready to move on to the next conversation. I think Paul had heard the Garth saga just one too many times as he grabbed my arm, held me back, looked me in the eyes and said, 'The problem with you, Tony, is that you give and give until there is nothing left for yourself.'

The truth of his statement struck me like a thunderbolt. I stood perfectly still. I looked at him, trying to grasp the full meaning of what he'd just said. It felt like the kind of statement that summarised months, possibly years of therapy.

'What did you say, Paul?' I asked, unsure that such a powerfully revealing comment could be made in a bar environment. He repeated his words slowly for emphasis this time. 'The problem —with you —is that you give— and give —until there is nothing left for yourself.'

'Do you realise what you just said, Paul?' his confrontational statement continuing to hit me at the very core of everything dysfunctional in me. For the next five minutes, I stood beside him with my hand on my chest, trying to catch my breath, as the truth permeated my being. Paul just smiled knowingly and watched the impact of his words. I was being taken into a realm of consciousness previously inaccessible to me. Just as snow cannot resist the warmth of the sun, his statement began melting away something dark inside me.

That statement of truth was the catalyst for a transformation that occurred over the next two weeks; my self-awareness increased and I resolved three major issues in my life. With my new awareness I was able to look back over the last three years of victim/co-dependent relationships and face the pattern that had developed in my life. I'd constantly complained about the way other guys treated me but now I could see it wasn't them, it was me. It was me who'd allowed them to use me, show me lack of respect, and take everything I'd given until there was nothing left. When they walked out of my life I was always left empty, destroyed and feeling used. How simple. Why had I never seen it before? More importantly, how had I ever become that type of person?

I realised that the source of this pattern came from a subconscious belief that I was not really worthy of love or happiness. I was a bad and undeserving person. These thoughts were ingrained in me after years of failing to be what the church and society wanted me to be. The public humiliation when I told the world that I was a complete and utter failure finally cemented the previous twenty-two years of feeling unworthy. This subconscious core belief of shamefulness, now chiselled into my psyche, had become a powerful force of destruction and the magnet that attracted tragedy after tragedy. It seemed so straightforward now, from that point onwards, to acknowledge who I was—a good person who was worthy of love and deserved respect. Surely I was entitled to correct the imbalance and begin to receive as much as I was willing to give?

With this new belief about myself, my relationship with Garth was the first thing that needed to go. I met with him for a meal to announce my decision that I would no longer allow people to treat me with disrespect by taking and never giving back. He could tell something was different about me. In fact, many people noticed the difference, often commenting, 'What's happened to you? You're looking really good!' We sat down to a late dinner at Eli's, the Italian restaurant next to the Oxford Hotel that we often frequented after the gym, and ordered our pasta. When the waiter left I made my declaration.

'Garth, we both want different things. You want a friendship and I want a relationship. This is never going to work so I'm finishing it. No more going out or staying at my place, I don't want you to call me again.'

Garth protested immediately. 'Can't we just be friends?' He knew he would lose my support and constant companionship.

'No, Garth. We've tried that and now for the first time in our relationship I'm thinking about what I want not what you want.'

He tilted his head in the puppy dog fashion that used to weaken me but this time it wasn't working. The cute look quickly turned to a scowl when he realised his power over me was broken and he said, 'You'll weaken. You'll call me.' How dare he think he could control and manipulate me like that? That statement made me even more determined to no longer be Garth's substitute partner.

'No, Garth. It's over.' I said goodbye and left. Walking down the back lane behind Oxford Street to my car I felt a new inner strength and knew I'd taken a major step to my restoration as a whole person. The darkness of self-hatred was disappearing inside me and self love, self honouring and self-respect were taking its place. I didn't weaken and the only time I saw Garth again was when we occasionally ran into each other in a nightclub or bar. From that point on, I would never date a man who was a 'project'.

I needed to get some perspective on what would bring me happiness in life. My sixteen years with Helen and the girls had been fantastic but now I'd accepted the fact I was gay, and I believed that once I found a partner I would be complete and fulfilled. What would happen, though, if I never found anyone? Would that mean I would spend the rest of my life being unhappy? I resolved that I could live a very fulfilled and rewarding life as a single person and would not wait for someone else to make me happy. I stopped searching and began enjoying life.

Deciding to march in the 1995 Mardi Gras Parade was my opportunity to extinguish my last fears regarding people's reaction to me being gay, knowing the parade would be seen by a live crowd of over 750,000 and a viewing audience in the millions on national television. After failing two auditions (just couldn't get that five, six, seven, eight! thing right) I saw an announcement on the noticeboard at the gym: 'Guys wanted to form a group called "Locker Room Boys"'. I knew at this late stage they would be more willing to take someone who lacked coordination.

For three hours every night for ten days our group of sixty guys rehearsed the dance routine to the Village People's 'YMCA'. Everyone worked hard to look fantastic; bodies were gym-toned, tanned and waxed. The two guys on either side of me were also marching for the first time. Mark, a striking, successful travel consultant on the left, and Anthony, a slim redhead and academic on my right, soon became friends. The combination of working with the unemployed and teaching sales, then rehearsals, and working out at the gym afterwards took me to near exhaustion point.

Excitement built as we gathered with the thousands of participants making up the two hundred floats and groups. It was a cold night, rain threatened and once again some churches encouraged Christians to pray for God to rain on our parade. It had been raining on and off all day but as it got closer to the parade's starting time, the rain stopped. Either God wasn't listening or He was on our side. The group in front moved off and the Locker Room Boys moved into position. The exhilaration as we marched into the crowds in Oxford Street was incredible. We repeated the dance routine nearly sixty times during the two-kilometre length of the parade and the crowd went wild when we'd throw off our towels to reveal our white Calvin Kleins.

Becky, my daughter, now nineteen, was somewhere in the crowd watching her first Mardi Gras Parade but I knew it would be almost impossible to see her among the crowds twelve deep along each side of the road. My eyes scanned the crowd looking for her familiar face at any opportunity, then at the halfway point as we turned at Taylor Square into Flinders Street for the last stretch, I saw her in the crowd. Her face beamed; she was totally distracted by the overwhelming variety of things vying for her attention. Then she suddenly saw me and threw caution to the wind. She jumped the barricade, pushed past the marshals and ran out to me. 'There's my Dad, there's my Dad!' I could hear her scream above the Village People booming from the speakers on the truck in front of us. We ran into each others arms like a scene from an old time movie and hugged over and over again in front of all those people. The emotion was overwhelming and with tears streaming down our faces, she said, 'Dad, I'm so proud of you. I love you.' I was proud of her that she was proud of me and thought that at last my little girl's broken heart was healed. No-one in the crowd would have known why we cried and danced or been aware of the pain we'd both gone through or the price we'd paid to arrive at that point where pride had replaced shame. My pain had become her pain and she'd continued to love me through confusion, humiliation and embarrassment.

Suddenly I realised that we were holding up the whole parade and the marshals were yelling 'move on', so I gave her one more big hug and ran up the street to catch up with the group and jumped back into the routine. Neither of us will ever forget that moment.

A few months later, a couple of weeks before Easter, I arrived home to find a note that Carolyn, now my flatmate, had written. 'Jason called, he'll call back tomorrow.' My heart sank. Jason, what did he want? It could only be bad news. The next night he rang again but this time I answered.

'Hi, it's Jason.' His voice was soft and weak.

'Yes,' I said coldly.

'I've just come out of hospital and I was going through my things and I found your letters. I thought I'd give you a call.' What was he talking about? It was a different Jason I was speaking to as he told me about the brain tumour the doctors had removed and his six months recovery in hospital. He was now living with his parents again in the Hunter Valley.

'I'm thinking of coming to Sydney for Easter and thought you might like to catch up.' Feeling sorry for him and sensing that this was a changed man from the one I had last seen two years earlier, I said he could stay with Carolyn and me.

Sitting in the car outside Central Station while my friends waited for me at the Beresford, I wondered what he would really be like. But I certainly wasn't prepared for the sight I saw as Jason hobbled through the huge sandstone arch of Central Station.

Jason, now thirty-three, looked like an old man. The handsome appearance had gone, replaced by a drained look, wrinkles, and leathery, dark skin, a side effect of the medication he'd been taking. His teeth had been removed to get to the tumour and the new plate was a poor fit, so that his teeth dropped down every time he smiled or tried to talk. They'd said they weren't really worth fixing. The walking stick was one of the first things I noticed. I jumped out of the car to help him with the bag he was struggling with. He gasped for air and dropped his walking stick as I slowly eased him into the car, reminding me of how

I had helped my father into the car the day before he passed away in January 1988.

'I'm meeting friends at the Beresford for a drink. Would you like to come?' I said cheerfully to begin the conversation. 'Just a couple,' he said between the deep breathing. 'I get tired easily.' I was shocked by his deterioration and wanted to know the worst but was afraid to ask the questions, 'Will you survive?' or 'How long have you got to live?' No matter how cruel he'd been to me, it was terrible to see him suffer in this way.

My network of friends who knew the story about Jason but had never met him, welcomed him with warmth and tried to make him feel at ease. Jason was embarrassed that his loose-fitting teeth stopped him from carrying on a conversation so after about half an hour we left for home.

I carried Jason's luggage as he struggled up the stairs and down the hall. His heavy breathing sounded like he was gulping for every bit of oxygen available to him; like that huge gulp of air you take after being underwater too long. My new apartment was such a contrast to the flat Jason and I had lived in; the spacious lounge room was bathed in light from the floor-to-ceiling glass that gave us a panoramic view of Drummoyne Bay. He commented on the spectacular view (as everyone did), as he collapsed into the lounge while I went to the kitchen to make us a drink.

Carolyn had gone away for the weekend and now we were finally alone. As I handed Jason his drink he said, 'So how did we meet?' I looked at him, bewildered by his question, 'What do you mean? Don't you remember?'

'Since the brain tumour was removed I've lost a lot of my memory. When I came out of the six months in hospital I was going through my things at home and found your letters, and thought I'd track you down so that I could try and get some memory back. So tell me, what happened between us?'

Horrified that our history together had been taken with a part of his brain, I began to tell him about our time together.

'We met in Brisbane, you'd just broken up with Charles and were starting a new life. I was a preacher, married with kids …' I continued the story, the pain of remembering the heartache making me cry. I'd purposely left those memories behind but now I was being faced again with every agonising detail.

'I loved you very much, Jason, but we had a very difficult time together. You stole from me because of your gambling habit, you bashed me, you had affairs behind my back. But I know everything now; the guys at the hotel you slept with, the drugs, everything and, Jason, I'm not afraid of you any more.' I wasn't trying to be cruel but knew this might be our last time together and honesty was the important thing if there was to be any resolution for either of us.

As I spoke Jason sat in silence, lifting his head occasionally to give me eye contact, trying to gauge my emotions about the events I was relaying.

I waited for a response, and the few moments of quiet made Jason's words come with greater power.

'I'm sorry,' he said. In all the years I'd known him I'd never heard those words come from his lips and knew he now he was a different Jason, not only externally but also on the inside. So I leant over, gave him a kiss on the cheek and said, 'I forgive you.' I got up from the lounge and walked into the kitchen to top up our glasses. Gripping the cold stainless steel edge of the sink I breathed deeply to gain control of the powerful emotions that could engulf me at any minute, and was startled when I turned around to see Jason now standing behind me, steadying himself between the fridge and the breakfast bench.

'You know I'm HIV-positive, don't you? I don't think I have much longer.' I moved over and put my arms around his fragile body, immediately feeling the bones protruding through the thin layers of flesh, so unlike the well-toned body I used to fall asleep holding. Still steadying himself on the bench for support, he placed one arm around me, and gave me a feeble hug.

'Yes, Jason darling, remember, you were diagnosed HIV-positive six months into our relationship?' I said, saddened that he'd forgotten such a significant detail.

He looked puzzled by my statement. 'No, I've been HIV-positive for twelve years,' he said.

I pulled away immediately, trying to make quick calculations in my mind. That made Jason a part of the first wave of diagnosed cases in Sydney. I moved back further towards the sink, the implications of his statement leaving me in total disbelief.

'You mean during the six months we had unsafe sex, you knew I could be infected? How could you do that to me? What were you thinking?' He didn't answer immediately then looked at me with a questioning and hopeful look in his eyes and said, 'You are okay, aren't you?'

'Yes,' I replied, still shaken by what I'd just heard. Jason looked relieved as he turned and ambled back to the lounge room. At last it all made sense. The constant tiredness, extreme mood swings, erratic behaviour, the tension that permeated every part of our relationship keeping Jason and I ever-distant, leaving me in constant confusion. Jason's guilt and deception had ensured that we never connected.

The next two days included moments of joy, sadness, resolution and closure, and unfortunately concluding with Jason stealing twenty dollars from my trousers. I challenged him but he denied it. Jason had changed in many ways but obviously not completely. This time I wasn't going to allow him to treat me like an idiot again or abuse my willingness to help. My coldness for the next few hours told Jason he'd stepped across the line.

Driving to the station, he complimented me on my wardrobe and told me how lucky I was to have such a circle of great friends. I knew he was guilty, I'd seen him switch to Mister Nice Guy too many times.

When we arrived at the station he said, 'If you need the twenty dollars I'll pay you back when I get my pension cheque next week.'

'It's not the money, Jason,' I said. 'All I ever wanted from you was for you to be honest with me and if you can't give me that, I don't want to have anything.' He slammed the car door as he shouted, 'Call me if you want to!' But I couldn't think of any reason why I should. I'd said my goodbyes.

Jason's name appeared in the *Sydney Star Observer* on World AIDS day in 1997 as one of the many who'd passed away since the epidemic began over a decade earlier. I really thought his death would come only a matter of weeks or months after he'd disappeared into the bustle of the station. Several years on, I was working in the Hunter Valley and had a feeling that I should call in and see Jason's parents. All was resolved but somehow I sensed it was important to make contact. Whilst resolving things on his last weekend in Sydney Jason promised that I could have the letters I'd written and I was hoping they might still be locked away somewhere. At least they would be a positive memory of our time together. Sitting in my car at nine o'clock in the morning outside the house I had visited eight years earlier, everything looked totally different. The changes in the garden and the new paint job made me wonder if Jason's parents still lived there any more. I began to doubt the sanity of what I doing. How would they react? Would this open up old wounds or would they even remember me? After sitting for ten minutes, I thought, if I'm meant to see them then they'll come out of the house.

As I finished that thought, Jason's parents stepped out the front door of the house and walked towards their car in the drive. They'd hardly changed in the last eight years. Hearing my car door slam in the quiet morning, they turned and watched me cross the road and walk up the path to introduce myself. It took a little while for them to put the pieces together and realise who I was and then they told me the story. Jason died alone on 5 May 1997 in Melbourne. His body was found

in a swimming pool; he'd had a seizure. When they went down to identify the body it took them a week to find his belongings, which had
been packed up in a shopping trolley he'd used as he was too weak to
carry them. So tragic.

'Where is Jason buried?' I asked cautiously. 'He was very significant
in my life and I would like to say my goodbyes.'

They gave me directions to the cemetery just out of Newcastle and
the memorial where his ashes had been placed; I left immediately. The
only other people at the cemetery at ten in the morning were a
handful of people in the distance laying a loved one to rest. For a brief
moment I thought how ludicrous it seemed to be here wanting to say
goodbye to the person who had caused so much misery in my life. I
walked around for twenty minutes, reading the little plaques on the
small cement blocks under the native bushes searching for Jason's lot. I
was beginning to thing it was an impossible task when finally I spotted
a small picture of Jason under a bottlebrush bush, probably placed there
by his sister who, years later, was still unable to come to terms with his
death. The laminated photo was of Jason in his prime and looked like
it had been taken around the time we'd met. Once again I felt the pain
of sorrow in my heart, even regret, that things had turned out so poorly
between us. I knew that beyond the impenetrable wall of lies, guilt and
deceit that separated Jason and me, there was love. Jason would never
have called me from the Hunter that night, would not have moved to
Sydney with me, or have contacted me again after the operation, if he
didn't love me. I'd seen the few tears no one else had seen. There was
just too much crap in the way, mine included, to find the depth that
could have held us together. Could things have been different? I
wondered, as I spoke softly, 'Goodbye, Jason.'

Jason gave you a gift.' The words came to me with amazing clarity,
breaking through the many other thoughts. It didn't make sense; I
shook my head as I thought of the heartache, stress, pain and black eyes
Jason had given me. What had he given me? Nothing! Not even a

birthday present because he was always broke. Walking back to the car the phrase continued to run over and over in my mind. '*Jason gave you a gift*.' And every time I wondered, what gift did Jason give me?

Stepping off the lawn onto the gravel car park the answer came with perfect clarity: *Jason gave you the gift of honesty*. I realised immediately the truth of that statement. Until I'd met Jason I'd lived in denial, deceiving my wife, children and friends, lying to myself and always pretending to be someone I wasn't. Then I met Jason and, for the first time in my life, I was forced to face the truth; then to live it by being honest with myself and others. Thank God for Jason, I thought, and imagined what my life would be like if I hadn't met him. I'd still be married, even more tortured I guessed, preaching words I couldn't live myself to others and constantly trying to do the right thing—but being a fake. A wholesome love for him emerged in my heart and, even more importantly, gratitude for the gift he brought into my life. I drove out of the cemetery released and empowered, having learnt that no matter how difficult or tragic a situation may appear, if you look deeper there will always be a treasure.

CHAPTER 19

James

In every major city around the world there is a strip or suburb where the gay community becomes visible. In New York it's Greenwich Village; San Francisco, the Castro; in Los Angeles, West Hollywood; London has Compton Street; in the Greek Islands it's Mykonos; in Melbourne it's Prahran; in Brisbane, the Valley, and Sydney has its famous Oxford Street. In these places young gay men and lesbians, and others not so young (like me), can more freely come to terms with their sexual orientation and experience the rites of passage of being gay. These communities provide a haven where gay and lesbian people can express their identity and enjoy the opportunity to evolve.

Many people wrongly judge the gay community, believing that gay life revolves around endless sexual encounters, bars, nightclubs, dance parties and drugs; this is often referred to by preachers and others as the 'gay lifestyle.' It's interesting to note that those who speak so knowledgeably about the 'gay lifestyle' actually don't know any gay men or lesbians. This knowledge is gained by observation from elevated ecclesiastical towers constructed to separate them from the world Jesus called them to minister to. In every major city there is also a red light or sex area where heterosexuals play and party, yet no one calls this a 'heterosexual lifestyle.' The majority of gay and lesbian people no more relate to zones like Oxford Street than heterosexuals do to red light areas like Sydney's Kings Cross. The party subculture exists in both worlds and has never been exclusively homosexual (although some think we do lights, music and costumes better, honey).

To say this 'gay lifestyle' is shared by the whole gay community demonstrates a person's ignorance, as this is only the tip of the iceberg. Underneath this visible expression are thousands, even millions, of gay men and lesbians who live everywhere, from the 'gay ghettoes' like Darlinghurst, to the suburbs, to the towns and rural areas. Whether single or partnered, they are just like everyone else, working as doctors, teachers, lawyers, labourers, business owners, mechanics, salespeople, factory workers, nurses, shop assistants. Some even have children! They live lives of unintentional activism, by gaining acceptance from neighbours and work colleagues as people of value just by being who they are—normal, decent, law-abiding citizens. Some have lived together as partners for ten, twenty, thirty, even fifty years, demonstrating that being gay or lesbian is not about what goes on the bedroom, partying or being outrageous. It's much deeper than that and we value the same things in life that heterosexuals do: love, friendships, happiness, companionship, intimacy, to make a difference where we can, and to treat people with respect.

By 1995, I was embracing my opportunity to enjoy the tip of the iceberg. I'd spent my life being responsible and now it was my turn to have some fun. With my new perspective about myself, things changed dramatically and within three weeks of ending the destructive relationship with Garth, I met Jay. I wasn't looking, it just happened, just as so many people said to me, 'When you're not looking, it will happen.' This advice had always been frustrating, as no-one could tell me how to get to that place of not looking.

I was upstairs at the Midnight Shift nightclub (a long-established gay venue with a great light show and dance music that can keep you on the floor for hours) with some of my friends on Saturday night. There was a particular place I called 'my magic spot', just on the edge of the dance floor, which was dark enough for me to be an observer but close enough to be part of the action. Almost every night I stood there, I met a cute guy.

You couldn't help but notice Jay; he was 188 centimetres normally but this night he'd chosen to wear boots that elevated him another five centimetres above everyone else in the club. In the limited nightclub lighting he appeared to be in his late twenties, with dark European features and eyelashes women would kill for. He'd brushed past several times already, smiling as he glided from the bar to the dance floor and stopping occasionally to dance in my magic spot. I had an opening line that always guaranteed an indication of a guy's interest, 'Having a good night?' If someone was interested, the conversation flowed; if not, they'd say yes then move on. Simple but effective.

Jay stayed to talk and within minutes we were dancing with each other on the dance floor. I moved closer to kiss him but his height made it difficult so I stretched up on tiptoes and Jay leant down and met me halfway. Connection. One by one my friends appeared next to us to see what was happening, the smile on my face clearly indicating what had occurred. At three in the morning, Jay predictably accepted my invitation to come home and continue our night of discovery.

The next day we met up with my friends for the usual Sunday afternoon meet-up at the Beresford where Jay's pleasant manner and good conversation meant everyone gave their stamp of approval. Jay was in. On Monday at the beach, Jay confessed he'd lied about his age and he wasn't twenty-eight but only twenty, which was difficult to imagine as his life experiences had blessed him with a mature outlook. Jay's father left when he was still too young to remember and he was brought up by his alcoholic mother. In his final years of high school he moved out to live with an older gay man only blocks from the family home. Jay's stories of what he'd been through shocked me but he was so different from other guys I'd previously been attracted to. He didn't need me to fix anything, he was doing just fine all by himself, successfully working through the issues that might have destroyed others.

We had a great five months together but Jay always said he didn't really want a long-term relationship. My previous experience with Garth stood me in good stead and I made sure the fondness and love I had for Jay never slipped into a strong romantic love. When I picked him up from work to come and stay the usual Tuesday night at my place I knew something had changed. When we got home we sat on the balcony overlooking the bay, scotch and cokes in our hands.

'There's something I want to tell you,' Jay said, 'but I'm worried about how you're going to react. I don't want to lose your friendship.'

'Go ahead, Jay,' I responded, knowing already where this conversation would go.

Jay explained his reasons for finishing our relationship but wanted to keep seeing each other as friends. In his mind Jay had obviously already made the switch from boyfriend to friend but it was going to take a little time for me.

'You've made your decision to finish our relationship but I'm not prepared to give my friendship at this stage, Jay. I'll have some things to work through. You can have my friendship when I feel I'm ready.'

Jay was shocked by my response. So was I, but for the first time I was looking after my own feelings and was not prepared to be hurt by seeing someone I still cared about move on to their next fling. I knew it was important for me to make that stand and the strength of my decision ensured Jay and I remain friends to this day. My relationship with Jay was the first wholesome one I'd had that began, continued and ended in a healthy way. I'd learnt the valuable lesson about never allowing romantic love and friendship love to mix. Like water and oil, it's impossible to mix the two and to try to maintain a friendship with a person to whom you're romantically attached only causes pain, placing you in the vulnerable position of becoming a victim.

It was a beautifully warm summer's night on Sunday 1 December 1996. As a married man, like many men in their thirties, I'd gone to seed—my waistline had increased each year and I had no tone. But as a body conscious gay man, I'd spent three years at the gym and transformed myself—I now had solid pecs, strong arms, a slimmer waist and broad shoulders. I made sure the clothes I wore showed off every moment of sweat and pain I'd put in at the gym and as I walked down Darlinghurst Road I thought I looked pretty hot in my tight black pants and muscle shirt. I enjoyed the smiles of acknowledgment from cute gay men as I passed them on my way to Gilligan's Cocktail Bar above the Oxford Hotel.

I'd planned on a big night, aiming to finish at Orb nightclub in Kings Cross around 3am. Sunday nights at Orb were organised by Jojo, a friend and promoter I'd met through Garth. Jojo had tried on several occasions to get crowds out on Sunday nights but with little success. This time, though, he was onto a winner and established a culture of Sunday nightclubbing in Sydney that still exits today—at that time, though, Orb was the place to be. Serious clubbers even stopped going out on Friday and Saturday nights so they could rage at Orb on Sunday nights, staggering out at five in the morning to go home and shower before work, or continuing on Monday morning in the darkness of a recovery venue. Orb, unlike many of the converted barns and overused venues of Oxford Street, had been built as a nightclub, was shiny and new and had 'chill-out' spaces and huge leather lounges. Week after week the best DJs Australia had to offer drove the crowd to screaming point with excitement, making it almost impossible to be sensible and go home for a sleep before work.

As I reached Oxford Street and turned right to begin the night at Gilligan's my attention was diverted by a loud, 'Mmmmmmmmmmmm!' to my left. The sound was too loud to ignore; looking around I saw a young guy striding towards me, leaving his friends behind on the corner.

James was only 170 centimetres tall and looked twenty at the most. He was such a cute package with his fresh face, blond wavy hair and cheeky smile. He became oblivious to his friends continuing their conversation behind us, as he walked beside me along the street, sticking to me like a magnet. James had been drinking (that was obvious) at the Albury and even though his interest in me was extremely flattering I was thinking how 'out there' this young man was. You'd be trouble with a capital 'T', I thought. When we arrived at Gilligan's I wished him well for the night and disappeared into the crowd.

Kendall, an actor and current boyfriend of ten months, arrived fifteen minutes later and we left to go to Kings Cross and Orb. We knew the security staff, which ensured we 'queue jumped'. At around midnight Kendall left, which was unusual for a party boy like him, but he had rehearsals the next morning. I moved through the dance floor, enjoying the high energy of 'handbag house', when I saw James dancing with another guy. I couldn't figure out whether he was a boyfriend or just a friend. Our eyes met and we attempted to make conversation above the deafening music. James was very keen; he gave me his business card and asked me to call.

This created a dilemma. Every gay relationship I'd been involved in had been monogamous and even though Kendall wanted ours to be open, I didn't feel comfortable with the arrangement, believing that being with another man would make me feel like I was cheating. My friend Mark, from the Locker Room Boys, encouraged me to take the opportunity, considering I had been given an open cheque, as it were, from Kendall. Maybe I was being too much of a prude and needed to be more liberal in my thinking? Was I being too inhibited? Maybe I could have a meaningful relationship and the freedom to have other sexual partners; others seemed to do it successfully. I'd always felt the decision to have an open relationship was a sign that the commitment was waning, or maybe I'd just bought into the traditional heterosexual model.

Considering the age difference, James's interest in me made me curious and so on the Thursday during my lunch break at work, I pulled the card out of my wallet and called him. The excited tone of his voice indicated he was glad I'd called.

'When would you like to meet up?' James asked, his eagerness adding to the mystery.

'How about coming over to my place for dinner next Tuesday night the twelfth?' I asked. His reply was a quick and definite yes.

As Tuesday approached I became more and more apprehensive, until an hour before James was due to arrive, I rang my friend Mark. 'I can't do this, Mark, it's not me.'

'You'll be fine,' he reassured me. 'You're not doing anything wrong. You shouldn't feel guilty. Enjoy.'

It was 8 o'clock and James was already thirty minutes late. I'd been quietly hoping he, like others I'd met, was irresponsible and wouldn't show up, then I wouldn't have to deal with the moral dilemma I was facing.

Apparently my directions to Drummoyne were difficult to follow and James had nearly given up. Still feeling uncomfortable when he finally arrived, I spent our first five minutes together trying everything I could think of to turn him off.

'I'm going to be totally honest with you, James. I'm in a relationship. My boyfriend wants an open relationship; I don't. I've been married and have two daughters that are around your age. I'm forty-five and if we had sex tonight I would have such an attack of the 'guilts' it would ensure nothing would happen. At the very least we may end up friends.'

That should be enough information, I thought, to ensure this doesn't go any further than a meal. Little did I know that my honesty was making me very attractive. The atmosphere immediately became more relaxed and we shared our life stories over dinner and discussed our perceptions of gay life. I kept the ex-preacher part out of the conversation as that part of my past was only reserved for people I really knew and trusted.

Like Jay, James's upbringing had not been easy, with constant violence in the home and other stories that shocked me, but he too seemed unaffected by the negative experiences. Even though he was twenty, his mature outlook was quite impressive. He was wise beyond his years and the more we talked I realised how unique he was; he possessed great depth of character and a strong sense of morality.

I thought of how fortunate he'd been, coming to terms with his sexuality at seventeen and his parents immediately accepting their gay son. James met Brian, his one and only partner, on his first night in a gay bar, which began a two-year relationship. Brian, also in midlife, had become very possessive and never let James out alone to enjoy himself, and always insisted that they go home together before 10pm. Eventually Brian's lack of trust drove a wedge between them and James left. James had also dealt with the drama of having an HIV-positive partner. Having only known what it was like to be in a relationship, James decided he'd have twelve months as a single gay man, and assured me he wasn't looking for a relationship either. I wondered if I was only hearing one side of the story and beneath the façade of wholesomeness he presented there were flaws that would be revealed; it was only a matter of time before the truth would come out. He was just too good to be true.

The conversation was unusually easy for two people who'd just met and the more we talked the more we discovered how much we had in common. Likes, dislikes, food, recreation, music, values. We were both Pisces; James born March ninth, and me the thirteenth. There was something beyond the physical I found magnetic, difficult to define yet so engaging. If this young man was really who he portrayed himself to be then he was exactly what I would look for in a partner; except he was too young.

After dinner we moved to the balcony for coffee. The wind had died down and the lights from the buildings across the bay glittered on the water, half a dozen joggers ran laps on the grey cement path surrounding the bay. We stood looking at each other, each of us already wanting to touch but cautious about taking that step. I leant over to kiss him.

James's kiss was perfect, gentle and responsive.

'I don't want to have sex and then you leave, James. I want you to stay the night,' I said, somehow knowing this was already more than just a casual encounter.

'Okay, I'll stay,' he said, without a moment's hesitation.

James was so different to other men; the conversation, the look in his eyes, the responses, the emotions, and I was still trying to understand what this young man was seeing in me. It was totally illogical. James went to the bathroom and I went to prepare the bedroom. I wanted it to be special. I lit the candles on the two bedside dressers, quickly searched for my favourite Enya CD and turned off the light. As I rolled back the doona I looked up to see James standing at the door.

'Make yourself comfortable, I'm just going to the bathroom.' When I returned to the doorway, James was lying on the bed, naked, smiling. I paused for a few moments to take in the vision before me. He looked gorgeous in the flickering, mellow light of the candles, every part of his body delightfully proportioned. The angelic, melodic, Celtic tones of Enya playing in the background added to the ambience being created and I sensed something coming from James; it was as though every cell in his body was saying the same thing: 'Love me'.

The enchantment of that moment held us both as I undressed and lay down beside him. Every movement, every touch and kiss had meaning. Slowly, affectionately and tenderly, we gave and received. James's touch was refreshing, meaningful and soothing.

We finally cuddled up together, our bodies spooning perfectly, waking every half hour to roll over, change positions and give each other a kiss on the shoulders, the palm, or back of the hand or neck. It was a pleasantly restless sleep. When we woke about 6.30am, James showered while I made coffee, both of us cautious about acknowledging how special our night together had been.

'I'll call you during the day,' James said as he left the apartment. Sure,

I thought, I've heard that a thousand times. Surprisingly, James was true to his word and called me at work. Of course I wanted to say, 'Would you like to come over tonight again?' but that would have appeared too keen. The monitoring, pacing and matching of interest and emotions in a new relationship is constant. The next day I called James at work and again we talked for an hour, as though we'd known each other for years. I thought I'd take the plunge, 'Would you like to come over for dinner tonight?' James's immediate and enthusiastic response was reassuring.

I was more relaxed when James arrived this time and when I asked, 'So how was your day?' it had a 'couple' air to it, like we'd been doing that routine for months already. The quality of the conversation was as good as at our first dinner. I loved James's outlook, his strength and his inner qualities, and I opened my heart more and more. I was becoming increasingly vulnerable, but at the same time I was aware of my tendency to be too trusting too soon.

By Friday night, Kendall still hadn't returned my calls, but I was used to him being too focused on rehearsing or performing, so I called James and we arranged to meet at the Beresford Hotel. I arrived early and met up with friends. They could tell by the way I was talking that I needed to be warned about any further involvement with this young man. Stan was especially strong in his advice to not take this any further.

'If I have two weeks or two months with James,' I said, 'I'll have a wonderful time.' This was my philosophy—take the risks when life presents opportunities and never live with regrets or what-ifs. After introducing James to my friends and having one drink I was keen to go home, which surprised everyone, as they knew how much I loved being out and having fun.

It was a blustery night and the large glass doors vibrated with the strength of the wind across the bay. James selected a CD, Elton John's CD of love songs, and I put it on. Sitting down on the lounge together, James laid down and put his head in my lap while I stroked his blond, wavy hair and gently drew lines with my fingertips across his forehead. The conversation that had come so easily was replaced by an equally comfortable silence as we became lost in each other's gaze. Oh shit! No, this wasn't supposed to happen. The growing fondness that I had for James and had been trying to keep in check suddenly spilled over into an overwhelming love. The words, 'I love you, James' seemed ridiculous, impulsive and reckless. I knew it was wrong to say such a thing. My friends had coached me to never say the 'L' word until you'd known someone for months, but the feeling was bursting to be expressed. 'I love you, James,' I said as casually as possible. James smiled. Could he be feeling the same thing, I wondered? We'd already agreed that nothing permanent would ever happen between us.

'What about Kendall?' James said softly, understanding the consequences of the last four words I'd spoken.

'I don't know, James, I don't understand it. When I'm with Kendall I feel a love for him but when we're away from each other I don't really miss him. All I know is, since we met, I feel so much love for you, it grows with every contact we have. It feels like it's too quick.'

'I'll wait for you. Even if it takes six or twelve months, I'll wait,' James responded. What was I hearing? Wait for me? If those words had come from the mouth of someone else I would have brushed them off but already I felt James was quite capable of following through with what he'd said. It was difficult though to comprehend that someone would value me that much.

We were both shocked at the speed at which our emotions had grown and the declarations made. It seemed like the appropriate thing that night was just to cuddle up together. We slept soundly, never letting go of each other's hands, waking occasionally again to give a reminder kiss of what we were feeling.

The next night, Kendall and I had arranged to go to a dance party at the Sydney Theatre Company at the Rocks. Most of the night I wandered about the party alone. Every time we met up again he asked if I was okay but I assured him I was fine, not knowing what to say or how to say it. We arrived home at Drummoyne as the sun was rising on the bay and Kendall had the courage to take the step I was unable to take.

'I think you have something to tell me?' he said, giving me the opportunity to come clean.

I took a deep breath. 'You know you wanted to have an open relationship? Well, I've taken up the option and I've met somebody and want to pursue a relationship with him. I can't do both.' My words sounded hollow as I said the words that are meant to be reassuring but never are; 'It's not you, it's me,' and, 'I really have valued the time we've had together.'

Kendall took the news with the sensibility and decorum of a mature gay man. We continued a polite conversation for an hour then I offered to drive him home. He decided to catch a cab. James had been waiting for my call and was over within a matter of minutes. Now that the Kendall issue was out of the way we could think more clearly about what would happen between us.

During the next week James stayed almost every night and we talked about everything. The age difference was a major issue; James had always been attracted to older men but I wanted to make sure his attraction to me was not to replace the lack of a healthy father/son relationship. I was not prepared to play that role and would only have a relationship in which we were equal. James spoke fondly of his love for his father and mother, so I knew that issue was dealt with. I was usually attracted to younger guys but felt I understood this recurring pattern—I enjoyed the dynamic of the younger brother relationship. The energy, freshness in thinking, and wanting to have fun were things I found difficult to find in men my own age. I'm sure the fact that I had previously done so much youth work that required staying young in my thinking influenced this as well. Another concern was that many of my friends had caringly warned me against any further involvement with younger men: 'No-one under thirty,' they said. I wondered how they'd react. But in the final analysis it wasn't what others thought of us but what we felt for each other. Looking back it seems ridiculous that we even discussed any possibility of not continuing. As if we could have stopped it.

As the week drew to a close, it was increasingly difficult to be separated and we spent every spare minute together or on the phone. We agreed to work at having an exceptional relationship, not by giving fifty-fifty but by both of us giving one hundred per cent to each other. It seemed the natural thing to live together so James left home and moved in that weekend. Within days it was Christmas Eve. Rebekah and Hannah had come to spend the night and a few friends had come over for drinks. James went out of his way to befriend the girls and help them deal with the situation of him being Dad's new boyfriend. Later in the evening I walked down the hall to find James and Hannah chatting on the bed, and then returned to my guests in the lounge room. Hannah reappeared without James so I walked down the hall again to make sure everything was okay and found him lying in the same position. He was deep in thought but he signalled for me to lie beside him.

'What were you and Hannah talking about, darling?' I said.

'We were talking about your life and she told me, "I don't know what you've done to Dad but I've never seen him so happy. You have my blessing, James".' Tears began to fill my eyes as he spoke. Suddenly all the hurt and pain of the last five years surfaced and I sobbed and sobbed as James held me tightly, surprised at the sudden outpouring of emotion.

'James, there have been times when I wondered if I could go on. I've never met anyone who loved me as much as I loved them, but I know how much you love me. It may sound strange but it almost feels like God's given you to me, James, and I feel like your love is healing me.' I couldn't say any more and we lay in each other's arms for another half an hour, James constantly telling me how much he cared for me. There are hurts inside us all that will only be healed by another's love.

It seemed we'd somehow found the very thing everyone looked for—true love … certainly an intensity of emotion beyond anything I'd experienced before.

I could never have picked anyone who was as perfect for me as James, and our meeting only twenty-five days earlier, on the corner of Oxford Street and Darlinghurst Road, was somehow meant to be. Every morning the alarm was set early so we had an extra half an hour together in bed to talk and cuddle while having coffee. When it was time for James to leave for work, usually an hour before me, we'd struggle for another five minutes saying goodbye, James running back inside several times for another kiss and to say, 'I love you soooooo much,' one more time.

So many things suddenly made sense and I understood what it meant to find a soul mate. How could I have listened to love songs on the radio all my life and never known what they really meant? I think at last I was beginning to discover what sex was really all about; an expression of love and devotion. Sex for sex's sake will give you a good physical feeling and release. Sex mixed with affection and intimacy takes it to another level. But James and I adored each other and it was not unusual, even three months into our relationship, to cry in each other's arms after making love, we were so happy. Finally, I was dealing with the years of negative conditioning, and the beauty, purity and selflessness of our love made me realise that if there was a God, He would never condemn two men or two women for loving each other. Love like that could never be evil—it has a sacredness to it. And to think I could have gone to the grave having never experienced this.

The scepticism of some of my friends quickly dissolved as they got to know James, and they were glad we'd found a special love, the kind of love found only once in a lifetime. Some outsiders made judgements and thought James was my toy boy but they were so far from the truth it was ridiculous. James was a giver not a taker. One night, my friend Mark was at Gilligan's when James and I walked in; some bitchy queen made a cutting remark about us so Mark immediately put them in their place.

'They're friends of mine and you've no idea what you are talking about. If more gay men had the kind of relationship they have, Sydney would be a better place.' Go, Mark!

Twelve months after we'd separated Helen met a man in the church and remarried. I was glad she'd found someone to love her, she deserved the best. She'd made such sacrifices when we were together and she'd been the innocent victim through all that happened. From my perspective today I can see how wrong it is for a gay man or ex-gay man to marry a woman believing marriage to be a part of the cure. The poor woman is in love with you and thinks you are attracted to her. She is giving the best years of her life to you and your children, and it's all a lie. Think of her— she deserves you to be honest with her.

Hannah also met a young man in the church and planned their wedding for February. James came to the celebration as my partner. Hannah glowed with the aura brides often have on their special day and as we turned into the church to walk down the aisle the whole congregation rose to their feet and cheered and clapped.

It appeared that my mother and sisters, after hearing about and finally meeting James, had come to a place of acceptance. At the reception, my brother in-law, Ian, took James aside and said, 'James, I want you to know we all think of you as one of the family.' This unsolicited comment and acceptance was more than I had ever dreamed of and even though I never felt any rejection from them, my sexuality and relationships were never mentioned. It was like there was a part of me, a very important part of me, that was a forbidden topic. There had been so much to tell them including my heartaches and joys but now for the first time I could share my life totally with my family. It was an amazing day of healing for us all.

I'd always wanted to be with a partner whose family were accepting, and to never have to hide or pretend. James told me many stories about how wonderful his family had been with his previous partner, Brian. James's family had previously been so accepting that his father introduced Brian as his son-in-law at family gatherings. I was looking forward to enjoying the same type of relationship, but there was a problem. Whilst Brian and James were together, James's parents had become quite close to Brian so when they did break up, the family remained loyal to Brian and saw me as the threat to them ever getting back together. It didn't seem fair that my family had welcomed James with open arms and James's was rejecting me, keeping me at a distance and doing whatever they could to discourage our relationship. If only they realised James could not have been with anyone in the world who loved, cherished and respected him more than I did. James finally decided that until they were willing to welcome me into the family, he would have nothing to do with them. It was a choice I didn't want him to make because I knew how much he loved them.

Over the next nine months we had the most magnificent time together. It felt like we had enough love for each other to last a lifetime, but of course this was something no-one could guarantee.

Towards November a number of pressures began to have an impact on our relationship. I was trying to extricate myself from my excessively social lifestyle but found it difficult because my social network was full of 'party animals'. James was stronger, usually leaving for home before me, knowing I could be trusted to resist the many temptations available each night out on the scene. Finances were becoming a pressure and James was finding it difficult to meet his weekly commitments. With Christmas approaching James began to miss his family, as it had been over nine months since they'd had any real contact. Our relationship was evolving from the highly charged emotional state of early romance into the more normal dynamic of a long-term relationship. As

James tried to deal with the pressures he became more distant—talking about these things would have helped but James found it difficult to discuss the fears and concerns going through his mind. He couldn't see any other way out but to leave and move back home again.

There was nothing I could do to help him realise that most of what we were experiencing were normal pressures and together we'd be able to work through them. This shouldn't be happening, I thought, James and I still love each other but I had to let him go. During our last few days together I often said, 'James, if only I could slot a chip in your brain to give you five more years' experience then you wouldn't be leaving now, we'd be supporting each other through these difficulties.' He left in November, just days before our first anniversary.

It was difficult to accept that something so wonderful and so right was over. Living alone in the apartment we'd moved to in Pyrmont and having Christmas and New Year without him was almost unbearable. I was trying desperately to move on in my life, once again dealing with loss. The connection we'd had still remained and I often knew what he was thinking or doing. I also had the strong feeling he was missing me as much as I was missing him. I didn't want to take on the role of the tragic lover but the shock of losing James plus the discovery that he was now seeing Mark, a hairdresser and close friend of mine, was too much. I'd always encouraged the friendship between Mark and James and they got on so well together. Mark often told me that friendships were more important to him than relationships as he'd had his heart broken several times before. I believed him. I'd left Mark and James alone in the apartment one day when I went off to work. Around 10.30am, sitting at my desk I had an awful feeling come over me that Mark and James were sleeping together at that moment. Immediately I put the thought out of my mind. Mark would never do that to me, I thought, he knows how much I love James and that would be the ultimate betrayal. Twelve months after our separation James confessed what had happened, apparently on the day and time I'd instinctively known.

Thoughts of ending the gnawing ache began infiltrating my thinking. Partying with my friends seemed the only way to deal with the loneliness, but the physical excesses of my lifestyle combined with the emotional trauma of losing James took its toll. It was as though my body said this is enough, I'm shutting you down for a while. My friend, Tim, had to come to my rescue. He'd discovered me in a tragic state after I took Normison to try and sleep, and Xanax to relieve the three days of uncontrollable hiccuping I'd been going through. Now I had internal bleeding and Tim had to take me to casualty. He called Becky at work. The doctor at the hospital had decided to give me Largactyl intravenously to settle me down and I remember stirring from my heavy sleep to see her sitting at my bedside. I turned away, embarrassed that she was seeing me in such a pathetic state, and then lapsed back into unconsciousness again.

After being released from the hospital, my friends monitored me twenty-four hours a day, looking after my every need and cooking meals. The wonderful group of genuine people I had gathered around me over the years were now shining like never before. I felt so blessed.

Within a week I was feeling better and knew it was time for some serious re-evaluation. My friend, Todd, asked me to go with him to the Gold Coast for a week in order to clear my head and start to think about a life and future without James.

CHAPTER 20

And the pieces finally fit ...

Like the proverbial phoenix, how many times can you rise out of the ashes or, in modern terminology, reinvent yourself? As many times as you choose to remain undefeated, leave the past behind and move on. The transformation can be endless, and from my experience, we either become bitter or better.

A geographical change, even for a few days, can give you a remarkably different perspective on your life and the week on the Gold Coast did that for me. Even though I still missed James dreadfully, I chose to focus my attention on a future without him and was determined to change the things in my life that remained incomplete. I don't think I had ever really sat down and thought about what I wanted my life to look like since I left the ministry. Away from the distractions of Sydney, clarity began to break through and three things became clear.

Firstly, I knew the experience with James, at its height, was possibly one of the most beautiful that two men could have with each other and I now understood the saying that people come into your life for a reason, a season or for life—the trick being to determine who is there for what. I would always be grateful for the richness of those twelve months and all that James had given me. Secondly, I'd learnt that gratefulness is much more empowering than regret and there was much in my life to be grateful for: my girls, my family and the wonderful circle of friends that now surrounded me. Thirdly, looking back, it became very clear that the party lifestyle of the last five years had robbed me of the ability to move forward in my life. As one of my friends put it so clearly, 'My time of partying gave me great times of fun, but during that time there was no creative energy left to move my life forward.'

I returned to Sydney with a new set of goals and determination. I knew the decisions and choices I'd made would take time to implement but I was about to gain a new understanding of the dynamics and the power of thought. In August 1998, I received a phone call from Tom, who'd found my details on an employment database, to see if I'd be interested in looking at a personal development business being introduced to Australia from Canada. Personal development, being a part of the content of my preaching in the past, had remained an interest of mine, so I agreed to meet with him. Tom assured me that the fourteen days I had to evaluate the self-study course would be sufficient time to discover its value.

'What have you got to lose? If you're not happy in fourteen days I'll give you your money back,' Tom reassured me. He was right, I had nothing to lose except possibly the things I really wanted to change about my life. If it worked for me then I'd have no problem marketing it to others.

As I worked through the self-study course, so much of the material resonated with me. It was spiritual but not religious, a unique combination of the basic and common principles found in every religion. Philosophy and universal truths were uniquely interwoven with scientific facts. The relaxation and visualisation exercises forced me to do something I hadn't done for a long time: STOP! STOP, be still, quieten the business of the mind and reflect. Within seven days something began to shift in my thinking as I was reminded of much that had become obsolete in my life. I was reading old familiar principles regarding cause and effect, sowing and reaping, giving, gratefulness, the power of thoughts, words and belief, and the benefits of forgiveness. All principles I'd preached and practised as a Christian but on the whole had ceased to be a part of my conscious thinking since I'd shut down my irreconcilable belief system in 1992. New concepts like 'allowingness' (a wonderful place of total non-judgement), creating greater awareness by learning to live in the present moment, and synchronicity, all opened up possibilities for a new way to think and live.

Having finished working with the unemployed I'd taken on additional teaching hours as well as working as an extra on various films and advertisements. The agency rang to let me know I'd been cast in a scene for *Heartbreak High* (an Australian soapie) which meant I'd spend the day on a ferry in Sydney Harbour. Being an extra and not a star, I knew there would be lots of time off the set, so decided to take the workbook with me and complete the final exercises, which were designed to apply the course principles individually and create a clear picture of the life you want. After filming the scene, I went to the back of the ferry and turned to the exercise on discovering your life's purpose. For most of my life I'd lived with a strong sense of destiny and purpose, believing I was doing something significant with my life, but leaving the ministry had meant rejecting that purpose. The previous six years had been spent learning about what it meant to be a gay man. Was it possible this exercise would help me rediscover that lost element that had made my life so rewarding and fulfilling? Was it possible to discover a higher purpose without God in my life?

Following the directions, I casually made a list of the things that motivated me, what made me special, what I wanted to change and what I wanted most out of life, finally prioritising them from one to ten. I was in a place where I was prepared to be totally honest and, working with the new prioritised list, began to write out ten purpose statements. The boat rocked as my pen clumsily formed the words on the page and after writing the statements I stopped, read it again and slammed the book shut. The impact of those words was too confronting. Surprisingly the word God had appeared in the statement at the top of my list.

There was a deep, inner, confirming response and I knew immediately that what I'd just written was true. It was so clear and simple, yet at the same time profound and powerful. The boat rocked even more from the wake of the large Manly ferry on its way back to Circular Quay. Gazing out of the window, watching the shoreline rise and fall with the movement of the boat, I reflected further on the meaning of what I'd inadvertently written. Possibly I'd never find a sense of fulfilment unless I lived according to the purpose on the page but the implications of the statement were enormous

Disturbing questions arose in my mind one after another, emerging from a belief system that had remained dormant for six years. Had I thrown the baby out with the bath water? Was God to be a part of my life again? Which God? The God who said I was supposed to change my sexual orientation before I would be acceptable to Him? Would this mean I would embrace again the Christian beliefs that had been the foundation of my life all those years? Would I have to go back to church? Would it be a gay friendly church or a gay rejecting denomination who would insist that I change? It was difficult to fully comprehend how this new awareness would play out. Six years earlier I'd been given a choice—choose God and keep denying who you are or be true to yourself and reject God. A bizarre choice to have to make in hindsight.

Terms used in the course like 'universal consciousness' reflected a much broader concept than I'd previously known but I felt somehow, no matter what term was used—universal consciousness, supreme being, divine intelligence, inner self, the source, the universe, or God— it was the same thing. It's hard to imagine that the source of this extensive universe would be hung up on spelling. I realised how limited my beliefs had been and that the most important thing was the connection not the title.

Accepting the truth that I was gay had severed that connection and, besides, God and I were not on speaking terms any more. I was angry with the God who'd not answered my prayers to make me straight and caused my life to be in continual conflict. Why should I communicate with a God who'd ignored my cries and let me down? At that moment, though, my openness and willingness to question caused something to happen—a barrier was removed.

I could see that for the last six years of my life I had been in a holding pattern. I'd been suspended like a plane circling over a city, waiting for the go-ahead from the control tower to land. It had been a time of enjoyment and I'd had many wonderful experiences. But, looking back, even though I'd evolved as a gay man, there had been no spiritual dimension to my life.

During that week, for no particular reason, I felt the need to write a description of my life at sixty-five and began with the words, 'The year is 2016 and I'm sixty-five years of age. The end of 1998 was a turning point for me …' The inspiration flowed as I detailed, very succinctly in two pages, my past, present and future, never stopping to edit, change or improve the words that effortlessly poured onto the page. One thing was clear: my journey had purpose, not just for me but for others as well. Some may call it inspired, prophetic or channelling, but whatever it was, I knew that those two pages were the blueprint of my life. Inspiration, passion and vision were returning to my life.

The following night I called Hannah to tell her about what had happened. Helen answered the phone. Thinking that she was probably visiting Hannah, I said, 'Hi, Helen, can I speak to Hannah?'

'She's not here,' Helen replied, 'You've called my place, not Hannah's.'

I had unknowingly dialled the wrong number, or was it the right number? Helen listened as I began to share what had happened over the last week and when I'd finished sharing the series of events, Helen responded in a caring voice. 'There's something I've been meaning to tell you for a while now. I forgive you for everything that's happened.'

We both cried as I replied, 'That means a lot to me. I never wanted to hurt you, I couldn't see any other way, I felt I had no other choice. If there was any other option I would have taken it. Thank you.' Further healing was coming to areas of my life I never thought possible.

The next weeks and months became a series of amazing incidents, as though another force was influencing, guiding, even directing my life. The most astounding experiences of synchronicity occurred as I frequently found myself in the right place at the right time to meet the right individual. It was as if the understanding I'd received and the willingness to live a life of purpose drew things to me effortlessly like a magnet. I discovered that there were many individuals who were a part of the growing group of people; people with a deep sense of spirituality.

Being committed to understanding more of the transformation I was experiencing, in May 1999 I decided to attend a seminar in Chichén Itzá, on the Yucatan Peninsula in Mexico, next to one of the Mayan sacred sites built around 600 AD. The course was going to clear my bank account of all my savings but I had a strong sense I was meant to go. I felt a little uneasy as I said goodbye to my friends and boarded the plane, aware the program would, in many ways, be confronting and challenging. The first night at Merida, Mexico, before boarding the buses to spend the week next to the great pyramid of the Mayans, jetlag made it difficult to sleep, so I decided to finish the last few pages of the book I'd been reading. In the final pages of the best-seller *The Celestine Prophecy*, I read James Redfield's theory that the Mayans had not been wiped out by the Spanish invaders but that they had evolved spiritually and moved into another dimension. It seemed a bizarre coincidence that I was reading those words alone in the early hours of the morning, knowing that tomorrow I would board a bus to the place I had just read about. Possibly I was in for a significant week.

When I arrived at Chichén Itzá the next day, I was immediately struck by the undeniable sense of calm and peace that permeated the area and the sincerity of those who had come from many parts of the world with such a passion to learn and grow. The week included ancient Mayan cleansing, nature and full moon ceremonies that previously I would have considered satanic or demonic. I'd preached against these things and now here I was participating in them. Every time we entered a sacred site or began a ritual my old belief system came raging to the surface, a block in my mind, limiting me to the possibility of more understanding and experience.

The very last pieces of my previously judgemental and condemning belief system were being challenged. One of the speakers made a statement that set me free from all the judgement, 'Whatever is sacred to a person is sacred,' and I finally saw how critical, judgemental and elitist I had been and that literally millions in the world lived with a deep sense of spirituality and connection. Who was I to judge? In fact, how dare I judge them or condemn them for their piety?

It was extremely hot and cooling off after lunch in one of the five pools at the resort was a welcome relief. I began a conversation with one of the participants from Canada, and listened as he shared his life journey, rejecting his Roman Catholic faith and then rediscovering it again with a deepened sense of spirituality. Up to this point, I had found it impossible to make sense of the various experiences of my life; it was like a jigsaw puzzle scattered across a table. I'd had so many wonderful experiences as a preacher and father, contrasted by numerous devastating ones, dark and light pieces that wouldn't match. The picture was not only unclear, it was confusing. I was transported as he spoke and could still hear his voice in the background whilst it seemed I was in another place. Like most, I'd often heard the term 'my life flashed before me' used to describe the experience before death when years are reduced to micro-seconds. In that moment my past, present and future merged in front of me playing out like a video, every step and experience fitting together perfectly like acts in a play—my journey finally made complete sense.

At the conclusion of the seminar, each participant was given the opportunity to share the significance of the week. Alone in my hotel room, further clarity came as I prepared my presentation of who I was and who I was to become.

In essence I am a good person. I have a strong sense of integrity, which gives me strength of character. After many years of being pressured to conform to what others would want me to be, I have developed an honesty and openness about what I feel and think. I confidently express my thoughts and emotions so that no-one is ever left guessing or assuming what is in my head and heart.

In essence I am a person of power. This power is expressed in many ways. It is revealed in my relationships by my commitment to my family and friends. It is evident in the way I have cut through the waves on the sea of life. In essence I am completely comfortable with my sexuality. I am not an activist but comfortable to the point where I no longer fear people's reaction to me being gay. So comfortable that if science developed a pill to make homosexual people heterosexual, I wouldn't take it. If I believed in rein-carnation and God sent me back as a homosexual, I would not be disap-pointed or feel ripped off. In fact, if I was given a choice I'd say, 'Please, can I be gay again this time?'

I paused for a moment and looked at the words that were flowing so easily onto the page. My sexuality? Why was I writing about that? It wasn't something I'd come all the way to the other side of the world to reflect on. Immediately I was reminded of the night in the Oxford Hotel when I'd envied the young gay man who had expressed a similar feeling. Occasionally I'd dreamed of feeling the same way but thought it impossible, and now it had come to pass. It was as if one chapter in my life had come to an end and now another was beginning. I contin-ued writing …

In essence my evolution as an individual has made me a people magnet that enriches others' lives by the encounter. My life has been of tremendous value and importance. My latter days are greater than my former.

Considering all the wonderful experiences I'd had over the years, I'd been living with the belief the best years of my life were behind me, but now for the first time, I could see a wonderful future brighter than anything I'd previously experienced. The completeness and the truth of those statements I wrote in May 1999 still affect me today.

When I returned to Sydney I had a strong feeling that I should go back to church but couldn't understand why or how, as a gay man, I could fit into a context that said I would go to hell because of who I was. I'd learnt how important it was to respond to the inner promptings that had now become a regular part of my life, so I went.

Walking into the church that Sunday night I was unsure of what reaction I'd get. Pastor Frank Houston was still pastoring the city campus of Hillsong Church at Waterloo, Sydney. I'd been a regular preacher there but since my 'fall from grace' had not been inside the building for many years.

Various members of the congregation instantly recognised me, including Pastor Frank, who came to say hi, each of them welcoming me with the same strange words, 'Hi, Tony, how are you? Haven't seen you for years! I heard you were dead.' For many fundamentalist Christians the emergence of AIDS around the world in the early 1980s was the judgement of God upon homosexuals. After I'd left the ministry a rumour spread throughout Australia that reflected that mentality. Tony is gay, gay men get AIDS, men with AIDS die, therefore Tony must be dead. The same thing had happened when I bumped into people on the streets who had known me as a preacher. Helen had even received calls from people around Australia offering their condolences when they'd heard the rumour I'd died.

'No,' I replied, a little shocked by such a confronting greeting. 'I'm very much alive and doing extremely well.' Walking out of the building that night I knew instantly why I was meant to go. It was obvious to me that the issues were resolved, the questions answered and nothing anyone could do or say could shake the belief I had in myself and my relationship with God. The overwhelming sense of peace was incredible. I would never again allow another person to condemn or judge me—no longer would anyone have this kind of power over my life.

I would have thought that a backslidden, former leader of the Assemblies of God returning to church would have been a relatively significant event. I certainly was not expecting a red carpet to be rolled out, or a fanfare of trumpets, but I thought someone would contact me to ask what had happened. It had certainly taken a great deal of courage to walk through those doors that night but it seemed that it was a bigger thing for me than it was for them. I tried to renew contact with some of my previous preacher friends and a couple returned my calls. Pat Mesiti met with me for coffee in Stanley Street, the Italian section of town. I told him of the peace and resolution I'd found and how once again God had become such a significant part of my life. He immediately burst into tears and said that he was apologising on behalf of the Assemblies of God and asking me to forgive them for the way I'd been treated. I thought at the time it was a strange reaction, but in hindsight I think Pat was possibly dealing with his own internal struggles and desired the freedom I'd found. I responded, gently consoling him. 'Pat,' I said, knowing Pat could often be overly enthusiastic, 'It's very nice of you to say sorry like this, but I don't really think you've been given that mandate by the denomination. And Pat, it's okay, I actually chose to forgive everyone for what happened seven years ago so it's no longer an issue for me.'

Within weeks the few who were prepared to make contact withdrew again, some finding it difficult to reconcile the fact that I, like the growing number around the world, could have a sexual orientation towards the same sex, and yet still be a good person and find peace and the resolution of my faith. Others never returned my calls, choosing to think of me as an apostate who should be shunned. From what I now know I think I understand every individual's response, which includes guilt because of their personal secrets or a simple case of ungodly homophobia. Those who have been brave enough to get close have discovered that I'm not the old Tony Venn-Brown, I'm better. They have shown the same love that can revolutionise lives because it's forgiving, welcoming, and non-judgemental. I thank them for taking the risk.

My life continued to take on a wonderful dimension of discovery and awareness. A number of months after this, I was on my way to have dinner with friends. Before I left I spent half an hour in meditation, being still, 'connecting' as I call it. I walked out of my apartment in Pyrmont and was very much aware that I was in a heightened state of perception. It was Saturday night and by the time I reached George Street in the city people were everywhere, going to the pictures and out partying. Looking at their faces it was as though I could look beyond that into their lives. When I walked into a hotel to pick up a bottle of wine for dinner, I saw people sitting alone drinking, some obviously passed the responsible alcohol limit recently introduced in bars and hotels. How sad, I thought, to be in this situation on a Saturday night, alone in a pub drinking yourself into oblivion. Others had lost looks on their faces. I got the impression that many of these people were not living but just existing, going through the motions. I saw the emptiness. In a moment, I realised that basically there are two types of people in this world: those who are asleep and those who are awake; those who are aware and conscious and those who live in a state of unknowing, living life on autopilot. I became intensely conscious that my new state of awareness had caused me to wake up and I'd begun to live life on a totally different dimension, with a deep level of fulfilment. As children we begin life with such innocence and purity, but some-where along the way we lose the very essence of who we are. We conform to what society, religion, parents, partners, the corporation and others want us to be, we're conditioned to become someone other than who we are. Either by conditioning or by choice we trade our true self for acceptance.

Looking at my life, I realised that I'd spent the last fourteen years of my life unlearning, unlearning everything I believed about myself. I had to unlearn in order to discover the truth. And this is what I discovered:

I am a good person. (Embarrassingly simple but for years difficult to acknowledge.)

I wasn't sick or in need of healing—there was a wholeness in me waiting to be discovered.

I wasn't broken or in need of fixing.

I wasn't an abomination to God—I was equal to every other human being who walks the planet and deserves the respect and rights that brings with it.

It wasn't homosexuality that had kept me bound but others' beliefs I embraced myself. I had learnt that homosexuality is not a curse but a blessing, a precious gift given to approximately somewhere between four to ten per cent of the population—that I should celebrate.

I didn't need to change, just accept.

Being a homosexual didn't mean being tormented; as a gay man I could find peace and resolution.

As a homosexual I was not destined to a life of loneliness; reward and fulfilment come to everyone, gay or straight, who is being true to themselves.

I didn't need someone else or a relationship to make me happy; I could find happiness and completeness in myself.

Homosexuality is not an act, it's an identity.

Saying you know the 'truth' makes everyone who thinks differently to you wrong, and puts you in the dangerous position of never being open to learning anything new.

Forgiveness brings transformation and freedom.

God is unfathomable.

I had learnt that I am not a human being having a spiritual experience but a spirit having a human experience.

My great discovery is that my alienation was a precious gift of freedom. Inside the safety of the city walls it's easier not to risk embarking on a journey of self-discovery. However, when you are rejected and thrust beyond the city's walls you are forced to find out who you are. What some outsiders discover on the other side is the courage to renounce self-contempt and the rules that others have made. At the moment a person questions the validity of the rules, the victim is no longer a victim.

Finally, in life's journey you are never off the path. Every detour, dead end, back alley, even road wrecks, looked at with insight are a possible part of a greater master plan.

Of course there is much more. Our journey of discovery will never end and that's what makes life so wonderful.

To some degree we are all living a life of unlearning. Unlearning the things we have accepted without question but which have no truth in our lives. Truth is internal, not external. People often want someone else to tell them what the truth is instead of finding it for themselves. They are afraid to trust that inner voice. Week after week, people sit in churches being told what they should believe but rarely challenging it—indeed they are afraid to doubt it. You will have to take responsibility to find it yourself and when you do you must live that truth: this is integrity. For me, the issue was my sexual orientation; your issues may be different. In my experience being true to yourself comes at a price. Had I known what was available on the other side, I would have willingly paid the price and laid down everything. When all the other garbage is swept away then you can live in authenticity and harmony. I've found being authentic, being true to yourself, to be a very powerful place. Look at those around you who live lives of integrity and authenticity. Observe the quality of their lives; they are truly blessed.

'The time will come when, with elation, you will greet yourself arriving at your own door, you will love again the stranger who was yourself, the stranger who has loved you all your life, whom you ignored for another, who knows you by heart.'

Extract from *Love After Love* by Derek Walcott.

And the pieces finally fit...

Chapter 21
Moving forward

The week after the launch of the first edition of *A Life of Unlearning*, I invited the Honourable Justice Michael Kirby to lunch. This would be a simple way of showing him how grateful I was that he had taken time out of his busy schedule to read my book and write the foreword.

In Australia and overseas Justice Kirby is highly respected and in the gay community has become somewhat of a hero. His appointments in the judicial system have been noteworthy but he is especially known as a Justice of the High Court of Australia. Justice Kirby received Australia's highest civil honour when he was made a Companion of the Order of Australia (AC) in 1991. Being a Companion of the Order of St Michael and St George (CMG), the United Nations Special Representative in Cambodia and the President of the International Commission of Jurists are other career highlights of note.

Justice Kirby has been open about his homosexuality since 1999, when he outed himself in Australia's *Who's Who*, naming Johan van Vloten as his long-term partner, now of thirty-seven years. He has often spoken publicly in support of gay rights and as an Anglican has expressed disappointment at his church's stance on homosexuality. On 2 May 2002, Justice Kirby was quoted in the Melbourne daily news-paper *The Age*, 'The churches, especially, must accept much of the blame for the homophobia that still exists in Australia, as in all communities. This is both the puzzle and the challenge. It is a puzzle, because such attitudes seem so incompatible with the basic lessons of a spiritual belief. The challenge is to expedite a change of view and to reiterate the universality of spiritual outreach. In the past there was perhaps an excuse for ignorance about sexuality. Today there is none. Homophobia has to stop. Silence and shame are the means by which oppression continues. That is why people like me must speak up.'[5]

Justice Kirby's willingness to speak so openly has not endeared him to everyone. In 2002 one of his critics, Liberal senator Bill Heffernan, under parliamentary privilege, accused Justice Kirby of using government vehicles to pick up male prostitutes. It appeared to many that this was an orchestrated attempt at character assassination, and Heffernan's evidence to support this claim was swiftly discovered to be a forgery. Senator Heffernan resigned his post as Parliamentary Secretary, and made a statement to the Senate in which he withdrew the claims. Even though the allegations were false I imagine this would have caused the judge personal hurt and stress and understandably deserved some justifiable retribution, but when Senator Heffernan eventually apologised, Justice Kirby simply responded, 'I accept Senator Heffernan's apology and reach out my hand in a spirit of reconciliation. I hope my ordeal will show the wrongs that hate of homosexuals can lead to.' Obviously the title, The Honourable, is not just a title—he is a man of great honour.

We had been corresponding via email for some time and had spoken briefly when he and Johan popped into my book launch, preferring to stand in the background while my daughters launched the book. I'd never met a High Court Judge before and was unsure how to address him. Justice, Judge, Your Honour—all seemed right and respectful but, being a more informal person, I chose to call him Michael. I must admit it felt a little awkward, but he didn't seem to mind.

We met for lunch at a café behind the Law Court building. We talked about the possibility of having been on a dance floor at the same time in 1973, before my Christian belief system took me back into the closet for another nineteen years. I thought for a moment about the contrast between our two journeys and wondered if I'd stayed true to my sexuality from those early days, would I have found a lifelong companion as he had? The conversation paused and he looked at me seriously, straightened up, and his eyes became more intense and focused. 'Now Anthony,' I knew I was in for an important statement, 'writing your book is not the end. Your role is to change the Pentecostals' view on homosexuality.' I thought it was a rather tall order and a tad flattering that he thought I could actually be that influential. I had already concluded that my work was done once I'd told my story. Now I could get on with my life, or so I thought. What more could I do?

Justice Kirby reminded me that people in Pentecostal churches are like most people in other denominations who are basically good and Christian people. Something I had also come to understand and believe from renewed contacts with various people and my years in the church. Confronted with scientific facts and actual human beings that they are hurting, they will eventually come to appreciate that there is a need to re-examine the scriptural texts presently taken as adverse to homosexuals. Possibly we may never see the dissolving of extremists groups like the Reverend Fred Phelps of www.godhatesfags.com and others. Regrettably we have seen too much hatred returned for hatred on both sides of the fence that continues to reinforce stereotypes and clouds rational debate. Justice Kirby continued with further details and as I listened intently to what he was saying, had a strong sense he was speaking prophetically. Deep down inside, his words resonated strongly with me and made perfect sense. As a former leader within the Assemblies of God, and having resolved my personal issues around the conflict between my sexual orientation and my faith, I was best qualified to speak about those issues. But how was I to do that?

In the two years since the book's publication I have received a steady stream of correspondence, often beginning the same way—'your story is my story'. These readers then go on to tell me of their own journey, in a one-paragraph email or a ten-page handwritten letter. Many felt that up to this point they could not talk to anyone about the ordeal they have gone through. Like me, their sense of shame and failure kept them silent. Not all yet have found the resolution I have, but they are on the way out of the dark and terrible closet that has kept them living in fear, shame and self-contempt. Analysing this overwhelming response, the picture is very clear. There is not one good thing that has come from the church maintaining the outdated, ill-informed belief that homosexuality is a sin, a perverse choice, or the result of a dysfunctional upbringing.

There was Trevor who told me how he had helped his Christian father build their multi-million dollar home, only to be disinherited when his father found out he was gay, giving everything to his heterosexual brother and sister. Or Greg, an ex-Baptist minister, who detailed his trip to a national park to gas himself in the car where he was saved only by a passing ranger. Jill and Trish recounted how they were in ministry in a mega-church and fell in love. When it became apparent, even though they had not slept together, they immediately had their positions of leadership stripped from them and the humiliation drove them from the church. Brian, who had done an ex-gay program and developed mental health issues, said that whilst struggling to be an ex-gay he attempted suicide three times. On a disability pension, he was unable to buy my book so he went to the city and read it in the reading room of a major bookshop. He was embarrassed as he sat and wept whilst reading, but returned the next day to finish the story. The resolution he found on those pages has somehow led to his healing. Every symptom of his illnesses are gone, he has a job and is living a wonderful life as a gay Christian. Jesus did say, 'You will know the truth and the truth shall set you free' (John 8:32).

Nineteen-year-old Reece told me about how his parents sent him to a Christian counsellor who put him on a lie detector as a way of monitoring his 'transformation'. His sister told him that unless he changed, he would not be allowed alone with her children. Reece eventually had to leave home. Peter and I had known each other in the ministry (I had never guessed he might be gay) but we had lost contact over the years. We reconnected after he had read my book, revealing he was living a tormented, closeted life. What would happen if he told the church leaders or his children? After marriage, serving in the ministry, some sexual involvement with another pastor who also suppressed his homosexuality, multiple physical and psychological problems, therapy, and depression, Peter was seriously considering that he should end his life. One night, I felt a strong impression to call him again and I'm glad I responded to that prompting. As a result of that phone call Peter has finally come out at the age of fifty. Though we've spoken of regret and what his life may have been like had he done this in his teens, he is at least now living free of the destructive, emotional and psychological consequences of his suppression.

Anthony broke down frequently as he read me the letters his twenty-six-year-old lover Michael had written to his Christian parents begging them to love him as he was and to accept Anthony, the man he loved, as his partner. In Michael's letters he pleads for acceptance but the response always comes back, 'We love you but … we don't want you to be gay. We love you but … we don't want you to be with Anthony.'

That one word made all the difference to Michael. 'BUT …'

A small word that means the world of difference between love or rejection. What Michael's parents should have said was, We love you, Michael. FULL STOP! No conditions. Then they would have been showing God's love. A person in the church in Perth had told Michael, 'If you don't change then you'll be dead before you reach twenty-six.' These words, like a curse, played on Michael's mind and even though he had a partner and friends who loved him, the inability to resolve his relationship with his Mum and Dad meant that when Anthony came home to celebrate Michael's twenty-sixth birthday, he found him dead in the car in the garage. Anthony doesn't think much of Christians.

Christine, the mother of a thirteen-year-old boy, revealed that her son spent six months in psychiatric treatment because his Christian teacher told him all homosexuals will burn in hell, then showed the class films of hell. She called it spiritual abuse and regrets ever sending her child to a Christian school.

I could compile a book of several volumes from the stories I have received. If my motive was to be sensational or cause scandal there are enough secrets in that correspondence to cause major embarrassment to individuals and denominations. My motive, though, is not to seek revenge or to create more heartache—I want change.

Finally, this email from Charles, twenty-three. When we met, I could see he was a lovely young man with great heart and potential. He had been previously serving God as a youth pastor at his local church, but knowing his church's official position about gays, he no longer attends and is trying to resolve that conflict that has been created by his faith and his sexuality:

Dear Anthony

*I still have my doubts about what it means to be gay and Christian. I have just started seeing a guy. He's soooo amazing, and he really likes me. It's really great! We've got a great beginning of a relationship. It's kinda cute. So, I told my parents about him. We've been seeing each other for a few weeks, and I met his family, so I was thinking mine should know about him also. It was good to tell them, but at the same time, it's really hard. I normally talk to my parents for hours, but since I've not talked to them much at all. They told me that they still don't believe I'm gay. It's not the way God made me, and that it's not right. **They have even offered to hire a prostitute for me, so I can try being straight** (my emphasis). I think this is ridiculous, but hey, that's what they're saying! What is really hard, is that they're pastors. It was expected after my baptism and years of Missionary work, that I would carry on the work. Obviously I can't, but I just don't know what to do! I'm really struggling to find what's right.*

It would be easy to be angry with Charles's parents but this situation only serves to remind us the enemy we fight is not people but ignorance. Receiving emails like this one regularly, I find it impossible to sit back and do nothing. Hopefully in some way I can make a difference. I think one of the most powerful things I can do is be. Be who I am. A person who loves life, loves God, and loves my tribe. As a former leader in the Assemblies of God and now Australia's first openly gay Pentecostal, I am an enigma to many people because apparently I am not who I am supposed to be. The problem is that I am happy, I enjoy the most wonderfully fulfilling life, I have an abundant network of quality people in my life, I have no mental health issues, no anger, no bitterness, just peace … and I'm not going to hell. I like to think of myself not so much as an activist, but as an ambassador.

Returning to the Pentecostal scene, I have discovered that change is occurring at the grass roots level. Some people have changed their attitudes, and some even their beliefs. These people have not yet acknowledged publicly their more informed belief about homosexuality because by doing so, in the current climate, that will mean loss of employment, rejection by friends or reprisals from leadership. They are not gay so why should they have to pay the price? I believe that things will change eventually, further up the hierarchies and even officially. I was surprised to find that gay and lesbian people exist in the congregations and have come to the understanding that their sexual orientation, although an issue to others, is not to them or their God. There are already Pentecostal churches in the United States and United Kingdom that are welcoming of GLBTI people, and a few with a lesbian or gay man as pastor. Despite many churches maintaining their outdated beliefs, God is moving amongst gay and lesbian people in what some have called 'The Rainbow Revival'. Gay Christians are a new phenomenon, but a growing one. A Google search of 'Gay Christian' results in about 281,000 pages today; tomorrow it will be more. However, while we wait for others to catch up, people are suffering and some of them dying. As some surveys have shown, GLBTI young people can be up to six times more likely to suicide; it's been estimated that one succeeds every five hours and forty-eight minutes in the US.

Some individuals reflect the change I've been speaking of, like Guy Sebastian. He used to attend Paradise Community Church in Adelaide, one of the largest Pentecostal churches in Australia with over 5,000 members, and currently attends Hillsong in Sydney. Guy rose to stardom when he won the first series of *Australian Idol* in 2003. In a news article[6] in September 2006, he talked about the homophobic remarks, the derogatory comments regarding his music career, and the physical harassment he'd received from members of the public. This so affected him working on his third album that he considered quitting singing altogether. Guy (a heterosexual) was experiencing something that GLBTI people encounter regularly. Instead of speaking negatively about the gay taunts, Guy said they offended him because 'thirty per cent of my friends are gay.' Fifteen years ago, a statement like that would have been unthinkable. As a high-profile Christian young person, Guy is to be commended, and his comments reflect what I'm discovering behind the scenes—things are changing.

Receiving so many distressing emails I felt it was important to send a letter to the National Executive of the Assemblies of God in Australia. My hope was that they would set up a committee to examine sexual orientation on a scientific, psychological and theological basis and do something about the terrible suffering people are experiencing unnecessarily. The majority of the men on the Executive were once my peers and closest friends. Some I hadn't seen for fourteen years. I met with them on 23 November 2005 as a response to my request and I offer this as an open letter to any church, Protestant or Catholic, that still maintains the belief 'the *Bible* says homosexuality is a sin', because that belief will be creating the same results in your worlds as well as Pentecostal Churches.

3 May 2005

Dear Executive Members

I'm writing to see if there is some way I may be of help to the Assemblies of God in Australia which will eventually assist those members and families facing difficulties and even alienation because of the issue of sexual orientation.

I never imagined I would be writing to you after all these years. In fact, I didn't expect to be alive. After leaving the church, my relationship with God, and my family, I planned to commit suicide before the age of 50 as I saw no hope in my life. I considered myself to be such a failure there was nothing to live for. Through a series of miraculous circumstances God has been the centre of my life again since 1998 ... something I thought impossible. That's quite a long story which I'd be happy to share with you any time. There was a time when I considered all of you to be friends and I trust that, as Christian men, you will relate to me with love and forgiveness.

Today I feel extremely blessed to have walked this path, one I would never have chosen but maybe in the wisdom of God the one set out for me. God's purpose is once again profoundly strong and I am currently honouring that in an informal way.

If asked what was the most important thing I've learnt in my 54 years on earth it's that God loves me as I am. My sexual orientation is not an issue to Him, only that I live my life according to His will and purpose.

You will sense, from the tone of this letter, that there is no aggression, bitterness or resentment but rather genuine concern to find a way forward and ensure we don't keep repeating the mistakes of the past.

I'm writing with a request. My unique situation means many people have told me their stories and it's important I bring to your attention these concerns. Over 500 emails, letters and phone calls show the consequences of our long held, uninformed and dated beliefs about sexual orientation. Although 500 may seem a small number, it is significant, considering the percentage of Pentecostal Christians who are same-sex-attracted. The emails continue to come with different stories but in essence contain similar themes.

The common themes are:

Suicides. *This would have to be the most horrific result of our church's current understanding of homosexuality. I know only too well the dark place that one can find oneself due to the conflict with your sexual orientation and your relationship with God. Too many have taken their lives because they were told God would never accept them they way they were and were unable to become heterosexual. I know of one Assemblies of God church in Melbourne where three young men (aged 18, 23 and 26) suicided in the space of two years. I'm under the impression that even some pastors have lost their sons this way. One life lost is one too many.*

A few weeks ago I received an email from a student in a Pentecostal bible college that you would all know well. He tells of his passion to serve God and the mental torment he is going through because he is same-sex-attracted. He has been considering suicide. I've tried to meet up with him and talk about how he might resolve his situation but he is too scared at this stage. I email him regularly to check if he is okay and see if he's comfortable about talking. He has sworn me to secrecy as he is very afraid of what might happen. I have to honour that confidentiality but it would be a terrible thing if he takes his own life.

I think it's tragic that people kill themselves when I know that it's possible to live a rewarding, fulfilling life of purpose as a gay man.

Parents rejecting their gay children. *There are very few Christian parents who know how to respond when their child is either exposed as gay or they pluck up the courage to tell the truth. Parents often feel a sense of shame and insist that the child must change, quoting scripture and sending them off for counselling or other therapies. Some kids have just left their homes knowing from the comments* of their Christian parents or in the church that they will never be accepted.

Recently I've read a book called 'Prayers for Bobby' where a Christian mother tells her story, based on her son's extensive diary chronicling the highs and lows of his four-year struggle with being gay and trying to live a Christian life. At the age of 20 he back-flipped off a freeway overpass, timing his leap so his body would be struck and killed by an oncoming truck. For four years before his death, his mother encouraged him to "cure" his homosexuality through prayer, constantly quoting scriptures and telling him that God didn't what him to be that way. Today Mrs Griffith has a very different view and has dedicated her life to helping other parents so they will not lose their children as she did.

Men and women marrying to solve the 'problem' of same-sex-attraction. Many of the stories received tell of them marrying with the belief that this action will and must change their attraction to the same sex. Whilst these marriages may last for years, eventually and most frequently in mid-life when all the unresolved issues must be dealt with, everything simply falls apart. One email, from a man in Perth, has just experienced this at the age of 62 after 27 years of marriage. It's difficult for most people to comprehend why you would bother at that age unless you were the person who lived a lie all your life. This leaves the partner and children with a terrible sense of betrayal that takes years to work through and resolve. Recently, in the foyer at Hillsong, I overheard a young man announcing his engagement to his friends. This young man displayed some key indicators that suggested he was probably gay - another tragedy in the making. My heart went out to him and the fiancée knowing that the marriage is doomed to failure as a result of this attempt to become 'normal'.

Deep emotional trauma. The emails are, at times, heart wrenching as people speak of their traumatic experience when churches, pastors and other individuals have handled the disclosure unwisely. Sadly, *many of these people still live with a very deep resentment towards the church and God. Something that would not be happening if there was love, grace and understanding. Philip Yancey speaks so beautifully about this in his book* What's So Amazing About Grace. *These people could still be vital members of our congregations and have a relationship with God.*

Another tragic result of this emotional trauma is that people are often left with feelings of self-hatred and shame which frequently leads to self-destructive behaviour. Some have shared with me that their initial reaction when leaving or being rejected by their churches was the contributing factor to them being HIV-positive today.

Inadequate counselling. *It appears that most pastors are inadequately equipped to counsel members of their congregations with same-sex-attraction. The worst case I've been told about involved a pastor suggesting, after his months of counselling had failed, that the guy try sex with a prostitute. [Author's note: I have since discovered that this is not uncommon.] Almost unbelievable I know, but true just the same, and demonstrates just how ill-equipped some of our leaders are to deal with this issue. Many people are given an endless number of strategies to deal with their temptation but find themselves living in constant failure when those strategies don't work. Others are simply told to pray about it and ask God to change them. When the answers don't come he/she is left with the constant feeling that I mustn't have enough faith or God has failed me. In my case, every time I sought help from pastors I can honestly say, not once was the situation handled in an intelligent manner.*

The damage and failure of ex-gay ministries. *The ex-gay ministries and Christian counsellors don't keep records of their success rate even though claims have been made of a 95% success rate while others say it's more like 10%.*

Exodus International has been operating now for three decades and even though there have been people who claim to now be heterosexu-

al, history tells us this is not true. Sixteen years of marriage didn't change me. Recently when the leader of the ex-gay ministry 'Living Waters' and I were interviewed together, he freely stated that he got sexually aroused just reading my book. He may be married but he is not free from his homosexual orientation, even though he claims that Jesus can do that. The promotion of this false hope leads people to years of unnecessary mental torture, interminable confusion and struggle. Thoughts of and attempts at suicide are common in these programs.

There is no scientific evidence that says sexual orientation can be changed permanently and that it is in fact damaging to try and change it (see below).

American Psychological Association -
http://www.apa.org/pubinfo/answers.html,
American Psychiatric Association -
http://www.psych.org/pnews/99-01-15/therapy.html.

Attempts to suppress, deny or reject one's true sexual identity are potentially harmful and often lead to mental health issues, addictions and/or deviant behaviour. This has become evident in some recent scandals involving ministers within our movement. It is my firm belief and experience that this would no longer happen if individuals are given proper counselling about accepting their sexual orientation.

The suffering, trauma and even deaths talked about above are the direct result of the churches stand against homosexuality. I hope that you see these as important concerns for individual pastors and also for you as leaders of the denomination.

Reaching the Gay Community. I've been in the gay community for 13 years and quickly discovered that all my beliefs and preconceptions were untrue. Popular misconceptions such as gay relationships not lasting, homosexuals being more promiscuous than heterosexuals, and gays and lesbians being sick and perverted are simply not true. I live, work and play with these people and I'm proud to call them my friends because of the lives they live and the kind of people they are. I *love them dearly for their continuing support when it has to be honest-ly admitted that my closest Christian friends ceased having any contact with me in my greatest time of need. Something I've never been able to understand in the light of the teachings of Jesus.*

Unfortunately the gay community has often not seen God's love because the majority of Christians have alienated themselves from them and even turned on them. Having already negatively judged gays and lesbians, it's difficult for Christians to reach out as love and judge-ment cannot exist in the heart at the same time. It's hard for gays and lesbians to see the love and grace of God when they are condemned at the first meeting, in the media or from the pulpit.

For years, we've quoted the words 'love the sinner, hate the sin' but the gay community has rarely seen this love because the church focuses on hating the sin and blocking every attempt gays and lesbians make to gain the same rights enjoyed by heterosexuals. Possibly, there is coming a day when the church will have to ask forgiveness for their attitude towards, and even hatred sometimes, of gays and lesbians. Before that day is reached there must be a change of attitude. I encour-age you to foster that.

The general impression is that the gay community is being targeted by our churches. I don't believe this is true, is it? Regrettably there is never any discussion. It's like a boxing match with each camp in the corner, the bell rings and we both come out to exchange blows. It would be more constructive for us to sit down at the table and dialogue. If we are going to reach these people with God's love, it's essential that an informed approach be taken.

Over the years I've come across many in my community who have a strong and living faith. The survival of that faith is a miracle itself. I know of many who would return to the Pentecostal fold as I have, if there was some indication they were welcome to do so.

I ask you to sincerely search your own hearts, do you genuinely love these people? God does. If the answer is yes then I have to ask what

are we doing to reach them? There is so much that churches and indi-
vidual Christians could do to demonstrate God's love in a practical way.
When seeking to renew contact with friends from my time in the
ministry, I've been the one to take the initiatives, make the contact and
follow up as no-one has really come to me or made me feel welcome. It's
a constant struggle but I persevere because I know God loves me
immensely and I refuse to allow others to think less of me than what I
am.

A Way Forward. *One of the first things that can be done would be*
to remove the Position Statement on Homosexuality and Lesbianism
from the Assemblies of God website. [Author's note: this statement has
since been removed from the Assemblies of God in Australia website.]

Although this is a long discussion I'll give you some brief reasons
why this needs to be removed.

'Homosexuality is referred to directly and specifically in the scriptures. The Old Testament also explicitly prohibited homosexuality'

This is not true. Currently there are several interpretations of those
famous six verses. In the light of the historical and cultural contexts of
the day we can only guess that what is talked about has to do with
abusive or exploitive relationships or the sexual practices used to
worship foreign gods. What is known as same-sex-attraction and love
today is not mentioned.

'The scripture also condemns Sodom for its homosexual practices'

Not really. Once again there are several interpretations. If you search
yourself through all the references to Sodom you'll see that the city was
judged for many things e.g. pride, not meeting the needs of the poor,
but never for homosexuality. Even Jesus' reference to it seems to be a
reference to their being inhospitable Luke 10:8-12. This is very diffi-
cult for us to understand in the 21st century but very real in the early
biblical culture. In Jewish historical writings, the Sodom and Gomorrah

story contains no sexual connotations before 90AD.

'Paul also lists homosexuality as a sin'

Unfortunately the translators in the middle of the 20th century have done us a great disservice by translating obscure Greek words more in the light of the popular thinking of their time and inserted the word homosexual instead of being true to the original language. The word didn't actually appear in the bible till 1946.

'Homosexuality is a chosen behaviour'

I think I can safely say that I know more gays and lesbians than the person who wrote this statement and I can tell you that not one of them chose it and they find this statement extremely offensive. It's totally illogical to think that a person would willingly choose to be rejected by their family, hated, discriminated against, ridiculed or physically harmed etc etc etc.

There is already a shift in some people's thinking within our churches. Mostly with those who through closer contact with gays and lesbians have found that their preconceived notions were unfounded. We have to admit that the Bible has been used in the past to promote beliefs we now know were wrong. One of those was the role of women in the church. When I joined the Assemblies of God not one woman was ordained. Today is a different story. There can be added to that list many other things such as dancing in and out of the church, going to the movies, behaviour on the Sabbath, dress codes and rock music to name a few. All these beliefs had a biblical basis for Pentecostal Christians and any erring from the way was once considered sin. Not any more. Each of us, having spent many years in the Assemblies of God movement, would freely admit that we got it wrong. It is challenging, but nevertheless important for us to consider if our stand on same-sex-attraction is another one of these situations.

Considering that since the early 70s the Psychiatric and Psychological Associations have believed that same-sex-attraction is not an illness or dysfunction, it's probably time for us in the church to have some informed and intelligent dialogue about the issue. Continuing to treat people any other way is outdated and more importantly, not in harmony with the values aspired to on the 'Love of People' page on the Assemblies of God in Australia website. Removing the page 'A Statement on Homosexuality and Lesbianism' would be a demonstration that we seek to treat the gay community with the dignity and respect they deserve.

There is a lot more that needs to be addressed and understood and that will take time. We are all aware of the controversy around this issue but ignoring it won't make it go away. It would be terrible to think that we just continue to repeat the mistakes of the past and damage other people's lives here.

As an ex ordained minister of the Assemblies of God and current member of Hillsong Waterloo I'm committed to working with you in any way to bring love, healing and reconciliation to all people, especially my tribe. 'You are all sons of God through faith in Jesus Christ, for all of you who were baptized into Christ have clothed yourself with Christ. There is neither Jew nor Greek, slave nor free, male nor female for you are all one in Christ Jesus' Galatians 3:28.

I'm happy to answer any questions you may ask me. I look forward to receiving your response to my requests.

Yours sincerely
Anthony Venn-Brown

A couple of weeks later I received a reply from the National Executive of the Assemblies of God in Australia thanking me for my openness, courage and graciousness. It went on to say, however, 'Following your openness the Executive want to reaffirm the commitment we have as a movement and as individuals to endeavour to show the love of Jesus Christ to all people regardless of culture, creed or sexual orientation when we deal with issues. At the same time we can only confirm that our theological position in relation to homosexuality has not changed.

We believe that it is based on a sound biblical basis and we must stand on our convictions.'

The erroneous belief that 'the *Bible* says homosexuality is a sin' still exists, but it will not exist forever. Every poll and survey reveals a gradual shift in society's attitudes and beliefs about same-sex orientation. The Australia Institute's survey of almost 25,000 people, 'Mapping of Homophobia in Australia,' released in July 2005, showed that change. Despite Pope Benedict XVI taking an obsessive anti-gay stand and calling homosexuality an 'intrinsic moral evil' only thirty-four per cent of Catholics believe homosexuality is immoral, revealing once again that church leaders are way out of step with current thinking in the pews. The numbers were similar in the Anglican and Uniting Churches. The study showed the less educated a person was the more likely they were to be homophobic; twenty-five per cent of those with tertiary education hold homophobic views compared to forty to fifty per cent among those who did not complete high school. The changes continue to grind along slowly as people become more informed and have more exposure to gay people. Individuals and denominations are moving along the continuum from hate—dislike—discomfort—tolerance— acceptance—affirmation and some to advocacy. I continue to engage people in an informed, intelligent, respectful dialogue where I can, leaving all the blame and anger outside the door to clear the space for productive communication. With the help of my friend Phill Wall we have commenced 'Freedom 2 b(e)' which provides support and a network for GLBTI people from Pentecostal and Charismatic backgrounds (www.freedom2b.org). What more needs to be done?

I can ask you, dear reader, to be involved at any level you desire, and help hasten the day when, as God intended, all people are treated equally no matter what their gender, race or sexual orientation. When you hear an individual, politician, church or denomination say something derogatory about GLBTI people take the opportunity to graciously correct the preconceived ideas and misconceptions about same-sex attracted people. Remind them they are speaking about your friend, brother, sister, mother, father, aunt, uncle, niece, nephew, son or daughter and, like us, be proud when you come out.

To my gay brothers and lesbian sisters: your life is already having an impact, and the way we live will either reinforce or dismantle the belief that being straight is normal while being gay is flawed. That means no more hiding or pretending you are straight. Stop fearing. Stop being ashamed and wondering what others will think if you tell them the truth. Have courage, face your fears and don't allow another to think less of you. Coming out is an empowering liberation from a host of destructive forces that deceive you into believing bad things about yourself and rejecting the wonderful person you are. How many politicians, celebrities and sports stars continue to reinforce outdated thinking and hide behind a façade of heterosexuality because they believe if they don't pretend then they would lose their careers?

In 1978, Harvey Milk of San Francisco was the first openly gay elected official in the United States. Harvey repeatedly said, 'Come out, and when you do, you will feel so much better.' Before he was assassinated in 1979 Harvey quite uncannily predicted he would be murdered, and had said, 'If a bullet should enter my brain, let that bullet destroy every closet door in the country.'

In 2000, Tammy Baldwin, a lesbian and a member of the United States House of Representatives from the district of Wisconsin, spoke from the stage of the Millennium March on Washington: 'If you dream of a world in which you can put your partner's picture on your desk, then put their picture on your desk and you will live in such a world.' In her inspiring speech to the hundreds of thousands attending, she continued to say that there are two things that keep homosexuals oppressed: them and us. In other words, we are half of the equation. We shouldn't wait around for some magical day when everything will be okay. It's up to us to make that day happen. We can all hasten that day by being true to ourselves.

It's your journey and it is not my place to tell you how to live your life. For many years I did that as a preacher. It we are honest with ourselves, deep down in our hearts, we all know the right thing to do. All we need is the courage and integrity to do it. My journey from rejection of self to embracing of self was twenty-eight years—more than half my life. Had I known the amazing sense of freedom, the peace through reconciliation, the liberation of bringing my secrets into the light, the power of living authentically, I would have smashed down the prison walls much earlier. My journey now it seems is to bridge the gap between the two worlds and the people I love and help them see the good in each other.

Notes

Chapter 3

1. *Sydney Morning Herald*, 14 October 1966, p.2.

Chapter 8

2. *Sydney Gay & Lesbian News*, vol. 1. no. 1, July 1972.

Chapter 13

3. http://www.smh.com.au/news/National/Church-expands-horizons/2005/05/03/1115092503070.html

4. *People for the American Way*, 'Hostile Climate,' 1997, p.15.

Chapter 21

5. Justice Michael Kirby, *The Age*, 2 May 2002. Permission to reproduce quote obtained from the author.

6. http://www.news.com.au/heraldsun/story/0,21985,20448603-661,00.html

Anthony Venn-Brown can be contacted by visiting his web site: www.anthonyvennbrown.com

Freedom 2 b(e)

Networking GLBTI people from Pentecostal and Charismatic backgrounds.

www.freedom2b.org

A LIFE OF UNLEARNING:
reviews of the first edition:

There is scarcely a page that does not engage you personally...nothing is held back. Some will find Anthony's story disturbing and confrontational and others will find it liberating and an example of the triumph of the individual human spirit. For those who want to understand human frailty, courage and personal redemption it is an invaluable resource. I highly recommend it.
Roger Fedyk, smh.com, Margo Kingston's Webdairy

In this well written autobiography, Anthony Venn-Brown takes the reader on a remarkable journey ... a heart felt story of someone attempting to reconcile two disparate, but equally powerful, elements of his life – his sexuality and his faith. Anthony wonderfully invokes growing up in Sydney in the nineteen fifties and his prose really rings true for a first time author. As our exploration of who we truly are always affects those closest to us, and it is their pain that echoes through this book. Through it all, however, we come to see the essential nature of 'character,' despite the dramatic changes of scenery along the way. Wellbeing Magazine.

A LIFE OF UNLEARNING:
emails from readers of the first edition:

'Thank you for enlightening my world. And I can confidently say changing it forever.' *Janet, a Christian mother whose son left the church and his marriage of three years, after accepting the fact that he was gay.*

'It is the most valuable book I will ever read. I have been in limbo not being able to understand him or what he was going through, but reading your story has helped put the pieces of the puzzle together.' *Margaret, whose husband came out at the age of 62 after 29 years of marriage.*

'The final chapters of your book broke my heart! I had to put it down almost every paragraph to refocus my puffy red eyes. I had a moment where something inside me wanted not to be broken anymore. For the first time I wasn't convincing myself that I was loved and valued and that everything was okay. I actually knew it.' *Matt, 22, London.*

'Wow! Thanks for writing your book which has given me insight & some much needed healing.' *Trish, a mother whose 15-year-old son required psychiatric treatment, after attending a Christian school and being taught 'all homosexuals will burn in hell'.*

'At 43 years old I attempted suicide. I believed that I was a worthless abomination to God. Thank you for your autobiography, which I hope, will help many.' *John, ex Baptist minister.*

'I have just finished reading your book. I am stunned, moved and about to cry!' *Bill from Canada who, after 30 years of fighting his homosexuality, has decided to finish his marriage and be true to himself his wife and children.*

'I'm 63. I too, have fought the battle. Your book gives hope to men like me.' *George from Canada.*

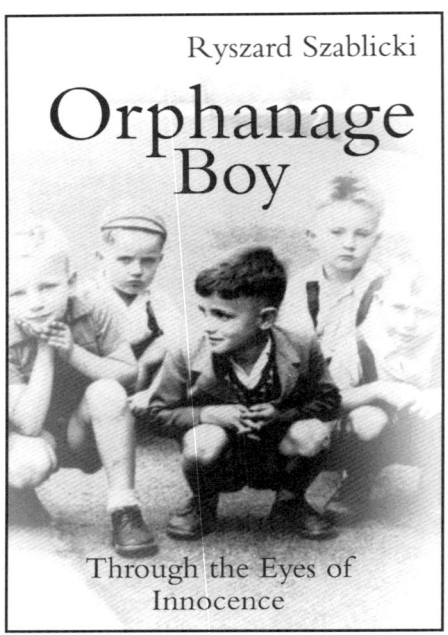

Ryszard Szablicki

Orphanage Boy

Through the Eyes of
Innocence

Ryszard Szablicki was born in Melbourne in 1952 and immediately placed in a foundling home ... by his mother. He remained in institutional care for over ten years.

In *Orphanage Boy: Through the Eyes of Innocence*, Ryszard recounts his early life in several Catholic institutions through the eyes of that boy, naïve and overwhelmed by the perverse corruption and indifference of a system he couldn't hope to understand.

In 1996, he joined a class action against the brutality and abuse of one of these institutions. A federal Senate inquiry followed in 2004, investigating similar allegations. Finally, Ryszard received an unreserved apology for these abuses—and some peace of mind.

It was through these processes that the memories began to spill out. The result is this book: a rare, haunting, tender and heart-rending account of a cold and often brutal world.

Orphanage Boy - Ryszard Szablicki
ISBN: 9781741105124